Microsoft Exchange Server PowerShell Cookbook

Third Edition

Over 120 recipes to help you manage and administrate
Exchange Server 2013 Service Pack 1 with PowerShell 5

Jonas Andersson

Mike Pfeiffer

[PACKT] enterprise 🏵
PUBLISHING   professional expertise distilled

BIRMINGHAM - MUMBAI

Microsoft Exchange Server PowerShell Cookbook

Third Edition

First published: July 2011
Second edition: May 2013
Third edition: July 2015

Production reference: 1240715

Published by Packt Publishing Ltd.
Livery Place
35 Livery Street
Birmingham B3 2PB, UK.

ISBN 978-1-78528-807-4

www.packtpub.com

Credits

Authors

Jonas Andersson

Mike Pfeiffer

Reviewers

Mark Andrews

Hakim Taoussi

Commissioning Editor

Amarabha Banerjee

Acquisition Editor

Vivek Anantharaman

Content Development Editor

Mamata Walkar

Technical Editor

Dhiraj Chandanshive

Copy Editor

Rashmi Sawant

Project Coordinator

Sanjeet Rao

Proofreader

Safis Editing

Indexer

Hemangini Bari

Production Coordinator

Shantanu N. Zagade

Cover Work

Shantanu N. Zagade

About the Authors

Jonas Andersson is a devoted person who is constantly developing himself and his skills. He started out in the IT business in 2004 and initially worked in a support center, where he got basic knowledge of the industry. In 2007, he started his career as a Microsoft Infrastructure consultant, and from 2008 onward, his focus has been on Microsoft Exchange.

Even though his focus is on Microsoft Exchange, his interests include migrations, backup, storage, archiving, and so on. At the start of 2010, he was employed at a large outsourcing company as a messaging specialist, specializing in Microsoft Exchange. His work includes designing, implementing, and developing messaging solutions for enterprise customers.

His unique knowledge makes him a key figure in large and complex migration projects, where he works on design and implementation. Examples of these projects include migrations from the IBM Domino mail platform to Microsoft Exchange 2007/2010/2013 and Office 365, using Quest Software with full coexistence between the systems for mail flow, directory synchronization, and free busy lookups.

In 2014, he joined Microsoft Consulting Services, and from then onward, his focus has been on Office 365 but also on-premises Exchange Server. At the start of 2015, he changed his role to a deployment consultant with Microsoft's Office 365 Global Practice EMEA team.

He writes articles on his blog (`http://www.testlabs.se/blog`), Twitter, and other forms of social media.

As a reward for his work in the community, he was awarded the Microsoft Most Valuable Professional for the Microsoft Exchange Server product in 2014. He was also awarded the Microsoft Community Contributor Award in both 2011 and 2012.

This is my second book. It's been a great experience and a great honor to once again get the opportunity to write an update of a book that Mike Pfeiffer initially wrote for Microsoft Exchange 2010. When writing this book, I've had a lot of help from my sidekicks: Hakim Taoussi, Steve Goodman, and Mark Andrews. I look forward to continuing with these kinds of side projects alongside my regular work.

There are a lot of people I would like to thank: firstly of course, my family, for the love and energy they keep giving me. Besides my family, I would like to thank Hakim Taoussi, Steve Goodman, and Mark Andrews for doing a great job on the technical reviews. I received lots of great feedback, which improved the content of this book.

I hope that you will enjoy the book and its content will help you develop your skills in the area.

Mike Pfeiffer is an accomplished IT architect, consultant, and conference speaker, with over 15 years of experience in the tech industry. He has published books, blogs, white papers, and training courses on a variety of topics related to infrastructure architecture, deployment automation, configuration management, and more. He has a passion for technology and enjoys learning as much as writing and teaching.

About the Reviewers

Mark Andrews has had a varied career in technology. Over the last 18 years, he has held several different positions, ranging from customer service to quality assurance. Throughout all of these positions, the responsibility of configuration management and build management has always fallen either on him personally or on one of the groups that he managed. Because of his "keeping a hand in" management style, he has been closely involved with the scripting and automation framework for these areas. Creating scripted frameworks that intercommunicate across machine/operating system/domain boundaries is his passion.

He has worked on *PowerShell 3.0 Advanced Administration Handbook*, *Windows PowerShell 4.0 for .NET Developers*, and *PowerShell for SQL Server Essentials*, all by Packt Publishing.

Hakim Taoussi is passionate about technologies, more specifically, Microsoft ones. He started early in the world of Microsoft messaging systems with MS Mail and Exchange 5.5 and went through all the versions to the actual ones, Exchange Server 2013/Exchange Online.

He is currently working at Nelite as a consultant/architect. He is involved in many migration and integration projects to/of Microsoft Exchange Server and Office 365.

www.PacktPub.com

Support files, eBooks, discount offers, and more

For support files and downloads related to your book, please visit www.PacktPub.com.

Did you know that Packt offers eBook versions of every book published, with PDF and ePub files available? You can upgrade to the eBook version at www.PacktPub.com and as a print book customer, you are entitled to a discount on the eBook copy. Get in touch with us at service@packtpub.com for more details.

At www.PacktPub.com, you can also read a collection of free technical articles, sign up for a range of free newsletters and receive exclusive discounts and offers on Packt books and eBooks.

PACKTLiB™

https://www2.packtpub.com/books/subscription/packtlib

Do you need instant solutions to your IT questions? PacktLib is Packt's online digital book library. Here, you can search, access, and read Packt's entire library of books.

Why subscribe?

- ▶ Fully searchable across every book published by Packt
- ▶ Copy and paste, print, and bookmark content
- ▶ On demand and accessible via a web browser

Free access for Packt account holders

If you have an account with Packt at www.PacktPub.com, you can use this to access PacktLib today and view 9 entirely free books. Simply use your login credentials for immediate access.

Instant updates on new Packt books

Get notified! Find out when new books are published by following @PacktEnterprise on Twitter or the *Packt Enterprise* Facebook page.

Table of Contents

Preface

This book is full of immediately usable task-based recipes for managing and maintaining your Microsoft Exchange 2013 environment with Windows PowerShell 5.0 and the Exchange Management Shell. The focus of this book is to show you how to automate routine tasks and solve common problems. While the Exchange Management Shell literally provides hundreds of cmdlets, we will not cover every single one of them individually. Instead, we'll focus on the common, real-world scenarios. You'll be able to leverage these recipes right away, allowing you to get the job done quickly, and the techniques that you'll learn will allow you to write your own amazing commands and scripts with ease.

What this book covers

Chapter 1, PowerShell Key Concepts, introduces several PowerShell core concepts, such as command syntax and parameters, working with the pipeline, loops, and conditional logic. The topics covered in this chapter lay the foundation for the remaining code samples in each chapter.

Chapter 2, Exchange Management Shell Common Tasks covers day-to-day tasks and general techniques for managing Exchange from the command line. The topics include configuring manual remote shell connections, exporting reports to external files, sending e-mail messages from scripts, and scheduling scripts to run with the Task Scheduler.

Chapter 3, Managing Recipients, demonstrates some of the most common recipient-related management tasks, such as creating mailboxes, distribution groups, and contacts. You'll also learn how to manage server-side inbox rules, Out of Office settings, and import user photos into Active Directory.

Chapter 4, Managing Mailboxes, shows you how to perform various mailbox management tasks that include moving mailboxes, importing and exporting mailbox data, and the detection and reparation of corrupt mailboxes. In addition, you'll learn how to delete and restore items from a mailbox and manage the new public folders.

Chapter 5, Distribution Groups and Address Lists, takes you deeper into distribution group management. The topics include distribution group reporting, distribution group naming policies, and allowing end users to manage distribution group membership. You'll also learn how to create Address Lists and Hierarchal Address Books.

Chapter 6, Mailbox Database Management, shows you how to set database settings and limits. Report generation for mailbox database size, average mailbox size per database, and backup status is also covered in this chapter.

Chapter 7, Managing Client Access, covers the management of ActiveSync, OWA, POP, and IMAP. It also covers the configuration of these components in Exchange 2013. We'll also take a look at controlling connections from various clients, including ActiveSync devices.

Chapter 8, Managing Transport Servers, explains the various methods used to control the mail flow within your Exchange organization. You'll learn how to create, send, and receive connectors, allow application servers to relay mail, and manage transport queues.

Chapter 9, High Availability, covers the implementation and management tasks related to Database Availability Groups. The topics include creating DAGs, adding mailbox database copies, and performing maintenance on DAG members. It also covers a new feature called Automatic Reseed.

Chapter 10, Exchange Security, introduces you to the new Role Based Access Control permissions model. You'll learn how to create custom RBAC roles for administrators and end users, and also how to manage mailbox permissions and implement SSL certificates.

Chapter 11, Compliance and Audit Logging, covers the new compliance and auditing features included in Exchange 2013. Topics such as archiving mailboxes and discovery search are covered here, as well as administrator and mailbox audit logging.

Chapter 12, Scripting with the Exchange Web Services Managed API, introduces you to advanced scripting topics that leverage Exchange Web Services. In this chapter, you'll learn how to write scripts and functions that go beyond the capabilities of the Exchange Management Shell cmdlets.

Appendix A, Common Shell Information, is a reference for the variables, scripts, and the filtering functions. These references will help you when writing scripts or running interactive scripts.

Appendix B, Query Syntaxes, is a reference for the Advanced Query Syntax. In this section, you will find lots of different examples that can be used in the real world.

What you need for this book

To complete the recipes in this book, you'll need the following:

- PowerShell v5, which is already installed by default on Windows 8.1 and Windows Server 2012 R2.
- A fully operational lab environment with an Active Directory forest and Exchange organization.
- Ideally, your Exchange Servers will run Windows Server 2012 R2, but they can run Windows Server 2008 R2 , if needed.
- You'll need to have at least one Microsoft Exchange 2013 server.
- It is assumed that the account you are using is a member of the Organization Management role group. The user account used to install Exchange 2013 is automatically added to this group.
- If possible, you'll want to run the commands, scripts, and functions in this book from a client machine. The 64-bit version of Windows 8.1 with the Exchange 2013 Management Tools installed is a good choice. You can also run the tools on Windows 7. Each client will need some additional prerequ sites in order to run the tools; see Microsoft's TechNet documentation for complete details.
- If you don't have a client machine, you can run the Exchange Management Shell from an Exchange 2013 server.
- *Chapter 12, Scripting with the Exchange Web Services Managed API*, requires the Exchange Web Services Managed API Version 2.2, which can be downloaded from `http://www.microsoft.com/en-us/download/details.aspx?id=42951`.

The code samples in this book should be run in a lab environment and fully tested before deployed into production. If you don't have a lab environment set up, the software can be downloaded from `http://technet.microsoft.com/en-us/exchange/`. Then, build the servers on your preferred virtualization engine.

Who this book is for

This book is for messaging professionals who want to learn how to build real-world scripts with Windows PowerShell 5.0 and the Exchange Management Shell. If you are a network or systems administrator responsible for managing and maintaining the on-premises version of Exchange Server 2013, then this book is for you.

The recipes in this Cookbook touch on each of the core Exchange 2013 server roles, and require a working knowledge of the supporting technologies, such as Windows Server 2008 R2, 2012 or 2012 R2, Active Directory, and DNS.

All of the topics in this book are focused on the on-premises version of Exchange 2013, and we will not cover Microsoft's hosted version of Exchange Online through Office 365. However, the concepts you'll learn in this book will allow you to hit the ground running with that platform since it will give you an understanding of PowerShell's command syntax and object-based nature.

Sections

In this book, you will find several headings that appear frequently (*Getting ready*, *How to do it*, *How it works*, *There's more*, and *See also*).

To give clear instructions on how to complete a recipe, we use these sections as follows:

Getting ready

This section tells you what to expect in the recipe, and describes how to set up any software or any preliminary settings required for the recipe.

How to do it...

This section contains the steps required to follow the recipe.

How it works...

This section usually consists of a detailed explanation of what happened in the previous section.

There's more...

This section consists of additional information about the recipe in order to make the reader more knowledgeable about the recipe.

See also

This section provides helpful links to other useful information for the recipe.

Conventions

In this book, you will find a number of styles of text that distinguish between different kinds of information. Here are some examples of these styles, and an explanation of their meaning.

Code words in text are shown as follows:

"We can read the content of an external file into the shell using the `Get-Content` cmdlet"

Commands and blocks of code are set as follows:

```
Get-Mailbox -ResultSize Unlimited | Out-File C:\report.txt
```

Commands like this can be invoked interactively in the shell, or from within a script or function.

Most of the commands you'll be working with will be very long. In order for them to fit into the pages of this book, we'll need to use line continuation. For example, the following is a command that creates a mailbox:

```
New-Mailbox -UserPrincipalName jsmith@contoso.com `
-FirstName John `
-LastName Smith `
-Alias jsmith `
-Database DB1 `
-Password $password
```

Notice that the last character on each line is the backtick (`` ` ``) symbol, also referred to as the grave accent. This is PowerShell's line continuation character. You can run this command as is, but make sure there aren't any trailing spaces at the end of each line. You can also remove the backtick and carriage returns and run the command on one line. Just ensure the spaces between the parameters and arguments are maintained.

You'll also see long pipeline commands formatted like the following example:

```
Get-Mailbox -ResultSize Unlimited |
Select-Object DisplayName,ServerName,Database |
Export-Csv c:\mbreport.csv -NoTypeInformation
```

PowerShell uses the pipe character (|) to send objects output from a command down the pipeline so it can be used as input by another command. The pipe character does not need to be escaped. You can enter the previous command as is, or you can format the command so that everything is on one line.

Any command-line input or output that must be done interactively at the shell console is written as follows:

```
[PS] C:\>Get-Mailbox administrator | ft ServerName,Database -Auto


ServerName Database
---------- --------
mbx1       DB01
```

New terms and **important words** are shown in bold. Words that you see on the screen, in menus or dialog boxes for example, appear in the text like this: "When a user logs into ECP, the very first thing they see is the **Account Information** screen".

[Warnings or important notes appear in a box like this.]

Reader feedback

Feedback from our readers is always welcome. Let us know what you think about this book—what you liked or disliked. Reader feedback is important for us as it helps us develop titles that you will really get the most out of.

To send us general feedback, simply e-mail feedback@packtpub.com, and mention the book's title in the subject of your message.

If there is a topic that you have expertise in and you are interested in either writing or contributing to a book, see our author guide at www.packtpub.com/authors.

Customer support

Now that you are the proud owner of a Packt book, we have a number of things to help you to get the most from your purchase.

Downloading the example code

You can download the example code files from your account at http://www.packtpub.com for all the Packt Publishing books you have purchased. If you purchased this book elsewhere, you can visit http://www.packtpub.com/support and register to have the files e-mailed directly to you.

Downloading the color images of this book

We also provide you with a PDF file that has color images of the screenshots/diagrams used in this book. The color images will help you better understand the changes in the output. You can download this file from `http://www.packtpub.com/sites/default/files/downloads/8074EN_ColorImages.pdf`.

Errata

Although we have taken every care to ensure the accuracy of our content, mistakes do happen. If you find a mistake in one of our books—maybe a mistake in the text or the code—we would be grateful if you could report this to us. By doing so, you can save other readers from frustration and help us improve subsequent versions of this book. If you find any errata, please report them by visiting `http://www.packtpub.com/submit-errata`, selecting your book, clicking on the **Errata Submission Form** link, and entering the details of your errata. Once your errata are verified, your submission will be accepted and the errata will be uploaded to our website or added to any list of existing errata under the Errata section of that title.

To view the previously submitted errata, go to `https://www.packtpub.com/books/content/support` and enter the name of the book in the search field. The required information will appear under the **Errata** section.

Piracy

Piracy of copyrighted material on the Internet is an ongoing problem across all media. At Packt, we take the protection of our copyright and licenses very seriously. If you come across any illegal copies of our works in any form on the Internet, please provide us with the location address or website name immediately so that we can pursue a remedy.

Please contact us at `copyright@packtpub.com` with a link to the suspected pirated material.

We appreciate your help in protecting our authors and our ability to bring you valuable content.

Questions

If you have a problem with any aspect of this book, you can contact us at `questions@packtpub.com`, and we will do our best to address the problem.

1
PowerShell Key Concepts

In this chapter, we will cover the following:

- ▶ Using the help system
- ▶ Understanding the command syntax and parameters
- ▶ Understanding the pipeline
- ▶ Working with variables and objects
- ▶ Working with arrays and hash tables
- ▶ Looping through items
- ▶ Creating custom objects
- ▶ Using the debugger functions
- ▶ Understanding the new execution policy
- ▶ Working with desired state configuration
- ▶ Using the Save-Help function
- ▶ Working with script repositories (a PowerShell v5 preview)

Introduction

So, your organization has decided to move to Exchange Server 2013 to take advantage of the many exciting new features, such as integrated e-mail archiving, discovery capabilities, and high availability functionality. Like it or not, you've realized that PowerShell is now an integral part of Exchange Server management, and you need to learn the basics to have a point of reference to build your own scripts. That's what this book is all about. In this chapter, we'll cover some core PowerShell concepts that will provide you with a foundation of knowledge to use the remaining examples in this book. If you are already familiar with PowerShell, you may want to use this chapter as a review or as a reference for later use after you've started writing scripts.

If you're completely new to PowerShell, its concept may be familiar if you've worked with UNIX command shells. Like UNIX-based shells, PowerShell allows you to string multiple commands together on one line using a technique called pipelining. This means that the output of one command becomes the input for another. However, unlike UNIX shells that pass the text output from one command to another, PowerShell uses an object model based on the .NET Framework, and objects are passed between commands in a pipeline, as opposed to plain text. From an Exchange perspective, working with objects gives us the ability to access very detailed information about servers, mailboxes, databases, and more. For example, every mailbox you manage within the shell is an object with multiple properties, such as an e-mail address, database location, or send and receive limits. The ability to access this type of information through simple commands means that we can build powerful scripts that generate reports, make configuration changes, and perform maintenance tasks with ease.

This book is based on the **Windows Management Framework (WMF)** 5.0 preview that was released in November 2014. Since this is a preview, the functionality may change in RTM and over time.

During the writing of this book, WMF 5.0 was not supported for Exchange 2013. This will probably change when the RTM gets released.

Performing some basic steps

To work with the code samples in this chapter, follow these steps to launch the Exchange Management Shell:

1. Log on to a workstation or server with the Exchange Management Tools installed.

2. You can connect using remote PowerShell, if you for some reason you don't have the Exchange Management Tools installed. Use the following command:

```
$Session = New-PSSession -ConfigurationName
Microsoft.Exchange

-ConnectionUri http://tlex01/PowerShell/
```

```
-Authentication Kerberos

Import-PSSession $Session
```

3. Open the Exchange Management Shell by navigating to **Start | All Programs | Microsoft Exchange Server 2013**. Or if you're using Windows Server 2012 R2, it can be found in the Apps list by clicking on the **Start** button and the arrow.

4. Click on the **Exchange Management Shell** shortcut.

> Remember to start the Exchange Management Shell using **Run as administrator** to avoid permission problems.
>
> In the chapter, notice that in the examples of cmdlets, I used the back tick (`` ` ``) character for breaking up long commands into multiple lines. The purpose is to make it easier to read. The back ticks are not required and should only be used if needed. Notice that the Exchange variables, such as $exscripts, are not available when using the preceding method.

Using the help system

The Exchange Management Shell includes over 780 cmdlets, each with a set of multiple parameters. For instance, the New-Mailbox cmdlet accepts more than 60 parameters, and the Set-Mailbox cmdlet has over 170 available parameters. It's safe to say that even the most experienced PowerShell expert would be at a disadvantage without a good help system. In this recipe, we'll take a look at how to get help in the Exchange Management Shell.

How to do it...

To get help information about a cmdlet, type Get-Help, followed by the cmdlet name. For example, to get help information about the Get-Mailbox cmdlet, run the following command:

```
Get-Help Get-Mailbox -full
```

How it works...

When running Get-Help for a cmdlet, a synopsis and description of the cmdlet will be displayed in the shell. The Get-Help cmdlet is one of the best discovery tools to use in PowerShell. You can use it when you're not quite sure how a cmdlet works or what parameters it provides.

You can use the following switch parameters to get specific information using the
`Get-Help` cmdlet:

- `Detailed`: This view provides parameter descriptions and examples and uses the
  following syntax:

  Get-Help <cmdletname> -Detailed

- `Examples`: You can view multiple examples of how to use a cmdlet by running the
  following syntax:

  Get-Help <cmdletname> -Examples

- `Full`: Use the following syntax to view the complete contents of the help file
  of a cmdlet:

  Get-Help <cmdletname> -Full

- `Online`: Use the following syntax to view the online version of the contents of the
  help file of a cmdlet:

  Get-Help <cmdletname> -Online

Some parameters accept simple strings as the input, while others require an actual object.
When creating a mailbox using the `New-Mailbox` cmdlet, you'll need to provide a secure
string object for the `-Password` parameter. You can determine the data type required for
a parameter using `Get-Help`:

```
                          Machine: tlex01.testlabs.se                    _  □  X

[PS] C:\>Get-Help New-Mailbox -Parameter Password

-Password <SecureString>
    The Password parameter specifies the initial password for the newly
    created user. This parameter isn't required if you're creating a
    linked mailbox, resource mailbox, or shared mailbox, because the user
    account for these types of mailboxes is disabled.

    Required?                    true
    Position?                    Named
    Default value
    Accept pipeline input?       False
    Accept wildcard characters?  false
```

From the output of the preceding command, you can see that we get several pieces of
key information about the `-Password` parameter. In addition to the required data type of
`<SecureString>`, we can see that this is a named parameter. It is required while running
the `New-Mailbox` cmdlet and it does not accept wildcard characters. You can use `Get-Help`
when examining the parameters for any cmdlet to determine whether or not they support
these settings.

You could run `Get-Help New-Mailbox -Examples` to determine the syntax required to create a secure string password object and how to use it to create a mailbox. This is also covered in detail in the recipe entitled *Adding, modifying, and removing mailboxes* in *Chapter 3, Managing Recipients*.

There's more...

There will be times when you'll need to search for a cmdlet without knowing its full name. In this case, there are a couple of commands you can use to find the cmdlets you are looking for.

To find all cmdlets that contain the word `Mailbox`, you can use a wildcard, as shown in the following command:

```
Get-Command *Mailbox*
```

You can use the `-Verb` parameter to find all cmdlets starting with a particular verb:

```
Get-Command -Verb Set
```

To search for commands that use a particular noun, specify the name with the `-Noun` parameter:

```
Get-Command -Noun Mailbox
```

The `Get-Command` cmdlet is a built-in PowerShell core cmdlet, and it will return commands from both Windows PowerShell as well as the Exchange Management Shell. The Exchange Management Shell also adds a special function called the `Get-Ex` command that will return only Exchange-specific commands.

In addition to getting cmdlet help for cmdlets, you can use `Get-Help` to view supplementary help files that explain general PowerShell concepts that focus primarily on scripting. To display the help file for a particular concept, type `Get-Help about_` followed by the concept name. For example, to view the help for the core PowerShell commands, type the following:

```
Get-Help about_Core_Commands
```

You can view the entire list of conceptual help files by using the following command:

```
Get-Help about_*
```

Don't worry about trying to memorize all the Exchange or PowerShell cmdlet names. As long as you can remember `Get-Command` and `Get-Help`, you can search for commands and figure out the syntax to do just about anything.

Getting help with cmdlets and functions

One of the things that can be confusing at first is the distinction between cmdlets and functions. When you launch the Exchange Management Shell, a remote PowerShell session is initiated to an Exchange server and specific commands, called proxy functions, are imported into your shell session. These proxy functions are essentially just blocks of code that have a name, such as `Get-Mailbox`, and that correspond to the compiled cmdlets installed on the server. This is true even if you have a single server and when you are running the shell locally on a server.

When you run the `Get-Mailbox` function from the shell, data is passed between your machine and the Exchange server through a remote PowerShell session.

The `Get-Mailbox` cmdlet is actually executing on the remote Exchange server, and the results are being passed back to your machine. One of the benefits of this is that it allows you to run the cmdlets remotely, regardless of whether your servers are on-premises or in the cloud. In addition, this core change in the toolset is what allows Exchange 2010 and 2013 to implement their new security model by allowing and restricting which cmdlets administrators and end users can actually use through the shell or the web-based control panel.

We'll get into the details of all this throughout the remaining chapters in the book. The bottom line is that, for now, you need to understand that, when you are working with the help system, the Exchange 2013 cmdlets will show up as functions and not as cmdlets.

Consider the following command and output:

```
Machine: tlex01.testlabs.se                    _  □  x

[PS] C:\>Get-Command Get-Service

CommandType      Name                                    Version
-----------      ----                                    -------
Cmdlet           Get-Service                             3.1.0.0
```

Here, we are running `Get-Command` against a PowerShell v5 core cmdlet. Notice that `CommandType` shows that this is a `Cmdlet`.

Now, try the same thing for the `Get-Mailbox` cmdlet:

```
Machine: tlex01.testlabs.se                    _  □  x

[PS] C:\>Get-Command Get-Mailbox

CommandType      Name                                    Version
-----------      ----                                    -------
Function         Get-Mailbox                             1.0
```

As you can see, CommandType for the Get-Mailbox cmdlet shows that it is actually a Function. So, there are a couple of key points to take away from this. First, throughout the course of this book, we will refer to the Exchange 2013 cmdlets as cmdlets, even though they will show up as functions when running Get-Command. Second, keep in mind that you can run Get-Help against any function name, such as Get-Mailbox, and you'll still get the help file for that cmdlet. However, if you are unsure of the exact name of a cmdlet, use Get-Command to perform a wildcard search as an aid in the discovery process. Once you've determined the name of the cmdlet you are looking for, you can run Get-Help against that cmdlet for complete details on how to use it.

Try using the help system before going to the Internet to find answers. You'll find that the answers to most of your questions are already documented within the built-in cmdlet help.

See also

▸ *Understanding command syntax and parameters*

▸ *Manually configuring remote PowerShell connections* in *Chapter 2, Exchange Management Shell Common Tasks*

▸ *Working with role-based access control* in *Chapter 10, Exchange Security*

Understanding command syntax and parameters

Windows PowerShell provides a large number of built-in cmdlets (pronounced command-lets) that perform specific operations. The Exchange Management Shell adds an additional set of PowerShell cmdlets used specifically for managing Exchange. We can also run these cmdlets interactively in the shell, or through automated scripts. When executing a cmdlet, parameters can be used to provide information, such as which mailbox or server to work with, or which attribute of those objects should be modified. In this recipe, we'll take a look at basic PowerShell command syntax and how parameters are used with cmdlets.

How to do it...

When running a PowerShell command, you type the cmdlet name, followed by any parameters required. Parameter names are preceded by a hyphen (-) followed by the value of the parameter. Let's start with a basic example. To get mailbox information for a user named `testuser`, use the following command syntax:

```
Get-Mailbox -Identity testuser
```

Alternatively, the following syntax also works and provides the same output, because the `-Identity` parameter is a positional parameter:

```
Get-Mailbox testuser
```

Most cmdlets support a number of parameters that can be used within a single command. We can use the following command to modify two separate settings on the `testuser` mailbox:

```
Set-Mailbox testuser -MaxSendSize 5mb -MaxReceiveSize 5mb
```

How it works...

All cmdlets follow a standard verb-noun naming convention. For example, to get a list of mailboxes, you use the `Get-Mailbox` cmdlet. You can change the configuration of a mailbox using the `Set-Mailbox` cmdlet. In both examples, the verb (`Get` or `Set`) is the action you want to take on the noun (`Mailbox`). The verb is always separated from the noun using the hyphen (-) character. With the exception of a few Exchange Management Shell cmdlets, the noun is always singular.

Cmdlet names and parameters are not case-sensitive. You can use a combination of upper and lowercase letters to improve the readability of your scripts, but it is not required.

Parameter input is either optional or required, depending on the parameter and cmdlet you are working with. You don't have to assign a value to the `-Identity` parameter since it is not required when running the `Get-Mailbox` cmdlet. If you simply run `Get-Mailbox` without any arguments, the first 1,000 mailboxes in the organization will be returned.

> If you are working in a large environment with more than 1,000 mailboxes, you can run the `Get-Mailbox` cmdlet, setting the `-ResultSize` parameter to `-Unlimited` to retrieve all of the mailboxes in your organization.

Notice that in the first two examples, we ran Get-Mailbox for a single user. In the first example, we used the -Identity parameter, but in the second example we did not. The reason we don't need to explicitly use the -Identity parameter in the second example is because it is a positional parameter. In this case, -Identity is in position 1, so the first argument received by the cmdlet is automatically bound to this parameter. There can be a number of positional parameters supported by a cmdlet, and they are numbered starting from one. Other parameters that are not positional are known as named parameters, which means that we need to use the parameter name to provide input for the value.

The -Identity parameter is included with most of the Exchange Management Shell cmdlets, and it allows you to classify the object you want to take an action on.

> The -Identity parameter used with the Exchange Management Shell cmdlets can accept different value types. In addition to the alias, the following values can be used: ADObjectID, Distinguished name, Domain\Username, GUID, LegacyExchangeDN, SmtpAddress, and **UserPrincipalName** (**UPN**).

When you run a cmdlet without providing an input for a required parameter, you will be prompted to enter the information before execution. This is because the cmdlet needs to know which mailbox it should modify when the command is executed.

> In order to determine whether a parameter is required, named or positional, supports wildcards, or accepts input from the pipeline, you can use the Get-Help cmdlet, which is covered in the next recipe in this chapter.
>
> Multiple data types are used for input, depending on the parameter you are working with. Some parameters accept string values, while others accept integers or Boolean values. Boolean parameters are used when you need to set a parameter value to either true or false. PowerShell provides built-in shell variables for each of these values using the $true and $false automatic variables. For a complete list of PowerShell v5 automatic variables, run Get-Help about_automatic_variables. Also see *Appendix A, Common Shell Information* for a list of automatic variables added by the Exchange Management Shell.

For example, you can enable or disable a send connector using the Set-SendConnector cmdlet with the -Enabled parameter:

```
Set-SendConnector Internet -Enabled $false
```

Switch parameters don't require a value. Instead, they are used to turn something on or off, or to either enable or disable a feature or setting. One common example of when you might use a switch parameter is when creating an archive mailbox for a user:

```
Enable-Mailbox testuser -Archive
```

PowerShell also provides a set of common parameters that can be used with every cmdlet. Some of the common parameters, such as the risk mitigation parameters (`-Confirm` and `-Whatif`), only work with cmdlets that make changes.

> For a complete list of common parameters, run `Get-Help about_CommonParameters`.

Risk mitigation parameters allow you to preview a change or confirm a change that may be destructive. If you want to see what will happen when executing a command without actually executing it, use the `–WhatIf` parameter:

```
Machine: tlex01.testlabs.se

[PS] C:\>Get-Mailbox –Database DB2 | Remove-Mailbox -WhatIf
What if: Removing mailbox "testlabs.se/Sales Users/Seattle/testuser" will r
emove the Active Directory user object and mark the mailbox and the archive
 (if present) in the database for removal.
[PS] C:\>
```

While making a change, such as removing a mailbox, you'll be prompted for confirmation, as shown in the following screenshot:

```
Machine: tlex01.testlabs.se

[PS] C:\>Remove-Mailbox -Identity testuser

Confirm
Are you sure you want to perform this action?
Removing mailbox "testuser" will remove the Active Directory user object
and mark the mailbox and the archive (if present) in the database for
removal.
[Y] Yes  [A] Yes to All  [N] No  [L] No to All  [?] Help
(default is "Y"):
```

To suppress this confirmation, set the `–Confirm` parameter to `false`:

```
Remove-Mailbox testuser -Confirm:$false
```

Notice here that when assigning the `$false` variable to the `-Confirm` parameter, we had to use a colon immediately after the parameter name and then the Boolean value. This is different to how we assigned this value earlier with the `-Enabled` parameter, when using the `Set-SendConnector` cmdlet. Remember that the `–Confirm` parameter always requires this special syntax, and while most parameters that accept a Boolean value generally do not require this, it depends on the cmdlet with which you are working. Fortunately, PowerShell has a great built-in help system that we can use when we run into these inconsistencies. When in doubt, use the help system, which is covered in detail in the next recipe.

Cmdlets and parameters support tab completion. You can start typing the first few characters of a cmdlet or a parameter name and hit the *Tab* key to automatically complete the name or tab through a list of available names. This is very helpful in terms of discovery and can serve as a bit of a time saver.

In addition, you only need to type enough characters of a parameter name to differentiate it from another parameter name. The following command using a partial parameter name is completely valid:

```
Set-Mailbox -id testuser -Office Sales
```

Here, we used `-id` as a shortcut for the `-Identity` parameter. The cmdlet does not provide any other parameters that start with `-id`, so it automatically assumes that you want to use the `-Identity` parameter.

Another helpful feature that some parameters support is the use of wildcards. When running the `Get-Mailbox` cmdlet, the `-Identity` parameter can be used with wildcards to return multiple mailboxes that match a certain pattern:

```
Get-Mailbox -id t*
```

In this example, all mailboxes starting with the letter `t` will be returned. Although this is fairly straightforward, you can refer to the help system for details on using wildcard characters in PowerShell by running `Get-Help about_Wildcards`.

[💡 Shortcuts for cmdlets might be great when doing interactive administrational tasks, but for future proofing the scripts, it's recommended that you use the full syntax of the cmdlets.]

There's more...

Parameter values containing a space need to be enclosed in either single or double quotation marks. The following command would retrieve all of the mailboxes in the `Sales Users` OU in Active Directory. Notice that since the OU name contains a space, it is enclosed in single quotes:

```
Get-Mailbox -OrganizationalUnit 'testlabs.se/Sales Users/Seattle'
```

Use double quotes when you need to expand a variable within a string:

```
$City = 'Seattle'
Get-Mailbox -OrganizationalUnit "testlabs.se/Sales Users/$City"
```

You can see here that we first create a variable containing the name of the city, which represents a sub OU under `Sales Users`. Next, we include the variable inside the string used for the organizational unit, when running the `Get-Mailbox` cmdlet. PowerShell automatically expands the variable name inside the double quoted string, where the value should appear, and all mailboxes inside the `Seattle` OU are returned by the command.

Quoting rules are documented in detail in the PowerShell help system. Run `Get-Help about_Quoting_Rules` for more information.

See also

- ▶ *Using the help system*
- ▶ *Working with variables and objects*

Understanding the pipeline

The single most important concept in PowerShell is the use of its flexible, object-based pipeline. You may have used pipelines in UNIX-based shells, or when working with the `cmd.exe` Command Prompt. The concept of pipelines is similar to that of sending the output from one command to another. Instead of passing plain text, PowerShell works with objects, and we can accomplish some very complex tasks in just a single line of code. In this recipe, you'll learn how to use pipelines to string together multiple commands and build powerful one-liners.

How to do it...

The following pipeline command would set the office location for every mailbox in the `DB1` database:

```
Get-Mailbox -Database DB2 | Set-Mailbox -Office "Headquarters"
```

How it works...

In a pipeline, you separate a series of commands using the pipe (|) character. In the previous example, the `Get-Mailbox` cmdlet returns a collection of mailbox objects. Each mailbox object contains several properties that contain information, such as the name of the mailbox, the location of the associated user account in Active Directory, and more. The `Set-Mailbox` cmdlet is designed to accept input from the `Get-Mailbox` cmdlet in a pipeline, and with one simple command, we can pass along an entire collection of mailboxes that can be modified in one operation.

You can also pipe the output to filtering commands, such as the `Where-Object` cmdlet. In this example, the command retrieves only the mailboxes with a `MaxSendSize` equal to 10 megabytes:

```
Get-Mailbox | Where-Object{$_.MaxSendSize -eq 10mb}
```

The code that the `Where-Object` cmdlet uses to perform the filtering is enclosed in curly braces ({ }). This is called a script block, and the code within this script block is evaluated for each object that comes across the pipeline. If the result of the expression is evaluated as `true`, the object is returned; otherwise, it is ignored. In this example, we access the `MaxSendSize` property of each mailbox using the `$_` object, which is an automatic variable that refers to the current object in the pipeline. We use the equals (`-eq`) comparison operator to check whether the `MaxSendSize` property of each mailbox is equal to 10 megabytes. If so, only those mailboxes are returned by the command.

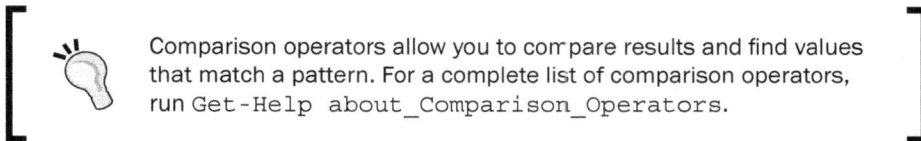

> Comparison operators allow you to compare results and find values that match a pattern. For a complete list of comparison operators, run `Get-Help about_Comparison_Operators`.

When running this command, which can also be referred to as a one-liner, each mailbox object is processed one at a time using stream processing. This means that as soon as a match is found, the mailbox information is displayed on the screen. Without this behavior, you would have to wait for every mailbox to be found before seeing any results. This may not matter if you are working in a very small environment, but without this functionality in a large organization with tens of thousands of mailboxes, you would have to wait a long time for the entire result set to be collected and returned.

One other interesting thing to note about the comparison being done inside our `Where-Object` filter is the use of the `mb` multiplier suffix. PowerShell natively supports these multipliers and they make it a lot easier for us to work with large numbers. In this example, we used `10mb`, which is the equivalent of entering the value in bytes because, behind the scenes, PowerShell is doing the math for us by replacing this value with `1024*1024*10`. PowerShell provides support for the following multipliers: `kb`, `mb`, `gb`, `tb`, and `pb`.

There's more...

You can use advanced pipelining techniques to send objects across the pipeline to other cmdlets that do not support direct pipeline input. For example, the following one-liner adds a list of users to a group:

```
Get-User |
Where-Object{$_.title -eq "Exchange Admin"} | Foreach-Object{
```

```
   Add-RoleGroupMember -Identity "Organization Management" `
   -Member $_.name
}
```

This pipeline command starts off with a simple filter that returns only the users that have their title set to Exchange Admin. The output from that command is then piped to the ForEach-Object cmdlet that processes each object in the collection. Similar to the Where-Object cmdlet, the ForEach-Object cmdlet processes each item from the pipeline using a script block. Instead of filtering, this time we are running a command for each user object returned in the collection and adding them to the Organization Management role group.

Using aliases in pipelines can be helpful because it reduces the number of characters you need to type. Let's take a look at the following command, where the previous command is modified to use aliases:

```
Get-User |
?{$_.title -eq "Exchange Admin"} | %{
   Add-RoleGroupMember -Identity "Organization Management" `
   -Member $_.name
}
```

Notice the use of the question mark (?) and the percent sign (%) characters. The ? character is an alias for the Where-Object cmdlet, and the % character is an alias for the ForEach-Object cmdlet. These cmdlets are used heavily, and you'll often see them used with these aliases because it makes the commands easier to type.

> You can use the Get-Alias cmdlet to find all of the aliases currently defined in your shell session and the New-Alias cmdlet to create custom aliases.

The Where-Object and ForEach-Object cmdlets have additional aliases. Here's another way you could run the previous command:

```
Get-User |
where{$_.title -eq "Exchange Admin"} | foreach{
   Add-RoleGroupMember -Identity "Organization Management" `
   -Member $_.name
}
```

Use aliases when you're working interactively in the shell to speed up your work and keep your commands concise. You may want to consider using the full cmdlet names in production scripts to avoid confusing others who may read your code.

See also

- ▸ *Looping through items*
- ▸ *Creating custom objects*
- ▸ *Dealing with concurrent pipelines in remote PowerShell* in *Chapter 2, Exchange Management Shell Common Tasks*

Working with variables and objects

Every scripting language makes use of variables as placeholders for data, and PowerShell is no exception. You'll need to work with variables often to save temporary data to an object so that you can work with it later. PowerShell is very different from other command shells in which everything you touch is, in fact, a rich object with properties and methods. In PowerShell, a variable is simply an instance of an object just like everything else. The properties of an object contain various bits of information depending on the type of object you're working with. In this recipe, we'll learn how to create user-defined variables and work with objects in the Exchange Management Shell.

How to do it...

To create a variable that stores an instance of the `testuser` mailbox, use the following command:

```
$mailbox = Get-Mailbox testuser
```

How it works...

To create a variable, or an instance of an object, you prefix the variable name with the dollar sign ($). To the right of the variable name, use the equals (=) assignment operator, followed by the value or object that should be assigned to the variable. Keep in mind that the variables you create are only available during your current shell session and will be destroyed when you close the shell.

Let's take a look at another example. To create a string variable that contains an e-mail address, use the following command:

```
$email = "testuser@contoso.com"
```

> In addition to user-defined variables, PowerShell also includes automatic and preference variables. To learn more, run `Get-Help about_Automatic_Variables` and `Get-Help about_Preference_Variables`.

Even a simple string variable is an object with properties and methods. For instance, every string has a `length` property that will return the number of characters that are in the string:

```
[PS] C:\>$email.length
20
```

When accessing the properties of an object, you can use dot notation to reference the property with which you want to work. This is done by typing the object name, then a period, followed by the property name, as shown in the previous example. You can access methods in the same way, except that the method names must always end with parenthesis `()`.

The string data type supports several methods, such as `Substring`, `Replace`, and `Split`. The following example shows how the `Split` method can be used to split a string:

```
[PS] C:\>$email.Split("@")
testuser
contoso.com
```

You can see here that the `Split` method uses the `"@"` portion of the string as a delimiter and returns two substrings as a result.

> PowerShell also provides a `-Split` operator that can split a string into one or more substrings. Run `Get-Help about_Split` for details.

There's more...

At this point, you know how to access the properties and methods of an object, but you need to be able to discover and work with these members. To determine which properties and methods are accessible on a given object, you can use the `Get-Member` cmdlet, which is one of the key discovery tools in PowerShell, along with `Get-Help` and `Get-Command`.

To retrieve the members of an object, pipe the object to the `Get-Member` cmdlet. The following command will retrieve all of the instance members of the `$mailbox` object we created earlier:

```
$mailbox | Get-Member
```

> To filter the results returned by `Get-Member`, use the `-MemberType` parameter to specify whether the type should be a `Property` or a `Method`.

Let's take a look at a practical example of how we can use `Get-Member` to discover the methods of an object. Imagine that each mailbox in our environment has a custom `MaxSendSize` restriction set, and we need to record the value for reporting purposes. When accessing the `MaxSendSize` property, the following information is returned:

```
[PS] C:\>$mailbox.MaxSendSize

IsUnlimited Value

----------- -----

False       10 MB (10,485,760 bytes)
```

We can see here that the `MaxSendSize` property actually contains an object with two properties: `IsUnlimited` and `Value`. Based on what we learned, we should be able to access the information for the `Value` property using the dot notation:

```
[PS] C:\>$mailbox.MaxSendSize.Value

10 MB (10,485,760 bytes)
```

That works, but the information returned contains not only the value in megabytes, but also the total number of bytes for the `MaxSendSize` value. For the purpose of what we are trying to accomplish, we only need the total number of megabytes. Let's see if this object provides any methods that can help us out with this, using `Get-Member`:

```
Machine: tlex01.testlabs.se                          _  □  X
[PS] C:\>$mailbox.MaxSendSize.Value | Get-Member -MemberType Method


    TypeName: Microsoft.Exchange.Data.ByteQuantifiedSize

Name          MemberType Definition
----          ---------- ----------
CompareTo     Method     int CompareTo(Microsoft.Exchange.Data.ByteQuan...
Equals        Method     bool Equals(System.Object obj), bool Equals(Mi...
GetHashCode   Method     int GetHashCode()
GetType       Method     type GetType()
RoundUpToUnit Method     uint64 RoundUpToUnit(Microsoft.Exchange.Data.B...
ToBytes       Method     uint64 ToBytes()
ToGB          Method     uint64 ToGB()
ToKB          Method     uint64 ToKB()
ToMB          Method     uint64 ToMB()
ToString      Method     string ToString(), string ToString(string form...
ToTB          Method     uint64 ToTB()
```

From the output shown in the preceding screenshot, we can see that this object supports several methods that can be used to convert the value. To obtain the `MaxSendSize` value in megabytes, we can call the `ToMB` method:

```
[PS] C:\>$mailbox.MaxSendSize.Value.ToMB()

10
```

In a traditional shell for Exchange on-premise, you would have to perform complex string parsing to extract this type of information, but PowerShell and the .NET Framework make this much easier. As you'll see over time, this is one of the reasons why PowerShell's object-based nature really outshines a typical text-based command shell.

An important thing to point about this last example is that it would not work if the mailbox had not had a custom `MaxSendSize` limitation configured. Nevertheless, this provides a good illustration of the process you'll want to use when you're trying to learn about an object's properties or methods.

Variable expansion in strings

As mentioned in the first recipe, *Using the help system*, in this chapter, PowerShell uses quoting rules to determine how variables should be handled inside a quoted string. When enclosing a simple variable inside a double-quoted string, PowerShell will expand that variable and replace the variable with the value of the string. Let's take a look at how this works by starting off with a simple example:

```
[PS] C:\>$name = "Bob"
[PS] C:\> "The user name is $name"
The user name is Bob
```

This is pretty straightforward. We stored the string value of `Bob` inside the `$name` variable. We then include the `$name` variable inside a double-quoted string that contains a message. When we hit return, the `$name` variable is expanded, and we get back the message we expect to see on the screen.

Now let's try this with a more complex object. Let's say that we want to store an instance of a mailbox object in a variable and access the `PrimarySmtpAddress` property inside the quoted string:

```
[PS] C:\>$mailbox = Get-Mailbox testuser
[PS] C:\>"The email address is $mailbox.PrimarySmtpAddress"
The email address is test user.PrimarySmtpAddress
```

Notice here that when we try to access the `PrimarySmtpAddress` property of our mailbox object inside the double-quoted string, we do not get back the information that we expect. This is a very common stumbling block when it comes to working with objects and properties inside strings. We can get around this using sub-expression notation. This requires that you enclose the entire object within the `$()` characters inside the string:

```
[PS] C:\>"The email address is $($mailbox.PrimarySmtpAddress)"
The email address is testuser@testlabs.se
```

Using this syntax, the `PrimarySmtpAddress` property of the `$mailbox` object is properly expanded and the correct information is returned. This technique will be useful later when we extract data from objects and generate reports or log files.

Strongly typed variables

PowerShell will automatically try to select the correct data type for a variable based on the value being assigned to it. You don't have to worry about doing this yourself, but we do have the ability to explicitly assign a type to a variable if needed. This is done by specifying the data type in square brackets before the variable name:

```
[string]$var2 = 32
```

Here, we assigned the value of 32 to the `$var2` variable. Had we not strongly typed the variable using the `[string]` type shortcut, `$var2` would have been created using the `Int32` data type, since the value we assigned was a number that was not enclosed in single or double quotes. Let's take a look at the following screenshot:

As you can see here, the `$var1` variable is initially created without any explicit typing. We use the `GetType()` method, which can be used on any object in the shell, to determine the data type of `$var1`. Since the value assigned was a number not enclosed in quotes, it was created using the `Int32` data type. When using the `[string]` type shortcut to create `$var2` with the same value, you can see that it has now been created as a string.

It is good to have an understanding of data types because when building scripts that return objects, you may need to have some control over this. For example, you may want to report on the amount of free disk space on an Exchange server. If we store this value in the property of a custom object as a string, we lose the ability to sort on that value. There are several examples throughout the book that use this technique.

> See *Appendix A, Common Shell Information* for a list of commonly-used type shortcuts.

Working with arrays and hash tables

Like many other scripting and programming languages, Windows PowerShell allows you to work with arrays and hash tables. An array is a collection of values that can be stored in a single object. A hash table is also known as an associative array and is a dictionary that stores a set of key-value pairs. You'll need to have a good grasp of arrays so that you can effectively manage objects in bulk and gain maximum efficiency in the shell. In this recipe, we'll take a look at how we can use both types of arrays to store and retrieve data.

How to do it...

You can initialize an array that stores a set of items by assigning multiple values to a variable. All you need to do is separate each value with a comma. The following command would create an array of server names:

```
$servers = "EX1","EX2","EX3"
```

To create an empty hash table, use the following syntax:

```
$hashtable = @{}
```

Now that we have an empty hash table, we can add key-value pairs:

```
$hashtable["server1"] = 1
$hashtable["server2"] = 2
$hashtable["server3"] = 3
```

Notice in this example that we can assign a value based on a key name, not by using an index number, as we saw with a regular array. Alternatively, we can create this same object using a single command, using the following syntax:

```
$hashtable = @{server1 = 1; server2 = 2; server3 = 3}
```

You can see here that we used a semicolon (;) to separate each key-value pair. This is only required if the entire hash table is created on one line.

You can break this up into multiple lines to make it easier to read:

```
$hashtable = @{
  server1 = 1
  server2 = 2
  server3 = 3
}
```

To create an empty array, use the following syntax:

```
$servers = @()
```

How it works...

Let's start off by looking at how arrays work in PowerShell. When working with arrays, you can access specific items and add or remove elements. In our first example, we assigned a list of server names to the $servers array. To view all of the items in the array, simply type the variable name and hit return:

```
[PS] C:\>$servers
EX1
EX2
EX3
```

Array indexing allows you to access a specific element of an array using its index number inside square brackets ([]). PowerShell arrays are zero-based, which means that the first item in the array starts at index zero. For example, use the second index to access the third element of the array, as shown next:

```
[PS] C:\>$servers[2]
EX3
```

To assign a value to a specific element of the array, use the equals (=) assignment operator. We can change the value from the last example using the following syntax:

```
[PS] C:\>$servers[2] = "EX4"
[PS] C:\>$servers[2]
EX4
```

Let's add another server to this array. To append a value, use the plus equals (+=) assignment operator, as shown here:

```
[PS] C:\>$servers += "EX5"
[PS] C:\>$servers
EX1
EX2
EX4
EX5
```

To determine how many items are in an array, we can access the Count property to retrieve the total number of array elements:

```
[PS] C:\>$servers.Count
4
```

We can loop through each element in the array with the `ForEach-Object` cmdlet and display the value in a string:

```
$servers | ForEach-Object {"Server Name: $_"}
```

We can also check for a value in an array using the `-Contains` or `-NotContains` conditional operator:

```
[PS] C:\>$servers -contains "EX1"
True
```

In this example, we are working with a one-dimensional array, which is what you'll be commonly dealing with in the Exchange Management Shell. PowerShell supports more complex array types, such as jagged and multidimensional arrays, but these are beyond the scope of what you'll need to know for the examples in this book.

Now that we have figured out how arrays work, let's take a closer look at hash tables. When we view the output for a hash table, the items are returned in no particular order. You'll notice this when we view the hash table we created earlier:

```
[PS] C:\>$hashtable
```

Name	Value
server2	2
server3	3
server1	1

If you want to sort the hash table, you can call the `GetEnumerator` method and sort by using the `Value` property:

```
[PS] C:\>$hashtable.GetEnumerator() | sort value
```

Name	Value
server1	1
server2	2
server3	3

Hash tables can be used when creating custom objects or to provide a set of parameter names and values using parameter splatting. Instead of specifying parameter names one by one with a cmdlet, you can use a hash table with keys that match the parameter's names and their associated values will automatically be used for input:

```
$parameters = @{
  Title = "Manager"
```

```
  Department = "Sales"

  Office = "Headquarters"

}
Set-User testuser @parameters
```

This command automatically populates the parameter values for `Title`, `Department`, and `Office` when running the `Set-User` cmdlet for the `testuser` mailbox.

For more details and examples for working with hash tables, run `Get-Help about_Hash_Tables`.

There's more...

You can think of a collection as an array created from the output of a command. For example, the `Get-Mailbox` cmdlet can be used to create an object that stores a collection of mailboxes, and we can work with this object just as we would with any other array. You'll notice that, when working with collections, such as a set of mailboxes, you can access each mailbox instance as an array element. Consider the following screenshot:

First, we retrieve a list of mailboxes that start with the letter `t` and assign that to the `$mailboxes` variable. From looking at the items in the `$mailboxes` object, we can see that the `testuser` mailbox is the second mailbox in the collection.

Since arrays are zero-based, we can access that item using the first index, as shown in the following screenshot:

In previous version(s) of the Exchange Server, we had an issue when the command only returned one item; the output could not be accessed using the array notation. If you face this, it can be solved using the following syntax:

```
$mailboxes = @(Get-Mailbox testuser)
```

You can see here that we wrapped the command inside the @() characters to ensure that PowerShell will always interpret the $mailboxes object as an array. This can be useful when you're building a script that always needs to work with an object as an array, regardless of the number of items returned from the command that created the object. Since the $mailboxes object has been initialized as an array, you can add and remove elements as needed.

We can also add and remove items to multivalued properties, just as we would with a normal array. To add an e-mail address to the testuser mailbox, we can use the following commands:

```
$mailbox = Get-Mailbox testuser
$mailbox.EmailAddresses += "testuser@testlabs.se"
Set-Mailbox testuser -EmailAddresses $mailbox.EmailAddresses
```

In this example, we created an instance of the testuser mailbox by assigning the command to the $mailbox object. We can then work with the EmailAddresses property to view, add, and remove e-mail addresses from this mailbox. You can see here that the plus equals (+=) operator was used to append a value to the EmailAddresses property.

We can also remove that value using the minus equals (-=) operator:

```
$mailbox.EmailAddresses -= "testuser@testlabs.se"
Set-Mailbox testuser -EmailAddresses $mailbox.EmailAddresses
```

> There is actually an easier way to add and remove e-mail addresses on recipient objects. See *Adding and removing recipient e-mail addresses* in *Chapter 3, Managing Recipients,* for details.

In this section, we covered the core concepts that you'll need to know while working with arrays. For more details, run Get-Help about_arrays.

See also

- *Working with variables and objects*
- *Creating custom objects*

Looping through items

Loop processing is a concept that you will need to master in order to write scripts and one-liners with efficiency. You'll need to use loops to iterate over each item in an array or a collection of items, and then run one or more commands within a script block against each of those objects. In this recipe, we'll take a look at how you can use `foreach` loops and the `ForEach-Object` cmdlet to process items in a collection.

How to do it...

The `foreach` statement is a language construct used to iterate through values in a collection of items. The following example shows the syntax used to loop through a collection of mailboxes, returning only the name of each mailbox:

```
foreach($mailbox in Get-Mailbox) {$mailbox.Name}
```

In addition, you can take advantage of the PowerShell pipeline and perform loop processing using the `ForEach-Object` cmdlet. This example produces the same result as the one shown previously:

```
Get-Mailbox | ForEach-Object {$_.Name}
```

You will often see the given command written using an alias of the `ForEach-Object` cmdlet, such as the percent sign (`%`):

```
Get-Mailbox | %{$_.Name}
```

How it works...

The first part of a `foreach` statement is enclosed in parentheses and represents a variable and a collection. In the previous example, the collection is the list of mailboxes returned from the `Get-Mailbox` cmdlet. The script block contains the commands that will be run for every item in the collection of mailboxes. Inside the script block, the `$mailbox` object is assigned the value of the current item being processed in the loop. This allows you to access each mailbox one at a time using the `$mailbox` variable.

When you need to perform loop processing within a pipeline, you can use the `ForEach-Object` cmdlet. The concept is similar, but the syntax is different because objects in the collection come across the pipeline.

The `ForEach-Object` cmdlet allows you to process each item in a collection using the `$_` automatic variable, which represents the current object in the pipeline. The `ForEach-Object` cmdlet is probably one of the most commonly used cmdlets in PowerShell, and we'll rely heavily on it in many examples throughout the book.

The code inside the script block used with both the looping methods can be more complex than just a simple expression. The script block can contain a series of commands or an entire script. Consider the following code:

```
Get-MailboxDatabase -Status | %{
  $DBName = $_.Name
  $whiteSpace = $_.AvailableNewMailboxSpace.ToMb()
  "The $DBName database has $whiteSpace MB of total white space"
}
```

In this example, we're looping through each mailbox database in the organization using the `ForEach-Object` cmdlet. Inside the script block, we created multiple variables, calculated the total megabytes of whitespace in each database, and returned a custom message that includes the database name and corresponding whitespace value. This is a simple example, but keep in mind that inside the script block, you can run other cmdlets, work with variables, create custom objects, and many more.

PowerShell also supports other language constructs for processing items, such as the `for`, `while`, and `do` loops. Although these can be useful in some cases, in the next recipe, we will use the `while` and `do` loops as examples. You can read more about them and view examples using the `get-help about_for`, `get-help about_while`, and `get-help about_do` commands in the shell.

There's more...

There are some key differences between the `foreach` statement and the `ForEach-Object` cmdlet that you'll want to be aware of when you need to work with loops. First, the `ForEach-Object` cmdlet can process one object at a time as it comes across the pipeline. When you process a collection using the `foreach` statement, this is the exact opposite. The `foreach` statement requires that all of the objects that need to be processed within a loop are collected and stored in memory before processing begins. We would want to take advantage of the PowerShell pipeline and its streaming behavior whenever possible, since it is much more efficient.

The other thing to take note of is that, in PowerShell, `foreach` is not only a keyword, but also an alias. This can be a little counterintuitive, especially when you are new to PowerShell and you run into a code sample that uses the following syntax:

```
Get-Mailbox | foreach {$_.Name}
```

At first glance, this might seem like we're using the `foreach` keyword, but we're actually using an alias for the `ForEach-Object` cmdlet. The easiest way to remember this distinction is that the `foreach` language construct is always used before a pipeline. If you use `foreach` after a pipeline, PowerShell will use the `foreach` alias, which corresponds to the `ForEach-Object` cmdlet.

Another common loop is the `for` loop, and it's ideal to use this loop when the same sequence of statements needs to be repeated a specific number of times. To explain the `for` loop, we illustrate this using the following example:

```
for (initialize; condition; increment) {
code block
}
```

The following are the various sections of PowerShell:

- ▶ **Initialize section**: In this section, you can set a variable to a starting value. You can also set one or more variables by separating them with commas.
- ▶ **Condition section**: This condition is tested each time by PowerShell before it executes the code. If the condition is found to be `true`, your body of code will be executed. If the condition is found to be `false`, PowerShell stops executing the code.
- ▶ **Increment section**: In this section, you can specify how you want a variable to be updated after each run of the loop. This can be an increment, a decrement, or any other change that you need. After the code has been executed once, PowerShell will update your variable.

The `for` loop keeps on looping until your condition turns `false`, which is similar to the following example.

```
for ($i = 1; $i -lt 11; $i++) {
Write-Host $i
}
```

In the preceding example, initially, `$i` is set to a value of `1`. The loop will run until `$i` is less than `11`. Our example will write the value for `$i` on the screen.

Other common loops are the `do while` and `while` loops. These loops executes until the condition value is `true`. These kinds of loop can be helpful when moving mailboxes and can then be used to verify that the move is proceeding as expected and has finished successfully. In this case, the move status would be the condition that the loop is using:

```
do { code block }
while (condition)
```

The preceding two sections shown are almost self-explanatory. Under the do section, the code is written, as our following example shows that we are using Write-Host.

Under the while section, the condition is set; in our example, the condition is that $i is less than 10:

```
do {
  Write-Host $i
  $i++
}
while ($i -le 10)
```

See also

- ▶ *Working with arrays and hash tables*
- ▶ *Understanding the pipeline*
- ▶ *Creating custom objects*

Creating custom objects

The fact that PowerShell is an object-based shell gives us a great deal of flexibility when it comes to writing one-liners, scripts, and functions. When generating detailed reports, we need to be able to customize the data output from our code so that it can be formatted or piped to other commands that can export the data in a clean, structured format. We also need to be able to control and customize the output from our code so that we can merge data from multiple sources into a single object. In this recipe, you'll learn a few techniques used to build custom objects.

How to do it...

The first thing we'll do is create a collection of mailbox objects that will be used as the data source for a new set of custom objects:

```
$mailboxes = Get-Mailbox
```

You can add custom properties to any object coming across the pipeline using calculated properties. This can be done using either the Select-Object or Format-Table cmdlets:

```
$mailboxes |
Select-Object Name,
Database,
@{name="Title";expression={(Get-User $_.Name).Title}},
@{name="Dept";expression={(Get-User $_.Name).Department}}
```

Another easy way to do this is by assigning a hash table to the `-Property` parameter of the `New-Object` cmdlet:

```
$mailboxes | %{
  New-Object PSObject -Property @{
    Name = $_.Name
    Database = $_.Database
    Title = (Get-User $_.Name).Title
    Dept = (Get-User $_.Name).Department
  }
}
```

You can also use the `New-Object` cmdlet to create an empty custom object, and then use the `Add-Member` cmdlet to tack on any custom properties that are required:

```
$mailboxes | %{
  $obj = New-Object PSObject
  $obj | Add-Member NoteProperty Name $_.Name
  $obj | Add-Member NoteProperty Database $_.Database
  $obj | Add-Member NoteProperty Title (Get-User $_.Name).Title
  $obj | Add-Member NoteProperty Dept (Get-User $_.Name).Department
  Write-Output $obj
}
```

Each of these three code samples will output the same custom objects that combine data retrieved from both the `Get-Mailbox` and `Get-User` cmdlets. Assuming that the `Title` and `Department` fields have been defined for each user, the output would look similar to the following screenshot:

How it works...

The reason we're building a custom object here is because we want to merge data from multiple sources into a single object. The `Get-Mailbox` cmdlet does not return the `Title` or `Department` properties that are tied to a user account; the `Get-User` cmdlet needs to be used to retrieve that information. Since we may want to generate a report that includes information from both the `Get-Mailbox` and `Get-User` cmdlets for each individual user, it makes sense to build a custom object that contains all of the required information. We can then pipe these objects to other cmdlets that can be used to export this information to a file.

We can modify one of our previous code samples and pipe the output to a CSV file used to document this information for the current user population:

```
$mailboxes |
Select-Object Name,
Database,
@{n="Title";e={(Get-User $_.Name).Title}},
@{n="Dept";e={(Get-User $_.Name).Department}} |
Export-CSV -Path C:\report.csv -NoType
```

Keep in mind that even though you can also create calculated properties using the `Format-Table` cmdlet, you'll want to use `Select-Object`, as shown previously, when converting these objects to CSV or HTML reports. These conversion cmdlets do not understand the formatting information returned by the `Format-Table` cmdlet, and you'll end up with a lot of useless data if you try to do this.

When building custom objects with the `Select-Object` cmdlet, we can select existing properties from objects coming across the pipeline and also add one or more calculated properties. This is done using a hash table that defines a custom property name in the hash table key and a script block within the hash table value. The script block is an expression where you can run one or more commands to define the custom property value. In our previous example, you can see that we called the `Get-User` cmdlet to retrieve both the `Title` and `Department` properties for a user that will be assigned to calculated properties on a new object.

The syntax to create a calculated property looks a little strange at first glance, since it uses the `name` and `expression` keywords to create a hash table that defines the calculated property. You can abbreviate these keywords, as shown next:

```
$mailboxes |
Select-Object Name,
Database,
```

```
@{n="Title";e={(Get-User $_.Name).Title}},
@{n="Dept";e={(Get-User $_.Name).Department}}
```

The property name uses the string value assigned to n, and the property value is assigned to e using a script block. Abbreviating these keywords with n and e just makes it easier to type. You can also use label or l to provide the calculated property name.

Using the New-Object cmdlet and assigning a hash table to the -Property parameter is a quick and easy way to create a custom object. The only issue with this technique is that the properties can be returned in a random order. This is due to how the .NET Framework assigns random numeric values to hash table keys behind the scenes, and the properties are sorted based on those values, not in the order that you defined them. The only way to get the properties back in the order you want is to continue to pipe the command to Select-Object and select the property names in order, or to use one of the other techniques shown in this recipe.

Creating an empty custom object and manually adding note properties with the Add-Member cmdlet can require a lot of extra typing, so generally this syntax is not widely used. This technique becomes useful when you want to add script methods or script properties to a custom object, but this is an advanced technique that we won't need to utilize for the recipes in the remainder of this book.

There's more...

There is another useful technique used to create custom objects, which utilizes the Select-Object cmdlet. Let's take a look at the following code:

```
$mailboxes | %{
  $obj = "" | Select-Object Name,Database,Title,Dept
  $obj.Name = $_.Name
  $obj.Database = $_.Database
  $obj.Title = (Get-User $_.Name).Title
  $obj.Dept = (Get-User $_.Name).Department
  Write-Output $obj
}
```

You can create a custom object by piping an empty string variable to the Select-Object cmdlet, specifying the property names that should be included. The next step is to simply assign values to the properties of the object using the property names that you defined. This code loops through the items in our $mailboxes object and returns a custom object for each one. The output from this code returns the exact same objects as all of the previous examples.

See also

- ▶ *Looping through items*
- ▶ *Working with variables and objects*
- ▶ *Exporting reports to text and CSV files* in *Chapter 2, Exchange Management Shell Common Tasks*
- ▶ *Dealing with concurrent pipelines in remote PowerShell* in *Chapter 2, Exchange Management Shell Common Tasks*

Using debugger functions

With PowerShell Version 5, we have great functions, such as debugging scripts, and code in PowerShell was added. This was introduced in the Windows Management Framework 5.0 preview. In this recipe, we will take a look at it in more depth. This recipe is more like a general PowerShell function but can, of course, be applied to Exchange scripts.

Let's take a look at two of these functions in detail and start with the basics and then advance from there. Both these examples can be used in the PowerShell console and in Windows PowerShell ISE.

The first method we are going to take a look at is called `Break All` and was introduced in PowerShell v5. This method gives us the option to debug the PowerShell workflow and supports command and tab completion. We can debug nested workflow functions both in local and remote sessions.

The second function in this recipe that we will use is the `Debug-Job` cmdlet inside more complex and advanced scripts. It uses the same basis as the `Break All` function.

How to do it...

First, we create a variable named `$i` with a value of 1, and then create a loop using the `Do While` operator. The loop will run until `$i` is less than or equal to 20. Within the loop, a text string is written to the console with a text `Value` and the value of `$i`:

```
$i = 1
Do {
Write-Host "Value: $i"
  $i++
  Start-Sleep -Milliseconds 200
}
While ($i -le 20)
```

As this is a basic example of how the debugger can be used, this method would be helpful for production, when executing scripts. The debugger mode can be used when the script is running by pressing *CTRL + Break* or *CTRL + B*. When breaking a script, it will look similar to the following screenshot:

```
Machine: tlex01.testlabs.se                       _  □  X
[PS] C:\Scripts>.\loop.ps1
Value: 1
Value: 2
Value: 3
Value: 4
Value: 5
Entering debug mode. Use h or ? for help.

At C:\Scripts\loop.ps1:5 char:2
+     Write-Host "Value: $i"
+     ~~~~~~~~~~~~~~~~~~~~~~~
[PS] C:\Scripts>_
```

We can see that the script called `loop.ps1` is stopped and has entered the debug mode. When pressing h or ?, the help information will show up.

In the debug mode, we can see the full source code (us ng 1) in the current script, we can also step through every row in the script (using s), go to the next statement (using v), and of course, continue running the script (using c) or stop the operation and exit the debug mode (using q).

How it works...

By initializing the debugging mode, the script is stopped until using either the `Continue` or `Quit` commands. The debugging can be very helpful; and for example, you can step through the code, view the source code, verify variables, view the environment state, and execute commands.

In the preceding screenshot, let's take a look at what the value in the $i variable is by typing the following command:

```
[PS] C:\Scripts>$i
```

```
5
```

Here, we see that the value is 5 as the loop was stopped at that stage.

One thing to mention here is that the script debugging method will only debug the executed script itself and cannot collect any information from external native commands or scripts and sends back the result in the debugging mode. For more advanced debugging, use the managed code together with Visual Studio or WinDbg.

There's more...

Together with the code debugger function, we can use the Debug-Job cmdlet that was introduced in Version 5 of PowerShell.

The Debug-Job cmdlet lets you break into the script debugger while running a job in a similar way, as the Break All function lets us break into a running script from the console or ISE.

A typical scenario where we could use Debug-Job is when we are running a long, complex script as a job, and for one reason or another, we suspect that the script is not executing correctly. It may take longer than expected or some of the output data doesn't seem right. Now we can drop the job in the debugger using the Debug-Job cmdlet, which allows us to verify that the code is being executed the way it's expected to be; it's a great and helpful function.

As you probably are aware of or the problem that you might face in the future is that while debugging scripts interactively, they work as expected but when they are running as jobs in production, they fail. However, this can now be debugged with this new feature by setting breakpoints or using the Wait-Debugger cmdlet.

In the following example, we are setting a breakpoint at Line 4 to debug the script and run it as a job, and use the Debug-Job cmdlet:

```
$job = Start-Job -ScriptBlock { Set-PSBreakpoint `
C:\Scripts\MyJob.ps1-Line 4; C:\Scripts\MyJob.ps1 `
}
$job

Debug-Job $job
```

By doing this, we will be able to enter the debugging mode and can reach variables, execute commands, view the environment state, view the source code, and step through the code:

```
                    Machine: tlex01.testlabs.se                  _  □  x
[PS] C:\Scripts>$job = Start-Job -ScriptBlock { Set-PSBreakpoint C:\Scripts
\MyJob.ps1 -Line 4; C:\Scripts\MyJob.ps1 }
[PS] C:\Scripts>$job

Id      Name            PSJobTypeName     State        HasMoreData     Locat
                                                                       ion
--      ----            -------------     -----        -----------     -----
2       Job2            BackgroundJob     AtBreakpoint True            lo...

[PS] C:\Scripts>Debug-Job $job
Entering debug mode. Use h or ? for help.

Hit Line breakpoint on 'C:\Scripts\MyJob.ps1:4'

At C:\Scripts\MyJob.ps1:4 char:22
+ foreach ($process in $Processes)
+                      ~~~~~~~~~~~
[DBG]: PS C:\Users\admins.TESTLABS\Documents>> _
```

The preceding screenshot shows you that the job state is `AtBreakpoint`, which means that it is waiting to be debugged. This method works in a similar way as the `Break All` method; it will only debug the script itself and cannot debug any external commands.

To continue with the process and leave the debugging mode, use the `detach` command.

See also

- *Understanding the new execution policy*
- *Creating custom objects*
- *Using the Save-Help function*

Understanding the new execution policy

Windows PowerShell implements script security to keep unwanted scripts from running in your environment. You have the option of signing your scripts with a digital signature to ensure that scripts that run are from a trusted source.

The policy has five (`Undefined`, `Restricted`, `AllSigned`, `RemoteSigned`, and `Unrestricted`) different states to be set in five different scopes (`MachinePolicy`, `UserPolicy`, `Process`, `CurrentUser`, and `LocalMachine`).

Here is a short description of the different policies and what they can or can't do:

- ► `Undefined`: There is no execution policy set for the current scope
- ► `Restricted`: No script either local, remote, or downloaded can be executed
- ► `AllSigned`: All scripts that are run require to be digitally signed
- ► `RemoteSigned`: All remote (UNC) or downloaded scripts require to be digitally signed
- ► `Unrestricted`: All scripts are allowed to be executed

Here is a description of the different scopes:

- ► `MachinePolicy`: This execution policy set by a group policy applies to all users
- ► `UserPolicy`: This execution policy set by a group policy applies to the current user
- ► `Process`: This execution policy applies to the current Windows PowerShell process
- ► `CurrentUser`: This execution policy applies to the current user
- ► `LocalMachine`: This execution policy applies to all users of the computer

It is possible to manage Exchange 2013 through PowerShell remoting on a workstation or server without the Exchange Tools installed. In this case, you'll need to make sure that your script execution policy is set to either `RemoteSigned` or `Unrestricted`. To set the execution policy, use the following command:

```
Set-ExecutionPolicy RemoteSigned
```

Make sure that you do not change the execution policy to `AllSigned` on machines where you'll be using the Exchange cmdlets. This will interfere with importing the commands through a remote PowerShell connection, which is required for the Exchange Management Shell cmdlets to run properly.

How to do it...

The following are some examples of cmdlets that can be used to configure the execution policy:

```
Get-ExecutionPolicy -List | Format-Table -AutoSize
Set-ExecutionPolicy AllSigned
Set-ExecutionPolicy -Scope CurrentUser -ExecutionPolicy `
RemoteSigned
```

How it works...

The default scope is set to `LocalMachine` if nothing is specified, which means that it will apply to everyone on this machine. If the execution policy is set to `Undefined` in all scopes, the effective execution policy is `Restricted`.

We started with listing the current policy settings and then continued with configuring the `LocalMachine` policy that requires scripts to be digita ly signed. Otherwise, they will be prohibited from being executed.

The last cmdlet was used to configure `CurrentUser` to `RemoteSigned` instead of `AllSigned`, which was configured to the `LocalMachine` policy.

Once this change is done, the configuration would look like the following screenshot:

This makes it possible to configure the execution policy to provide digital signatures for scripts that are executed by everyone, except the currently logged-in user.

If you are uncertain on which user is logged on, use the `whoami` command.

There's more...

Since the default execution policy is configured to `RemoteSigned`, all remote (UNC) or downloaded scripts require to be digitally signed.

It is very common that when a script is downloaded, we need to unblock this file before it can be executed, when the policy is set to default settings.

Of course, it's recommended that before you unblock any downloaded file, you need to test it in a test environment so that it doesn't harm any production environment or add any malicious code in some way:

```
Unblock-File -Path C:\Scripts\HarmlessScript.ps1
```

```
Get-ChildItem C:\DownloadFolder | Unblock-File
```

The first line unblocks the specified downloaded file, while the second line retrieves all files from a folder called `DownloadFolder` and then unblocks them. This makes it possible to execute these files with the default configuration.

`Unblock-File` performs the same operation as the **Unblock** button in the **Properties** dialog box in File Explorer.

For more detailed information, use the `Get-Help about_Execution_Policies` cmdlet.

See also

▸ *Working with Desired State Configuration*

▸ *Working with script repositories*

▸ *Using the Save-Help function*

Working with Desired State Configuration

Desired State Configuration (**DSC**) was first introduced in PowerShell Version 4. With PowerShell Version 5, it has, of course, been developed a lot. Some of the new functions that would be interesting from an Exchange on-premise perspective are as follows:

▸ ThrottlingLimit (`PSDesiredStateConfiguration`) specifies the number of target computers or devices on which we want the command to run simultaneously

▸ Centralized DSC error reporting

▸ Improvements to DSC resourcing lists all DSC resources, automatic completion, the `DependsOn` property, and tab completion

▸ DSC can now be run with a specified user by adding the `PSDscRunAsCredential` cmdlet to the node block

▸ 32-bit support was added

▸ Partial configuration can now deliver configuration documents to a node in fragments

▸ New cmdlets such as `Get-DscConfigurationStatus`, `Compare-DscConfiguration`, `Publish-DscConfiguration`, `Test-DscConfiguration`, and `Update-DscConfiguration` were introduced

Now we have all the great functionality added into the last version of PowerShell for DSC.

Before we go deep into this recipe, we should be aware of what the purpose of DSC is and what DSC is all about.

DSC can in some way be compared to Active Directory **Group Policies Objects** (**GPO**). The main purpose of both of them is to make sure that settings are configured according to the configuration. In that sense, DSC can pretty much be compared to GPO, and DSC will make sure that the settings are equally the same over the specified nodes and that the settings will remain so.

The DSC system has two configuration modes: push or pull using HTTP(S) or SMB. A typical setup would be to have one server acting as the DSC server, where the configurations and modules are located.

In push mode, the MOF configuration is pushed to its intended targets, called nodes. The opposite is done in pull mode; the nodes then pull the configuration from the DSC server, which has to be configured, and get the required modules and resources. The pull nodes have a scheduled task that takes the actions.

In this recipe, we concentrate on pull mode, and the default setting for the pull interval is 15 minutes.

In this recipe, we will install and configure the DSC server. With the DSC server in place, we will take it to the next level and see how DSC can help us manage Exchange on-premises.

How to do it...

Our first example is an example of how to configure the DSC Pull Server. One thing to mention, as a prerequisite, is that winrm needs to be configured. This is done by running the following command winrm quickconfig.

So, let's install and configure the DSC Pull server using the following example. Save the following script as PullServerConfig.ps1 and run it:

```
configuration CreatePullServer
{
  param
    (
      [string[]]$ComputerName = 'localhost'
    )
  Import-DSCResource -ModuleName xPSDesiredStateConfiguration
  Node $ComputerName
    {
      WindowsFeature DSCServiceFeature
        {
          Ensure = "Present"
          Name   = "DSC-Service"
        }
      xDscWebService PSDSCPullServer
        {
            Ensure = "Present"
            EndpointName = "PSDSCPullServer"
            Port = 8080
            PhysicalPath = "$env:SystemDrive\inetpub\wwwroot\ `
PSDSCPullServer"
            CertificateThumbPrint = "AllowUnencryptedTraffic"
            ModulePath = "$env:PROGRAMFILES\WindowsPowerShell\ `
DscService\Modules"
```

```
              ConfigurationPath = "$env:PROGRAMFILES\ `
WindowsPowerShell\DscService\Configuration"
              State = "Started"
              DependsOn = "[WindowsFeature]DSCServiceFeature"
          }
        xDscWebService PSDSCComplianceServer
          {
              Ensure = "Present"
              EndpointName = "PSDSCComplianceServer"
              Port = 9080
              PhysicalPath = "$env:SystemDrive\inetpub\wwwroot\ `
PSDSCComplianceServer"
              CertificateThumbPrint = "AllowUnencryptedTraffic"
              State = "Started"
              IsComplianceServer = $true
              DependsOn = ("[WindowsFeature]DSCServiceFeature","[xDSCWeb
Service]PSDSCPullServer")
          }
      }
}
CreatePullServer -ComputerName dscsrv.testlabs.se
```

This wasn't too hard. Was it? So, let's continue with the configuration for our Exchange server. In the following example, we are going to configure the execution policy to a value of RemoteSigned. We are also going to make sure that the MSExchangeFrontEndTransport service is running. So, let's create the script and finally one for pulling the configuration from the DSC server:

```
Configuration CompliantExchange
{
  param ($MachineName)
  Import-DSCResource -ModuleNamePSDesiredStateConfiguration, `
xPowerShellExecutionPolicy
  Node $MachineName
  {
    xPowerShellExecutionPolicy SetPSExecutionPolicyToRemoteSigned
    {
      ExecutionPolicy = "RemoteSigned"
    }
  Service MSExchangeFrontEndTransport
    {
      Name = "MSExchangeFrontEndTransport"
      StartupType = "Automatic"
```

```
        State = "Running"
      }
    }
}
CompliantExchange -MachineName tlex01.testlabs.se
$guid = [guid]::NewGuid()
$source = "CompliantExchange\tlex01.testlabs.se.mof"
$dest = "\\dscsrv.testlabs.se\c`$\program
files\windowspowershell\dscservice\configuration\$guid.mof"
copy $source $dest
New-DSCChecksum $dest
```

So, let's create the script to pull the configuration from the DSC server to our Exchange server.
This should be executed on the Exchange on-premises server:

```
Configuration SetPullMode
{
   param([string]$guid)
   Node tlex01.testlabs.se
     {
        LocalConfigurationManager
         {
           ConfigurationMode = 'ApplyAndAutoCorrect'
           ConfigurationID = $guid
           RefreshMode = 'Pull'
           DownloadManagerName = 'WebDownloadManager'
           DownloadManagerCustomData = @{
              ServerUrl = 'http://dscsrv.testlabs.se:8080/
PSDSCPullServer.svc';
              AllowUnsecureConnection = 'true' }
         }
      }
}
SetPullMode -guid $guid
Set-DSCLocalConfigurationManager -Computer tlex01.testlabs.se `
-Path ./SetPullMode -Verbose
```

How it works...

The first part in this recipe was the script to create the DSC Pull server, don't forget about the
prerequisite (winrm quickconfig). To create the pull server in this example, we did import
the DSC module named xPSDesiredStateConfiguration and use the resource named
xDscWebService. Make sure to place the xPSDesiredStateConfiguration module into
the $env:ProgramFiles\WindowsPowerShell\Modules folder.

We saved the script as `PullServerConfig.ps1` and started it by running
`.\PullServerConfig.ps1`. A folder will be created with the configuration name; in
this case, it was called `CreatePullServer`. Inside the folder, we now have a file called
`nodename.domain.mod`; in our example, it was named `dscsrv.testlabs.se.mof`.

Finally, to configure the server, we started the DSC configuration by running
`Start-DscConfiguration .\CreatePullServer -Wait`. The reason we are
using the `Wait` parameter is that it's easier for us to follow if everything runs as expected.
The following screenshot shows you an ongoing configuration:

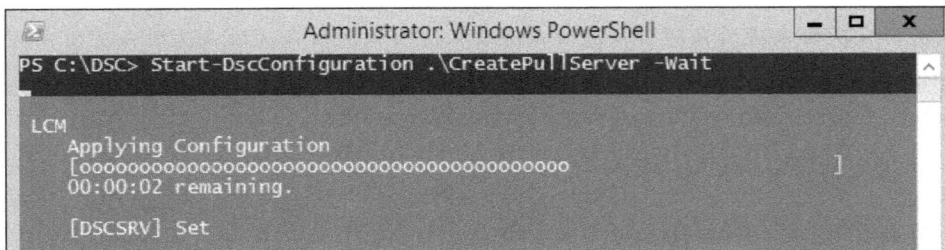

When our DSC server was created successfully, the second script that we used was made
with the purpose to make sure that the execution policy was always set to `RemoteSigned`
and that the Microsoft Exchange service named `MSExchangeFrontEndTransport` was
always running. However, these two were just used to illustrate an example of what DSC
could be used for.

First, we imported the DSC modules that are going to be used. One thing to
mention here is that these modules need to be deployed to our pull clients/nodes,
in the same folder as the DSC server. The modules should be placed in the
`$env:ProgramFiles\WindowsPowerShell\Modules` folder.

In the second script, we specified which node we are going to configure with the resource
and what setting.

Before deploying these scripts to the DSC server, we need to make sure to follow the third
script, where we created a new guide and published the `configuration/mof` file in the
`$env:ProgramFiles\WindowsPowerShell\DscService\Configuration` folder.
This is basically done because the DSC server uses GUIDs and now node names.

With the MOF files in place, the last step for the configuration is to create a checksum for
the MOF file. This is done using the `New-DSCChecksum` cmdlet.

The final step to allow the DSC server and its client/nodes to take the necessary actions,
we need to configure the nodes. In our example, the Exchange server needs to pull the
configuration from the DSC server. Once the pull mode has been configured, give the node
30 minutes to retrieve the configuration. The following screenshot shows you when to
configure the Exchange server in order to use the pull method instead of the push method:

```
Administrator: Windows PowerShell                        ‒  ☐  x

PS C:\DSC> .\SetPullMode.ps1


    Directory: C:\DSC\SetPullMode

Mode            LastWriteTime          Length Name
----            -------------          ------ ----
-a----          1/18/2015    9:44 PM     2062 tlex01.testlabs.se.meta.m
                                              of
VERBOSE: Performing the operation "Start-DscConfiguration:
SendMetaConfigurationApply" on target "MSFT_DSCLocalConfigurationManager".
VERBOSE: Perform operation 'Invoke CimMethod' with following parameters,
''methodName' = SendMetaConfigurationApply,'className' =
MSFT_DSCLocalConfigurationManager,'namespaceName' =
root/Microsoft/Windows/DesiredStateConfiguration'.
VERBOSE: An LCM method call arrived from computer DSCSRV with user sid
S-1-5-21-2583573880-4118140427-1284315487-500.
VERBOSE: [TLEX01]: LCM:  [ Start  Set      ]
VERBOSE: [TLEX01]: LCM:  [ Start  Resource ]  [MSFT_DSCMetaConfiguration]
VERBOSE: [TLEX01]: LCM:  [ Start  Set      ]  [MSFT_DSCMetaConfiguration]
VERBOSE: [TLEX01]: LCM:  [ End    Set      ]  [MSFT_DSCMetaConfiguration]
  in 0.0150 seconds.
VERBOSE: [TLEX01]: LCM:  [ End    Resource ]  [MSFT_DSCMetaConfiguration]
VERBOSE: [TLEX01]: LCM:  [ End    Set      ]   in  0.0310 seconds.
VERBOSE: Operation 'Invoke CimMethod' complete.
VERBOSE: Set-DscLocalConfigurationManager finished in 0.257 seconds.
```

After applying the pull configuration settings, give the node at least 30 minutes, then you can go ahead and check whether the configuration has taken place by running the `Get-DscConfigurationStatus` cmdlet. This cmdlet will show you if the configuration was successfully deployed or if there were any issues. Also, the `Get-DscConfiguration` cmdlet can be helpful to see which configuration was deployed and its status.

See also

▸   *Understanding the new execution policy*

▸   *Working with script repositories*

Using the Save-Help function

The useful help cmdlet `Get-Help` can provide useful information and examples. By default, PowerShell retrieves the help files from the Internet if they are not available locally.

In PowerShell Version 4 of Windows Management Framework, the function was introduced that made it possible to save the help files and import them to another server or client, which is great when a server or client is prohibited from having Internet access.

This can be done with the following few commands; these commands will be described in the *How it works* section.

How to do it...

Let's take a look at the following example to update the help files for the modules that has anything to do with `Microsoft.PowerShell`:

```
Get-Module -Name Microsoft.PowerShell*

Save-Help -Module Microsoft.PowerShell* -DestinationPath `
"C:\HelpFiles"

Update-Help-SourcePath "C:\Help" -Force

Update-Help -SourcePath "\\fileserver\HelpFilesShare" -Force
```

How it works...

Once the help files are downloaded, each module contains a XML and CAB file. These can be updated per module or all at once. This is a basic task to perform.

In the previous example, we are first retrieving the modules, which are available, that have a name `Microsoft.PowerShell` followed by something. Then, the help files are downloaded for these modules and saved in a local folder called `Help`.

If we do not specify any modules, all the help files for PowerShell will be downloaded to the specified folder.

Finally, these help files are then imported to another server or client, simply where they are needed using the `Update-Help` cmdlet.

As shown in the preceding example, the `Update-Help` function can either be pointing at a local folder or a UNC path or share.

Be aware that when running the `Update-Help` cmdlet, you may require to use the **Run as administrator** option or else it might not have the access needed to import the files into the system:

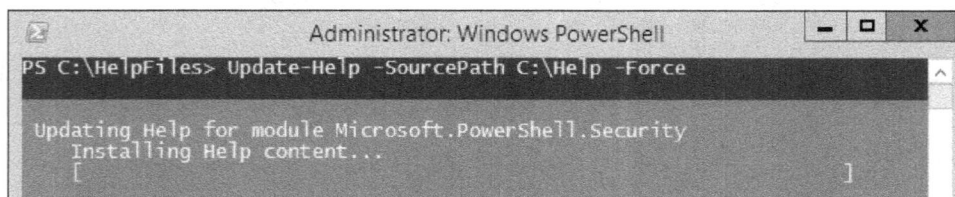

> Note that `-DestinationPath` and `-SourcePath` should be pointed to a folder and not to a file. The help files contain a pair of XML and CAB files per module.

A good idea would be to always keep these help files up to date and update them in the PowerShell profile to make sure that it's the current version.

See also

- ▶ *Using the help system*
- ▶ *Using debugger functions*
- ▶ *Creating custom objects*

Working with script repositories

Windows Management Framework Version 5 includes a package manager called PowerShellGet, which enables functionalities, such as the `find`, `get`, `install`, and `uninstall` packages from internal and public sources. However, this recipe is not specific to Exchange; see this recipe as a tips and tricks recipe, since it's more PowerShell gereral than Exchange-specific.

PowerShellGet is a package manager for Windows PowerShell. Basically, it is a wrapper around the OneGet component that simplifies the package management for PowerShell modules. PowerShellGet is built on top of the well-known package management solution NuGet.

OneGet is a unified package management component that allows you to search for software installation, uninstallation, and inventory for any type of software that it supports through its provider interface.

OneGet works with the community-based software repository called Chocolatey. Currently, Chocolatey has over 2,600 unique packages.

There are a bunch of galleries (also referred to as provicers) to use and select from, such as PowerShell Resource Gallery (Microsoft supported), MyGet, Inedo ProGet, JFrog Artifactory, and many more.

For a better understanding, let's take a look at the first example.

How to do it...

In this example, we will use OneGet to install two example modules from Chocolatey:

```
Import-Module -Name OneGet
Get-Command -Module OneGet
Find-Package | Out-GridView
Find-Package -Name "notepadplusplus"
Find-Package -Name "7zip"
Install-Package -Name "7zip"
Install-Package -Name "notepadplusplus"-Force
Get-Package
```

How it works...

For illustrating how OneGet works we have seen the preceding example.

First, we imported the module of OneGet to use the cmdlets for the package manager. We then used the `Get-Command` cmdlet to see what commands are available with this module.

With the `Find-Package` cmdlet, we searched for available packages. First, we piped the results to a `GridView`, since this can be user friendly to watch instead of text. Once we find the packages we are looking for; in this example, Notepad++ and 7zip, we will use the `Install-Package` cmdlet to install these packages. The following screenshot shows you when the installation had taken place, the packages that are now available for use and can be found at the start button:

```
Machine: tlex01.testlabs.se                          _ □ X

[PS] C:\Scripts>Find-Package -Name "notepadplusplus"

Name     Version   Status      ProviderName    Source       Summar
                                                             y
----     -------   ------      ------------    ------       ------
note...  6.7.4     Available   Chocolatey      chocolatey   Not...

[PS] C:\Scripts>Install-Package -Name "notepadplusplus" -Force

Name     Version   Status      ProviderName    Source       Summar
                                                             y
----     -------   ------      ------------    ------       ------
note...  6.7.4     Installed   Chocolatey      chocolatey   Not...
note...  6.7.4     Installed   Chocolatey      chocolatey   Not...
```

Once the packages are in place, and we have verified that everything has worked as expected, we can finalize this by uninstalling them. The following are some examples of cmdlets used to uninstall packages:

```
Uninstall-Package –Name "notepadplusplus"
Uninstall-Package –Name "7zip"
```

There's more...

Chocolatey is great in many ways, but most companies or at least enterprise companies probably want to have their own internal, more trusted, and reliable repository but still hosted on the Internet.

So, let's take a look at how this can be established. First, let's sign up for an account at an optional provider.

In my case, I used `http://www.myget.org` as the provider and created a feed when the account was created.

Now, let's see how the feed can be used as a repository. The feed that was created got an URL as `https://www.myget.org/F/tlpowershell/`, Once it's created, we have to register it as a repository in PowerShell using the `Register-PSRepository` cmdlet:

```
Register-PSRepository -Name MyGet -SourceLocation `
https://www.myget.org/F/tlpowershell/api/v1 `
-PublishLocation https://www.myget.org/F/tlpowershell/ `
-InstallationPolicy Trusted
Find-Package -Source MyGet
```

Since the `MyGet` repository is brand new, there are currently no packages. So, the next action is to upload a package to `MyGet`. To upload a module, the module itself should have a file extension of `.psm1` together with the module manfest using an extension of `.psd1`. In the manifest, you need to include the values of `Author` and `Description`, but I want to recommend that you also include the values of `RootModule`, `ModuleVersion`, and `CompanyName`. The following examples show how the manifest was created and also how the modules were published to `MyGet`:

```
New-ModuleManifest -Path `
C:\Windows\System32\WindowsPowerShell\v1.0\Modules\mailboxes.psd1`
-Author "Jonas Andersson" -CompanyName "Testlabs, Inc." `
-RootModule "mailboxes" -Description `
"Module that lists mailboxes" -ModuleVersion "1.0"

Import-Module PowerShellGet
$PSGalleryPublishUri = 'https://www.myget.org/F/tlpowershell/api/v2/
package'
```

```
$PSGallerySourceUri = 'https://www.myget.org/F/tlpowershell/api/v2'

Publish-Module -Name mailboxes -NuGetApiKey `
a2d5b281-c862-4125-9523-be42ef21f55a -Repository MyGet

Find-Package -Source MyGet

Install-Package -Name "mailboxes" -Source MyGet
```

Before we end this recipe, we might want to remove the repository for some reason. This is done simply by running the following cmdlet:

```
Unregister-PSRepository -Name MyGet
```

See also

- ▶ *Understanding the new execution policy*
- ▶ *Creating custom objects*
- ▶ *Working with Desired State Configuration*

2

Exchange Management Shell Common Tasks

In this chapter, we will cover the following topics:

- ▶ Manually configuring remote PowerShell connections
- ▶ Using explicit credentials with PowerShell cmdlets
- ▶ Transferring files through remote shell connect ons
- ▶ Managing domains or an entire forest using the recipient scope
- ▶ Exporting reports to text and CSV files
- ▶ Sending SMTP e-mails through PowerShell
- ▶ Scheduling scripts to run at a later time
- ▶ Logging shell sessions to a transcript
- ▶ Automating tasks with the scripting agent
- ▶ Scripting an Exchange Server installation

Introduction

Microsoft introduced some radical architectural changes in Exchange 2007, including a brand new set of management tools. PowerShell v1, along with an additional set of Exchange-Server-specific cmdlets, finally gave administrators an interface that could be used to manage the entire product from a command-line shell. This was an interesting move, and at that time, the entire graphical management console was built on top of this technology.

The same architecture still existed with Exchange 2010, and PowerShell was even more tightly integrated with this product. Exchange 2010 used PowerShell v2, which relied heavily on its new remoting infrastructure. This provides seamless administrative capabilities from a single seat with the Exchange Management Tools, whether your servers are on-premises or in the cloud.

Initially, with Exchange 2013, PowerShell Version 3 was used, but now when using PowerShell Version 5 together with cumulative updates, there are a lot of new cmdlets, core functionality changes, and even more integrations with the cloud services. When Exchange 2013 was introduced (RTM), we had 764 cmdlets and after application of Service Pack 1 and Cumulative Update 7, a total of 806 Exchange cmdlets are available. This demonstrates more features and functionalities have been added over time.

In this chapter, we'll cover some of the most common topics, as well as common tasks that will allow you to effectively write scripts with this latest release. We'll also take a look at some general tasks, such as scheduling scripts, sending e-mails, generating reports, and many more.

Performing some basic steps

To make use of all the examples in this chapter, we'll need to use the Exchange Management Shell, the Exchange Management console, and a standard PowerShell console.

You can launch the Exchange Management Shell using the following steps:

1. Log on to a workstation or server with the Exchange Management Tools installed.
2. Open the Exchange Management Shell by navigating to **Start** | **All Programs** | **Exchange Server 2013**.
3. Click on the **Exchange Management Shell** shortcut.

To launch a standard PowerShell console, use the following steps:

1. On Windows 8 or Windows 8.1, click on the Windows button, and select **Windows PowerShell** under **Windows System**.
2. On Windows Vista, Windows 7, or Windows Server 2008 R2, open a standard PowerShell console by navigating to **Start** | **All Programs** | **Accessories**, click on the `Windows PowerShell` folder, and then click on the **Windows PowerShell** shortcut.
3. On Windows XP and Windows Server 2003, navigate to **Start** | **Programs** | **Accessories**, click on the `Windows PowerShell` folder, and then click on the **Windows PowerShell** shortcut.

> Remember to start the Exchange Management Shell using **Run as administrator** to avoid permission problems. In the chapter, notice that in the examples of cmdlets, I have used the back tick (`` ` ``) character to break up long commands into multiple lines. The purpose is to make it easier to read. The back ticks are not required and should only be used if needed.

Manually configuring remote PowerShell connections

Just like Exchange 2010, Exchange 2013 is very reliable on remote PowerShell for both on-premises and cloud services. When you double-click on the Exchange Management Shell shortcut on a server or workstation with the Exchange Management Tools installed, you are connected to an Exchange server using a remote PowerShell session.

PowerShell remoting also allows you to remotely manage your Exchange servers from a workstation or a server, even when Exchange Management Tools are not installed. In this recipe, we'll create a manual remote shell connection to an Exchange server using a standard PowerShell console.

Getting ready

To complete the steps in this recipe, you'll need to log on to a workstation or a server and launch Windows PowerShell.

How to do it...

Let's see how to manually configure remote PowerShell connections, using the following steps:

1. First, create a credential object using the `Get-Credential` cmdlet. When running this command, you'll be prompted with a Windows authentication dialog box. Enter a username and password for an account that has an administrative access to your Exchange organization. Make sure that you enter your user name in the DOMAIN\ USERNAME or UPN format:

    ```
    $credential = Get-Credential
    ```

2. Next, create a new session object and store it in a variable. In this example, the Exchange server that we are connecting to is specified using the `-ConnectionUri` parameter. Replace the server FQDN in the following example with one of your own Exchange servers:

    ```
    $session = New-PSSession -ConfigurationName
    Microsoft.Exchange

    -ConnectionUri http://tlex01.testlabs.se/PowerShell/ `
    -Credential $credential
    ```

3. Finally, import the session object:

    ```
    Import-PSSession $session
    ```

4. After you execute the preceding command, the Exchange Management Shell cmdlets will be imported into your current PowerShell session, as shown in the following screenshot:

```
Administrator: Windows PowerShell                          _ □ x

PS C:\Scripts> $credential = Get-Credential

cmdlet Get-Credential at command pipeline position 1
Supply values for the following parameters:
Credential
PS C:\Scripts> $session = New-PSSession -ConfigurationName Microsoft.Exchan
ge -ConnectionUri http://tlex01.testlabs.se/PowerShell/ -Credential $creden
tial
PS C:\Scripts> Import-PSSession $session
WARNING: The names of some imported commands from the module
'tmp_cxcbf3zz.0xj' include unapproved verbs that might make them less
discoverable. To find the commands with unapproved verbs, run the
Import-Module command again with the Verbose parameter. For a list of
approved verbs, type Get-Verb.

ModuleType Version    Name                            ExportedCommands
---------- -------    ----                            ----------------
Script     1.0        tmp_cxcbf3zz.0xj                {Add-ADPermis...
```

How it works...

Each server runs IIS and supports remote PowerShell sessions via HTTP. Exchange Servers host a PowerShell virtual directory in IIS. This contains several modules that perform authentication checks and determine which cmdlets and parameters are assigned to the user that make the connection. This happens when running both the Exchange Management Shell with the tools installed and when creating a manual remote connection. The IIS virtual directory that is used to connect is shown in the following screenshot:

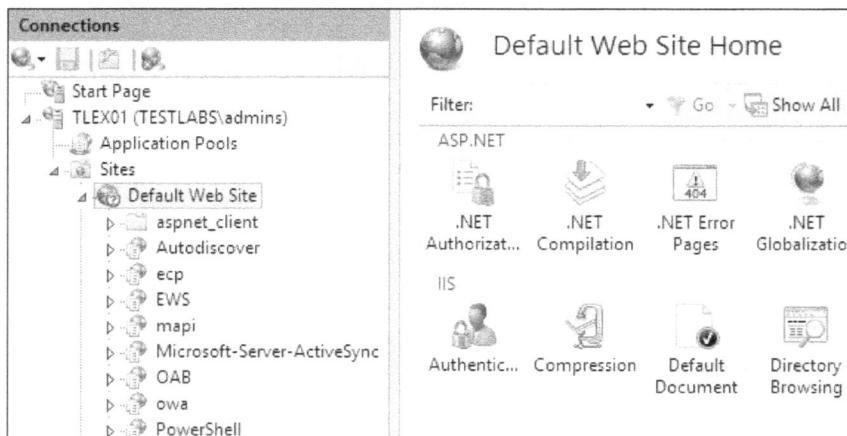

The IIS virtual directories can also be retrieved using PowerShell with the `Get-WebVirtualDirectory` cmdlet, and to get the information on the web applications, use the `Get-WebApplication` cmdlet.

Remote PowerShell connections to Exchange 2013 servers use the same special feature as Exchange 2010 did, implicit remoting, that allows us to import remote commands into the local shell session. With this feature, we can use the Exchange PowerShell snap-in installed on the server in our local PowerShell session without installing the Exchange tools.

> You'll need to allow the execution of scripts in order to create a manual remote shell connection on a machine that does not have the Exchange tools installed. For more details, refer to the *Understanding the new execution policy* recipe in *Chapter 1, PowerShell Key Concepts*.

You may be curious to know as to why Exchange uses remote PowerShell, even when the tools are installed and when running the shell from the server. There are a couple of reasons for this, but some of the main factors are permissions. The Exchange 2010 and 2013 permissions model have been completely transformed in this latest version and use a new feature called **Role Based Access Control** (**RBAC**), which defines what administrators can and cannot do. When you make a remote PowerShell connection to an Exchange 2013 server, the RBAC authorization module in IIS determines which cmdlets and parameters you have access to. Once this information is obtained, only the cmdlets and parameters that have been assigned to your account via an RBAC role are loaded into your PowerShell session using implicit remoting.

There's more...

In the previous example, we explicitly set the credentials used to create the remote shell connection. This is optional and not required if the account you are currently logged on with has the appropriate Exchange permissions assigned. To create a remote shell session using your currently logged on credentials, use the following syntax to create the session object:

```
$session = New-PSSession -ConfigurationName Microsoft.Exchange `
-ConnectionUri http://tlex01.testlabs.se/PowerShell/
```

Once again, import the session:

```
Import-PSSession $session
```

When the tasks have been completed, remove the session:

```
Remove-PSSession $session
```

Here, you can see that the commands are almost identical to the previous example, except that this time, we removed the `-Credential` parameter and used the assigned credential object. After this is done, you can simply import the session, and the commands will be imported into your current session using implicit remoting.

> Although you can manually load the Exchange snap-in within a standard PowerShell console on a machine with the Exchange tools installed, this is not supported. You may also have mixed results when doing this, since this method bypasses remoting; and therefore, the RBAC system may be required to give you the appropriate rights.

In addition to implicit remoting, Exchange 2013 servers running PowerShell v3 or above can also be managed using fan-out remoting. This is accomplished using the `Invoke-Command` cmdlet, and it allows you to execute a script block on multiple computers in parallel. For more details, run `Get-Help Invoke-Command` and `Get-Help about_remoting`.

Connecting to the Exchange online is more common, and it's very similar to connecting to a remote PowerShell on-premises. The following prerequisites are required: .NET Framework 4.5 or 4.5.1, and then either Windows Management Framework 3.0 or 4.0.

We will now create a variable of the credentials by running the following command:

```
$UserCredential = Get-Credential
```

We then create a session variable as follows:

```
$Session = New-PSSession -ConfigurationName Microsoft.Exchange `
-ConnectionUri https://outlook.office365.com/powershell-liveid/ `
-Credential $UserCredential -Authentication Basic `
-AllowRedirection
```

Finally, we import the session:

```
Import-PSSession $Session
```

You can then perform the tasks you want to do by running the following command:

```
Get-Mailbox
```

When the tasks have been completed, remove the session:

```
Remove-PSSession $session
```

You may also want to check out the *Administrator's Guide to Windows PowerShell Remoting*. Even though this is intended for PowerShell Version 2, it still applies to newer versions. It is a great resource that covers PowerShell remoting in depth, and it can be downloaded from http://powershell.com/cs/media/p/4908.aspx.

See also

▸ *Using explicit credentials with PowerShell commands*

Using explicit credentials with PowerShell cmdlets

There are several PowerShell and Exchange Management Shell cmdlets that provide a credential parameter that allows you to use an alternate set of credentials when running a command. You may need to use alternate credentials when making manual remote shell connections, sending e-mail messages, working in cross-forest scenarios, and many more. In this recipe, we'll take a look at how you can create a credential object that can be used with commands that support the `-Credential` parameter.

How to do it...

To create a credential object, we can use the `Get-Credential` cmdlet. In this example, we store the credential object in a variable that can be used by the `Get-Mailbox` cmdlet:

```
$credential = Get-Credential
Get-Mailbox -Credential $credential
```

How it works...

When you run the `Get-Credential` cmdlet, you are presented with a Windows authentication dialog box requesting your username and password. In the previous example, we assigned the `Get-Credential` cmdlet to the `$credential` variable. After typing your username and password in the authentication dialog box, the credentials are saved as an object that can then be assigned to the `-Credential` parameter of a cmdlet. The cmdlet that utilizes the credential object will then run using the credentials of the specified user.

Supplying credentials to a command doesn't have to be an interactive process. You can programmatically create a credential object within your script without using the `Get-Credential` cmdlet:

```
$user = "testlabs\administrator"
$pass = ConvertTo-SecureString -AsPlainText P@ssw0rd01 -Force
$credential = New-Object `
System.Management.Automation.PSCredential `
-ArgumentList $user,$pass
```

You can see here that we created a credential object from scratch without using the `Get-Credential` cmdlet. In order to create a credential object, we need to supply the password as a secure string type. The `ConvertTo-SecureString` cmdlet can be used to create a secure string object. We then use the `New-Object` cmdlet to create a credential object, specifying the desired username and password as arguments.

If you need to prompt a user for their credentials, but you do not want to invoke the Windows authentication dialog box, you can use this alternative syntax to prompt the user in the shell for their credentials:

```
$user = Read-Host "Please enter your username"

$pass = Read-Host "Please enter your password" -AsSecureString

$credential = New-Object `
System.Management.Automation.PSCredential-ArgumentList `
$user,$pass
```

This syntax uses the `Read-Host` cmdlet to prompt the user for both their username and password. Notice that when creating the `$pass` object, we use `Read-Host` with the `-AsSecureString` parameter to ensure that the object is stored as a secure string.

There's more...

After you have created a credential object, you may need to access the properties of that object in order to retrieve the username and password. We can access the username and password properties of the `$credential` object created previously using the following commands:

```
[PS] C:\Scripts>$credential.UserName
testlabs\administrator
[PS] C:\Scripts>$credential.GetNetworkCredential().Password
P@ssw0rd01
[PS] C:\Scripts>
```

You can see here that we can simply grab the username stored in the object by accessing the `UserName` property cmdlet of the credential object. Since the `Password` property is stored as a secure string, we need to use the `GetNetworkCredential` method to convert the credential to a `NetworkCredential` object that will expose the `Password` property as a simple string.

Another powerful method used to manage passwords for scripts is to encrypt them and store them in a text file. This can be easily done using the following example.

The password is stored in a variable as follows:

```
$secureString = Read-Host -AsSecureString "Enter a secret password"
```

The variable gets converted from SecureString and saved to a text file:

```
$secureString | ConvertFrom-SecureString | Out-File .\storedPassword.txt
```

The contents in the text file are retrieved and converted to a SecureString value:

```
$secureString = Get-Content .\storedPassword.txt | ConvertTo-SecureString
```

See also

▶ *Transferring files through remote shell connections*

▶ *Manually configuring remote PowerShell connections*

Transferring files through remote shell connections

Since the Exchange 2013 Management Shell commands are executed through a remote PowerShell session, importing and exporting files require a new special syntax. There are a handful of shell cmdlets that require this. In this recipe, we'll take a look at the syntax that needs to be used to transfer files through a remote she l connection.

How to do it...

Let's say that we are about to import a certificate to the client access server. We can import the file using the Get-Content cmdlet, using a syntax similar to the following:

```
[byte[]]$data = Get-Content -Path ".\ExportedCert.pfx" `
-Encoding Byte `
-ReadCount 0
$password = Get-Credential
Import-ExchangeCertificate -FileData $data -Password
$password.Password
```

In this example, the file data is first read into a variable called $data. The certificate import is done using the Import-ExchangeCertificate cmdlet by assigning the $data variable as a value to the -FileData parameter.

How it works...

When you launch the Exchange 2013 Management Shell, special commands called proxy functions are imported into your local shell session. These proxy functions represent the compiled cmdlets that are actually installed on your Exchange server. When you run these commands, any data required for the input through parameters is transferred through a remote connection from your machine to the server and the command is then executed. Since the commands are actually running on the server and not on your machine, we cannot use a local path for files that need to be imported.

In the previous example, you could see that we first stored the data file in a variable. What we are doing here is reading the file content into the variable using the `Get-Content` cmdlet in order to create a byte-encoded object. This variable is then assigned to the cmdlet's `-FileData` parameter, which requires a byte-encoded value.

There are a number of Exchange Management Shell cmdlets that include a `-FileData` parameter used to provide external files as input:

- `Import-DlpPolicyCollection`: This is used to import DLP policy collections into the organization
- `Import-DlpPolicyTemplate`: This is used to import DLP policy templates into the organization
- `Import-ExchangeCertificate`: This is used to import certificates
- `Import-JournalRuleCollection`: This is used to import a collection of journal rules
- `Import-RecipientDataProperty`: This is used to import photos or audio into Active Directory
- `Import-TransportRuleCollection`: This allows you to import a collection of transport rules
- `Import-UMPrompt`: This is used to import custom audio files into the UM feature

This is a good example of how remote PowerShell sessions have changed things in Exchange 2010/2013. For example, if you have worked with the shell in Exchange 2007, you may remember the `Import-ExchangeCertificate` cmdlet. This cmdlet is used to accept a local file path when importing a certificate into a server, but due to the new remoting functionality, the commands used to perform this task have changed, even though the cmdlet name is still the same.

There's more...

We also have to take remote shell connections into consideration when exporting data. For example, let's say that we need to export the user photo associated with a mailbox from Active Directory. The command would look something like this:

```
Export-RecipientDataProperty -Identity tdawson-Picture | %{
   $_.FileData | Add-Content C:\pics\tdawson.jpg -Encoding Byte
}
```

When using the `Export-RecipientDataProperty` cmdlet with the `-Picture` switch parameter, the photo can be retrieved from the `FileData` property of the object returned. The photo data is stored in this property as a byte array. In order to export the data, we need to loop through each element stored in this property, and use the `Add-Content` cmdlet to reconstruct the image to an external file.

When dealing with cmdlets that import or export data, make sure that you utilize the help system. Remember, you can run `Get-Help <cmdlet name> -Examples` with any of these cmdlets to determine the correct syntax.

See also

▶ *Using the help system* in *Chapter 1, PowerShell Key Concepts*

▶ *Manually Configuring Remote PowerShell Connections*

Managing domains or an entire forest using the recipient scope

The Exchange Management Tools can be configured to use specific portions of your Active Directory hierarchy using a specific recipient scope. When you set the recipient scope to a location in the Active Directory, such as a domain or an organizational unit, the Exchange Management Shell will only allow you to view the recipients that are stored in that location and any containers beneath it. In this recipe, we'll look at how to set the recipient scope when working with the Exchange Management Shell.

How to do it...

Let's see how to manage domains using the recipient scope using the following steps:

1. We can set the recipient scope in the Exchange Management Shell using the `Set-AdServerSettings` cmdlet. For example, to set the recipient scope to the `sales` OU in the `contoso.com` domain, use the following command:

   `Set-AdServerSettings -RecipientViewRoot contoso.com/sales`

2. We can also specify the value using the distinguished name of the OU:

   `Set-AdServerSettings -RecipientViewRoot `
   `"OU=sales,DC=contoso,DC=com"`

How it works...

In Exchange 2007, the recipient scope was set using the `AdminSessionADSettings` global session variable. With Exchange 2010 and 2013, we use the `Set-AdServerSettings` cmdlet. When you first start the Exchange Management Shell, the default recipient scope is set to the domain of the computer that is running the shell. If you change the recipient scope, the setting will not be retained when you restart the shell. The default domain scope will always be used when you launch the shell. You can override this by adding these commands to your PowerShell profile to ensure that the setting is always initially configured as needed.

In the previous example, we set the recipient scope to a specific OU in the domain. If you are working in a multidomain forest, you can use the `-ViewEntireForest` parameter so that all recipient objects in the forest can be managed from your shell session. Use the following command to view the entire forest:

`Set-AdServerSettings -ViewEntireForest $true`

To change the recipient scope to a specific domain, set the `-RecipientViewRoot` cmdlet to the fully qualified domain name of the Active Directory domain:

`Set-AdServerSettings -RecipientViewRoot corp.contoso.com`

There's more...

If you're working in a large environment with multiple domains and OUs, setting the recipient scope can improve the speed of the Exchange Management Shell, since it will limit the total number of recipients returned by your commands.

If you have Exchange recipients in multiple Active Directory domains or sites, you may have to take replication latency into account when working with a broad recipient scope. To handle this, you can use the `Set-AdServerSettings` cmdlet to specify the domain controllers and global catalog servers that you want to work with.

To set the preferred domain controllers and global catalog that should be used with your recipient scope, use the `-SetPreferredDomainControllers` and `-PreferredGlobalCatalog` parameters to specify the FQDN of the servers:

```
Set-AdServerSettings -ViewEntireForest $true `
-SetPreferredDomainControllers dc1.contoso.com `
-PreferredGlobalCatalog dc1.contoso.com
```

Setting the preferred domain controller can be useful to ensure that your commands will read the latest list of recipients in Active Directory. If you have a provisioning process that uses a specific domain controller when creating recipients, it may take some time to replicate this information throughout the forest. Setting the preferred domain controllers can be used to ensure that you are working with the latest set of recipients available, even if they haven't been replicated throughout the forest.

Exporting reports to text and CSV files

One of the added benefits of the Exchange Management Shell is the ability to run very detailed and customizable reports. With the hundreds of `Get-*` cmdlets provided between Windows PowerShell and the Exchange Management Shell, the reporting capabilities are almost endless. In this recipe, we'll cover how to export command output to plain text and CSV files that can be used to report on various resources throughout your Exchange environment.

How to do it...

To export command output to a text file, use the `Out-File` cmdlet. To generate a report of mailboxes in a specific mailbox database that can be stored in a text file, use the following command:

```
Get-Mailbox | Select-Object Name,Alias | Out-File c:\report.txt
```

You can also save the output of the previous command as a CSV file that can then be opened and formatted in Microsoft Excel:

```
Get-Mailbox | Select-Object Name,Alias | `
Export-CSV c:\report.csv -NoType
```

How it works...

The `Out-File` cmdlet is simply a redirection command that will export the output of your command to a plain text file. Perhaps, one of the most useful features of this cmdlet is the ability to add data to the end of an existing file using the `-Append` parameter. This allows you to continuously update a text file when processing multiple objects or creating persistent log files or reports.

> [💡 You can also use the `Add-Content`, `Set-Content`, and `Clear-Content` cmdlets to add, replace, or remove data from files.]

By your command, the `Export-CSV` cmdlet converts the object's output into a collection of comma-separated values and stores them in a CSV file. When we ran the `Get-Mailbox` cmdlet in the previous example, we filtered the output, selecting only the `Name` and `Alias` properties. When exporting this output using `Export-CSV`, these property names are used for the column headers. Each object returned by the command will be represented in the CSV file as an individual row, therefore populating the `Name` and `Alias` columns with the associated data.

You may have noticed in the `Export-CSV` example that we used the `-NoType` switch parameter. This is commonly used and is a shorthand notation for the full parameter name `-NoTypeInformation`. If you do not specify this switch parameter, the first line of the CSV file will contain a header, specifying the .NET Framework type of the object that was exported. This is rarely useful. If you end up with a strange-looking header in one of your reports, remember to run the command again using the `-NoTypeInformation` switch parameter.

There's more...

One of the most common problems that Exchange administrators run into with `Export-CSV` is when exporting objects with multivalued properties. Let's say we need to run a report that lists each mailbox and its associated e-mail addresses. The command would look something like the following:

```
Get-Mailbox | `
Select-Object Name,EmailAddresses | `
Export-CSV c:\report.csv -NoType
```

The problem here is that each mailbox can contain multiple e-mail addresses. When we select the `EmailAddresses` property, a multivalued object is returned. The `Export-CSV` cmdlet does not understand how to handle this, and when you import the CSV file in PowerShell, you'll end up with a CSV file that looks like the following:

```
Machine: tlex01.testlabs.se

[PS] C:\Scripts>Import-Csv C:\report.csv

Name                                EmailAddresses
----                                --------------
admins                              Microsoft.Exchange.Data.ProxyAddr...
DiscoverySearchMailbox {D919BA05-4... Microsoft.Exchange.Data.ProxyAddr...
testuser                            Microsoft.Exchange.Data.ProxyAddr...
Jonas Andersson                     Microsoft.Exchange.Data.ProxyAddr...
Sofie Andersson                     Microsoft.Exchange.Data.ProxyAddr...
Indie Andersson                     Microsoft.Exchange.Data.ProxyAddr...
Ann Andersson                       Microsoft.Exchange.Data.ProxyAddr...
Klas Andersson                      Microsoft.Exchange.Data.ProxyAddr...
Terrance Randolph                   Microsoft.Exchange.Data.ProxyAddr...
Tomas Dawson                        Microsoft.Exchange.Data.ProxyAddr...
```

In the preceding screenshot, you can see that on the first line, we have our header names that match the properties selected during the export. In the first column, the `Name` property for each mailbox has been recorded correctly, but, as you can see, there is a problem with the values listed in the `EmailAddresses` column. Instead of the e-mail addresses, we get the .NET Framework type name of the multivalued property. To get around this, we need to help the `Export-CSV` cmdlet understand what we are trying to do and specifically reference the data that needs to be exported.

One of the best ways to handle this is to use a calculated property and join each value of the multivalued property as a single string:

```
Get-Mailbox | `
Select-Object Name,@{n="Email";e={$_.EmailAddresses -Join ";"}}`
| Export-CSV c:\report1.csv -NoType
```

In this example, we modified the previous command by creating a calculated property that will contain each e-mail address for the associated mailbox. Since we need to consolidate the `EmailAddresses` property data into a single item that can be exported, we use the `-Join` operator to create a string containing a list, separated by semicolons, of every e-mail address associated with each mailbox. The command is then piped to the `Export-CSV` cmdlet, and the report is generated in a readable format that can be viewed using the `Import-CSV` cmdlet:

As you can see in the preceding screenshot, each e-mail address for a mailbox is now listed in the `Email` column and is separated using a semicolon. Each address has an SMTP prefix associated with it. An SMTP prefix in all capital letters indicates that the address is the primary SMTP address for the mailbox. Any remaining secondary addresses will use an SMTP prefix in lowercase characters. If you do not want to export the prefixes, we can make further modifications to our code as follows:

```
Get-Mailbox | `
select-Object Name, `
@{n="Email"; `
  e={($_.EmailAddresses | %{$_.SmtpAddress}) -Join ";"} `
} | Export-CSV c:\report2.csv -NoType
```

Here you can see that, within the expression of the calculated property, we're looping through the `EmailAddresses` collection and retrieving only the `SmtpAddress` cmdlet, which does not include the SMTP prefix and returns only the e-mail addresses. Once the data is exported to a CSV file, we can review it using the `Import-CSV` cmdlet:

```
Machine: tlex01.testlabs.se                        _  □  x

[PS] C:\Scripts>Import-Csv C:\report2.csv

Name                              Email
----                              -----
admins                            admins@testlabs.se
DiscoverySearchMailbox {D919BA05-4...   DiscoverySearchMailbox{D919BA05-4...
testuser                          testuser@testlabs.se
Jonas Andersson                   jonand@testlabs.se
Sofie Andersson                   sofand@testlabs.se
Indie Andersson                   indand@testlabs.se
Ann Andersson                     annand@testlabs.se
Klas Andersson                    klaand@testlabs.se
Terrance Randolph                 trandolph@testlabs.se
Tomas Dawson                      tdawson@testlabs.se
```

As you can see here, we now get each e-mail address associated with each mailbox, without the SMTP prefix within the `Email` column of our CSV file.

See also

▸ *Working with arrays and hash tables* in *Chapter 1, PowerShell Key Concepts*

▸ *Creating custom objects* in *Chapter 1, PowerShell Key Concepts*

Sending SMTP e-mails through PowerShell

As an Exchange administrator, you will probably need an automated solution to send e-mails from your PowerShell scripts. Whether it's used to send notifications to users in a specific database or e-mail the output of your scripts to a reporting mailbox, the transmission of messages such as these will prove very useful while performing common day-to-day administrative scripting tasks. In this recipe, we'll take a look at how you can send SMTP e-mail messages from PowerShell to the recipients in your Exchange organization.

How to do it...

PowerShell v2 and later includes a core cmdlet that can be used to send e-mail messages via SMTP to one or more recipients. Use the following syntax to send an e-mail message:

```
Send-MailMessage -To user1@contoso.com `
-From administrator@contoso.com `
-Subject "Test E-mail" `
-Body "This is just a test" `
-SmtpServer ex01.contoso.com
```

How it works...

In PowerShell v1, the `Send-MailMessage` cmdlet didn't exist. In the early days before Exchange 2007 SP2 and PowerShell v2 support, we had to use the classes in the `System.Net.Mail` namespace in the .NET Framework to send SMTP e-mail messages. This was difficult for some administrators because working with .NET classes can be confusing without prior programming experience. The good news is that the `Send-MailMessage` cmdlet utilizes the same .NET classes that allow you to create rich e-mail messages that can contain one or more attachments, using an HTML formatted message body, support message priority, and many more. Here are some of the most useful parameters that can be used with the `Send-MailMessage` cmdlet:

- ▶ `Attachments`: This specifies the path to the file that should be attached. It separates multiple attachments with a comma.

- ▶ `Bcc`: This allows you to specify a blind copy recipient. It separates multiple recipients using a comma.

- ▶ `Body`: This specifies the content of a message.

- ▶ `BodyAsHtml`: This is a switch parameter that ensures that the message will use an HTML-formatted message body.

- ▶ `Cc`: This allows you to specify a carbon copy recipient. It separates multiple recipients using a comma.

- ▶ `Credential`: You can provide a `PSCredential` object created by the `Get-Credential` cmdlet to send the message using the credentials of another user.

- ▶ `DeliveryNotificationOption`: This specifies the delivery notification options for the message. The default value is **None**, but other valid options are **OnSuccess**, **OnFailure**, **Delay**, and **Never**.

- ▶ `Encoding`: This specifies the encoding of the e-mail, such as an S/MIME and non-MIME character set.

- ▶ `From`: This is the e-mail address of the sender. You can define a display name using the `Dave <dave@contoso.com>` format.

- ▶ `Priority`: This specifies the importance of the message. The default value is **Normal**. The remaining valid values are **High** and **Low**.

- ▶ `SmtpServer`: This needs to be the name or IP address of your SMTP server. When working in an Exchange environment, this will be set to one of your Hub Transport servers.

- ▶ `Subject`: This is the subject of the e-mail message.

- ▶ `To`: This allows you to specify an e-mail recipient. It separates multiple recipients with a comma.

There's more...

When using this cmdlet, you need to specify an SMTP server in order to submit the message. Unless you are already using some type of mail relay system within your environment, you'll want to use a Mailbox server in your Exchange organization. Out of the box, Exchange servers will not allow workstations or untrusted servers to relay e-mail messages. Depending on where you are sending the message from, you may need to allow the machine running your scripts to relay e-mails.

PowerShell v2 and later includes a preference variable called `$PSEmailServer` that can be assigned the name or IP address of an SMTP server. When this variable is defined, you can omit the `-SmtpServer` parameter when using the `Send-MailMessage` cmdlet. You can add this variable assignment to your PowerShell profile, so that the setting will persist across all of your shell sessions.

Sending messages with attachments

You may want to write a script that generates a report to a text or CSV file, and then e-mail that data to an administrator mailbox. The `-Attachment` parameter can be used with the `Send-MailMessage` cmdlet to do this. For example, let's say that you've generated a CSV report file for the top 10 largest mailboxes in your environment and this needs to be e-mailed to your staff. The following command syntax could be used in this scenario:

```
Send-MailMessage -To support@contoso.com `
-From powershell@contoso.com `
-Subject "Mailbox Report for $((Get-Date).ToShortDateString())" `
-Body "Please review the attached mailbox report." `
-Attachments c:\report.csv `
-SmtpServer ex01.contoso.com
```

Notice that all we need to do here is provide the path and filename to the `-Attachment` parameter. You can send multiple message attachments this way by providing a comma-separated list of files.

Sending command output in the body of a message

Instead of exporting command data to an external file and sending it as an attachment, you may want to add this information to the body of an e-mail. In this example, we'll send a message that displays the top 10 largest mailboxes in the organization in the body of an HTML-formatted message:

```
[string]$report = Get-MailboxDatabase |
Get-MailboxStatistics| ?{(!$_.DisconnectDate) -and `
($_.DisplayName -notlike "HealthMailbox*")} |
Sort-Object TotalItemSize -Desc |
```

```
Select-Object DisplayName,Database,TotalItemSize -First 10 |
ConvertTo-Html
Send-MailMessage -To support@contoso.com `
-From powershell@contoso.com `
-Subject "Mailbox Report for $((Get-Date).ToShortDateString())" `
-Body $report `
-BodyAsHtml `
-SmtpServer ex01.contoso.com
```

Here, you can see that the report data is generated with a fairly sophisticated one-liner, and the output is saved in a string variable called `$report`. We need to strongly type the `$report` variable as a string because that is the data type required by the `-Body` parameter of the `Send-MailMessage` cmdlet. Notice that we're using the `ConvertTo-Html` cmdlet at the end of the one-liner to convert the objects to an HTML document. Since the `$report` variable will simply contain raw HTML, we can assign this value to the `-Body` parameter, and use the `-BodyAsHtml` switch parameter to send the report data in the body of an HTML-formatted message.

See also

▸ *Allowing application servers to relay mail* in *Chapter 8, Managing Transport Servers*

▸ *Sending e-mail messages with EWS* in *Chapter 12, Scripting with the Exchange Web Services Managed API*

▸ *Reporting on the mailbox size* in *Chapter 4, Managing Mailboxes*

Scheduling scripts to run at a later time

One of the most common tasks that Exchange administrators perform is scheduling scripts to run at a later time. This can be useful when performing maintenance after hours or running monitoring scripts on a regular basis. In this recipe, you'll learn how to schedule your PowerShell scripts to run with the Windows Task Scheduler. In PowerShell Version 4, we have some powerful new cmdlets to manage Windows Task Scheduler.

How to do it...

To create a scheduled task that runs from one of your Exchange servers, perform the following steps:

1. Open the Windows Task Scheduler by navigating to **Start** | **All Programs** | **Accessories**, click on the `System Tools` folder, and then click on the **Task Scheduler** shortcut.

2. From the **Action** menu, click on **Create Basic Task**.

3. Give your task a name and description and click on **Next**.

4. On the **Trigger** screen, select how often you'd like the script to run (**Daily**, **Weekly**, **Monthly**, and so on).

5. When asked what action you want the task to perform, select **Start a Program**.

6. Use the following syntax in the **Program/Script** field and click on **Next**:

```
C:\Windows\System32\WindowsPowerShell\v1.0\powershell.exe - `
command ". 'C:\Program Files\Microsoft\Exchange `
Server\V15\bin\RemoteExchange.ps1'; Connect-ExchangeServer `
-auto; c:\Scripts\MoveMailboxes.ps1".
```

7. You will receive a prompt that says **It appears as though arguments have been included in the program text box. Do you want to run the following program?** Click on **Yes**.

8. This will bring you to a **Summary** screen, where you can click on **Finish**.

How it works...

The syntax used in this example may look a little strange at first. What we are actually doing here is scheduling `PowerShell.exe` and using the `-Command` parameter to execute multiple statements. This allows us to pass the contents of a PowerShell script to `PowerShell.exe`. In this case, our script has multiple lines and each statement is separated by a semicolon.

The first thing we do is dot-source the `RemoteExchange.ps1` script located in the Exchange Server bin directory. This file initializes some Exchange shell variables and imports several Exchange-specific functions.

The next line of the task calls the `Connect-ExchangeServer` function using the `-Auto` parameter, allowing the Exchange Management Shell environment to automatically load from the best Exchange Server in the local AD site.

Finally, we provide the path to our `.ps1` script that utilizes any required Exchange Management Shell cmdlets and the script is executed, carrying out whatever it is that we need to be done.

It's worth mentioning here that you do not have to use a `.ps1` script file with this syntax. You can replace the call with the `MoveMailboxes.ps1` file with any valid PowerShell commands. If you have a script that contains multiple lines, you can continue to separate each line using a semicolon.

When using this method, make sure that you configure the scheduled task to run as a user that has administrative access to your Exchange organization. In addition, RBAC should be considered to minimize and use the least required privileges when dealing with accounts that are used to run actions within the task scheduler.

Also, if you have **User Account Control (UAC)** enabled, you may need to enable the option to **Run with highest privileges** in the properties of the scheduled task, this for using elevated privileges. Additionally, you will probably want to enable the option to **Run whether user is logged on or not** in the properties of the scheduled task.

There's more...

The previous example demonstrated scheduling a task from an Exchange server using the installed Exchange Management Shell tools. Since all of the Exchange Management Shell connections utilize PowerShell remoting, it is possible to schedule a script to run from a workstation or server that does not have the Exchange tools installed. The only requirement is that the machine must be running PowerShell v2 or later.

To schedule a task from a machine that does not have the Exchange tools installed, use the steps from the previous example, but use the following syntax for the program action:

```
C:\Windows\System32\WindowsPowerShell\v1.0\powershell.exe -command `
"$s = New-PSSession -ConfigurationNameMicrosoft.Exchange - `
ConnectionUri http://ex01.contoso.com/PowerShell/; Import- `
PSSession $s ; c:\Scripts\MoveMailboxes.ps1"
```

You can see here again that we are scheduling the `PowerShell.exe` program and specifying the script using the `-Command` parameter. The difference is that this time, we are not using the locally installed Exchange tools. Instead, we are creating a manual implicit remoting connection to a particular Exchange server. The length of the command line wrapping makes it difficult to read, but keep in mind that this is all done on one line.

When using this method, you can configure the scheduled task to run as a user that has administrative access to your Exchange organization, or you can provide the explicit credentials used to create the session object and run the script as another user.

Scheduled tasks can since Version 4 of PowerShell can also be added using the cmdlets.

An example of this would look like the following:

```
$TaskCommand = `
"c:\windows\system32\WindowsPowerShell\v1.0\powershell.exe"

$TaskArg = '-command "$s = New-PSSession -ConfigurationName `
Microsoft.Exchange -ConnectionUri `
http://ex01.contoso.com/PowerShell/; Import-PSSession $s; `
c:\Scripts\MoveMailboxes.ps1"'

$TaskStartTime = [datetime]::Now.AddMinutes(15)

$TaskAction = New-ScheduledTaskAction -Execute "$TaskCommand" `
-Argument "$TaskArg"

$TaskTrigger = New-ScheduledTaskTrigger -At $TaskStartTime -Once `
```

```
Register-ScheduledTask -Action $TaskAction -Trigger $Tasktrigger `
-TaskName "Scheduled task - Move Mailboxes" -User `
"contoso\administrator" -
RunLevel Highest
```

We created a variable named `TaskCommand`, which refers to `powershell.exe`, including the full path. Secondly, we are creating the `TaskArg` variable, which is used to decide what arguments in `powershell.exe` should be used. `TaskStartTime` is using the current time, plus 15 minutes Finally, we use these variables and register the scheduled task.

See also

► *Manually configuring remote PowerShell connections*

► *Using explicit credentials with PowerShell cmdlets*

Logging shell sessions to a transcript

You may find it useful at times to record the output of your shell sessions in a log file. This can help you save the history of all the commands you've executed and determine the success or failure of automated scripts. In this recipe, you'll learn how to create a PowerShell transcript.

How to do it...

To create a transcript, perform the following steps:

1. Execute the `Start-Transcript` cmdlet:

   ```
   Start-Transcript c:\logfile.txt
   ```

2. You can stop recording the session using the `Stop-Transcript` cmdlet:

   ```
   Stop-Transcript
   ```

How it works...

When starting a PowerShell transcript, you can specify a path and a filename that will be used to record your commands and their output. The use of the `-Path` parameter is optional; if you do not provide a file path, the cmdlet will create a transcript file with a random name in the default documents folder in your profile path, as shown in the following screenshot:

```
Machine: tlex01.testlabs.se                                    _  □  x

[PS] C:\Scripts>Start-Transcript
Transcript started, output file is C:\Users\admins.TESTLABS\Documents\Powe
rShell_transcript.TLEX01.c9asN2SZ.20150122194218.txt
[PS] C:\Scripts>
```

When you are done, you can run the `Stop-Transcript` cmdlet or simply exit the shell. You can use the `-Append` parameter with the `Start-Transcript` cmdlet to add a new transcript to an existing log file. When doing so, you'll need to specify the name of the file you want to append to using the `-Path` parameter.

You can record your entire session every time you start the Exchange Management Shell by adding the `Start-Transcript` cmdlet to your user profile. If you choose to do this, make sure you that specify the same log file to use every time the shell starts and use the `-Append` parameter, so that each session is added to the log file every time.

There's more...

By default, only the output from PowerShell cmdlets will be recorded in your transcript. If you execute an external program, such as the Exchange `eseutil.exe` utility, the output from this command will not be saved in your transcript file, even though it was run within the current shell session. You can pipe external programs to the `Out-Default` cmdlet and this will force the output to be stored in your transcript.

See also

▸ *Exporting reports to text and CSV files*
▸ *Automating tasks with the scripting agent*

Automating tasks with the scripting agent

The scripting agents were introduced in Exchange 2010 and still remain in Exchange 2013. Exchange 2010 introduced the concept of cmdlet extension agents is to extend the functionality of the Exchange Management Tools. The scripting extension agent can be used to trigger custom commands, as changes are made by administrators from the management console or the shell. In this recipe, we'll take a look at how to use the scripting agent to automate a task in the Exchange Management Shell.

Getting ready

To complete the steps in this recipe, you'll need to create an XML file. You can simply use Notepad or any XML editor of your choice.

How to do it...

To automate a task in the Exchange Management Shell using the scripting agent, perform the following steps:

1. Let's say that you need to enable a single item recovery for every mailbox that gets created in your organization. By default, a single item recovery is disabled when you create a mailbox. To automatically enable a single item recovery for each mailbox as it is created, add the following code to a new file:

```
<?xml version="1.0" encoding="utf-8" ?>
<Configuration version="1.0">
<Feature Name="MailboxProvisioning" Cmdlets="New-Mailbox">
<ApiCall Name="OnComplete">
  if($succeeded) {
    $mailbox =
$provisioningHandler.UserSpecifiedParameters["Name"]
    Set-Mailbox $mailbox -SingleItemRecoveryEnabled $true
  }
</ApiCall>
</Feature>
</Configuration>
```

2. Next, make sure to save the file as `ScriptingAgentConfig.xml` on all Exchange servers in the `<install path>\V15\Bin\CmdletExtensionAgents` directory.

3. Finally, you need to enable the scripting agent using the following command:

```
Enable-CmdletExtensionAgent "Scripting Agent"
```

If you have multiple Exchange servers in your environment, make sure that you copy the `ScriptingAgentConfig.xml` file to each server in the `CmdletExtentionAgents` directory, as described previously.

How it works...

When the scripting agent is enabled, it is called every time a cmdlet is run in your Exchange environment. This includes cmdlets that run from within the shell or any of the graphical management tools.

You can see from the code that, in this example, we're using the `OnComplete` API, which runs immediately after the cmdlet has been completed. Using the `Feature` tag, we specified that this block of code should only be executed on completion of the `New-Mailbox` cmdlet.

After the `New-Mailbox` cmdlet has completed, we check the built-in `$succeeded` variable to ensure that the command was successful. If so, we retrieve the value that was used with the `-Name` parameter and store the result in the `$mailbox` variable. This value is then used to specify the identity when running the `Set-Mailbox` cmdlet to enable a single item recovery.

There's more...

You can add multiple scripts to the XML file if needed by defining multiple `Feature` tags under the configuration tag. Each block of code within the `Feature` tag should have an `ApiCall` tag, as shown in the previous example.

The state of the scripting agent is an organization-wide setting. If you enable the scripting agent, it is important that `ScriptingAgentConfig.xml` is copied to every Exchange server in your organization.

Using multiple cmdlets with the OnComplete API

Let's take a look at another example. Imagine that, in addition to enabling a single item recovery for all newly-created mailboxes, we also want to disable the ActiveSync protocol for each mailbox. This means that, in addition to calling the `Set-Mailbox` cmdlet to enable a single item recovery, we'll also need to call the `Set-CASMailbox` cmdlet to disable ActiveSync. Also, mailboxes can be created using both the `New-Mailbox` and `Enable-Mailbox` cmdlets. Since we'd like our custom settings to be applied regardless of how the mailbox is created, we can use the following code in our XML file:

```xml
<?xml version="1.0" encoding="utf-8" ?>
<Configuration version="1.0">
<Feature Name="Mailboxes" Cmdlets="new-mailbox,enable-mailbox">
<ApiCall Name="OnComplete">
  if($succeeded) {
    $id = $provisioningHandler.UserSpecifiedParameters["Alias"]
    Set-Mailbox $id -SingleItemRecoveryEnabled $true
    Set-CASMailbox $id -ActiveSyncEnabled $false
  }
</ApiCall>
</Feature>
</Configuration>
```

This code is similar to our previous example, except in this version, we specified that our custom code will be called when both the `New-Mailbox` and `Enable-Mailbox` cmdlets are used. The code in the `ApiCall` tag captures `Alias` of the mailbox, and then uses `Set-Mailbox` and `Set-CASMailbox` to modify the settings as required.

There are multiple scripting agent APIs that can be used to extend the Exchange Management Shell functionality even further. For examples on how to use these APIs, refer to the `ScriptingAgentConfig.xml` sample file in the `<installpath>\V15\Bin\CmdletExtensionAgents` folder.

See also

- ▸ *Adding, modifying, and removing mailboxes* in *Chapter 3, Managing Recipients*
- ▸ *Managing ActiveSync, OWA, POP3, and IMAP4 mailbox settings* in *Chapter 7, Managing Client Access*

Scripting an Exchange server installation

If you are performing mass deployment of Exchange servers in a large environment, automating the installation process can minimize administrator error and speed up the overall process. The `setup.exe` utility can be used to perform an unattended installation of Exchange, and when combined with PowerShell and just a little bit of scripting logic, it can create a fairly sophisticated installation script. This recipe will provide a couple of examples that can be used to script the installation of an Exchange server.

Getting ready

You can use a standard PowerShell console from the server to run the scripts in this recipe.

How to do it...

Let's see how to create an automated installation script that installs Exchange based on the hostname of the server:

1. Using Notepad or your favorite scripting editor, add the following code to a new file:

```
Param($Path)
if(Test-Path $Path) {
  switch -wildcard ($env:computername) {
    "*-EX-*" {$role = "CA,MB" ; break}
    "*-MB-*"  {$role = "MB" ; break}
    "*-CA-*"  {$role = "CA" ; break}
  }
  $setup = Join-Path $Path "setup.exe"
```

```
    Invoke-Expression "$setup /mode:install `
/r:$role /IAcceptExchangeServerLicenseTerms `
/InstallWindowsComponents"
}
else {
  Write-Host "Invalid Media Path!"
}
```

2. Save the file as `InstallExchange.ps1`.

3. Execute the script from a server, where you want to install Exchange using the following syntax:

    `InstallExchange.ps1 -Path D:`

The value provided for the `-Path` parameter should refer to the Exchange 2013 media, either on DVD or extracted to a folder.

How it works...

One of the most common methods to automate an Exchange installation is to determine the required roles based on the hostname of the server. In the previous example, we assume that your organization uses a standard server naming convention. When executing the script, the switch statement will evaluate the hostname of the server and determine the required roles. For example, if your mailbox servers use a server name, such as CONTOSO-MB-01, the mailbox server role will be installed. If your CAS servers use a server name, such as CONTOSO-CA-02, the CAS role will be installed, and so on.

It's important to note that Exchange 2013 requires several Windows operating system hotfixes, such as .NET Framework 4.5, Filter Pack 2.0, and Unified Communications API 4.0. These should all be installed prior to running this script.

When calling the `Setup.exe` installation program within the script, we use the `/InstallWindowsComponents` and `/IAcceptExchangeServerLicenseTerms` switches, which are new `Setup.exe` features in Exchange Server 2013. This will allow the setup program to load any prerequisite Windows roles and features, such as IIS, and so on, before starting the Exchange installation. The accept agreement switch is required when using the unattended installation method.

There's more...

Scripting the installation of Exchange based on the server names may not be an option for you. Fortunately, PowerShell gives us plenty of flexibility. The following script uses a similar logic, but performs the installation based on different criteria.

Let's say that your core Exchange infrastructure has already been deployed. Your corporate headquarters already has the required CAS and Hub Transport server infrastructure in place; and therefore, you only need to deploy mailbox servers in the main Active Directory site. All remaining remote sites will contain multirole Exchange servers. Replace the code in the InstallExchange.ps1 script with the following:

```
param($Path)
$site = [DirectoryServices.ActiveDirectory.ActiveDirectorySite]
if(Test-Path $Path) {
  switch ($site::GetComputerSite().Name) {
    "Headquarters" {$role = "MB"}
    Default {$role = "CA,MB"}
  }
  $setup = Join-Path $Path "setup.exe"
  Invoke-Expression "$setup /mode:install /r:$role
/IAcceptExchangeServerLicenseTerms /InstallWindowsComponents"
}
else {
  Write-Host "Invalid Media Path!"
}
```

This preceding example determines the current Active Directory site of the computer executing the script. If the computer is in the Headquarters site, only the Mailbox role is installed. If it is located at any of the other remaining Active Directory sites, the Client Access and Mailbox server roles are installed.

As you can see, combining the Setup.exe utility with a PowerShell script can give you many more options when performing an automated installation.

See also

- ▶ *Looping through items* in *Chapter 1, PowerShell Key Concepts*
- ▶ *Creating custom objects* in *Chapter 1, PowerShell Key Concepts*
- ▶ *Working with Desired State Configuration* in *Chapter 1, PowerShell Key Concepts*

3

Managing Recipients

In this chapter, we will cover the following topics:

- ▶ Adding, modifying, and removing mailboxes
- ▶ Working with contacts
- ▶ Managing distribution groups
- ▶ Managing resource mailboxes
- ▶ Creating recipients in bulk using a CSV file
- ▶ Working with recipient filters
- ▶ Adding and removing recipient e-mail addresses
- ▶ Hiding recipients from address lists
- ▶ Configuring recipient moderation
- ▶ Configuring message delivery restrictions
- ▶ Managing automatic replies and Out of Office settings for a user
- ▶ Adding, modifying, and removing server-side inbox rules
- ▶ Managing mailbox folder permissions
- ▶ Importing user photos into Active Directory

Introduction

If you are like many other administrators, you would probably spend the majority of your time performing recipient-related management tasks when dealing with Exchange. If you work in a large environment with thousands of recipients, to create, update, and delete recipients will probably be a cumbersome and time-consuming process. Of course, the obvious solution to this is to use the Exchange Management Shell. By utilizing the Exchange Management Shell, you can automate all of your recipient management tasks and drastically speed up your work.

The concept of an Exchange recipient is more than just a user with a mailbox. An Exchange recipient is any Active Directory object that has been mail-enabled and can receive messages within the Exchange organization. This can be a distribution group, a contact, a mail-enabled public folder, and so on. These object types include individual sets of cmdlets that can be used to completely automate the administration of the Exchange recipients in your environment.

The goal of this chapter is to show you some common solutions that can be used when performing day-to-day recipient management from the shell. Quite often, Exchange recipients are provisioned or updated in bulk through an automated process driven by a PowerShell script. The recipes in this chapter will provide solutions for these types of scripts that you can use right away. You can also use these concepts as a guide to build your own scripts from scratch to automate recipient-related tasks in your environment.

Performing some basic steps

To work with the code samples in this chapter, we'll need to launch the Exchange Management Shell using the following steps:

1. Log on to a workstation or server with the Exchange Management tools installed.

2. Open the Exchange Management Shell by navigating to **Start | All Programs | Exchange Server 2013**.

3. Click on the **Exchange Management Shell** shortcut.

If any additional steps are required, they will be listed at the beginning of the recipe in the *Getting ready* section.

> Remember to start the Exchange Management Shell using **Run as administrator** to avoid permission problems.
>
> In this chapter, notice that in the examples of cmdlets, I have used the back tick (`` ` ``) character to break up long commands into multiple lines. The purpose of this is to make it easier to read. The back ticks are not required and should only be used if needed.

Adding, modifying, and removing mailboxes

One of the most common tasks performed within the Exchange Management Shell is mailbox management. In this recipe, we'll take a look at the command syntax required to create, update, and remove mailboxes from your Exchange organization. The concepts outlined in this recipe can be used to perform basic day-to-day tasks and will be useful for more advanced scenarios, such as creating mailboxes in bulk.

How to do it...

Let's see how to add, modify, and delete mailboxes using the following steps:

1. Let's start off by creating a mailbox-enabled Active Directory user account. To do this, we can use the `New-Mailbox` cmdlet, as shown in the following example:

```
$password = ConvertTo-SecureString -AsPlainText P@ssw0rd `
-Force

New-Mailbox -UserPrincipalName dave@contoso.com `

-Alias dave `

-Database DAGDB1 `

-Name 'Dave Jones' `

-OrganizationalUnit Sales `

-Password $password `

-FirstName Dave `

-LastName Jones `

-DisplayName 'Dave Jones'
```

2. Once the mailbox has been created, we can modify it using the `Set-Mailbox` cmdlet:

```
Set-Mailbox -Identity dave `

-UseDatabaseQuotaDefaults $false `

-ProhibitSendReceiveQuota 5GB `

-IssueWarningQuota 4GB
```

3. To remove the Exchange attributes from the Active Directory user account and mark the mailbox in the database for removal, use the `Disable-Mailbox` cmdlet:

```
Disable-Mailbox -Identity dave -Confirm:$false
```

How it works...

When running the `New-Mailbox` cmdlet, the `-Password` parameter is required, and you need to provide a value for it, using a secure string object. As you can see from the code, we used the `ConvertTo-SecureString` cmdlet to create a `$password` variable that stores a specified value as an encrypted string. This `$password` variable is then assigned to the `-Password` parameter when running the cmdlet. It's not required to first store this object in a variable; we could have done it inline, as shown next:

```
New-Mailbox -UserPrincipalName dave@contoso.com `

-Alias dave `
```

```
-Database DAGDB1 `

-Name 'Dave Jones' `

-OrganizationalUnit Sales `

-Password (ConvertTo-SecureString -AsPlainText P@ssw0rd -Force) `

-FirstName Dave `

-LastName Jones `

-DisplayName 'Dave Jones'
```

Keep in mind that the password used here needs to comply with your Active Directory password policies, which may enforce a minimum password length and have requirements for complexity.

Only a few parameters are actually required when running `New-Mailbox`, but the cmdlet itself supports several useful parameters that can be used to set certain properties when creating the mailbox. You can run `Get-Help New-Mailbox -Detailed` to determine which additional parameters are supported.

The `New-Mailbox` cmdlet creates a new Active Directory user and then mailbox-enables that account. We can also create mailboxes for existing users with the `Enable-Mailbox` cmdlet, using a syntax similar to the following:

```
Enable-Mailbox steve -Database DAGDB1
```

The only requirement when running the `Enable-Mailbox` cmdlet is that you need to provide the identity of the Active Directory user that should be mailbox-enabled. In the previous example, we specified the database in which the mailbox should be created, but this is optional. The `Enable-Mailbox` cmdlet supports a number of other parameters that you can use to control the initial settings for the mailbox.

You can use a simple one-liner to create mailboxes in bulk for existing Active Directory users:

```
Get-User -RecipientTypeDetails User | Enable-Mailbox -Database DAGDB1
```

Notice that we run the `Get-User` cmdlet, specifying `User` as the value for the `-RecipientTypeDetails` parameter. This will retrieve only the accounts in Active Directory that have not been mailbox-enabled. We then pipe those objects down to the `Enable-Mailbox` cmdlet and mailboxes will be created for each of those users in one simple operation.

Once the mailboxes have been created, they can be modified with the `Set-Mailbox` cmdlet. As you may recall from our original example, we used the `Set-Mailbox` cmdlet to configure the custom storage quota settings after creating a mailbox for Dave Jones. Keep in mind that the `Set-Mailbox` cmdlet supports over 100 parameters, so anything that can be done to modify a mailbox can be scripted.

Bulk modifications to mailboxes can be done easily by taking advantage of the pipeline and the `Set-Mailbox` cmdlet. Instead of configuring storage quotas on a single mailbox, we can do it for multiple users at once:

```
Get-Mailbox -OrganizationalUnit contoso.com/sales |
Set-Mailbox -UseDatabaseQuotaDefaults $false `
-ProhibitSendReceiveQuota 5GB `
-IssueWarningQuota 4GB
```

Here, we are simply retrieving every mailbox in the `sales` OU using the `Get-Mailbox` cmdlet. The objects returned from this command are piped down to `Set-Mailbox`, which then modifies the quota settings for each mailbox in one shot.

The `Disable-Mailbox` cmdlet will strip the Exchange attributes from an Active Directory user and will disconnect the associated mailbox. By default, disconnected mailboxes are retained for 30 days. You can modify this setting on the database that holds the mailbox. In addition to this, you can also use the `Remove-Mailbox` cmdlet to delete both the Active Directory account and the mailbox at once:

```
Remove-Mailbox -Identity dave -Confirm:$false
```

After running this command, the mailbox will be purged once it exceeds the deleted mailbox retention setting on the database. One common mistake is when administrators use the `Remove-Mailbox` cmdlet when the `Disable-Mailbox` cmdlet should have been used. It's important to remember that the `Remove-Mailbox` cmdlet will delete the Active Directory user account and mailbox, while the `Disable-Mailbox` cmdlet only removes the mailbox, but the Active Directory user account still remains.

There's more...

When we ran the `New-Mailbox` cmdlet in the previous examples, we assigned a secure string object to the `-Password` parameter using the `ConvertTo-SecureString` cmdlet. This is a great technique to use when your scripts need complete automation, but you can also allow an operator to enter this information interactively. For example, you might build a script that prompts an operator for a password when creating one or more mailboxes. There are a couple of ways you can do this. First, you can use the `Read-Host` cmdlet to prompt the user running the script to enter a password:

```
$pass = Read-Host "Enter Password" -AsSecureString
```

Once a value has been entered in the shell, your script can assign the `$pass` variable to the `-Password` parameter of the `New-Mailbox` cmdlet.

Alternatively, you can supply a value for the `-Password` parameter using the `Get-Credential` cmdlet:

```
New-Mailbox -Name Dave -UserPrincipalName dave@contoso.com `
-Password (Get-Credential).password
```

You can see that the value we are assigning to the `-Password` parameter in this example is actually the `password` property of the object returned by the `Get-Credential` cmdlet. Executing this command will first launch a Windows authentication dialog box, where the caller can enter a username and password. Once the credential object has been created, the `New-Mailbox` cmdlet will run. Even though a username and password must be entered in the authentication dialog box, only the password value will be used when the command executes.

Setting the Active Directory attributes

Some of the Active Directory attributes that you may want to set when creating a mailbox might not be available when using the `New-Mailbox` cmdlet. Good examples of this are a user's city, state, company, and department attributes. In order to set these attributes, you'll need to call the `Set-User` cmdlet after the mailbox has been created:

```
Set-User -Identity dave -Office IT -City Seattle -State Washington
```

You can run `Get-Help Set-User -Detailed` to view all of the available parameters supported by this cmdlet.

> Notice that the `Set-User` cmdlet is an Active Directory cmdlet and not an Exchange cmdlet.
>
> In the examples using the `New-Mailbox` cmdlet to create new mailboxes, it is not required to use all these parameters from the example. The only required parameters are `UserPrincipalName`, `Name`, and `Password`.

See also

▸ *Using the help system* in *Chapter 1, PowerShell Key Concepts*

▸ *Creating recipients in bulk using a CSV file*

▸ *Managing distribution groups*

Working with contacts

Once you've started managing mailboxes using the Exchange Management Shell, you'll probably notice that the concepts and command syntax used to manage contacts are very similar. The difference, of course, is that we need to use a different set of cmdlets. In addition, we also have two types of contacts to deal with in Exchange. We'll take a look at how you can manage both of them in this recipe.

How to do it...

Let's see how to work with contacts using the following steps:

1. To create a mail-enabled contact, use the `New-MailContact` cmdlet:

```
New-MailContact -Alias rjones `
-Name "Rob Jones" `
-ExternalEmailAddress rob@fabrikam.com `
-OrganizationalUnit sales
```

2. Mail-enabled users can be created with the `New-MailUser` cmdlet:

```
New-MailUser -Name 'John Davis' `
-Alias jdavis `
-UserPrincipalName jdavis@contoso.com `
-FirstName John `
-LastName Davis `
-Password (ConvertTo-SecureString -AsPlainText P@ssw0rd `
-Force) `
-ResetPasswordOnNextLogon $false `
-ExternalEmailAddress jdavis@fabrikam.com
```

How it works...

Mail contacts are useful when you have external e-mail recipients that need to show up in your global address list. When you use the `New-MailContact` cmdlet, an Active Directory contact object is created and mail-enabled with the external e-mail address assigned. You can mail-enable an existing Active Directory contact using the `Enable-MailContact` cmdlet.

Mail users are similar to mail contacts in the way that they have an associated external e-mail address. The difference is that these objects are mail-enabled Active Directory users and this explains why we need to assign a password when creating the object. You might use a mail user for a contractor who works onsite in your organization and needs to be able to log on to your domain. When users in your organization need to e-mail this person, they can select them from the global address list and messages sent to these recipients will be delivered to the external address configured for the account.

When dealing with mailboxes, there are a couple of things that should be taken into consideration when it comes to removing contacts and mail users. You can remove the Exchange attributes from a contact using the `Disable-MailContact` cmdlet. The `Remove-MailContact` cmdlet will remove the contact object from the Active Directory and Exchange. Similarly, the `Disable-MailUser` and `Remove-MailUser` cmdlets work in the same fashion.

There's more...

Like mailboxes, mail contacts and mail-enabled user accounts have several Active Directory attributes that can be set, such as the job title, company, department, and so on. To update these attributes, you can use the `Set-*` cmdlets that are available for each respective type. For example, to update our mail contact, we can use the `Set-Contact` cmdlet with the following syntax:

```
Set-Contact -Identity rjones `
-Title 'Sales Contractor' `
-Company Fabrikam `
-Department Sales
```

To modify the same settings for a mail-enabled user, use the `Set-User` cmdlet:

```
Set-User -Identity jdavis `
-Title 'Sales Contractor' `
-Company Fabrikam `
-Department Sales
```

Both cmdlets can be used to modify a number of different settings. Use the help system to view all of the available parameters.

See also

▶ *Using the help system* in *Chapter 1, PowerShell Key Concepts*

▶ *Adding, modifying, and removing mailboxes*

Managing distribution groups

In many Exchange environments, distribution groups are heavily relied upon and require frequent changes. This recipe will cover the creation of distribution groups and how to add members to groups, which might be useful when performing these tasks interactively in the shell or through automated scripts.

How to do it...

Let's see how to create distribution groups using the following steps:

1. To create a distribution group, use the `New-DistributionGroup` cmdlet:

   ```
   New-DistributionGroup -Name Sales
   ```

2. Once the group has been created, adding multiple members can be done easily using a one-liner, as follows:

```
Get-Mailbox -OrganizationalUnit Sales |
Add-DistributionGroupMember -Identity Sales
```

3. We can also create distribution groups whose memberships are set dynamically:

```
New-DynamicDistributionGroup -Name Accounting `
-Alias Accounting `
-IncludedRecipients MailboxUsers,MailContacts `
-OrganizationalUnit Accounting `
-ConditionalDepartment accounting,finance `
-RecipientContainer contoso.com
```

How it works...

There are two types of distribution groups that can be created with Exchange. Firstly, there are regular distribution groups, which contain a distinct list of users. Secondly, there are dynamic distribution groups, whose members are determined at the time a message is sent based on a number of conditions or filters that have been defined. Both types have a set of cmdlets that can be used to add, remove, update, enable, or disable these groups.

By default, when creating a standard distribution group, the group scope will be set to `Universal`. You can create a mail-enabled security group using the `New-DistributionGroup` cmdlet by setting the `-Type` parameter to `Security`. If you do not provide a value for the `-Type` parameter, the group will be created using the `Distribution` group type.

You can mail-enable an existing Active Directory universal distribution group using the `Enable-DistributionGroup` cmdlet.

After creating the `Sales` distribution group in our previous example, we added all of the mailboxes in the `Sales` OU to the group using the `Add-DistributionGroupMember` cmdlet. You can do this in bulk, or for one user at a time, using the `–Member` parameter:

```
Add-DistributionGroupMember -Identity Sales -Member administrator
```

> Distribution groups is a large topic, and we're merely covering the basics here. See *Chapter 5, Distribution Groups and Address Lists* for in-depth coverage of distribution groups.

Dynamic distribution groups determine their membership based on a defined set of filters and conditions. When we created the `Accounting` distribution group, we used the `-IncludedRecipients` parameter to specify that only the `MailboxUsers` and `MailContacts` object types would be included in the group. This eliminates resource mailboxes, groups, or mail users from being included as members. The group will be created in the `Accounting` OU based on the value used with the `-OrganizationalUnit` parameter. Using the `–ConditionalDepartment` parameter, the group will only include users that have a department setting of either `Accounting` or `Finance`. Finally, since the `-RecipientContainer` parameter is set to the FQDN of the domain, any user located in the Active Directory can potentially be included in the group. You can create more complex filters for dynamic distribution groups using a recipient filter; for example, see the recipe titled *Working with recipient filters*, later in this chapter.

> You can modify both group types using the `Set-DistributionGroup` and `Set-DynamicDistributionGroup` cmdlets.

There's more...

When dealing with other recipient types, there are a couple of things that should be taken into consideration when it comes to removing distribution groups. You can remove the Exchange attributes from a group using the `Disable-DistributionGroup` cmdlet. The `Remove-DistributionGroup` cmdlet will remove the group object from the Active Directory and Exchange.

See also

- *Working with recipient filters*
- *Reporting on distribution group membership* in Chapter 5, *Distribution Groups and Address Lists*
- *Adding members to a distribution group from an external file* in Chapter 5, *Distribution Groups and Address Lists*
- *Previewing dynamic distribution group membership* in Chapter 5, *Distribution Groups and Address Lists*

Managing resource mailboxes

In addition to mailboxes, groups, and external contacts, recipients can also include specific rooms or pieces of equipment. Locations such as a conference room or a classroom can be given a mailbox so that they can be reserved for meetings. Equipment mailboxes can be assigned to physical, non-location specific resources, such as laptops or projectors, and can then be checked out to individual users or groups by booking a time with the mailbox. In this recipe, we'll take a look at how you can manage resource mailboxes using the Exchange Management Shell.

How to do it...

When creating a resource mailbox from within the shell, the syntax is similar to creating a mailbox for a regular user. For example, you still use the `New-Mailbox` cmdlet when creating a resource mailbox:

```
New-Mailbox -Name "CR23" -DisplayName "Conference Room 23" `
-UserPrincipalName CR23@contoso.com -Room
```

How it works...

There are two main differences when it comes to creating a resource mailbox, as opposed to a standard user mailbox. First, you need to use either the `-Room` switch parameter or the `-Equipment` switch parameter to define the type of resource mailbox that will be created. Second, you do not need to provide a password value for the user account. When using either of these resource mailbox switch parameters to create a mailbox, the `New-Mailbox` cmdlet will create a disabled Active Directory user account that will be associated with the mailbox.

The entire concept of room and equipment mailboxes revolves around the calendars used by these resources. If you want to reserve a room or a piece of equipment, you book a time through Outlook or OWA with these resources for the duration that you'll need them. The requests sent to these resources need to be accepted, either by a delegate or automatically using the Resource Booking Attendant.

To configure the room mailbox created in the previous example, to automatically accept new meeting requests, we can use the `Set-CalendarProcessing` cmdlet to set the Resource Booking Attendant for that mailbox to `AutoAccept`:

```
Set-CalendarProcessing CR23 -AutomateProcessing AutoAccept
```

When the Resource Booking Attendant is set to `AutoAccept`, the request will be immediately accepted as long as there is no conflict with another meeting. If there is a conflict, an e-mail message will be returned to the requestor, which explains that the request was declined due to scheduling conflicts. You can allow conflicts by adding the `-AllowConflicts` switch parameter to the previous command.

When working with resource mailboxes with `AutomateProcessing` set to `AutoAccept`, you'll get an automated e-mail response from the resource after booking a time. This e-mail message will explain whether the request was accepted or declined, depending on your settings. You can add an additional text to the response message that the meeting organizer will receive using the following syntax:

```
Set-CalendarProcessing -Identity CR23 `
-AddAdditionalResponse $true `
-AdditionalResponse 'For Assistance Contact Support at Ext. #3376'
```

This example uses the `Set-CalendarProcessing` cmdlet to customize the response messages sent from the CR23 room mailbox. You can see here that we added a message that tells the user the help desk number to call if assistance is required. Keep in mind that you can only add an additional response text, when the `AutomateProcessing` property is set to `AutoAccept`.

If you do not want to automate the calendar processing for a resource mailbox, then you'll need to add delegates that can accept or deny meetings for that resource. Again, we can turn to the `Set-CalendarProcessing` cmdlet to accomplish this:

```
Set-CalendarProcessing -Identity CR23 `
-ResourceDelegates "joe@contoso.com","steve@contoso.com" `
-AutomateProcessing None
```

In this example, we added two delegates to the resource mailbox and have turned off automated processing. When a request comes into the CR23 mailbox, both Steve and Joe will be notified and can accept or deny the request on behalf of the resource mailbox.

There's more...

When it comes to working with resource mailboxes, another useful feature is the ability to assign custom resource properties to rooms and equipment resources. For example, you may have a total of 5, 10, or 15 conference rooms, but maybe only four of these have whiteboards. It might be useful for your users to know this information when booking a resource for a meeting, where they will be conducting a training session.

Using the shell, we can add custom resource properties to the Exchange organization by modifying the resource schema. Once these custom resource properties have been added, they can then be assigned to specific resource mailboxes.

You can use the following code to add a whiteboard resource property to the Exchange organization's resource schema:

```
Set-ResourceConfig -ResourcePropertySchema 'Room/Whiteboard'
```

Now that the whiteboard resource property is available within the Exchange organization, we can add this to our Conference Room 23 mailbox using the following command:

```
Set-Mailbox -Identity CR23 -ResourceCustom Whiteboard
```

When users access the **Select Rooms** or **Add Rooms** dialog box in Outlook 2007, 2010, or 2013, they will see that Conference Room 23 has a whiteboard available.

Converting mailboxes

If you've moved from an old version, you may have a number of mailboxes that were used as resource mailboxes. Once these mailboxes have been moved they will be identified as `Shared` mailboxes. You can convert them to different types using the `Set-Mailbox` cmdlet so that they'll have all of the properties of a resource mailbox:

```
Get-Mailbox conf* | Set-Mailbox -Type Room
```

You can run the `Set-Mailbox` cmdlet against each mailbox one at a time and convert them to `Room` mailboxes, using the `-Type` parameter. Or, if you use a common naming convention, you may be able to do them in bulk by retrieving a list of mailboxes using a wildcard and piping them to `Set-Mailbox`, as shown previously.

See also

- *Adding, modifying, and removing mailboxes*
- *Creating recipients in bulk using a CSV file*

Creating recipients in bulk using a CSV file

One of the most common bulk provisioning techniques used in the Exchange Management Shell makes use of CSV files. These files act like a database table. Each record in this table is represented by one line in the file, and each field value is separated by a comma, which is used as a delimiter. In this recipe, you'll learn how to set up a CSV file and create recipients in bulk using the Exchange Management Shell.

Getting ready

In addition to the Exchange Management Shell, you'll need to use Microsoft Excel to create a CSV file.

How to do it...

Let' see how to create recipients in bulk using the following steps:

1. We'll enter some data into Excel that will include the settings for five new mailboxes:

2. Go to **File | Save As** and select **CSV (Comma delimited) (*.csv)** for the file type. Save the file as `C:\mailboxes1.csv`.

3. Within the Exchange Management Shell, create a secure password object to be used as an initial password for each mailbox:

```
$pass = ConvertTo-SecureString -AsPlainText P@ssw0rd01 `
-Force
```

4. Import the CSV file and create the mailboxes:

```
Import-CSV C:\mailboxes1.csv | % {
   New-Mailbox -Name $_.Name `
   -Alias $_.Alias `
   -UserPrincipalName $_.UserPrincipalName `
   -OrganizationalUnit $_.OrganizationalUnit `
   -Password $pass `
   -ResetPasswordOnNextLogon $true
}
```

How it works...

In this example, we're importing the CSV file into the shell and piping that information to the `ForEach-Object` cmdlet (using the `%` alias). For each record in the CSV file, we're running the `New-Mailbox` cmdlet, providing values for the `-Name`, `-Alias`, `-UserPrincipalName`, and `-OrganizationalUnit` parameters. The properties for each record can be accessed inside the loop using the `$_` variable, which is the automatic variable that refers to the current object in the pipeline. The property names for each record match the header names used in the CSV file. As we create each mailbox, the password is set to the `$pass` variable. The `-ResetPasswordOnNextLogon` parameter is set to `$true`, which will require each user to reset their password after their first logon.

Using this technique, you can literally create thousands of mailboxes in a matter of minutes. This concept can also be applied to other recipient types, such as distribution groups and contacts. You just need to specify the appropriate parameter values in the CSV file and use the corresponding cmdlet for the recipient type. For example, if you want to bulk provision contacts from a CSV file, use the code from the previous example as a guide, and instead of using the `New-Mailbox` cmdlet, use the `New-MailContact` cmdlet and whatever parameters are required based on your settings.

There's more...

Let's take a look at an alternative approach to the previous example. Let's say that you don't want to set an initial password for each user and instead, you want to include this information in the CSV file so that each new mailbox gets a unique password. Again, you'll need to set up a CSV file with the required values. For this example, your CSV file would look something like this:

	A	B	C	D	E	F	G
1	Name	Alias	UserPrincipalName	Password			
2	Pete Dickson	pdickson	Pdickson@contoso.com	4::N2IQzXe			
3	Emanuel Moss	emoss	Emoss@contoso.com	:$IG%FXxRw			
4	Lee Sanders	lsanders	Lsanders@contoso.com	Hez9sJz&zX			
5	Arlene Finley	afinley	Afinley@contoso.com	9X,/LNKsny			
6	Ruben Mcleod	rmcleod	Rmcleod@contoso.com	qD-*:Z(ku(			

mailboxes2

In the preceding screenshot, we are using different column names for this new file. We removed the `OrganizationalUnit` column and now have a `Password` column that will be used to create each mailbox with a unique password. After you're done creating the file, save it again as `C:\mailboxes2.csv`.

Next, you can use the following code to create the mailboxes, specifying the path and filename to the CSV file created in the previous step:

```
Import-CSV C:\Mailboxes.CSV | % {
  $pass = ConvertTo-SecureString -AsPlainText $_.Password -Force
  New-Mailbox -Name $_.Name `
  -Alias $_.Alias `
  -UserPrincipalName $_.UserPrincipalName `
  -Password $pass
}
```

As we loop through each record in the CSV file, we create a secure password object that can be used with the `-Password` parameter. The main difference here compared to the previous example is that each user gets a unique password, and they do not need to reset their password the first time they log in.

Taking it a step further

When provisioning recipients, you'll probably need to do multiple things, such as set Active Directory attributes and configure distribution group membership. Let's take our previous example a step further:

```
Import-CSV C:\NewMailboxes.csv | % {
  New-Mailbox -Name $_.Name `
  -FirstName $_.FirstName `
  -LastName $_.LastName `
  -Alias $_.Alias `
  -UserPrincipalName $_.UserPrincipalName `
  -Password (ConvertTo-SecureString -AsPlainText P@ssw0rd `
  -Force) `
  -OrganizationalUnit $_.OrganizationalUnit `
  -Database DB1
  Set-User -Identity $_.Name `
  -City $_.City `
  -StateOrProvince $_.State `
```

```
-Title $_.Title `
-Department $_.Department
Add-DistributionGroupMember -Identity DL_Sales `
-Member $_.Name
Add-DistributionGroupMember -Identity DL_Marketing `
-Member $_.Name
}
```

Here, we're still using a CSV file, but as we loop through each record, we call multiple cmdlets to first create the mailbox, set some of the Active Directory attributes, and then add the mailbox to two separate distribution groups. In order to use this code, we would just need to create a CSV file that has columns for all of the values we're setting.

Now that we have this framework in place, we can add as many columns as we need to the CSV file, and we can call any number of cmdlets for each record in the CSV.

See also

▶ *Looping through items* in *Chapter 1, PowerShell Key Concepts*

▶ *Adding, modifying, and removing mailboxes*

▶ *Managing distribution groups*

Working with recipient filters

Starting with Exchange 2007 and continuing with Exchange 2010 and 2013, address lists, dynamic distribution groups, e-mail address policies, and global address lists can be customized with recipient filters that use the OPATH filtering syntax. This replaces the legacy LDAP filtering syntax that was used in earlier versions of Exchange. We can also perform server-side searches using filters, which can greatly speed up our work. In this recipe, you'll learn how to work with these filters in the Exchange Management Shell.

How to do it...

Let's see how to work with recipient filters using the following steps:

1. We can filter the results from the recipient `Get-*` cmdlets using the `-Filter` parameter:

    ```
    Get-Mailbox -Filter {Office -eq 'Sales'}
    ```

2. In addition, we can use attribute filters to create distribution groups, e-mail address policies, and address lists using the `-RecipientFilter` parameter:

```
New-DynamicDistributionGroup -Name DL_Accounting `
-RecipientFilter {
  (Department -eq 'Accounting') -and
  (RecipientType -eq 'UserMailbox')
}
```

How it works...

In our first example, you can see that we used the `Get-Mailbox` cmdlet to retrieve only the users that have the `Office` property set to the `Sales` value. This is more efficient than performing the following command, which would return the same results:

```
Get-Mailbox | ?{$_.Office -eq 'Sales'}
```

This command uses the `Where-Object` cmdlet (using the `?` alias) to retrieve only the mailboxes with their `Office` property set to `Sales`. We get the same results, but it is less efficient than our original example. When filtering with `Where-Object`, every mailbox in the organization must be retrieved and evaluated before any results are returned. The benefit of using the `-Filter` parameter with the `Get-Mailbox` cmdlet is that the filtering is done on the server and not on our client machines. The `-Filter` method is preferred when working in large environments.

There are a number of cmdlets that support this parameter. You can get an entire list with a simple one-liner:

```
get-excommand | ?{$_.parameters.keys -eq 'filter'}
```

This uses the `get-excommand` shell function to retrieve a list of Exchange Management Shell cmdlets that support the `-Filter` parameter. If you are writing scripts or functions that need to query a large amount of recipients, you'll want to try to use server-side filtering whenever possible.

Unfortunately, there are only a certain set of properties that can be filtered. For instance, we were able to filter using the `Office` property, when using the `Get-Mailbox` cmdlet. Based on this, you may assume that since `OrganizationalUnit` is a property of a mailbox object that you can filter on that as well, but that is not the case. The `Get-Mailbox` cmdlet provides an `-OrganizationalUnit` parameter that can be used to accomplish this task, so it's not always safe to assume that a particular property can be used within a filter. To view a list of common filterable properties that can be used with the `-Filter` parameter, see *Appendix A, Common Shell Information* at the end of this book.

In our second example, we used the `New-DynamicDistributionGroup` cmdlet to create a query-based group. The membership of this group is determined using the OPATH filter defined with the `-RecipientFilter` parameter. The syntax is similar and the same PowerShell operators can be used. Based on the settings used with our filter when we created the `DL_Accounting` group, only mailboxes with their `Department` attributes set to `Accounting` will be included. Other recipient types, such as mail contacts and mail users, will not be included in the group, even though they may be in the `Accounting` department.

Dynamic distribution groups, address lists, and e-mail address policies can be configured with these filters. Again, to get the list of cmdlets that support this functionality, use the `get-excommand` shell variable:

```
get-excommand | ?{$_.parameters.keys -eq 'recipientfilter'}
```

These cmdlets also have a limited number of filterable properties that can be used. To view a list of the most common properties used with the `-RecipientFilter` parameter, see *Appendix A, Common Shell Information* at the end of this book.

There's more...

Instead of using the `-RecipientFilter` parameter, you have the option of using precanned filters. In some cases this may be easier, as it allows you to simply use a set of parameters and values as opposed to an OPATH filter. The following command would create our `DL_Accounting` distribution group with the same members using the precanned filter parameters:

```
New-DynamicDistributionGroup -Name DL_Accounting `
-IncludedRecipients MailboxUsers `
-ConditionalDepartment Accounting
```

As you can see, this is a little easier to read, and probably easier to type in the shell. Although, there are only a few precanned parameters available, and they may not always be useful, depending on what you are trying to do, but it helps you to be aware of this functionality. You can use `Get-Help` to view the entire list of available parameters for each cmdlet that supports recipient filters.

Understanding variables in filters

One of the issues you may run into when working in the shell is the expansion of variables used within a filter. For example, this syntax is completely valid but will not currently work correctly in the Exchange Management Shell:

```
$office = "sales"
Get-Mailbox -Filter {Office -eq $office}
```

You might get some results from this command, but they will probably not be what you are expecting. This is because when running the `Get-Mailbox` cmdlet, the value of the `$office` variable will not be expanded prior to the command being executed through the remote shell. What you end up with instead is a filter that checks for a `$null` value. In order to fix this, you need to use a syntax similar to the following:

```
$office = "sales"
Get-Mailbox -Filter "Office -eq '$office'"
```

This syntax will force any variables assigned within the `-Filter` parameter to be expanded before sending the command through the remote session, and you should get the correct results.

See also

> ▸ *Managing distribution groups*
>
> ▸ *Using the help system* in *Chapter 1, PowerShell Key Concepts*
>
> ▸ *Previewing dynamic distribution group membership* in *Chapter 5, Distribution Groups and Address Lists*

Adding and removing recipient e-mail addresses

There are several recipient types in Exchange 2013, and each one of them can support multiple e-mail addresses. Of course, the typical user mailbox recipient type is probably the first that comes to mind, but we also have distribution groups, contacts, and public folders, each of which can have one or more e-mail addresses. The syntax used to add and remove e-mail addresses to each of these recipient types is essentially identical; the only thing that changes is the cmdlet that is used to set the address. In this recipe, you'll learn how to add or remove an e-mail address from an Exchange recipient.

How to do it...

Let's see how to add and remove recipient e-mail addresses using the following steps:

1. To add a secondary e-mail address to a mailbox, use the following command syntax:

   ```
   Set-Mailbox dave -EmailAddresses
   @{add='dave@west.contoso.com'}
   ```

2. Multiple addresses can also be added using this technique:

   ```
   Set-Mailbox dave -EmailAddresses @{
     add='dave@east.contoso.com',
   ```

```
    'dave@west.contoso.com',

    'dave@corp.contoso.com'

}
```

3. E-mail addresses can also be removed using the following syntax:

```
Set-Mailbox dave -EmailAddresses
@{remove='dave@west.contoso.com'}
```

4. We are able to add multiple e-mail addresses at once. We can do the same when removing an address:

```
Set-Mailbox dave -EmailAddresses @{

    remove='dave@east.contoso.com',

    'dave@corp.contoso.com'

}
```

How it works...

Adding and removing e-mail addresses was more challenging in the Exchange Management Shell of Exchange Server 2007, because it required that you work directly with the `EmailAddresses` collection, which is a multivalued property. In order to modify the collection, you first have to save the object to a variable, modify it, and then write it back to the `EmailAddresses` object on the recipient. This made it impossible to update the e-mail addresses for a recipient with one command.

The `Set-*` cmdlets used to manage recipients in Exchange 2013 now support a new syntax that allows us to use a hash table to modify the `EmailAddresses` property. As you can see from the previous code samples, we can simply use the `Add` and `Remove` keys within the hash table, and the assigned e-mail address values will be either added or removed as required. This is a nice change that makes it easier to do this in scripts, especially when working interactively in the shell.

The `Add` and `Remove` keywords are interchangeable with the plus (+) and minus (-) characters that serve as aliases:

```
Set-Mailbox dave -EmailAddresses @{

    '+'='dave@east.contoso.com'

    '-'='dave@west.contoso.com'

}
```

In the previous example, we added and removed e-mai addresses from the mailbox. Notice that the + and - keywords need to be enclosed in quotes so that PowerShell does not try to interpret them as the += and -= operators.

This syntax works with all of the `Set-*` cmdlets that support the `-EmailAddresses` parameter:

- ▶ `Set-CASMailbox`
- ▶ `Set-DistributionGroup`
- ▶ `Set-DynamicDistributionGroup`
- ▶ `Set-Mailbox`
- ▶ `Set-MailContact`
- ▶ `Set-MailPublicFolder`
- ▶ `Set-MailUser`
- ▶ `Set-RemoteMailbox`

Keep in mind that in most cases, the best way to add an e-mail address to a recipient is through the use of an e-mail address policy. This may not always be an option, but should be used first if you find yourself in a situation where addresses need to be added to a large number of recipients. Having said that, it is possible do this in bulk using a simple `foreach` loop:

```
foreach($i in Get-Mailbox -OrganizationalUnit Sales) {
  Set-Mailbox $i -EmailAddresses @{
    add="$($i.alias)@west.contoso.com"
  }
}
```

This code simply iterates over each mailbox in the `Sales` OU and adds a secondary e-mail address using the existing alias at `west.contoso.com`. You can use this technique and modify the syntax as needed to perform bulk operations.

There's more...

Imagine a situation where you need to remove all the e-mail addresses under a certain domain from all of your mailboxes. These could be secondary addresses that were added manually to each mailbox or could be used to be applied as part of an e-mail address policy that no longer applies. The following code can be used to remove all the e-mail addresses from mailboxes under a specific domain:

```
foreach($i in Get-Mailbox -ResultSize Unlimited) {
  $i.EmailAddresses |
  ?{$_.SmtpAddress -like '*@corp.contoso.com'} | %{
    Set-Mailbox $i -EmailAddresses @{remove=$_}
  }
}
```

This code iterates through each mailbox in the organization and simply uses a filter to discover any e-mail addresses at `corp.contoso.com`. If any exist, the `Set-Mailbox` cmdlet will attempt to remove each of them from the mailbox.

See also

- ▶ *Adding, modifying, and removing mailboxes*
- ▶ *Working with contacts*
- ▶ *Managing distribution groups*

Hiding recipients from address lists

There may be times when you'll need to hide a particular mailbox, contact, or distribution group from your Exchange address lists. This is a common task that is required to be done when you have mailboxes, contacts, or public folders used by applications or staff in your IT department that should not be seen by end users. In this recipe, we'll take a look at how you can disable these recipient types from the address lists using the Exchange Management Shell.

How to do it...

To hide a mailbox from the Exchange address lists, use the `Set-Mailbox` command:

```
Set-Mailbox dave –HiddenFromAddressListsEnabled $true
```

How it works...

As you can see, hiding a mailbox from address lists is pretty straightforward, as it requires only a simple PowerShell one-liner. The `–HiddenFromAddressListsEnabled` parameter accepts a Boolean value, either `$true` or `$false`. To enable this setting, set the value to `$true`, and to disable it, set the value to `$false`.

There are multiple recipient types that can be hidden from address lists. Each of the following cmdlets supports the `-HiddenFromAddressListsEnabled` parameter:

- ▶ `Set-DistributionGroup`
- ▶ `Set-DynamicDistributionGroup`
- ▶ `Set-Mailbox`
- ▶ `Set-MailContact`
- ▶ `Set-MailPublicFolder`
- ▶ `Set-MailUser`
- ▶ `Set-RemoteMailbox`

There's more...

Once you've hidden your recipients from the address lists, you may need to generate a report to list the objects that currently have the `HiddenFromAddressListsEnabled` setting enabled. Use the following command syntax to obtain this information:

```
Get-Mailbox -Filter {HiddenFromAddressListsEnabled -eq $true}
```

This searches for all the mailboxes that have been hidden from address lists. It makes use of the `-Filter` parameter, which keeps you from having to perform the filtering on the client side with the `Where-Object` cmdlet.

See also

▶   *Working with recipient filters*

Configuring recipient moderation

The recipient moderation allows you to require approval for all e-mail messages sent to a particular recipient by a designated moderator. In this recipe, you'll learn how to configure the moderation settings on recipients using the Exchange Management Shell.

How to do it...

Let's see how to configure recipient moderation settings using the following steps:

1. To enable moderation for a distribution group, use the `Set-DistributionGroup` cmdlet:

    ```
    Set-DistributionGroup -Identity Executives `
    -ModerationEnabled $true `
    -ModeratedBy administrator `
    -SendModerationNotifications Internal
    ```

2. These same parameters can be used to configure moderation for a mailbox, when using the `Set-Mailbox` cmdlet:

    ```
    Set-Mailbox -Identity dave `
    -ModerationEnabled $true `
    -ModeratedBy administrator `
    -SendModerationNotifications Internal
    ```

How it works...

When you enable moderation for a recipient, any e-mail message sent to that recipient must be reviewed by a moderator. When a message is sent to a moderated recipient, the moderator will receive the message and determine whether or not it should be accepted. This is done by the moderator through Outlook or OWA by clicking on an **Approve** or a **Reject** button in the e-mail message. If the moderator accepts the message, it is delivered to the group. If it is rejected, the message is deleted, and depending on the SendModerationNotifications setting, the sender may receive an e-mail informing them that the message has been rejected.

Moderation can be enabled for any recipient, whether it's a mailbox, mail contact, mail user, distribution group, or mail-enabled public folder. The cmdlets for each of these recipient types can be used to configure moderation, when a recipient is being created with the New-* cmdlets, or after the fact using the Set-* cmdlets. To view the list of cmdlets that can be used to enable moderation, run the following command:

```
get-excommand | ?{$_.parameters.keys -eq 'ModerationEnabled'}
```

In our first example, we enabled moderation for the Executives distribution group, specifying that the administrator account will be used as the moderator for the group. As you can see in the example, we used multiple parameters when running the command, but only the -ModerationEnabled parameter is required to change the moderation setting for the group. If no value is specified for the -ModeratedBy parameter, the group owner will review and approve the messages sent to the group. You can specify one or more owners when running the Set-DistributionGroup cmdlet with the -ManagedBy parameter.

The -SendModerationNotifications parameter allows you to control the status messages sent to the originator of a message that was sent to a moderated recipient. We have the option to use the following values for this parameter:

- ▶ Always: Notifications are sent to all internal and external senders
- ▶ Internal: Notifications are only sent to users within the organization
- ▶ Never: Notifications are not sent at all

If no value is provided for the -SendModerationNotifications parameter when you enable moderation for a group, the setting will default to Always.

There's more...

There is an exception to every rule; and of course, there may be times where we need to bypass moderation for certain recipients. Let's say that we need to bypass specific users from moderation on the `Executives` distribution group. The group moderator or group owners are already exempted from moderation. To exclude others, we can specify a list of one or more recipients using the `-BypassModerationFromSendersOrMembers` parameter when running the `Set-DistributionGroup` cmdlet.

For example, to exclude a recipient named Bob from moderation on the `Executives` distribution group, run the following command:

```
Set-DistributionGroup -Identity Executives `
-BypassModerationFromSendersOrMembers bob@contoso.com
```

If you want the members of the moderated group, or any other distribution group, to be excluded from moderation, simply use the previous syntax and assign the identity of the group to the `-BypassModerationFromSendersOrMembers` parameter. You can assign multiple users or distribution groups at once by separating each value with a comma.

Keep in mind that running the previous command will overwrite the existing list of bypassed members if any have been defined. For example, to see how to add a new item to a multivalued property, refer to the *Working with arrays and hash tables* in *Chapter 1, PowerShell Key Concepts*.

Additionally, you may need to bypass moderation for a group of several individual recipients. While you could add them one by one, this could be very time consuming if you are dealing with a large number of recipients. Let's say that you want to exclude all the users in the San Diego office from moderation:

```
$exclude = Get-Mailbox -Filter {Office -eq 'San Diego'} |
Select-Object -ExpandProperty alias
Set-DistributionGroup -Identity Executives `
-BypassModerationFromSendersOrMembers $exclude
```

In this example, we create a collection that contains the alias for each mailbox in the San Diego office. Next, we use the `Set-DistributionGroup` cmdlet to exclude all of those recipients from moderation using a single command. While this might be useful in certain situations, it's easier to bypass moderation based on groups. If a group has been bypassed for moderation, you can simply manage the membership of the group, and you don't need to worry about continuously updating individual recipients that are on the bypass list.

See also

▶   *Managing distribution groups*

Configuring message delivery restrictions

Since distribution groups contain multiple members, you may want to place restrictions on who can send messages to these recipients. Exchange allows you to tightly control these settings and provides several options when it comes to placing message delivery restrictions on groups. We can also place restrictions on other recipient types in the organization. This recipe will show you how to configure these options from the Exchange Management Shell.

How to do it...

Let's see how to configure restrictions on message delivery using the following steps:

To restrict who can send messages to a group, use the `Set-DistributionGroup` cmdlet:

```
Set-DistributionGroup -Identity Sales `
-AcceptMessagesOnlyFrom 'Bob Smith','John Jones'
```

After running this command, only the users Bob Smith and John Jones can send messages to the `Sales` distribution group.

How it works...

The `-AcceptMessagesOnlyFrom` parameter allows you to specify one or more recipients who are allowed to send messages to a distribution group. These recipients can be regular users with mailboxes or contacts.

You can add individual recipients and distribution groups to the accepted senders list, using the following syntax:

```
Set-DistributionGroup -Identity Sales `
-AcceptMessagesOnlyFromSendersOrMembers Marketing,bob@contoso.com
```

In this example, we're allowing both the `Marketing` distribution group and Bob, an individual recipient, to the accepted senders list for the `Sales` distribution group. Doing so will allow Bob and any members of the `Marketing` distribution group to send messages to the `Sales` group.

When using these parameters, keep in mind that any existing accepted recipients that have been configured will be overwritten. For example, to see how to add a new item to a multivalued property, see the section *Working with arrays and hash tables* in *Chapter 1, PowerShell Key Concepts*.

Delivery restrictions can be placed on any recipient, whether it's a mailbox, mail contact, mail user, distribution group, or mail-enabled public folder. The `Set-*` cmdlets for each of these recipient types can be used to configure delivery restrictions. To view the list of cmdlets that can be used to do this, run the following command:

```
get-excommand | ?{$_.parameters.keys -eq 'AcceptMessagesOnlyFrom'}
```

If you need to add a large list of users to the accepted senders list, you can create a collection and assign it to the -`AcceptMessagesOnlyFrom` parameter:

```
$finance = Get-Mailbox -Filter {Office -eq 'Finance'}
Set-DistributionGroup -Identity Sales `
-AcceptMessagesOnlyFrom $finance
```

You can wipe out these settings and allow messages from all senders by setting the value to `$null`:

```
Set-DistributionGroup -Identity Sales `
-AcceptMessagesOnlyFromSendersOrMembers $null
```

Similar to the previous examples, we can reject messages from a specific user or member of a distribution list using the -`RejectMessagesFromSendersOrMembers` parameter:

```
Set-DistributionGroup -Identity Executives `
-RejectMessagesFromSendersOrMembers HourlyEmployees
```

In this example, Exchange will reject any message sent from a member of the `HourlyEmployees` distribution group to the `Executives` group.

There's more...

When you create a distribution group, the default configuration is to reject messages from senders who are not authenticated. This means that users outside your organization will not be able to send messages to your distribution groups. Generally, this is the desired configuration, but if needed, you can modify this setting on a distribution group to accept messages from external users using the following syntax:

```
Set-DistributionGroup -Identity HelpDesk `
-RequireSenderAuthenticationEnabled $false
```

You can see here that we have disabled sender authentication for the `HelpDesk` distribution group. You can re-enable it at any time by setting the previous parameter value to `$true`.

See also

► *Managing distribution groups*

Managing automatic replies and Out of Office settings for a user

In Exchange 2010, we were introduced to a new set of cmdlets that can be used to manage and automate the configuration of a user's Out of Office settings. In this recipe, we'll take a look at how to use these cmdlets from the Exchange Management Shell for Exchange 2013.

How to do it...

Let's see how to manage automatic replies and Out of Office settings using the following steps:

1. To view the Out of Office settings for a mailbox, use the following syntax:

   ```
   Get-MailboxAutoReplyConfiguration dave
   ```

2. You can change the Out of Office settings for a mailbox. For example, to disable the Out of Office settings for a mailbox, use the following command:

   ```
   Set-MailboxAutoReplyConfiguration dave `
   -AutoReplyState Disabled
   ```

How it works...

Retrieving the settings for a mailbox simply requires that you run the `Get-MailboxAutoReplyConfiguration` cmdlet and specify the identity of the mailbox, as shown in the previous example. The `Set-MailboxAutoReplyConfiguration` cmdlet supports multiple parameters that can be used to customize the settings used for the mailbox autoreply configuration:

```
Set-MailboxAutoReplyConfiguration dave `

-AutoReplyState Scheduled `

-StartTime 1/26/2015 `

-EndTime 2/2/2015 `

-ExternalMessage "I will be out of the office this week"
```

In this command, we set `AutoReplyState`, specify a `StartTime` and `EndTime`, and set `ExternalMessage`. When the `StartTime` date is reached, the mailbox will proceed to automatically reply to messages using the specified `ExternalMessage` cmdlet until the `EndTime` date is reached. If you want automatic replies to be enabled indefinitely, set `AutoReplyState` to `Enabled`.

To view the settings configured in the previous command, we can use the `Get-MailboxAutoReplyConfiguration` cmdlet, as shown in the following screenshot:

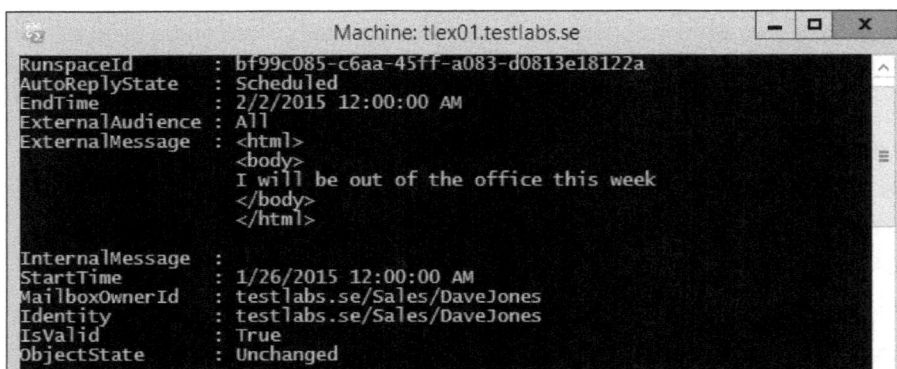

You can notice that in the mailbox auto-reply settings for this mailbox, only external replies are enabled. To enable internal Out of Office messages, you can run the previous set command and specify a message using the `-InternalMessage` parameter. Or, you can use them both using a single command.

The `-InternalMessage` and `-ExternalMessage` parameters support HTML-formatted messages. If you want to set custom HTML code when configuring the auto-reply configuration from the shell, you can use the following command syntax:

```
Set-MailboxAutoReplyConfiguration dave `
-ExternalMessage (Get-Content C:\oof.html)
```

This command will read in a custom HTML-formatted message from an external file and use that data when setting the internal or external message. This will allow you to work on the file from the HTML editor of your choice and import the code using a simple command from the shell.

By default, the `-ExternalAudience` parameter will be set to `All` if no value is specified. The remaining options are `Known` and `None`. Setting the external audience to `Known` will only send automatic replies to external users who are listed as contacts in the users mailbox.

There's more...

These cmdlets can be useful when making mass updates and running reports. For example, to determine all of the users that currently have the Out of Office settings enabled, you can run the following command:

```
Get-Mailbox -ResultSize Unlimited |
Get-MailboxAutoReplyConfiguration |
?{$_.AutoReplyState -ne "Disabled"} |
Select Identity,AutoReplyState,StartTime,EndTime
```

This one-liner will check every mailbox in the organization and return only the mailboxes with the auto-reply state set to either `Enabled` or `Scheduled`.

> Notice that the Out of Office configuration set by administrators will override any configuration done by the end user.

Adding, modifying, and removing server-side inbox rules

In Exchange 2010, we were introduced to a new set of cmdlets that can be used to manage server-side inbox rules for mailboxes in your organization. We now have the ability to add, remove, update, enable, and disable the inbox rules for mailboxes from within the Exchange Management Shell. This new functionality allows administrators to quickly resolve mailbox issues related to inbox rules and allows them to easily deploy and manage inbox rules in bulk using just a few simple commands. In this recipe, you'll learn how to work with the inbox rules cmdlets in Exchange 2013.

How to do it...

Let's see how to add, modify, and remove server-side inbox rules using the following steps:

1. To create an inbox rule, use the `New-InboxRule` cmdlet:

   ```
   New-InboxRule -Name Sales -Mailbox dave `
   -From sales@contoso.com `
   -MarkImportance High
   ```

2. You can change the configuration of an inbox rule using the `Set-InboxRule` cmdlet:

```
Set-InboxRule -Identity Sales -Mailbox dave `
-MarkImportance Low
```

3. Use the `Enable-InboxRule` and `Disable-InboxRule` cmdlets to turn a rule on or off:

```
Disable-InboxRule -Identity Sales -Mailbox dave
```

4. The `Get-InboxRule` cmdlet will return all of the server-side rules that have been created for a specified mailbox. The output from the command is shown in the following screenshot:

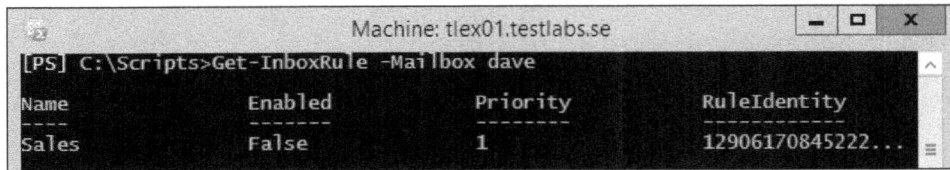

```
Machine: tlex01.testlabs.se                    _  □  X
[PS] C:\Scripts>Get-InboxRule -Mailbox dave

Name            Enabled        Priority        RuleIdentity
----            -------        --------        ------------
Sales           False          1               12906170845222...
```

5. To remove an inbox rule, use the `Remove-InboxRule` cmdlet:

```
Remove-InboxRule -Identity Sales -Mailbox dave `
-Confirm:$false
```

How it works...

Inbox rules are used to process messages sent to a mailbox based on a certain set of criteria and to then take an action on that message if the condition is met. In the previous example, we created an inbox rule for the mailbox that would mark messages from the sales@contoso.com address with high importance. The `New-InboxRule` cmdlet provides a number of rule predicate parameters that allow you to define the conditions used for the rules you create.

Let's take a look at another example. Let's say that we want to create a rule that will check the subject or body of all the incoming messages for a certain keyword. If there is a match, we'll send the message to the deleted items folder:

```
New-InboxRule -Name "Delete Rule" `

-Mailbox dave `

-SubjectOrBodyContainsWords "Delete Me" `

-DeleteMessage $true
```

In addition to conditions and actions, we can also add exceptions to these rules. Consider the following example:

```
New-InboxRule -Name "Redirect to Andrew" `
-Mailbox dave `
-MyNameInToOrCcBox $true `
-RedirectTo "Andrew Castaneda" `
-ExceptIfFrom "Alfonso Mcgowan" `
-StopProcessingRules $true
```

In this example, once again we're creating an inbox rule in Dave's mailbox. The condition `MyNameInToOrCcBox` is set to `$true` so that any message with the mailbox name in the `To` or `CC` field will be processed by this rule. The action is the `RedirectTo` setting and this will redirect the message to Andrews's mailbox, except if the message was sent from Alfonso's mailbox. Finally, the `-StopProcessingRules` parameter is set to `$true`, which means that, once this rule is processed, Exchange will not process any other rules in this mailbox. The `-StopProcessingRules` parameter is an optional setting and is provided to give you another level of flexibility when it comes to controlling the way the rules are applied.

> It's important to note that when you add, remove, update, enable, or disable server-side rules using the `*-InboxRule` cmdlets, any client-side rules created by Outlook will be removed.

In all of these examples, we specified the mailbox identity and configured the rules of a single mailbox. If you do not provide a value for the `-Mailbox` parameter, the `*-InboxRule` cmdlets will execute against the mailbox that belongs to the user that is running the command.

There's more...

Now, let's take a look at a practical example of how you might create inbox rules in bulk. The following code will create an inbox rule for every mailbox in the `Sales` OU:

```
$sales = Get-Mailbox -OrganizationalUnit contoso.com/sales
$sales | %{
  New-InboxRule -Name Junk `
  -Mailbox $_.alias `
  -SubjectContainsWords "[Spam]" `
  -MoveToFolder "$($_.alias):\Junk Email"
}
```

What we are doing here is using the `-SubjectContainsWords` parameter to check for a subject line that starts with `Spam`. If there is a match, we move the message to the junk e-mail folder within that user's mailbox. As you can see, we loop through each mailbox using the `ForEach-Object` cmdlet (using the `%` alias), and within the loop, we specify the identity of the user when creating the inbox rule and specifying the folder ID, using the `$_.alias` property.

Even if you are logged in using an account in the Organization Management group, you may receive errors when trying to use the `-MoveToFolder` parameter, when creating an inbox rule in another user's mailbox. Assigning the `FullAccess` permissions to the mailbox in question should resolve this issue. For more details, refer to the *Granting administrators full access to mailboxes* recipe in *Chapter 10, Exchange Security*.

> Make sure to verify the folder names; these vary depending on the selected language and are set per mailbox.

See also

> ▶ *Granting users full access permissions to mailboxes* in *Chapter 10, Exchange Security*

Managing mailbox folder permissions

Exchange 2010 introduced a new set of cmdlets that can be used to manage the permissions on the folders inside a mailbox. When it comes to managing recipients, one of the most common tasks that administrators and support personnel perform on a regular basis is updating the permissions on the calendar of a mailbox. In most corporate environments, calendars are shared among employees, and often, special rights need to be delegated to other users that will allow them to add, remove, update, or change the items on a calendar. In this recipe, we'll cover the basics of how to manage mailbox folder permissions from within the shell, but we will focus specifically on calendar permissions, since that is a common scenario. Keep in mind that the cmdlets used in this recipe can be used with any folder within a mailbox.

How to do it...

Let's see how to manage folder permissions of a mailbox using the following steps:

To allow users to view the calendar for a specific mailbox, use the following command:

```
Set-MailboxFolderPermission -Identity dave:\Calendar `
-User Default `
-AccessRights Reviewer
```

How it works...

In this example, we're giving the `Default` user the ability to read all items in the calendar of the specified mailbox by assigning the `Reviewer` access right. This would give every user in the organization the ability to view the calendar items for this mailbox. There are four cmdlets in total that can be used to manage the mailbox folder permissions:

- `Add-MailboxFolderPermission`
- `Get-MailboxFolderPermission`
- `Remove-MailboxFolderPermission`
- `Set-MailboxFolderPermission`

The `Add` and `Set-MailboxFolderPermission` cmdlets both provide an `-AccessRights` parameter that is used to set the appropriate permissions on the folder specified in the command. In the previous example, instead of assigning the `Reviewer` role, we could have assigned the `Editor` role to the `Default` user, giving all users the ability to completely manage the items in the calendar. The possible values that can be used with the `-AccessRights` parameter are as follows:

- `ReadItems`: The user assigned with this right can read items within the designated folder.
- `CreateItems`: The user assigned with this right can create items within the designated folder.
- `EditOwnedItems`: The user assigned with this right can edit the items that the user owns in the designated folder.
- `DeleteOwnedItems`: The user assigned with this right can delete items that the user owns in the designated folder.
- `EditAllItems`: The user assigned with this right can edit all the items in the designated folder.
- `DeleteAllItems`: The user assigned with this right can delete all the items in the designated folder.
- `CreateSubfolders`: The user assigned with this right can create subfolders in the designated folder.
- `FolderOwner`: The user assigned with this right has the right to view and move the folder and create subfolders. The user cannot read items, edit items, delete items, or create items.
- `FolderContact`: The user assigned with this right is the contact for the designated folder.
- `FolderVisible`: The user assigned with this right can view the specified folder, but can't read or edit the items within it.

The following roles are made up by one or more of the permissions specified in the previous list and can also be used with the `-AccessRights` parameter:

- ▶ **None**: `FolderVisible`
- ▶ **Owner**: `CreateItems, ReadItems, CreateSubfolders, FolderOwner, FolderContact, FolderVisible, EditOwnedItems, EditAllItems, DeleteOwnedItems, DeleteAllItems`
- ▶ **PublishingEditor**: `CreateItems, ReadItems, CreateSubfolders, FolderVisible, EditOwnedItems, EditAllItems, DeleteOwnedItems, DeleteAllItems`
- ▶ **Editor**: `CreateItems, ReadItems, FolderVisible, EditOwnedItems, EditAllItems, DeleteOwnedItems, DeleteAllItems`
- ▶ **PublishingAuthor**: `CreateItems, ReadItems, CreateSubfolders, FolderVisible, EditOwnedItems, DeleteOwnedItems`
- ▶ **Author**: `CreateItems, ReadItems, FolderVisible, EditOwnedItems, DeleteOwnedItems`
- ▶ **NonEditingAuthor**: `CreateItems, ReadItems, FolderVisible`
- ▶ **Reviewer**: `ReadItems, FolderVisible`
- ▶ **Contributor**: `CreateItems, FolderVisible`

There's more...

Using the `*-MailboxFolderPermission` cmdlets makes it easier to perform bulk operations on many mailboxes at once. For example, let's say that you need to assign the `Reviewer` permissions to all employees on every mailbox calendar in the organization. You can use the following code to accomplish this task:

```
$mailboxes = Get-Mailbox -ResultSize Unlimited
$mailboxes | %{
$calendar = Get-MailboxFolderPermission `
"$($_.alias):\Calendar" -User Default
if(!($calendar.AccessRights)) {
  Add-MailboxFolderPermission "$($_.alias):\Calendar" `
  -User Default -AccessRights Reviewer
}
  if($calendar.AccessRights -ne "Reviewer") {
```

```
    Set-MailboxFolderPermission "$($_.alias):\Calendar" `
    -User Default -AccessRights Reviewer
  }
}
```

First, we use the Get-Mailbox cmdlet to retrieve all the mailboxes in the organization and store that result in the $mailboxes variable. We then loop through each mailbox in the $mailboxes collection. Within the loop, we retrieve the current calendar settings for the Default user using the Get-MailboxFolderPermission cmdlet and store the output in the $calendar variable. If the Default user has not been assigned any rights to the calendar, we use the Add-MailboxFolderPermission cmdlet to add the Reviewer access right.

If the Default user has been assigned calendar permissions, we check to see if the access rights are set to Reviewer. If not, we modify the existing setting for the Default user to the Reviewer access right.

See also

> *Granting users full access permissions to mailboxes in Chapter 10, Exchange Security*

Importing user photos into Active Directory

One of the most popular new features in Exchange 2010 was the ability to view user photos in Outlook 2010. Even though Outlook 2013 has a built-in social connector, this may be applicable to Outlook 2013 as well for organizations. This feature is based on the possibility by importing an image to the thumbnailPhoto attribute for a given user account in Active Directory. This image can then be displayed when viewing a message or browsing the Global Address List within Outlook 2010 or Outlook 2013. This was a long-awaited enhancement, and the addition of this new feature makes it easier, especially in large organizations, to identify coworkers and get to know the people you are working with. In this recipe, we'll take a look at how you can import user photographs to Active Directory.

Getting ready

In addition to the Exchange Management Shell, you will need access to the Active Directory administration tools for this recipe. The Remote Server Administration Tools pack (RSAT-ADDS) is a prerequisite required by the Exchange 2013 setup, so it will already be installed on an Exchange 2013 server, and you can use the tools from there, if needed.

How to do it...

First, you need to update the Active Directory schema to ensure that the `thumbnailPhoto` attribute will be replicated to the Global Catalog. Your account will need to be a member of the schema admins group in Active Directory. On a machine with the Active Directory administration tools installed, do the following:

1. In the Exchange Management Shell or a cmd console, run the following command to register the Active Directory schema extension:

   ```
   Regsvr32 schmmgmt.dll.
   ```

2. Start the MMC console by clicking on **Start | Run**, type MMC, and click on **OK**.

3. Go to **File** and click on **Add/Remove Snap-in**.

4. Add the Active Directory Schema snap-In and click on **OK**.

5. Under Active Directory Schema, highlight the **Attributes** node and locate the **thumbnailPhoto** attribute.

6. Right-click on the **thumbnailPhoto** attribute and click on **Properties**.

7. On the **Properties** page, select **Replicate this attribute to the Global Catalog**, and click on **OK**.

At this point, the required Active Directory steps have been completed and you can now import a photo to Active Directory using the `Import-RecipientDataProperty` cmdlet:

```
Import-RecipientDataProperty -Identity dave `
-Picture `
-FileData (
  [Byte[]] (
    Get-Content -Path C:\dave.jpg `
    -Encoding Byte `
    -ReadCount 0
  )
)
```

How it works...

Each user account or contact object in Active Directory has a `thumbnailPhoto` attribute that can be used to store binary data. The `Get-Content` cmdlet is used to read a `.jpeg` file into a byte array, and we then use the `Import-RecipientDataProperty` cmdlet to load that data into the `thumbnailPhoto` attribute of the user account or contact in Active Directory, using the `-FileData` parameter. Once the data has been imported to Active Directory, Outlook 2010/2013 will query the `thumbnailPhoto` attribute of each user and display their photo when you receive an e-mail message from them, or when you view their information in the Global Address List.

> If you need to remove a photo for a user or a contact, use the -RemovePicture switch parameter with the Set-Mailbox or Set-MailContact cmdlet.

There are a few things to keep in mind when you decide to load photos into Active Directory for your users. First, the -FileData parameter is limited to 10 kb, so you need to ensure that the images you are trying to import are not too large. Also, the image file must be in a JPEG format. The recommended thumbnail photo size in pixels is 96x96 pixels. Finally, be conscious about the size of your NTDS database in Active Directory. If you only have a small number of users, then this will probably not be a big issue. If you have hundreds of thousands of users, there will be some serious replication traffic if you suddenly import photos for each of those users. Make sure to plan accordingly.

There's more...

Outlook clients operating in cached mode will use the thumbnailPhoto attribute configuration of the **Offline Address Book** (**OAB**) to determine how to access photos. By default, the thumbnailPhoto attribute is an Indicator attribute, which means that it points Outlook to Active Directory to retrieve the image. f you want to disable thumbnail photos for cached-mode clients, remove the attribute using the Remove method of the ConfigureAttrbutes collection:

```
$oab = Get-OfflineAddressBook 'Default Offline Address Book'

$oab.ConfiguredAttributes.Remove('thumbnailphoto,indicator')

Set-OfflineAddressBook 'Default Offline Address Book' `
-ConfiguredAttributes $oab.ConfiguredAttributes
```

If you want offline clients to be able to view thumbnail photos, you can add the thumbnailPhoto attribute as a value attribute using the Add method:

```
$oab = Get-OfflineAddressBook 'Default Offline Address Book'

$oab.ConfiguredAttributes.Add('thumbnailphoto,value')

Set-OfflineAddressBook 'Default Offline Address Book' `
-ConfiguredAttributes $oab.ConfiguredAttributes
```

If you work in a medium or large organization, this could make for an extremely large OAB. Again, make sure to plan accordingly. Use the following command to update the OAB after these configuration changes have been made:

```
Update-OfflineAddressBook 'Default Offline Address Book'
```

Taking it a step further

If you are going to take advantage of this function, you are likely going to do this in bulk for existing employees, or as new employees are hired, and this may require some automation. Let's say that your company issues a security badge with a photo for each employee. You have each of these photos stored on a file server in a JPEG format. The filenames of the photos use the Exchange alias for the user's associated mailbox. The following script can be used in this scenario to import the photos in bulk:

```
$photos = Get-ChildItem \\server01\employeephotos -Filter *.jpg
foreach($i in $photos) {
  [Byte[]]$data = gc -Path $i.fullname -Encoding Byte -ReadCount 0
  Import-RecipientDataProperty $i.basename -Picture -FileData $data
}
```

First, this code creates a collection of JPEG files in the \\server01\employeephotos location, and then shares and stores the results in the $photos object. We're using the -Filter parameter with the Get-ChildItem cmdlet so that the command only returns files with a .jpg extension. The items returned from the Get-ChildItem cmdlet are the FileInfo objects, which contain several properties that include detailed information about each file, such as the filename and the full path to the file.

As we loop through each photo in the collection, you can see that inside the loop, we cast the output from Get-Content (using the gc alias) to [Byte[]] and store the result in the $data variable. We can determine the path to the file using the FullName property of the FileInfo object that represents the current .jpeg file being processed in the loop. We then use the Import-RecipientDataProperty cmdlet to import the data for the current user in the loop. The BaseName property of a FileInfo object returns the filename without the extension; therefore, we use this property value to identify which user we're importing the photo for when executing the Import-RecipientDataProperty cmdlet.

See also

▸ *Transferring files through remote PowerShell* in *Chapter 2, Exchange Management Shell Common Tasks*

4
Managing Mailboxes

In this chapter, we will cover the following topics:

- ▸ Reporting on the mailbox size
- ▸ Working with move requests and performing mailbox moves
- ▸ Email notification on mailbox moves
- ▸ Importing and exporting mailboxes
- ▸ Deleting messages from mailboxes
- ▸ Managing disconnected mailboxes
- ▸ Reporting on mailbox creation time
- ▸ Setting storage quotas for mailboxes
- ▸ Finding inactive mailboxes
- ▸ Detecting and fixing corrupt mailboxes
- ▸ Restoring deleted items from mailboxes
- ▸ Managing public folder mailboxes
- ▸ Reporting on public folder statistics
- ▸ Managing user access to public folders

Introduction

The concept of the mailbox is the core feature of any Exchange solution, and it's likely that almost everything you do as an Exchange administrator will revolve around this component. Now in Exchange 2013, the architecture has changed, and lots of new cmdlets and features were introduced that make life much easier for any Exchange administrator, allowing you to do just about anything you can think of when it comes to managing mailboxes through scripts and one-liners. This includes tasks such as moving, importing, exporting, removing, and reconnecting mailboxes, just to name a few. In this chapter, you will learn how to generate reports, perform bulk mailbox changes, repair corrupt mailboxes, and more.

Performing some basic steps

To work with the code samples in this chapter, follow these steps to launch the Exchange Management Shell:

1. Log on to a workstation or server with the Exchange Management Tools installed.

2. Open the Exchange Management Shell by navigating to **Start | All Programs | Exchange Server 2013**.

3. Click on the **Exchange Management Shell** shortcut.

> Remember to start the Exchange Management Shell using **Run as administrator** to avoid permission problems.
>
> In this chapter, you might notice that in the examples of cmdlets, I have used the back tick (`` ` ``) character to break up long commands into multiple lines. The purpose of this is to make it easier to read. The back ticks are not required and should only be used if needed.

Reporting on the mailbox size

Using cmdlets from both the Exchange Management Shell and Windows PowerShell gives us the ability to generate detailed reports. In this recipe, we will use these cmdlets to report on all of the mailboxes within an organization and their total size.

How to do it...

Let's see how to generate and export the report of a mailbox using the following steps:

1. Use the following command to generate a report of each mailbox in the organization and the total mailbox size:

```
Get-MailboxDatabase | Get-MailboxStatistics |
?{!$_.DisconnectDate} |
Select-Object DisplayName,TotalItemSize
```

2. Pipe the command even further to export the report to a CSV file that can be opened and formatted in Excel:

```
Get-MailboxDatabase | Get-MailboxStatistics |
?{!$_.DisconnectDate} |
Select-Object DisplayName,TotalItemSize |
Export-CSV c:\mbreport.csv -NoType
```

How it works...

In both the commands, we're using the Get-MailboxDatabase cmdlet to pipe each database in the organization to the Get-MailboxStatistics cmdlet. Notice that in the next stage of the pipeline, we are filtering on the DisconnectDate property. Inside the filter, we are using the exclamation (!) character, which is a shortcut for the -not operator in PowerShell. So we are basically saying to give us all the mailboxes in the organization that are not in a disconnected state. This can be standard mailboxes as well as archive mailboxes. We then select the DisplayName and TotalItemSize properties that give us the name and total mailbox size of each mailbox.

There's more...

When using the first example to view the mailboxes and their total size, you will see that the output in the shell is similar to the following screenshot:

Here, you can see that we get the total size in megabytes, as well as in bytes. If you find that this additional information is not useful, you can extend the previous one-liner using a calculated property:

```
Get-MailboxDatabase | Get-MailboxStatistics |
?{!$_.DisconnectDate} |
Select-Object DisplayName,
@{n="SizeMB";e={$_.TotalItemSize.value.ToMb()}} |
Sort-Object SizeMB -Descending
```

Running the preceding one-liner will provide the output similar to the following:

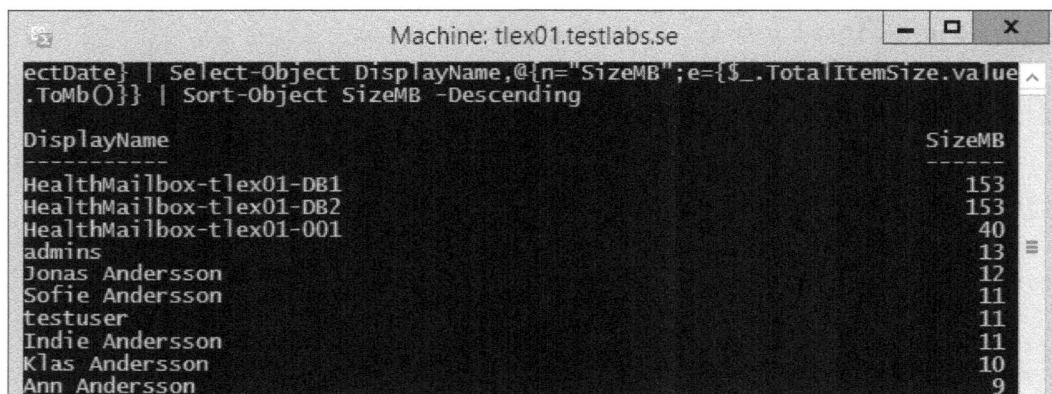

Notice that we now have a custom property called `SizeMB` that reports only the mailbox size in megabytes. We have also sorted this property in the `Descending` order and the mailboxes are now listed from largest to smallest. You can continue to pipe this command down to the `Export-CSV` cmdlet to generate a report that can be viewed outside the shell.

See also

- ▸ *Adding, modifying, and removing mailboxes* in *Chapter 3, Managing Recipients*
- ▸ *Working with move requests and performing mailbox moves*
- ▸ *Reporting on mailbox database size* in *Chapter 6, Mailbox Database Management*
- ▸ *Finding the total number of mailboxes in a database* in *Chapter 6, Mailbox Database Management*
- ▸ *Determining the average mailbox size per database* in *Chapter 6, Mailbox Database Management*

Working with move requests and performing mailbox moves

Even if you performed mailbox moves with PowerShell in Exchange 2007 or 2010, it's important that you understand that the process has evolved with new features, such as the ability to move reports together with batch move requests. There is a new set of cmdlets available for performing and managing mailbox moves. The architecture used by Exchange to perform mailbox moves uses a new concept known as move requests, which have been implemented in Exchange 2010 and have been further developed in Exchange 2013. In this recipe, you will learn how to manage move requests from the Exchange Management Shell.

How to do it...

To create a move request and move a mailbox to another database within the Exchange organization, use the `New-MoveRequest` cmdlet, as shown in the following command:

```
New-MoveRequest –Identity testuser –TargetDatabase DB2
```

How it works...

Mailbox moves are performed asynchronously with this method; the `New-MoveRequest` cmdlet does not perform the actual mailbox move. Mailbox moves are handled by mailbox servers that run the Microsoft Exchange **Mailbox Replication Service** (**MRS**). This is a major improvement because the mailbox data does not move through an administrative workstation when performing a move; instead, the service is responsible for transferring the data from one database to another. Not only does this make mailbox moves faster, but it also allows you to kick off one or more mailbox moves from any machine in the organization. You can later check on the status of these move requests from any other machine with PowerShell or the Exchange Management Tools installed.

When you create a new move request with the `New-MoveRequest` cmdlet, the command places a special message in the target mailbox database's system mailbox. The MRS scans the system mailboxes on a regular basis, looking for queued mailbox move requests and, once they are found, the MRS will start the move process. Once the move has been completed, a record of the mailbox move is saved and can be viewed using the `Get-MoveRequest` cmdlet.

This recipe only covers local move requests that are performed within an Exchange organization. It is possible to use the `New-MoveRequest` cmdlet to perform a mailbox move across Active Directory forest boundaries. For more details, see the *Prepare mailboxes for cross-forest move requests* on TechNet at `http://technet.microsoft.com/en-us/library/ee633491.aspx`.

If you automate mailbox moves using the Exchange Management Shell, it is likely that you will be doing so in bulk. The following example shows how you can move all of the mailboxes from one database to another:

```
Get-Mailbox -Database DB1 | New-MoveRequest -TargetDatabase DB2
```

In this example, we are retrieving all of the mailboxes in the DB1 database and creating a new move request for each one that will then be moved to the target database of DB2. The -TargetDatabase parameter is actually an optional parameter. If you have multiple mailbox databases in your organization, you can omit the -TargetDatabase parameter in the previous command, and the mailboxes will be moved evenly across the available mailbox databases, as long as those databases have not been suspended or excluded from provisioning and as long as the **Mailbox Resources Management** agent is enabled, which is the default setting.

There's more...

In order to view the detailed information about move requests, you can use the Get-MoveRequestStatistics cmdlet. This will return a great deal of useful information of a given move request, such as the move status, percent complete, the total bytes transferred, and more. You can also use the -IncludeReport switch parameter when running the cmdlet to provide debug level details of mailbox moves. This can be very beneficial when troubleshooting an issue.

One of the greatest uses of this cmdlet is to report on the current status of mailbox moves in progress, especially during large migrations. The following command can be used to gather the statistics of the currently running mailbox moves and can be run periodically throughout the migration to check the status:

```
Get-MoveRequest |
?{$_.Status -ne 'Completed'} |
Get-MoveRequestStatistics |
select DisplayName,PercentComplete,BytesTransferred
```

The preceding command will produce an output for each mailbox, which is similar to the following screenshot:

In this example, we're selecting just a few of the properties from the output of the command. Alternatively, it may be useful to export this information to a CSV file or to mail the results to an administrator mailbox. Either way, it gives you a method to monitor the status of your mailbox moves interactively in the shell or through an automated script.

If you just want to do some basic interactive monitoring from the shell to determine when all moves are complete, you can use the following code:

```
while($true) {
  Get-MoveRequest| ?{$_.Status -ne 'Completed'}
  Start-Sleep 5
  Clear-Host
}
```

The output from this command will give you a view of all the incomplete move requests and will refresh every five seconds. This is done using an endless `while` loop that runs `Get-MoveRequest`, waits for 5 seconds, clears the screen, and starts over again. Once all the moves are completed, just press *Ctrl + C* to break out of the loop.

Removing the move requests

You cannot perform a move request for a mailbox if there is an existing move request associated with that mailbox. This is true regardless of the move request status, whether it is complete, pending, canceled, or failed. You can use the `Remove-MoveRequest` cmdlet to delete an existing move request for a single mailbox, using the following syntax:

Remove-MoveRequest -Identity testuser -Confirm:$false

If you perform frequent moves, you may find it necessary to regularly delete all the existing move requests in the organization. To do this, use the following command:

Get-MoveRequest -ResultSize Unlimited |

Remove-MoveRequest -Confirm:$false

Keep in mind that stored move requests can provide detailed information, which can be used for monitoring or generating reports for mailbox moves. Make sure you no longer need this information before removing these move requests from your organization.

Moving the archive mailboxes

Consider the `testuser` account has a mailbox in the DB1 database, and also a personal archive mailbox in the DB1 database. We can use the following command to move `testuser` to DB2:

New-MoveRequest testuser -TargetDatabase DB2

In this case, both the primary mailbox and the archive mailbox will be moved to `DB2`. We can customize this behavior using some additional parameters that are made available by the `New-MoveRequest` cmdlet. For example, if we want to only move this user's primary mailbox and leave the archive mailbox in its current location, we can use the following command:

```
New-MoveRequest testuser -TargetDatabase DB2 -PrimaryOnly
```

This command adds the `-PrimaryOnly` switch parameter, which will indicate to the `New-MoveRequest` cmdlet that we do not want to move the archive mailbox, but we do want to move the primary mailbox to the `DB2` database. Use the following command to move only the archive mailbox:

```
New-MoveRequest testuser -ArchiveOnly -ArchiveTargetDatabase DB2
```

This time, we have added the `-ArchiveOnly` switch parameter so that only the archive mailbox will be moved. The `-ArchiveTargetDatabase` parameter is also used to specify that we want to move the archive mailbox to the `DB2` database.

Moving the mailboxes in batches

When performing migrations or moving multiple mailboxes in bulk, it can be useful to move them in batches. The `New-MoveRequest` cmdlet provides a `-BatchName` parameter to group multiple mailbox moves into a single, logical collection. Let's say that we are migrating multiple mailboxes to several different databases and we want to easily track the mailbox moves based on a certain criteria, using the following command:

```
$mailboxes = Get-Mailbox `
-RecipientTypeDetails UserMailbox `
-Database DB1 |
Get-MailboxStatistics |
?{$_.TotalItemSize -gt 2gb}
$mailboxes | %{
  New-MoveRequest -Identity $_.Alias `
  -BatchName 'Large Mailboxes' `
  -TargetDatabase DB2
}
```

Here, we are retrieving all the mailboxes in the `DB1` database that are larger than two gigabytes and storing the results in the `$mailboxes` variable. We then pipe the `$mailboxes` object to the `ForEach-Object` cmdlet (using the `%` alias) and loop through each item. As each mailbox in the collection is processed within the loop, we create a new move request for that mailbox, indicating that it should be included in the `Large Mailboxes` batch and moved to the `DB2` database. At this point, we can easily track the moves in the batch using a simple command:

```
Get-MoveRequest -BatchName 'Large Mailboxes'
```

The preceding command will return each move request included in the `Large Mailboxes` batch and will provide several details, including the display name, move status, and target database.

Moving mailboxes with corrupt items

When migrating from a previous version of Exchange, or when migrating large mailboxes, it's not uncommon to run into problems with users that have corrupted items in their mailbox. You can use the `-BadItemLimit` parameter to specify the acceptable number of corrupt, or bad, items to skip when performing a mailbox move. Keep in mind that if you set the `-BadItemLimit` parameter to a value higher than 50, then you need to also use the `-AcceptLargeDataLoss` switch parameter, as shown in the following example:

```
New-MoveRequest -Identity testuser `
-BadItemLimit 100 `
-AcceptLargeDataLoss `
-TargetDatabase DB2
```

When executing this command, a move request will be created for the `testuser` mailbox. Up to 100 corrupt items in the source mailbox will be allowed to perform a successful move to the new database. You will see a warning in the shell when using these parameters, and any corrupt items found in the source mailbox will be skipped when the mailbox is moved.

See also

- *Reporting on the mailbox size*
- *Managing archive mailboxes in Chapter 11, Compliance and Audit Logging*
- *Adding, modifying, and removing mailboxes in Chapter 3, Managing Recipients*

E-mail notification on mailbox moves

Exchange 2013 introduced the new `New-MigrationBatch` cmdlet, which includes a built-in automatic reporting feature for moving mailboxes, together with a more flexible way of moving collections of mailboxes. In this recipe, we will take a look at how to move mailboxes with the new features and check out the report.

How to do it...

To create a migration batch (move request) for moving a collection of mailboxes to another database within the Exchange organization, use the `New-MigrationBatch` cmdlet, as shown in the following command:

```
New-MigrationBatch -Name "Move Batch" -CSVData `
([System.IO.File]::ReadAllBytes("C:\localmove.csv")) `
-Local -TargetDatabase DB2 -NotificationEmails `
'administrator@contoso.com','dave@contoso.com' -AutoStart
Get-MigrationUser |
Get-MigrationUserStatistics | ft -Autosize
Complete-MigrationBatch -Identity "Move Batch"
```

The following is a screenshot with the migration statistics:

```
Machine: tlex01.testlabs.se                                    _  □  x

[PS] C:\Scripts>Get-MigrationUser | Get-MigrationUserStatistics | ft -Autos
ize

Identity            Batch        Status Items Synced Items Skipped
--------            -----        ------ ------------- -------------
testuser@testlabs.se Move Batch Synced 454           0
```

The following screenshot shows an example from a notification report that was sent after a migration batch was completed:

Migration batch Move Batch has completed successfully.

Microsoft Outlook
Sun 2/1/2015 6:39 PM

To: admins; Dave Jones;

Migration batch Move Batch has completed successfully.

How it works...

Using the `New-MigrationBatch` cmdlet, we create a collection of mailboxes that are going to be moved to another mailbox database. What's important to know is that the full filepath to the CSV needs to be specified. The `-Local` parameter means that it's a local move; the `-NotificationEmails` parameter needs to be used in case a move report is required. The cmdlet for creating the migration batch, by default it won't start the move, which is good in some cases. For example, when creating a couple of migration batches, and then manually starting each of them. In the preceding example, using the `-AutoStart` parameter, the mailbox data synchronization will start right away when the batch is created successfully.

You need to be aware that the move will be paused right before the finalization of the move. The completion of the move needs to be done using the `Complete-MigrationBatch` cmdlet. A parameter for the completion can be used; it's called `-AutoComplete` and can be added at the end of the initial cmdlet.

There's more...

As it was described in the previous section, I would like to give you an example of how to create, start, and complete the migration batch using the following command:

```
New-MigrationBatch -Name "Move Batch #2" -CSVData `
([System.IO.File]::ReadAllBytes("C:\localmove.csv")) -Local `
-TargetDatabase DB2 -NotificationEmails `
'administrator@contoso.com','dave@contoso.com' -AutoStart `
-AutoComplete
```

This command will create a migration batch called `Move Batch #2`; the CSV file is located under `C:\` in this example. All the mailboxes that exists in the `localmove.csv` file will be moved to `DB2` and the notification e-mail will be sent to the `administrator` and `dave` mailbox. With this command, the migration batch will start moving the mail data immediately, and when everything is done, it will finalize the move by making sure that all the data is moved and the last step will be to update the Active Directory attributes.

> Be aware that even if the mailbox move has been completed, it can take a while for the Active Directory to replicate the information. In such cases, the clients may get interrupted. Read more about Active Directory replication at `http://technet.microsoft.com/en-us/library/cc755994.aspx`.

See also

▶ *Reporting on the mailbox size*

▶ *Managing archive mailboxes* in *Chapter 11, Compliance and Audit Logging*

▶ *Adding, modifying, and removing mailboxes* in *Chapter 3, Managing Recipients*

Importing and exporting mailboxes

If you have worked with Exchange for a long time, you have probably used utilities, such as ExMerge or the Exchange 2007 Management Shell, to import and export data between mailboxes and PST files. While these tools were useful for their time, they had some limitations. For example, ExMerge was the main import and export utility, starting with Exchange 5.5 and continuing on to Exchange 2003, but it was difficult to automate. Exchange 2007 included the `Import-Mailbox` and `Export-Mailbox` cmdlets that made it easier to automate these tasks through PowerShell scripts. Unfortunately, the `Export-Mailbox` cmdlet required both a 32-bit workstation running the 32-bit version of the Exchange 2007 Management tools and Microsoft Outlook 2003 Service Pack 2 or later.

With the release of Exchange 2010 and 2013, we have a new set of cmdlets that can be used to manage the import and export operations for Exchange mailboxes. These new cmdlets have no dependencies on a management workstation and there is no requirement to install Outlook to perform these tasks. The Microsoft Exchange MRS runs on the Mailbox Server role. Exchange 2010 introduced a new concept called mailbox import and export requests that implements this functionality as a server-side process. In this recipe, you will learn how to configure your environment and use these cmdlets to automate mailbox import and export requests.

How to do it...

Let's see how to import and export a mailbox using the following steps:

1. Let's start off by exporting a mailbox to a PST file. First, you need to add an RBAC role assignment to your account. Assign the `Mailbox Import Export` role to your account using the following command. You will need to restart the shell after running this command for the assigned cmdlets to be visible:

   ```
   New-ManagementRoleAssignment -Role `
   "Mailbox Import Export" -User administrator
   ```

2. Next, you will need to create a network share that can be used to store the PST file. When you create the share, make sure that the Exchange Trusted Subsystem group in Active Directory has at least read/write NTFS permissions on the folder and also has modify share permissions.

3. The last step is to use the `New-MailboxExportRequest` cmdlet to export the data for a mailbox, using the following syntax:

```
New-MailboxExportRequest -Mailbox testuser `
-Filepath \\contoso-ex01\export\testuser.pst
```

How it works...

By default, the built-in `Mailbox Import Export` role is not assigned to anyone, including the administrators. This means that, out of the box, you will not be able to run the `*-MailboxExportRequest` cmdlets, even if you are a member of the `Organization Management` role group. Therefore, the first step in the process is to assign your account to this role using the `New-ManagementRoleAssignment` cmdlet. In the previous example, you can see that we created a direct assignment in the user account of `administrator`. This can be your administrative account or an actual role group that you are already a member of. If needed, you can specify that the role be assigned to a role group or an Active Directory security group using the `-SecurityGroup` parameter.

The location used for imported and exported PSTs must be a valid UNC path that the Exchange Trusted Subsystem group has access to. This is because the cmdlets that you execute are actually running under the security context of the Exchange servers in this group. This is required to implement the new RBAC security model, and therefore, the share and NTFS permissions must be assigned to this group and not to your user account specifically.

The syntax for the import and export commands is fairly straightforward. If you take a look at the command used in the previous example, you can see that we were able to easily create an export request for a specified mailbox using a specific file share on the network.

Using additional parameters, we can do other interesting things, such as only exporting specific folders of a mailbox to a PST:

```
New-MailboxExportRequest -Mailbox testuser `
-IncludeFolders "Sent Items" `
-FilePath \\contoso-ex01\export\testuser_sent.pst `
-ExcludeDumpster
```

As you can see from the preceding command, we are only exporting the `Sent Items` folder from the `testuser` mailbox, and we are excluding the items in the dumpster.

Here is another example that exports data from an archive mailbox:

```
New-MailboxExportRequest -Mailbox testuser `
-ContentFilter {Received -lt "01/01/2014"} `
-FilePath \\contoso-ex01\export\testuser_archive.pst `
-ExcludeDumpster `
-IsArchive
```

Here, we are specifying that we want to only export data from the archive mailbox using the `-IsArchive` switch parameter. In addition, we are limiting the amount of data exported from the mailbox using the `-ContentFilter` parameter. We are only including items that were received before 01/01/2014. In addition to the `Received` property, the `-ContentFilter` parameter allows you to highly customize the data that is exported.

> You can create up to 10 mailbox export requests per mailbox, without manually specifying a name for the export request. Once you have reached this limit, you either need to specify a unique name for the export request, or delete some of the previous export requests using the `Remove-MailboxExportRequest` cmdlet.

Using the `-ContentFilter` parameter, you can filter the recipient, types of attachments that were included in a message, text in the body, and more. For a complete list of available property names, check out the *Filterable properties for the -ContentFilter parameter* on TechNet. It can be found at `http://technet.microsoft.com/en-us/library/ff601762.aspx`.

There's more...

You can use the `Get-MailboxImportRequest` and `Get-MailboxExportRequest` cmdlets to view the status of your import and export tasks. To view all requests, simply run the appropriate `Get-*` cmdlet. If you want to narrow your search, you can use the `-Mailbox` and `-Status` parameters:

`Get-MailboxExportRequest -Mailbox testuser -Status Failed`

This command will return all of the export requests made for the `testuser` mailbox that have a failed status. You can use the same syntax with the import version of this cmdlet to review similar information.

When it comes to advanced reporting of import or export requests, there are two cmdlets available that you can use. `Get-MailboxExportRequestStatistics` and `Get-MailboxImportRequestStatistics` can be used to provide detailed information about the tasks associated with a particular operation. For example, let's take a look at the following script:

```
foreach($i in Get-MailboxExportRequest) {
  Get-MailboxExportRequestStatistics $i |
  select-object SourceAlias,Status,PercentComplete
}
```

This will provide a brief report of each export request. This can be useful when you are performing multiple import or export operations and need to check the status of each one.

Importing data into mailboxes

The `New-MailboxImportRequest` cmdlet works similar to the `New-MailboxExportRequest` cmdlet. Most of the parameters shown in the previous examples are available with both cmdlets. For example, we can import data into a specific folder in an inbox with the following command:

```
New-MailboxImportRequest -Mailbox sysadmin `
-TargetRootFolder "Recover" `
-FilePath \\contoso-ex01\export\testuser_sent.pst
```

This command imports the `testuser` PST into the `Recover` folder of the `sysadmin` mailbox. In addition to exporting data from archive mailboxes, we can also import data into archive mailboxes with the `-IsArchive` switch parameter.

Taking it a step further

Let's create a script that will export all of the mailboxes in your organization to individual PST files stored in a central location. Create a new file called `Export.ps1` and save it in the `C:\` drive. Using a text editor, open the file and add the following code, and then save the file:

```
param($Path, $BatchName)
foreach($i in Get-Mailbox -ResultSize Unlimited) {
  $filepath = Join-Path -Path $Path -ChildPath "$($i.alias).pst"
  New-MailboxExportRequest -Mailbox $i `
  -FilePath $filepath `
  -BatchName $BatchName
}
```

This script provides a couple of parameters used to control the behavior of the mailbox export requests. First, the `-Path` parameter will allow us to specify a UNC share for our exported mailboxes. Secondly, the `-BatchName` parameter is used to logically group the export requests using a friendly common name.

As we loop through each mailbox, we are doing a few things. We are using the value of the `-Path` parameter as the root directory of the PST file, and we are using the `alias` property of the mailbox for the base filename. This will ensure that each PST file is stored centrally in the required location using a unique filename that matches the mailbox alias.

To execute the preceding script, the command might look something like the following:

```
$batch = "Export for (Get-Date).ToShortDateString()"
.\Export.ps1 -Path \\contoso\ex01\export -BatchName $batch
```

This will create each mailbox export request using a batch name, such as `Export for 2/1/2015`. Then, you can easily check the status of all the mailbox export requests that are grouped into that batch name using the following command:

```
Get-MailboxExportRequestStatistics |
?{$_.BatchName -eq "Export for 2/1/2015"} |
select SourceAlias,Status,PercentComplete
```

This one-liner will give you a brief report on each of the export requests performed in the batch created on 2/1/2015 that can be reviewed in the shell, exported to a text or CSV file, or e-mailed to another user.

See also

▶ *Exporting reports to text and CSV files* in *Chapter 2, Exchange Management Shell Common Tasks*

▶ *Sending SMTP e-mails through PowerShell* in *Chapter 2, Exchange Management Shell Common Tasks*

Deleting messages from mailboxes

At some point, you are bound to find yourself in a situation where you need to remove an e-mail message from one or more mailboxes. This may be due to a message being sent to one of your distribution lists or as a part of some kind of spam or virus-related outbreak. If you have worked with Exchange 2007, you may be familiar with the `Export-Mailbox` cmdlet that could previously be used to perform this task. With Exchange 2010 SP1, the cmdlet called `Search-Mailbox` was introduced. This has been even more enveloped. The `Search-Mailbox` cmdlet can be used to clean up the mailboxes in our environment. In Exchange 2013, this cmdlet includes some new features as well, and in this recipe, we will take a look at how to use it to delete messages from mailboxes.

How to do it...

Let's see how to delete messages from mailboxes using the following steps:

1. If you have not already done so, you will need to use the following command syntax to assign your account the Mailbox Import Export RBAC role. You will need to restart the shell after running this command for the assigned cmdlet to be visible:

```
New-ManagementRoleAssignment -Role `

"Mailbox Import Export" -User administrator
```

2. Next, use the `Search-Mailbox` cmdlet to delete items from a mailbox. In this example, we will use a search query to delete items with a specific phrase in the subject line:

```
Search-Mailbox -Identity testuser `

-SearchQuery "Subject:'suppress'" `

-DeleteContent `

-Force
```

How it works...

The key to deleting items from a mailbox is the `-DeleteContent` switch parameter used with the `Search-Mailbox` cmdlet. When executing the command in the previous example, any message matching the subject specified in the search query will be deleted without any confirmation, and an output similar to the following will be displayed:

```
Machine: tlex01.testlabs.se                              _  □  X

[PS] C:\Scripts>Search-Mailbox -Identity testuser -SearchQuery "Subject:'su
ppress'" -DeleteContent -Force
WARNING: The Search-Mailbox cmdlet returns up to 10000 results per mailbox
 if a search query is specified. To return more than 10000 results, use
the New-MailboxSearch cmdlet or the In-Place eDiscovery & Hold console in
the Exchange Administration Center.


RunspaceId       : 9ad249df-24c2-4509-9722-fa00715958aa
Identity         : testlabs.se/Sales/Seattle/testuser
TargetMailbox    :
Success          : True
TargetFolder     :
ResultItemsCount : 2
ResultItemsSize  : 315.4 KB (322,925 bytes)
```

As you can see, there is a lot of useful information returned that indicates whether or not the delete operation was successful, how many the items were deleted, the total item size of the deleted messages, and so on.

Keep in mind that the `Search-Mailbox` cmdlet will include messages in a user's archive mailbox and the dumpster within their primary mailbox as part of the search. To exclude these, use the following syntax:

```
Search-Mailbox -Identity testuser `
-SearchQuery "Subject:'free ipad'" `
-DoNotIncludeArchive `
-SearchDumpster:$false `
-DeleteContent `
-Force
```

There's more...

The `-SearchQuery` parameter is used to specify the criteria of your search using **Advanced Query Syntax** (**AQS**), which is the same query syntax used with Windows Search, Exchange Search, and the Instant Search box in Outlook. When composing a command, you need to use the property name, followed by a colon, and then the text you want to query. There are several AQS properties that can be used; some of the most common properties are `Subject`, `Body`, `Sent`, `To`, `From`, and `Attachment`. See *Appendix B, Query Syntaxes* at the end of this book for a list of AQS properties and common search queries.

Running reports before deleting data

Of course, permanently deleting data from someone's mailbox is not something that should be done without total confidence. If you are unsure of the results, or you just want to cover your bases, you can use the following syntax to generate a report of the items that will be deleted:

```
Get-Mailbox |
Search-Mailbox -SearchQuery "from:spammer@contoso.com" `
-EstimateResultOnly | Export-CSV C:\report.csv -NoType
```

This example uses the `-EstimateResultOnly` parameter when executing the `Search-Mailbox` cmdlet. You can see here that we are executing a one-liner that will search each mailbox for messages sent from `spammer@contoso.com`. The estimate of the result is exported to a CSV file that you can use to determine how much data will be cleaned up out of each individual mailbox.

If you need a more detailed report, we can use the logging capabilities of the `Search-Mailbox` cmdlet. The following command performs a search on the `testuser` mailbox and generates some reports that we can use to determine exactly what will be deleted:

```
Search-Mailbox -Identity testuser `
-SearchQuery "Subject:'Accounting Reports'" `
-TargetMailbox sysadmin `
-TargetFolder "Delete Log" `
-LogOnly `
-LogLevel Full
```

This is made possible by the `-LogOnly` switch parameter. This will generate a message in a target mailbox folder that you specify. In this example, you can see that the target folder of the report is the `Delete Log` folder in the `sysadmin` mailbox. This report will provide you with a summary of the items that will be deleted in the search, if you were to run this command with the `-DeleteContent` parameter. When setting the `-LogLevel` parameter value to `Full`, a ZIP file containing a CSV report that lists each of the items returned by the search will be attached to this message.

Deleting messages in bulk

Most likely, you will need to delete items from several mailboxes in a bulk operation. The following one-liner can be used to delete messages from every mailbox in the organization:

```
Get-Mailbox -ResultSize Unlimited |
Search-Mailbox -SearchQuery 'from:spammer@contoso.com' `
-DeleteContent -Force
```

In this example, we are piping all the mailboxes in the organization to the `Search-Mailbox` cmdlet. Any messages sent from the `spammer@contoso.com` e-mail address will be deleted.

See also

- *Restoring deleted items from mailboxes*
- *Performing a discovery search* in *Chapter 11, Compliance and Audit Logging*
- *Deleting e-mail items from a mailbox with EWS* in *Chapter 12, Scripting with the Exchange Web Services Managed API*

Managing disconnected mailboxes

Exchange allows us to disassociate a mailbox from an Active Directory user account, and later reconnect that mailbox to an Active Directory account. For some organizations, a mailbox database has a low deleted mailbox retention setting, and once a mailbox has been removed from a user, it is forgotten about and purged from the database once the retention period elapses. However, if you maintain your deleted mailboxes for any amount of time, having the ability to retrieve these mailboxes after they have been removed from a user can, at times, be very helpful. In this recipe, we will take a look at how to manage disconnected mailboxes using the Exchange Management Shell.

How to do it...

To reconnect a disconnected mailbox to a user account, use the `Connect-Mailbox` cmdlet. The following command reconnects a disconnected mailbox to the `tuser1009` account on the Active Directory:

```
Connect-Mailbox -Identity 'Test User' `
-Database DB1 `
-User 'contoso\tuser1009' `
-Alias tuser1009
```

How it works...

When you use the `Remove-Mailbox` or `Disable-Mailbox` cmdlets to delete a mailbox for a user, that mailbox can actually be retained in its source database for a period of time. This is determined by the deleted mailbox retention setting of the database the mailbox resides in. For example, let's say that the deleted mailbox retention for the database hosting the `testuser` mailbox is set to 30 days. After the `testuser` mailbox has been deleted, this gives us 30 days to reconnect that mailbox to an Active Directory user account before the retention period is met and the mailbox is permanently purged.

The `-Identity` parameter, used with the `Connect-Mailbox` cmdlet, specifies the mailbox that should be connected to an Active Directory account and can accept the `MailboxGuid`, `DisplayName`, or `LegacyExchangeDN` values as input. Finding this information requires a little digging, as there is no `Get` cmdlet when it comes to searching for disconnected mailboxes. You can find this information with the `Get-MailboxStatistics` cmdlet:

```
Get-MailboxDatabase |
Get-MailboxStatistics |
?{$_.DisconnectDate} |
fl DisplayName,MailboxGuid,LegacyExchangeDN,DisconnectDate
```

This command will search each database for mailboxes that have a `DisconnectDate` variable defined. The values that can be used to identify a disconnected mailbox when running the `Connect-Mailbox` cmdlet will be displayed in the list format.

> It is possible that there could be multiple disconnected mailboxes with the same `DisplayName` property. In this case, you can use the `MailboxGuid` value to identify the disconnected mailbox that should be reconnected.

The previous command will return both disconnected mailboxes and also disconnected archive mailboxes, so you may need to filter those out if you have implemented personal archives in your environment, for example:

Get-MailboxDatabase |

Get-MailboxStatistics |

?{$_.DisconnectDate -and $_.IsArchiveMailbox -eq $false} |

fl DisplayName,MailboxGuid,LegacyExchangeDN,DisconnectDate

This one-liner will search for disconnected mailboxes in all the databases that do not have their `IsArchiveMailbox` property set to `$true`.

All of these commands can be a little cumbersome to type, and if you use them often, it might make sense to write the custom code that makes this easier. Let's take a look at the following function that has been written to automate the process:

```
function Get-DisconnectedMailbox {
  param(
    [String]$Name = '*',
    [Switch]$Archive
  )
  $databases = Get-MailboxDatabase
  $databases | %{
    $db = Get-Mailboxstatistics -Database $_ |
    ?{$_.DisconnectDate -and $_.IsArchiveMailbox -eq $Archive}
    $db | ?{$_.displayname -like $Name} |
    Select DisplayName,
    MailboxGuid,
    Database,
    DisconnectReason
  }
}
```

This function can be added to your PowerShell profile, and it will then be available every time you start the Exchange Management Shell. You can then run the function just like a regular cmdlet. By default, if you run the cmdlet without parameters, all of the disconnected mailboxes in your environment will be returned. You can also narrow your search using wildcards, as shown in the following screenshot:

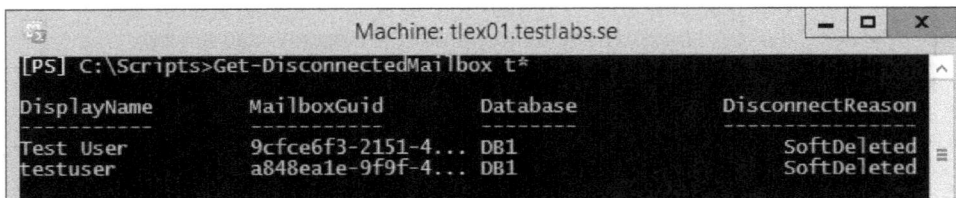

Here, you can see that we have used a wildcard with the function to find all the disconnected mailboxes starting with the letter t. To use the function and to find disconnected archive mailboxes, simply use the -Archive switch parameter.

There's more...

When the move request was introduced in Exchange 2010 SP1, some new functionality was added that you will need to be aware of when managing disconnected mailboxes. When you use the New-MoveRequest cmdlet to move a mailbox from one database to another, the mailbox in the source database is not deleted, and instead, is disconnected and marked as Soft-Deleted. You can check the value of the DisconnectReason property when working with a disconnected mailbox using the Get-MailboxStatistics cmdlet. The Get-DisconnectedMailbox function included earlier in this recipe will also return the value of this property for each disconnected mailbox.

If you move or remove mailboxes frequently, you may end up with hundreds or even thousands of disconnected mailboxes at any given time. Disconnected mailboxes can be purged using the Remove-StoreMailbox cmdlet by specifying the identity of the mailbox, the database it is located in, and the disconnect state that it is in, as shown in the following example:

```
Remove-StoreMailbox -Identity `
1c097bde-edec-47df-aa4e-535cbfaa13b4 `
-Database DB1 `
-MailboxState SoftDeleted `
-Confirm:$false
```

Keep in mind that if you want to delete every single disconnected mailbox in your environment, you will need to run the `Remove-StoreMailbox` cmdlet for mailboxes in both the `Disabled` and `SoftDeleted` state. If you want to purge every disconnected mailbox from the organization, regardless of the location or the reason of disconnection, you can use the following code:

```
$mb = Get-MailboxDatabase |
Get-MailboxStatistics |
?{$_.DisconnectDate}
foreach($i in $mb) {
   Remove-StoreMailbox -Identity $i.MailboxGuid `
   -Database $i.Database `
   -MailboxState $i.DisconnectReason.ToString() `
   -Confirm:$false
}
```

Mailboxes within a recovery database will be reported by the `Get-MailboxStatistics` cmdlet as disconnected and disabled. You cannot purge them with the `Remove-StoreMailbox` cmdlet; if you try to do so, you will get an error.

See also

- ▸ *Managing archive mailboxes* in *Chapter 11, Compliance and Audit Logging*
- ▸ *Restoring data from a recovery database* in *Chapter 6, Mailbox Database Management*

Reporting on mailbox creation time

If you work in an environment that frequently hires new employees, you may have a process in place to provision your mailboxes in bulk. You may have already used this book to help you do this. Now you might like to generate reports or retrieve a list of mailboxes that were created during a specific time frame or after a specific date. In this recipe, you will learn a couple of ways to do this using the Exchange Management Shell.

How to do it...

Let's start off with a simple example. To generate a report of mailboxes created in the last week, execute the following command:

```
Get-Mailbox -ResultSize Unlimited |
?{$_.WhenMailboxCreated -ge (Get-Date).AddDays(-7)} |
Select DisplayName, WhenMailboxCreated, Database |
Export-CSV C:\mb_report.CSV -NoType
```

How it works...

This one-liner searches through every mailbox in the organization by checking the `WhenMailboxCreated` property. If the date is within the last seven days, we select a few useful properties for each mailbox and export the list to a CSV file.

Mailboxes also have a property called `WhenCreated`, so why don't we just check this property instead? This is because the `WhenCreated` property is an Active Directory attribute that stores the creation date of the user account and not the mailbox. It is quite possible that your user accounts are created in Active Directory long before they are mailbox-enabled, so using this property may not be reliable in your environment.

There's more...

The `WhenMailboxCreated` property returns a `DateTime` object that can be compared to other `DateTime` objects. In the previous example, we used the following filter with the `Where-Object` cmdlet:

```
$_.WhenMailboxCreated -ge (Get-Date).AddDays(-7)
```

When running the `Get-Date` cmdlet without any parameters, a `DateTime` object for the current date and time is returned. Every `DateTime` object provides an `AddDays` method that can be used to create a new `DateTime` object. So, to get the `DateTime` object from seven days ago, we simply provide a negative value when calling this method, and the result is the date and time from a week ago. We compare the `WhenMailboxCreated` date to this value, and if it is greater than or equal to the date seven days ago, the command retrieves the mailbox.

You can use other `DateTime` properties when performing a comparison. For example, let's say that the last month was October, the tenth month of the year. We can use the following command to retrieve all the mailboxes created in October:

```
Get-Mailbox | ?{$_.WhenMailboxCreated.Month-eq 10}
```

This gives us the ability to generate very customizable reports, such as reporting only on mailboxes that were created on Mondays in October:

```
Get-Mailbox | ?{
  ($_.WhenMailboxCreated.DayOfWeek -eq "Monday") -and `
  ($_.WhenMailboxCreated.Month -eq 10)
}
```

As you can see, there is a lot of flexibility here that you can use to customize the output in order to meet your needs. This is a good example of how we can extend the Exchange Management Shell by tapping into the capabilities of the .NET Framework.

See also

▸ *Working with variables and objects* in Chapter 1, *PowerShell Key Concepts*

▸ *Exporting reports to text and CSV files* in Chapter 2, *Exchange Management Shell Common Tasks*

Setting storage quotas for mailboxes

One thing that has been around for several versions of Exchange is the concept of storage quotas. Using quotas, we can control the size of each mailbox to ensure that our mailbox databases don't grow out of control. In addition to setting storage quotas at the database level, we can also configure storage quotas on a per-mailbox basis. In this recipe, we will take a look at how to configure mailbox storage quotas from the Exchange Management Shell.

How to do it...

Use the following command syntax to set custom limits on mailboxes:

```
Set-Mailbox -Identity testuser `
-IssueWarningQuota 1024mb `
-ProhibitSendQuota 1536mb `
-ProhibitSendReceiveQuota 2048mb `
-UseDatabaseQuotaDefaults $false
```

How it works...

The `Set-Mailbox` cmdlet is used to configure the quota warning and send and receive limits for each mailbox. In this example, we are setting the `-IssueWarningQuota` parameter to one gigabyte. When the user's mailbox exceeds this size, they will receive a warning message from the system that they are approaching their quota limit.

The `-ProhibitSendQuota` parameter is set to 1.5 gigabytes, and when the total mailbox size exceeds this limit, the user will no longer be able to send messages, although new incoming e-mail messages will still be received.

We've set the `-ProhibitSendReceiveQuota` parameter value to two gigabytes. Once this mailbox reaches this size, the user will no longer be able to send or receive e-mails.

It's important to point out here that we have disabled the option to inherit the storage quota limits from the database by setting the `-UseDatabaseQuotaDefaults` parameter to `$false`. If this setting was set to `$true`, the custom mailbox quota settings would not be used.

There's more...

By default, mailboxes are configured to inherit their storage quota limits from their parent database. In most cases this is ideal, since you can centrally control the settings of each mailbox in a particular database. However, it is unlikely that having a single quota limit for the entire organization will be sufficient. For example, you will probably have a group of managers, VIP users, or executives that require a larger amount of space for their mailboxes.

Even though you could create a separate database for these users with higher quota values, this might not make sense in your environment; and instead, you may want to override the database quota defaults with a custom setting on an individual basis. Let's say that all the users with their `Title` property set to `Manager` should have a custom quota setting. We can use the following commands to make this change in bulk:

```
Get-User -RecipientTypeDetails UserMailbox `
-Filter {Title -eq 'Manager'} |
Set-Mailbox -IssueWarningQuota 2048mb ` -ProhibitSendQuota 2560mb `
-ProhibitSendReceiveQuota 3072mb `
-UseDatabaseQuotaDefaults $false
```

What we are doing here is searching Active Directory with the `Get-User` cmdlet and filtering the results so that only mailbox-enabled users with their `Title` property set to `Manager` are returned. This command is piped further to get the `Set-Mailbox` cmdlet, which configures the mailbox quota values and disables the option to use the database quota defaults.

See also

▶ *Restoring deleted items from mailboxes*

Finding inactive mailboxes

If you support a large Exchange environment, it's likely that users come and go frequently. In this case, it's quite possible that, over the time, you will end up with multiple unused mailboxes. In this recipe, you will learn a couple of techniques used when searching for inactive mailboxes with the Exchange Management Shell.

How to do it...

The following command will retrieve a list of mailboxes that have not been logged on to in over 90 days:

```
$mailboxes = Get-Mailbox -ResultSize Unlimited
$mailboxes | ?{
  (Get-MailboxStatistics $_).LastLogonTime -and `
  (Get-MailboxStatistics $_).LastLogonTime -le `
  (Get-Date).AddDays(-90)
}
```

How it works...

You can see here that we're retrieving all of the mailboxes in the organization using the Get-Mailbox cmdlet and storing the results in the $mailboxes variable. We then pipe this collection to the Where-Object cmdlet (using the ? alias) and use the Get-MailboxStatistics cmdlet to build a filter. This first part of this filter indicates that we only want to retrieve mailboxes that have a value set for the LastLogonTime property. If this value is $null, it indicates that these mailboxes have never been used, and have probably been recently created, which means that they will probably soon become active mailboxes. The second part of the filter compares the value for the LastLogonTime property. If this value is less than or equal to the date 90 days ago, then we have a match and the mailbox will be returned.

There's more...

Finding unused mailboxes in your environment might be as simple as searching for disabled user accounts in Active Directory that are mailbox-enabled. If that is the case, you can use the following one-liner to discover these mailboxes:

```
Get-User -ResultSize Unlimited -RecipientTypeDetails UserMailbox |
?{$_.UserAccountControl -match 'AccountDisabled'}
```

This command uses the Get-User cmdlet to search through all of the mailbox-enabled users in Active Directory. Next, we filter the results even further by piping these results to the Where-Object cmdlet to find any mailboxes where the UserAccountControl property contains the AccountDisabled value, indicating that the associated Active Directory user account has been disabled.

See also

▶ *Working with variables and objects* in *Chapter 1, PowerShell Key Concepts*

▶ *Looping through items* in *Chapter 1, PowerShell Key Concepts*

Detecting and fixing corrupt mailboxes

For years, Exchange administrators have used the Information Store Integrity Checker, more commonly known as the ISInteg utility, to detect and repair the mailbox database corruption. You may have used ISInteg in previous versions of Exchange to correct a corruption issue, preventing a user from opening their mailbox, or from opening a particular message. Unfortunately, in order to repair a mailbox with ISInteg, you have to dismount the database hosting the mailbox, taking it offline for everyone else that has a mailbox stored on that database. Obviously, taking an entire mailbox database down for maintenance when it is only affecting one user is less than ideal. In Exchange 2010 SP1, a new cmdlet called `New-MailboxRepairRequest` was introduced that replaced the ISInteg tool and allows you to detect and repair the mailbox corruption, while the database is online and mounted. In this recipe, we will take a look at how to use these cmdlets and automate the detection and repair of corrupt mailboxes.

How to do it...

Let's see how to detect and fix corrupt mailboxes using the following steps:

1. To detect corruption for a single mailbox, use the `New-MailboxRepairRequest` cmdlet with the following syntax:

```
New-MailboxRepairRequest -Mailbox testuser `
-CorruptionType SearchFolder `
-DetectOnly
New-MailboxRepairRequest -Mailbox testuser `
-CorruptionType ProvisionedFolder `
-DetectOnly
New-MailboxRepairRequest -Mailbox testuser `
-CorruptionType FolderView `
-DetectOnly
New-MailboxRepairRequest -Mailbox testuser `
-CorruptionType AggregateCounts `
-DetectOnly
```

2. The `-DetectOnly` switch parameter indicates that we do not want to perform a repair and that we only want to check for corruption within this mailbox. To perform a repair, simply remove the `-DetectOnly` switch parameter from the previous command:

```
New-MailboxRepairRequest -Mailbox testuser `
-CorruptionType SearchFolder
New-MailboxRepairRequest -Mailbox testuser `
-CorruptionType ProvisionedFolder
New-MailboxRepairRequest -Mailbox testuser `
-CorruptionType FolderView
New-MailboxRepairRequest -Mailbox testuser `
-CorruptionType AggregateCounts
```

> Notice the change between Exchange 2010 and 2013 and the previous commands; it only accepts one parameter value per command.

How it works...

The `New-MailboxRepairRequest` cmdlet can be run against a single mailbox or an entire mailbox database. In the previous example, we specified the `testuser` mailbox using the `-Mailbox` parameter. If needed, we can instead use the `-Database` parameter and provide the name of a database that we want to check or repair.

The `-CorruptionType` parameter accepts only one of the outlined values in following list:

- `SearchFolder`: This is used to detect and repair links to folders that no longer exist
- `AggregateCounts`: This specifies the aggregate counts on folders that do not indicate the correct values that should be repaired or detected
- `FolderView`: This is used to detect and repair views with incorrect content
- `ProvisionedFolder`: This specifies the links between provisioned and unprovisioned folders that should be detected and repaired

In the previous examples, we specified only one value of the `SearchFolder`, `ProvisionedFolder`, `FolderView`, and `AggregateCounts` corruption types, when performing mailbox repair detection for the `testuser` mailbox. The `-CorruptionType` parameter is required, so you need to provide one of the preceding values when running the cmdlet.

As always, we can take advantage of the PowerShell pipeline to perform operations in bulk. Perhaps you want to perform detection on a group of mailboxes, but not on every mailbox in the entire database. Just pipe the results of the `Get-Mailbox` cmdlet to the `New-MailboxRepairRequest` cmdlet:

```
Get-Mailbox -OrganizationalUnit "OU=Sales,DC=contoso,DC=com" |
New-MailboxRepairRequest `
-CorruptionType SearchFolder `
-DetectOnly
```

In this example, we're only performing detection on mailboxes in the `Sales` OU. This is just one example of how you can do this. Use the `-Filter` parameter in combination with the `Get-Mailbox` or the `Where-Object` cmdlet to limit which mailboxes are sent to the pipeline.

The `New-MailboxRepairRequest` cmdlet can also be used against archive mailboxes when using the `-Archive` switch parameter.

There's more...

After working with mailbox move requests and mailbox import requests, you might assume that there is an entire set of cmdlets that allow you to get, set, or remove mailbox repair requests, but that was not the case with Exchange 2010 and it's the same in Exchange 2013. In this version, all we have to work with is a single `New-MailboxRepairRequest` cmdlet. Fortunately, detailed information about the mailbox repair requests are written to the event log, so you can still check the status of these operations, but it will either require that you manually check the logs or write some PowerShell code that will check the logs for you.

The following event IDs will be written to the application log, depending on the parameters used with your command:

- ▶ `4003`: The mailbox repair request started
- ▶ `4004`: The mailbox repair request finished
- ▶ `4006`: Started processing mailbox repair request
- ▶ `4008`: Finished processing mailbox repair request
- ▶ `9017`: Mailbox assistant entering a work cycle
- ▶ `9018`: Mailbox assistant completed the work cycle

In order to provide some automation when reviewing the logs, we can use the `Get-EventLog` cmdlet, which is a PowerShell core cmdlet. We can retrieve the logs from the mailbox server, where the mailbox resides, by filtering the `RequestIDs` and the `EventIDs`. One way of doing this is by saving the repair request in a variable:

```
$repair = New-MailboxRepairRequest -Mailbox testuser `
-CorruptionType SearchFolder
```

Next, if we want to retrieve the status for `EventIDs` 4003, 4004, 4006, 4008, 9017, and 9018, we can use the following command syntax:

```
Get-EventLog -LogName Application -ComputerName ex01 | ?{
  ('4003','4004','4006','4008','9017','9018' -contains $_.EventID) - `
and `
  ($_.Message -match $repair.RequestID)
}
```

What we should get back here is all events that match the `EventIDs` and the mailbox repair `RequestID` for the `testuser` mailbox. Of course, you can extend this to support multiple mailboxes and simply use PowerShell's looping constructs to iterate through each mailbox repair request and check the logs for each one.

See also

▸ *Looping through items* in *Chapter 1, PowerShell Key Concepts*

Restoring deleted items from mailboxes

One of the most common requests that Exchange administrators are asked to perform is to restore deleted items from a user's mailbox. In the previous versions of Exchange, there were usually a couple of ways to handle this. First, you can use your traditional brick-level backup solution to restore individual items in a mailbox. Of course, there is also the more time-consuming process of exporting data from a mailbox located in a recovery database. Exchange 2010 reduced the complexity of restoring deleted items by implementing a feature called single item recovery. When this feature is enabled, administrators can recover the purged data from an end user's mailbox using the `Search-Mailbox` cmdlet. In this recipe, we will take a look at how this restore process works from within the Exchange Management Shell.

How to do it...

Let's see how to restore deleted items from mailboxes using the following steps:

1. If you have not already done so, you will need to use the following command syntax to assign the Mailbox Import Export RBAC role to your account. You will need to restart the shell after running this command for the assigned cmdlet to be visible:

   ```
   New-ManagementRoleAssignment -Role `
   "Mailbox Import Export" -User administrator
   ```

2. To restore the deleted data from an end user's mailbox, use the `Search-Mailbox` cmdlet:

```
Search-Mailbox -Identity testuser `
-SearchQuery "subject:'Expense Report'" `
-TargetMailbox restoremailbox `
-TargetFolder "Test Restore" `
-SearchDumpsterOnly
```

How it works...

The `Search-Mailbox` cmdlet provides the capability to search only the dumpster containing the deleted items for a given mailbox using the `-SearchDumpsterOnly` switch parameter. In this example, we used the `-SearchQuery` parameter to limit the search results to items that contain the term `Expense Report` within the subject line. After this command has been run, an administrator can access the target mailbox to retrieve the restored data. The items that matched the search query will be restored to a subfolder of the target folder in the target mailbox specified.

> To learn more about *Single Item Recovery in Exchange Server 2010*, see the Exchange Team blog post at `http://blogs.technet.com/b/exchange/archive/2009/09/25/3408389.aspx`.

The `-SearchQuery` parameter uses **Advanced Query Syntax** (**AQS**) to define the conditions for your search. See *Appendix B, Query Syntaxes,* at the end of this book for a list of AQS properties and common search queries.

There's more...

You can perform very granular searches with AQS and the `-SearchQuery` parameter. Let's say that we want to restore all the deleted items from the mailbox that were received after a certain date. We can use the following command to accomplish this:

```
Search-Mailbox -Identity testuser `
-SearchQuery "received:>2/5/2015" `
-TargetMailbox administrator `
-TargetFolder "Testuser Restore" `
-SearchDumpsterOnly
```

Similar to the previous example, we are restoring data from the `testuser` mailbox to the same target folder in the administrator mailbox. The difference is that, this time, the search query is only going to look for messages that have been received after February 5, 2015. You can see here that we are using the greater than (>) symbol to indicate that any message older than `2/5/2015` should be restored.

You can open the target mailbox in Outlook to retrieve the restored messages or export them using the `New-MailboxExportRequest` cmdlet.

Keep in mind that the `-SearchQuery` parameter is optional. If you want to restore all of the end user's deleted items, you can simply omit this parameter for the commands in the previous examples. Also, you can restore messages when performing a discovery search with the `New-MailboxSearch` cmdlet.

See also

▶ *Performing a discovery search* in Chapter 11, *Compliance and Audit Logging*
▶ *Restoring data from a recovery database* in Chapter 6, *Mailbox Database Management*
▶ *Importing and exporting mailboxes*

Managing public folder mailboxes

For how many years has Microsoft said that public folders should be removed in future releases of Exchange? I don't know for sure. What I know is that the public folders are here to stay, at least they will remain in Exchange 2013. Microsoft got rid of the public folder database, and therefore also the public folder replication. The legacy public folder architecture has now been replaced; in Exchange 2013, the public folder mailbox is introduced.

This also means that we now have the availability to use the **Database Availability Group** (**DAG**) for replicating the public folder mailboxes between servers, just like normal mailboxes.

In this recipe, we are going to create a structure of public folders and finally, mail-enable one of them.

How to do it...

To create the initial public folder hierarchy and a structure, use the following commands:

```
New-Mailbox -Name PF_Master_Hierarchy -Alias PF_Master_Hierarchy- `
Database DB1 -OrganizationalUnit "CN=Users,DC=contoso,DC=com" `
-PublicFolder
New-PublicFolder "Top Folder" -Path "\"
New-PublicFolder "AMER" -Path "\Top Folder"
New-PublicFolder "USA" -Path "\Top Folder\AMER"
New-PublicFolder "Projects" -Path "\Top Folder\AMER\USA"
Enable-MailPublicFolder -Identity "\Top Folder\AMER\USA\Projects"
```

How it works...

In this example, we are creating an initial public folder hierarchy mailbox that handles the public folder contents; it's created in the DB1 database. We are also creating a couple of folders and subfolders. Finally, the Projects folder is mail-enabled, which means that by default it shows up in the address list and therefore can be used for sending mails too.

Let's take a look at the example in the following screenshot:

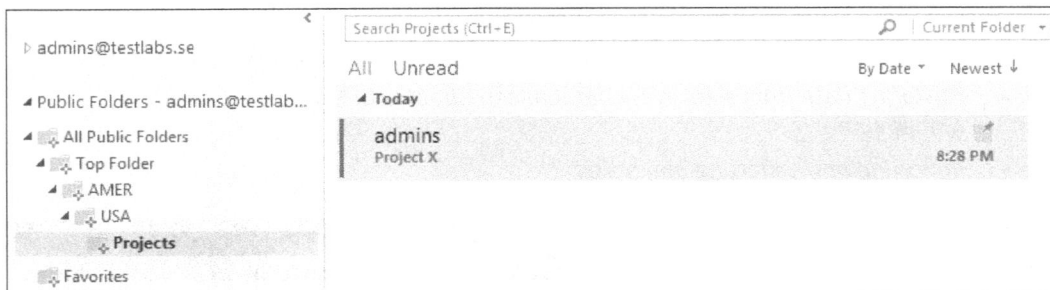

> In the current version, when this book has been written (CU7), the public folders can't be reached using OWA. The Outlook client needs to be used for this. This might change over time in the upcoming cumulative updates. Some of you might wonder how you can migrate your public folders from Exchange 2010 SP3 to Exchange 2013. Microsoft has created a guide that can be found at http://technet.microsoft.com/en-us/library/jj150486.aspx.

There's more...

Since public folders have been totally rebuilt, there are lots of changes. One of them that needs to be pointed out is that the quota and retention settings are now configured using the Set-OrganizationConfig cmdlet.

For example, if you want to configure DefaultPublicFolderIssueWarningQuota to 5 GB, this can be done using the following command:

```
Set-OrganizationConfig -DefaultPublicFolderIssueWarningQuota 5GB
```

See also

▶ *Reporting on public folder statistics*

▶ *Managing user access to public folders*

Reporting on public folder statistics

Since the public folder structure got created in the earlier recipe, it's now time for taking out statistics of the public folders and retrieving information about the contents.

This is basically done using the Get-Mailbox and Get-PublicFolderStatistics cmdlets.

In this recipe, we will also take a look at exporting the statistics to a CSV file and finally, we will check out the quota settings.

How to do it...

The following commands will give you the possibility to retrieve the statistics information about the public folder structure:

```
Get-Mailbox -PublicFolder | Get-MailboxStatistics | ft `
DisplayName,TotalItemSize -AutoSize
Get-PublicFolderStatistics | ft `
Name,ItemCount,TotalItemSize,TotalDeletedItemSize,FolderPath,`
MailboxOwnerId -AutoSize
Get-Mailbox -PublicFolder | Get-MailboxStatistics | Select `
DisplayName,TotalItemSize |
Export-CSV C:\pf_hierarchy.csv -Notype
Get-PublicFolderStatistics | Select `
Name,ItemCount,TotalItemSize,TotalDeletedItemSize,FolderPath,`
MailboxOwnerId | Export-CSV C:\pf.csv -Notype
```

How it works...

In the first of these examples, we are querying for all the public folder mailboxes and selecting to view the DisplayName and TotalItemSize values for all of them.

The second command is used for retrieving the statistics information about the public folder contents; how many items, the size, but also which public folder the contents are placed in, and the path.

In the last two examples, we are selecting the information we want and exporting it to a CSV file.

There's more...

By default, the quota limits are configured on an organizational level; using the `Get-OrganizationConfig` cmdlet, the quota limits can be viewed.

There is only a warning quota and a prohibit quota that can be configured at this level; note that there is one quota that can be configured called `MaxItemSize`, which means that each item has a maximum size, and it can't be larger than that.

Let's say that we do need to configure the quota for `DefaultPublicFolderIssueWarningQuota` to 5 GB and `DefaultPublicFolderProhibitPostQuota` to 10 GB.

This is done simply using the following command:

```
Set-OrganizationConfig -DefaultPublicFolderIssueWarningQuota 5GB - `
DefaultPublicFolderProhibitPostQuota 10GB.
```

See also

 ▸ *Managing public folder mailboxes*
 ▸ *Managing user access to public folders*

Managing user access to public folders

Now that we have a public folder structure, we realize that the default permissions aren't appropriate. So we want to change them a little bit.

First, we don't want end users to create items in folders they shouldn't create objects in.

The `Default` user is given author permissions, which in short means that they can read and create items in that folder. A full permission list can be found in this section.

In this recipe, we will start by changing the permissions for the `Default` user, and later on, we will configure some security groups with public folder permissions.

How to do it...

The following commands remove the permissions for the `Default` user and the second one will add new permissions:

```
Get-PublicFolder -Recurse | Get-PublicFolderClientPermission

Remove-PublicFolderClientPermission -Identity "\" -User Default

Remove-PublicFolderClientPermission -Identity "\Top Folder" `
```

```
-User Default
Add-PublicFolderClientPermission -Identity "\" -User Default `
-AccessRights Reviewer
Add-PublicFolderClientPermission -Identity "\Top Folder" `
-User Default -AccessRights Reviewer
```

How it works...

Our mission with this recipe was to change the permissions for the `Default` user.

We start off by checking the default permissions for the public folders.

The second command removes the default permissions from the root folder and the following folder. These examples can be used for all folders; they are just used for illustrating a couple of examples.

Finally, we add the permission to the `Default` user, but this time, it's not the `Author` permissions, instead we use the `Reviewer` permission. The difference between them is that the `Reviewer` isn't able to create items in the folder, which was the mission.

You might wonder which permissions can be used and what kind of access they provide. The possible values that can be used with the `-AccessRights` parameter are as follows:

- `ReadItems`: The user assigned with this right can read items within the designated folder.
- `CreateItems`: The user assigned with this right can create items within the designated folder.
- `EditOwnedItems`: The user assigned with this right can edit the items that the user owns in the designated folder.
- `DeleteOwnedItems`: The user assigned with this right can delete items that the user owns in the designated folder.
- `EditAllItems`: The user assigned with this right can edit all items in the designated folder.
- `DeleteAllItems`: The user assigned with this right can delete all items in the designated folder.
- `CreateSubfolders`: The user assigned with this right can create subfolders in the designated folder.
- `FolderOwner`: The user assigned with this right has the right to view and move the folder and create subfolders. The user cannot read items, edit items, delete items, or create items.

> ▸ `FolderContact`: The user assigned with this right is the contact for the designated folder.

> ▸ `FolderVisible`: The user assigned with this right can view the specified folder, but can't read or edit items within it.

The following roles are made up by one or more of the permissions specified in the previous list and can also be used with the `-AccessRights` parameter:

> ▸ `None`: This role has the `FolderVisible` permission

> ▸ `Owner`: This role has `CreateItems`, `ReadItems`, `CreateSubfolders`, `FolderOwner`, `FolderContact`, `FolderVisible`, `EditOwnedItems`, `EditAllItems`, `DeleteOwnedItems`, and `DeleteAllItems` permissions

> ▸ `PublishingEditor`: This role has `CreateItems`, `ReadItems`, `CreateSubfolders`, `FolderVisible`, `EditOwnedItems`, `EditAllItems`, `DeleteOwnedItems`, and `DeleteAllItems` permissions

> ▸ `Editor`: This role has `CreateItems`, `ReadItems`, `FolderVisible`, `EditOwnedItems`, `EditAllItems`, `DeleteOwnedItems`, and `DeleteAllItems` permissions

> ▸ `PublishingAuthor`: This role has `CreateItems`, `ReadItems`, `CreateSubfolders`, `FolderVisible`, `EditOwnedItems`, and `DeleteOwnedItems` permissions

> ▸ `Author`: This role has `CreateItems`, `ReadItems`, `FolderVisible`, `EditOwnedItems`, and `DeleteOwnedItems` permissions

> ▸ `NonEditingAuthor`: This role has `CreateItems`, `ReadItems`, and `FolderVisible` permissions

> ▸ `Reviewer`: This role has `ReadItems` and `FolderVisible` permissions

> ▸ `Contributor`: This role has `CreateItems` and `FolderVisible` permissions

There's more...

Dealing with permissions in large environments isn't always that easy, and it's recommended to use groups because it is much easier to manage; this also applies to the public folders.

I've created two universal security groups, which are mail-enabled and included one member in each of them. In my example, they are called `PF_Top Folder_Owner` and `PF_AMER_USA_Projects_Owner`. Let's use these two universal security groups by adding them as `Owners`. Use the following command:

```
Add-PublicFolderClientPermission -Identity "\Top Folder" `
-User "PF_Top Folder_Owner" -AccessRights Owner
Add-PublicFolderClientPermission -Identity `
"\Top Folder\AMER\USA\Projects" -User ` "PF_AMER_USA_Projects_Owner" `
-AccessRights Owner
```

Using groups instead of specific user permissions, it's at least a little bit easier to administrate the permissions. Make sure to plan the structure very well if it's a larger infrastructure.

See also

- ▸ *Managing public folder mailboxes*
- ▸ *Managing user access to public folders*

5

Distribution Groups and Address Lists

In this chapter, we will cover the following topics:

- ▶ Reporting on distribution group membership
- ▶ Adding members to a distribution group from an external file
- ▶ Previewing dynamic distribution group membership
- ▶ Excluding hidden recipients from a dynamic distribution group
- ▶ Converting and upgrading distribution groups
- ▶ Allowing managers to modify group permissions
- ▶ Removing disabled users from distribution groups
- ▶ Working with distribution group naming policies
- ▶ Working with distribution group membership approval
- ▶ Creating address lists
- ▶ Exporting an address list membership to a CSV file
- ▶ Configuring hierarchical address books

Introduction

In *Chapter 3, Managing Recipients*, we looked at managing recipients, which covered the process of creating and modifying the membership of both regular and dynamic distribution groups. In this chapter, we are going to dive deeper into distribution group management within the Exchange Management Shell. The recipes in this chapter provide solutions to some of the most common distribution group management tasks that can, and sometimes must, be handled from the command line. Some of the topics we'll cover include the implementation of group naming policies, allowing group managers to modify the memberships of distribution groups, and more. We'll also cover the process of some basic address list management that can be automated through the shell.

Performing some basic steps

To work with the code samples in this chapter, follow these steps to launch the Exchange Management Shell:

1. Log on to a workstation or server with the Exchange Management Tools installed.

2. Open the Exchange Management Shell by navigating to **Start | All Programs | Exchange Server 2013**.

3. Click on the **Exchange Management Shell** shortcut

> Remember to start the Exchange Management Shell using **Run as administrator**, to avoid permission problems.
>
> In this chapter, notice that in the examples of cmdlets, I have used the back tick (`) character to break up long commands into multiple lines. The purpose of this is to make it easier to read. The back ticks are not required and should only be used if needed.

Reporting on distribution group membership

One of the common requests that you are likely to receive as an Exchange administrator is to generate a detailed report of which recipients are members of one or more distribution groups. In this recipe, we'll take a look at how to retrieve this information from the Exchange Management Shell.

How to do it...

To view a list of each distribution group member interactively, use the following code:

```
foreach($i in Get-DistributionGroup -ResultSize Unlimited) {
  Get-DistributionGroupMember $i -ResultSize Unlimited |
  Select-Object @{n="Member";e={$_.Name}},
  RecipientType,
  @{n="Group";e={$i.Name}}
}
```

This will generate a list of Exchange recipients and their associated distribution group membership.

How it works...

This code loops through each item returned from the `Get-DistributionGroup` cmdlet. As we process each group, we run the `Get-DistributionGroupMember` cmdlet to determine the member list for each group, and then use `Select-Object` to construct a custom object that provides the `Member`, `RecipientType`, and `Group` properties. Notice that, when running both Exchange cmdlets, we're setting the `-ResultSize` parameter to `Unlimited` to ensure that the details will be retrieved in the event that there are more than 1,000 groups or group members. The result of the preceding cmdlets will look similar to the following screenshot:

There's more...

The previous code sample will allow you to view the output in the shell. If you want to export this information to a CSV file, use the following code:

```
$report=foreach($i in Get-DistributionGroup -ResultSize Unlimited) {
  Get-DistributionGroupMember $i -ResultSize Unlimited |
  Select-Object @{n="Member";e={$_.Name}},
  RecipientType,
  @{n="Group";e={$i.Name}}
}
$report | Export-CSV c:\GroupMembers.csv –NoType
```

The difference is that the output from our code is saved in the `$report` variable. Once the report has been generated, the `$report` object is then exported to a CSV file that can be opened in Excel.

See also

▸ *Previewing dynamic distribution group membership*

▸ *Adding members to a distribution group from an external file*

Adding members to a distribution group from an external file

When working in large or complex environments, performing bulk operations is the key to efficiency. By using PowerShell core cmdlets, such as `Get-Content` and `Import-CSV`, we can easily import external data into the shell, and use this information to perform bulk operations on hundreds or thousands of objects in a matter of seconds. Obviously, this can vastly reduce the time we spend on routine tasks and greatly increase our efficiency. In this recipe, we'll use these concepts to add members to distribution groups in bulk from a text or CSV file using the Exchange Management Shell.

How to do it...

Let's see how to add members to a distribution group from an external file using the following steps:

1. Create a text file called `c:\Scripts\users.txt` that lists the recipients in your organization that you want to add to a group. Make sure you enter them one line at a time, as shown in the following screenshot:

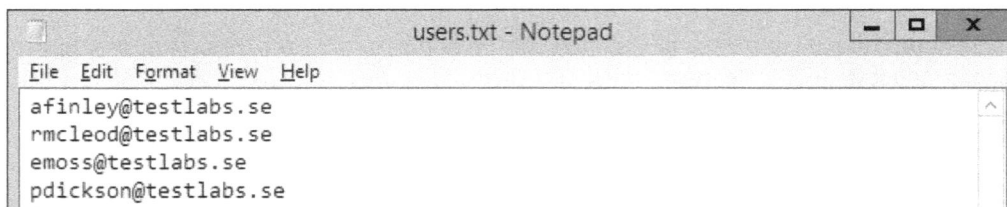

2. Next, execute the following code to add the list of recipients to a distribution group:

```
Get-Content c:\Scripts\users.txt | ForEach-Object {
  Add-DistributionGroupMember -Identity Sales -Member $_
}
```

When the code runs, each user listed in the `c:\Scripts\users.txt` file will be added to the `Sales` distribution group.

How it works...

When importing data from a plain text file, we use the `Get-Content` cmdlet, which will read the content of the file into the shell one line at a time. In this example, we pipe the content of the file to the `ForEach-Object` cmdlet, and as each line is processed, we execute the `Add-DistributionGroupMember` cmdlet.

Inside the `ForEach-Object` script block, we use the `Add-DistributionGroupMember` cmdlet and assign the `$_` object, which is the current recipient item in the pipeline, to the `-Member` parameter.

> To remove recipients from a distribution group, you can use the `Remove-DistributionGroupMember` cmdlet.

Keep in mind that this text file does not have to contain the SMTP address of the recipient. You can also use the Active Directory account name, User Principal Name, Distinguished Name, GUID, or LegacyExchangeDN values. The important thing is that the file contains a valid and unique value for each recipient. If the identity of the recipient cannot be determined, the `Add-DistributionGroupMember` command will fail.

There's more...

In addition to using plain text files, we can also import recipients from a CSV file and add them to a distribution group. Let's say that you have a CSV file setup with multiple columns, such as `FirstName`, `LastName`, and `EmailAddress`. When you import the CSV file, the data can be accessed using the column headers as the property names for each object. Let's take a look at the following screenshot:

```
Machine: tlex01.testlabs.se                                    _ □ x
[PS] C:\Scripts>Import-Csv .\users.csv

FirstName               LastName               EmailAddress
---------               --------               ------------
Alexander               Lucas                  alucas@testlabs.se
Alejandro               Jones                  ajones@testlabs.se
Charlene                Munoz                  cmunoz@testlabs.se
Alex                    Knowles                aknowles@testlabs.se
Cassandra               Peck                   cpeck@testlabs.se
```

Here, you can see that each item in this collection has an `EmailAddress` property. As long as this information corresponds to the recipient data in the Exchange organization, we can simply loop through each record in the CSV file and add these recipients to a distribution group:

```
Import-Csv C:\Scripts\users.csv | ForEach-Object {
  Add-DistributionGroupMember Sales -Member $_.EmailAddress
}
```

The given code uses the `Import-CSV` cmdlet to loop through each item in the collection. As we process each record, we add the recipient to the `Sales` distribution group using the `$_.EmailAddress` object.

See also

▶ *Managing distribution groups* in *Chapter 3, Managing Recipients*

Previewing dynamic distribution group membership

The concept of the dynamic distribution group was introduced with the initial release of Exchange 2007 and included a new way to create and manage distribution groups. Unlike regular distribution groups, whose members are statically defined, a dynamic distribution group determines its members based on a recipient filter. These recipient filters can be very complex, or they can be based on simple conditions, such as including all the users with a common value set for their `Company` or `Department` attributes in Active Directory. Since these dynamic groups are based on a query, they do not actually contain group members, and if you want to preview the results of the groups query in the shell, you need to use a series of commands. In this recipe, we'll take a look at how to view the membership of dynamic distribution groups in the Exchange Management Shell.

How to do it...

Imagine that we have a dynamic distribution group named `Legal` that includes all of the users in Active Directory with a `Department` attribute set to the word `Legal`. We can use the following commands to retrieve the current list of recipients for this group:

```
$legal= Get-DynamicDistributionGroup -Identity legal
Get-Recipient -RecipientPreviewFilter $legal.RecipientFilter
```

How it works...

Recipient filters for dynamic distribution groups use OPATH filters that are accessible through the `RecipientFilter` property of a dynamic distribution group object. As you can see here, we have specified the `Legal` group's OPATH filter when running the `Get-Recipient` cmdlet with the `-RecipientPreviewFilter` parameter. Conceptually, this would be similar to running the following command:

```
Get-Recipient -RecipientPreviewFilter "Department -eq 'Legal'"
```

Technically, there is a little bit more to it than that. If we were to actually look at the value for the `RecipientFilter` property of this dynamic distribution group, we would see much more information in addition to the filter defined for the `Legal` department. This is because Exchange automatically adds several additional filters when it creates a dynamic distribution group that excludes system mailboxes, discovery mailboxes, arbitration mailboxes, and more. This ends up being quite a bit of information, and creating an object instance of the dynamic distribution group gives us easy access to the existing OPATH filter that can be previewed with the `Get-Recipient` cmdlet.

There's more...

When working with regular distribution groups, you may notice that there is a cmdlet called `Get-DistributionGroupMember`. This allows you to retrieve a list of every user that is a member of a distribution group. Unfortunately, there is no equivalent cmdlet for dynamic distribution groups, and we need to use the method outlined previously that uses the `Get-Recipient` cmdlet to determine the list of recipients in a dynamic distribution group.

If you find yourself doing this frequently, it probably makes sense to wrap these commands up into a function that can be added to your PowerShell profile. This will allow you to determine the members of a dynamic distribution group using a single command that will be available to you, every time you start the shell. Here is the code for a function called `Get-DynamicDistributionGroupMember`, which can be used to determine the list of recipients included in a dynamic distribution group:

```
function Get-DynamicDistributionGroupMember {
  param(
  [Parameter(Mandatory=$true)]
  $Identity
  )
  $group = Get-DynamicDistributionGroup -Identity $Identity
  Get-Recipient -RecipientPreviewFilter $group.RecipientFilter
}
```

Once this function is loaded into your shell session, you can run it just like a cmdlet as shown in the following screenshot:

You can see here that the command returns the recipients that match the OPATH filter for the `Legal` distribution group, and it is much easier to type than the original example.

See also

▶ *Reporting on distribution group membership*

▶ *Working with recipient filters* in *Chapter 3, Managing Recipients*

Excluding hidden recipients from a dynamic distribution group

When creating dynamic distribution groups through the Exchange Management Console, you can specify which recipients should be included in the group using a basic set of conditions. If you want to do more advanced filtering, such as excluding hidden recipients, you will need to configure the OPATH filters for your dynamic distribution groups through the Exchange Management Shell. In this recipe, you'll learn how to use the shell to create a recipient filter that excludes hidden recipients from dynamic distribution groups.

How to do it...

Let's say that we need to set up a distribution group for our `TechSupport` department. The following commands can be used to create a dynamic distribution group that includes all the mailboxes for the users in the `TechSupport` OU that are not hidden from address lists:

```
New-DynamicDistributionGroup -Name TechSupport `
-RecipientContainer contoso.com/TechSupport `
-RecipientFilter {
  HiddenFromAddressListsEnabled -ne $true
}
```

How it works...

When you want to exclude a mailbox, contact, or distribution group from an address list, you set the `HiddenFromAddressListsEnabled` property of the recipient to `$true`. This is often done for special-purpose recipients that are used for applications or services that should not be visible by the general end-user population. While this takes care of address lists, it does not affect your dynamic distribution groups, and if you want to exclude these recipients, you'll need to use a similar filter to the one shown in the previous example. When we created the `TechSupport` dynamic distribution group, we used a very basic configuration that included all the recipients that exist within the `TechSupport` OU in Active Directory. Our custom recipient filter specifies that the `HiddenFromAddressListEnabled` property of each recipient can't be equal to `$true`. With this filter in place, only recipients that are not hidden from Exchange address lists are included as dynamic distribution group members.

Keep in mind that when you create a dynamic group using the `-RecipientFilter` parameter, any future changes will have to be made through the Exchange Management Shell. If you need to change the recipient filter at any time, you cannot use the Exchange Admin Center and will need to use the `Set-DynamicDistributionGroup` cmdlet to make the change.

There's more...

Updating a recipient filter for an existing dynamic distribution group can be a bit tricky. This is because the recipient filters are automatically updated by Exchange to exclude certain types of resource and system mailboxes. Let's go through the process of creating a new dynamic distribution group, and then we'll modify the recipient filter after the fact, so that you can understand how this process works.

First, we'll create a new dynamic distribution group for the `Marketing` department using a basic filter. Only users with e-mail addresses that contain the word `Marketing` will be members of this group:

```
New-DynamicDistributionGroup -Name Marketing `
-RecipientContainer contoso.com/Marketing `
-RecipientFilter {
   EmailAddresses -like '*marketing*'
}
```

Now that the group has been created, let's verify the recipient filter by accessing the `RecipientFilter` property of that object:

```
[PS] C:\Scripts>(Get-DynamicDistributionGroup Marketing).recipientfilter
((EmailAddresses -like '*marketing*') -and (-not(Name -like 'SystemMailbox
{*')) -and (-not(Name -like 'CAS_{*')) -and (-not(RecipientTypeDetailsValu
e -eq 'MailboxPlan')) -and (-not(RecipientTypeDetailsValue -eq 'DiscoveryM
ailbox')) -and (-not(RecipientTypeDetailsValue -eq 'PublicFolderMailbox'))
 -and (-not(RecipientTypeDetailsValue -eq 'ArbitrationMailbox')) -and (-no
t(RecipientTypeDetailsValue -eq 'AuditLogMailbox')))
[PS] C:\Scripts>_
```

As you can see from the output, we get a lot more back than we originally put in. This is how Exchange prevents the dynamic distribution groups from displaying recipients, such as system and discovery mailboxes in your dynamic distribution lists. You do not need to worry about this extraneous code when you update your filters, as it will automatically be added back in for you when you change the recipient filter.

Now that we understand what's going on here, let's update this group so that we can also exclude hidden recipients. To do this, we need to construct a new filter, and use the `Set-DynamicDistributionGroup` cmdlet, as shown here:

```
Set-DynamicDistributionGroup -Identity Marketing `
-RecipientFilter {
  (EmailAddresses -like '*marketing*') -and
  (HiddenFromAddressListsEnabled -ne $true)
}
```

Using this command, we specified the previously configured filter in addition to the new one that excludes hidden recipients. For recipients to show up in this dynamic distribution group, they must have the word `Marketing` somewhere in their e-mail address and their account must not be hidden from address lists.

See also

 ▶ *Hiding recipients from address lists* in *Chapter 3, Managing Recipients*
 ▶ *Working with recipient filters* in *Chapter 3, Managing Recipients*

Converting and upgrading distribution groups

Earlier, when migrating to Exchange 2010 from Exchange 2003, you may be carrying over several mail-enabled, non-universal groups. These groups will still function, but the administration of these objects within the Exchange tools will be limited. In addition, several distribution group features provided by Exchange 2010 or 2013 will not be enabled for a group until it has been upgraded. If, by chance, you haven't upgraded your groups before, it's about time now. That's why this recipe is included in this book. This recipe covers the process of converting and upgrading these groups within the Exchange Management Shell.

How to do it...

Let's see how to convert and upgrade distribution groups using the following steps:

1. To convert all of your non-universal distribution groups to universal, use the following command:

```
Get-DistributionGroup -ResultSize Unlimited `
-RecipientTypeDetails MailNonUniversalGroup |
Set-Group -Universal
```

2. Once all of your distribution groups have been converted to universal, you can upgrade them using the following command:

```
Get-DistributionGroup -ResultSize Unlimited |
Set-DistributionGroup -ForceUpgrade
```

How it works...

The first command will retrieve all the non-universal, mail-enabled distribution groups in your organization and pipe the results to the Set-Group cmdlet, which will then convert them using the -Universal switch parameter. It may not be a big deal to modify a handful of groups, but if you have hundreds of mail-enabled, non-universal groups, then the command in the previous example can save you a lot of time.

If you have a large number of groups to convert, you may find that some of them are members of another global group and cannot be converted. Keep in mind that a universal group cannot be a member of a global group. If you run into errors because of this, you can convert these groups individually using the Set-Group cmdlet. Then, you can run the command in the previous example again to convert any remaining groups in bulk.

Even after converting non-universal groups to universal, you'll notice that, when viewing the properties of a distribution group created by Exchange 2003, you cannot manage things, such as message moderation and membership approval. In order to fully manage these groups, you need to upgrade them using the -ForceUpgrade parameter with the Set-DistributionGroup cmdlet. Keep in mind that after the upgrade, these objects can no longer be managed using anything other than the Exchange 2010 or 2013 management tools.

There's more...

The Exchange Management tools, both the graphical console and the shell, can only be used to create distribution groups using a universal group scope. Additionally, you can only mail-enable existing groups with a universal group scope. If you've recently introduced Exchange in your environment, you can convert existing non-universal, non-mail enabled groups in bulk using the following command:

```
Get-Group -ResultSize Unlimited `
-RecipientTypeDetails NonUniversalGroup `
-OrganizationalUnit Sales |
Where-Object {$_.GroupType -match 'global'} |
Set-Group -Universal
```

As you can see in this example, we are retrieving all non-mail enabled, non-universal global groups from the `Sales` OU and converting them to universal in a single command. See the following screenshot for the outcome of the preceding cmdlets:

```
                          Machine: TLEX01.testlabs.se          [ _ ][ □ ][ X ]

[PS] C:\>Get-Group -ResultSize unlimited -RecipientTypeDetails NonUniversal
Group -OrganizationalUnit Sales | Where-Object {$_.GroupType -match 'global
'}

Name                 DisplayName          SamAccountName       GroupType
----                 -----------          --------------       ---------
Global-NonUnive...                        Global-NonUnive... Global
Global-NonUnive...                        Global-NonUnive... Global, Securi...


[PS] C:\>Get-Group -ResultSize unlimited -RecipientTypeDetails NonUniversal
Group -OrganizationalUnit Sales | Where-Object {$_.GroupType -match 'global
'} | Set-Group -Universal
[PS] C:\>
```

You can change the OU or use additional conditions in your filter based on your needs. Once the group is converted, it can be mail-enabled using the `Enable-Distribution` group cmdlet, and it will show up in the list of available groups when creating new distribution groups.

See also

▸ *Managing distribution groups* in *Chapter 3, Managing Recipients*

▸ *Allowing managers to modify group membership*

Allowing managers to modify group membership

Many organizations like to give specific users rights to manage the membership of designated distribution groups. This has been a common practice for years in previous versions of Exchange. While users have typically modified the memberships of the groups they have rights to from within Outlook, they now have the added capability to manage these groups from the web-based **Exchange Control Panel** (**ECP**). Exchange 2010 introduced a new security model that changed the way you can delegate these rights. In this recipe, we'll take a look at what you need to do in Exchange 2013 in order to allow managers to modify the memberships of distribution groups.

How to do it...

Let's see how to allow managers to modify group membership using the following steps:

1. The first thing you need to do is assign the built-in `MyDistributionGroups` role to `Default Role Assignment Policy`:

   ```
   New-ManagementRoleAssignment -Role MyDistributionGroups `
   -Policy "Default Role Assignment Policy"
   ```

2. Next, set the `ManagedBy` property of the distribution group that needs to be modified:

   ```
   Set-DistributionGroup Sales -ManagedBy bobsmith
   ```

After running the given command, Bob Smith has the ability to modify the membership of the `Sales` distribution group through ECP, Outlook, or the Exchange Management Shell.

How it works...

In order to allow managers to modify the membership of a group, we need to do some initial configuration through the Exchange 2013 security model called **Role Based Access Control** (**RBAC**). The `MyDistributionGroups` role is an RBAC management role that allows end users to view, remove, and add members to distribution groups where they have been added to the `ManagedBy` property.

By default, the `MyDistributionGroups` management role is not assigned to anyone. In the first step, we added this role to `Default Role Assignment Policy` that is assigned to all users by default.

> In addition to using the shell, you can assign the `MyDistributionGroups` management role to the `Default Role Assignment Policy` using ECP.

In the next step, we will assign a user to the `ManagedBy` property of the `Sales` distribution group. The `ManagedBy` attribute is a multivalued property that will accept multiple users if you need to allow several people to manage a distribution group.

The reason that the `MyDistributionGroups` role is not enabled by default is because, in addition to allowing users to modify the groups that they own, it also allows them to create new distribution groups from within the ECP. While some organizations may like this feature, others may not be able to allow this since the provisioning of groups may need to be tightly controlled. Make sure you keep this in mind before implementing this solution.

There's more...

If you need to prevent users from creating their own distribution groups, then you will not want to assign the MyDistributionGroups role. Instead, you'll need to create a custom RBAC role. This can only be accomplished using the Exchange Management Shell.

To implement a custom RBAC role that will only allow users to modify distribution groups that they own, we need to perform a few steps. The first thing we need to do is create a child role based on the existing MyDistributionGroups management role, as shown next:

New-ManagementRole -Name MyDGCustom -Parent MyDistributionGroups

After running this command, we should now have a new role called MyDGCustom that contains all of the cmdlets that will allow the user to add and remove distribution groups. Using the following commands, we'll remove those cmdlets from the role:

Remove-ManagementRoleEntry MyDGCustom\New-DistributionGroup

Remove-ManagementRoleEntry MyDGCustom\Remove-DistributionGroup

This modifies the role so that only the cmdlets that can get, add, or remove distribution group members are available to the users.

Finally, we can assign the custom role to Default Role Assignment Policy, which, out of the box, is already applied to every mailbox in the organization:

New-ManagementRoleAssignment -Role MyDGCustom `

-Policy "Default Role Assignment Policy"

Now that this custom RBAC role has been implemented, we can simply add users to the ManagedBy property of any distribution group and they will be able to add members to and remove members from that group. However, they will be unable to delete the group or create a new distribution group, which accomplishes the goal.

See also

- ▶ *Working with Role Based Access Control* in *Chapter 10, Exchange Security*
- ▶ *Troubleshooting RBAC* in *Chapter 10, Exchange Security*

Removing disabled user accounts from distribution groups

A standard practice among most organizations when users leave, or have been let go, is to disable their associated Active Directory user account. This allows an administrator to easily re-enable the account in the event that the user comes back to work, or if someone else needs access to the account. Obviously, this has become a common practice because the process of restoring a deleted Active Directory user account is a much more complex alternative. Additionally, if these user accounts are left mailbox-enabled, you can end up with distribution groups that contain multiple disabled user accounts. This recipe will show you how to remove these disabled accounts using the Exchange Management Shell.

How to do it...

To remove disabled Active Directory user accounts from all the distribution groups in the organization, use the following code:

```
$groups = Get-DistributionGroup -ResultSize Unlimited
foreach($group in $groups){
 Get-DistributionGroupMember $group |
   ?{$_.RecipientType -like '*User*' -and $_.ResourceType -eq
$null} |
   Get-User | ?{$_.UserAccountControl -match 'AccountDisabled'} |
   Remove-DistributionGroupMember $group -Confirm:$false
}
```

How it works...

This code uses a `foreach` loop to iterate through each distribution group in the organization. As each group is processed, we retrieve only the members whose recipient type contains the word `User`. We're also filtering out resource mailboxes, as these are tied to disabled Active Directory accounts. These filters will ensure that we only pipe objects with Active Directory user accounts down to the `Get-User` cmdlet, which will determine whether or not the account is disabled by checking the `UserAccountControl` property of each object.

If the account is disabled, it will be removed from the group. For example, see the following screenshot:

There's more...

Instead of performing the remove operation, we can use a slightly modified version of the previous code to simply generate a report based on disabled Active Directory accounts that are members of a specific distribution group. Use the following code to generate this report:

```
$groups = Get-DistributionGroup -ResultSize Unlimited
$report = foreach($group in $groups){
 Get-DistributionGroupMember $group |
  ?{$_.RecipientType -like '*User*' -and $_.ResourceType -eq
$null} |
  Get-User | ?{$_.UserAccountControl -match 'AccountDisabled'} |
  Select-Object Name,RecipientType,@{n='Group';e={$group}}
}
$report | Export-CSV c:\disabled_group_members.csv -NoType
```

After running this code, a report will be generated using the specified file name that will list the disabled account name, Exchange recipient type, and the associated distribution group of which it is a member.

See also

▶ *Managing distribution groups* in *Chapter 3, Managing Recipients*

Working with distribution group naming policies

Using group naming policies, you can see that the distribution group names in your organization follow a specific naming standard. For instance, you can specify that all distribution group names are prefixed with a certain word, and you can block certain words from being used within group names. In this recipe, you'll learn how to work with group naming policies from within the Exchange Management Shell.

How to do it...

To enable a group naming policy for your organization, use the `Set-OrganizationConfig` cmdlet, as shown in the following command:

```
Set-OrganizationConfig -DistributionGroupNamingPolicy `
"DL_<GroupName>"
```

How it works...

Since Exchange 2010 gives your users the ability to create and manage their own distribution groups, you may want to implement a naming policy that matches your organization's naming standards. In addition, you can implement naming policies, so that your administrators are required to follow a specific naming convention when creating groups.

Your distribution group naming policy can be made up of text that you specify, or it can use specific attributes that map to the user, who creates the distribution group. In the previous example, we specified that all distribution groups should be prefixed with DL_, followed by the group name. The `<GroupName>` attribute indicates that the group name provided by the user should be used. So, if someone were to create a group named Help Desk, Exchange would automatically configure the name of the group as DL_Help Desk.

The following attributes can be used within your group naming policies:

- Company
- CountryCode
- CountryorRegion
- CustomAttribute1 - 15
- Department
- Office
- StateOrProvince
- Title

Let's take a look at another example to see how we can implement some of these attributes within a group naming policy. Using the following command, we'll update the group naming policy to include both `Department` and `State` of the user creating the group:

```
Set-OrganizationConfig -DistributionGroupNamingPolicy `
"<Department>_<GroupName>_<StateOrProvince>"
```

Now let's say that we have an administrator named Dave who works in the IT department in the Arizona office. Based on this information, we know that his `Department` attribute will be set to `IT` and his `State` attribute will be set to `AZ`. When Dave uses the `New-DistributionGroup` cmdlet to create a group for the maintenance department, specifying `Maintenance` for the `–Name` parameter value, Exchange will automatically apply the group naming policy, and the distribution group name will be `IT_Maintenance_AZ`.

In addition, we can exclude a list of names that can be used when creating distribution groups. This is also specified by running the `Set-OrganizationConfig` cmdlet. For example, to block a list of words, we can use the following syntax:

```
Set-OrganizationConfig `
-DistributionGroupNameBlockedWordsList badword1,badword2
```

If a user tries to create a group using one of the blocked names, they'll receive an error that says the group name contains a word which isn't allowed in group names in your organization. Please rename your group.

There is one more parameter to be aware of, which could be very useful.

It's used to provide a default organization unit where the distribution groups are placed by default. See the following command:

```
Set-OrganizationConfig `
-DistributionGroupDefaultOU "contoso.com/Test"
```

This setting can be overridden by using the `-OrganizationalUnit` parameter when creating the distribution groups.

There's more...

When a group naming policy is applied in your organization, it is possible to override it from within the Exchange Management Shell. Both the `New-DistributionGroup` and the `Set-DistributionGroup` cmdlets provide an `-IgnoreNamingPolicy` switch parameter that can be used when you are creating or modifying a group. To create a distribution group that will bypass the group naming policy, use the following syntax:

```
New-DistributionGroup -Name Accounting -IgnoreNamingPolicy
```

The Graphical Management Tools can be used to create distribution groups, but if a naming policy is applied to your organization, and you need to override it, you must use the shell, as shown previously.

You can also force administrators to use group naming policies, even if they have access to the Exchange Management Shell. If you plan on doing this, you will need to assign them to the `New-DistributionGroup` and `Set-DistributionGroup` cmdlets using a custom **Role Based Access Control** (**RBAC**) role that does not allow them to use the `-IgnoreNamingPolicy` switch parameter.

See also

▸ *Managing distribution groups* in *Chapter 3*, Managing Recipients

Working with distribution group membership approval

You can allow end users to request distribution group membership through the Exchange Control Panel. Additionally, you can configure your distribution groups so that users can join a group automatically, without having to be approved by a group owner. We'll take a look at how to configure these options in this recipe.

How to do it...

To allow end users to add and remove themselves from a distribution group, you can set the following configuration using the `Set-DistributionGroup` cmdlet:

```
Set-DistributionGroup -Identity CompanyNews `
-MemberJoinRestriction Open `
-MemberDepartRestriction Open
```

This command will allow any user in the organization to join or leave the `CompanyNews` distribution group without needing an approval from a group owner.

How it works...

The two parameters that control the membership approval configuration for a distribution group are `-MemberJoinRestriction` and `-MemberDepartRestriction`. The `-MemberJoinRestriction` parameter can be set to one of the following values:

▸ Open: This allows the user to add or remove their account from the group, without needing an approval from the group owner

- ▶ `Closed`: Here, users cannot join or leave the group
- ▶ `ApprovalRequired`: Here, requests to join or leave a group must be approved by a group owner

While the `-MemberDepartRestriction` parameter can only be set to the following values:

- ▶ `Open`: This allows the user to add or remove their account from the group without an approval from the group owner
- ▶ `Closed`: Here, users cannot join or leave the group

These settings are not mutually exclusive. For example, you can allow users to join a group without needing an approval, but you will require an approval when users try to leave the group, or vice versa. By default, the `MemberJoinRestriction` property is set to `Closed` and the `MemberDepartRestriction` property is set to `Open`.

There's more...

When a member joins or leaves, restrictions are set to `ApprovalRequired`. A group owner will receive a message informing them of the request, and they can approve or deny the request using the **Accept** or **Reject** buttons in Outlook or OWA. The user who created the distribution group will automatically be the owner, but you can change the owner, if needed, using the `-ManagedBy` parameter when running the `Set-DistributionGroup` cmdlet, as shown in the following command:

```
Set-DistributionGroup -Identity AllEmployees `
-ManagedBy dave@contoso.com,john@contoso.com
```

As you can see, the `-ManagedBy` parameter will accept one or more values. If you are setting multiple owners, just separate each one with a comma, as shown previously.

See also

- ▶ *Reporting on distribution group membership*
- ▶ *Managing distribution groups* in *Chapter 3, Managing Recipients*

Creating address lists

Just like dynamic distribution groups, Exchange address lists can be comprised of one or more recipient types and are generated using a recipient filter or a set of built-in conditions. You can create one or more address list(s), made up of users, contacts, distribution groups, or any other mail-enabled objects in your organization. This recipe will show you how to create an address list using the Exchange Management Shell.

How to do it...

Let's say that we need to create an address list for the sales representatives in our organization. We can use the `New-AddressList` cmdlet to accomplish this, as shown next:

```
New-AddressList -Name 'All Sales Users' `
-RecipientContainer contoso.com/Sales `
-IncludedRecipients MailboxUsers
```

How it works...

This example uses the `New-AddressList` cmdlet's built-in conditions to specify the criteria for the recipients that will be included in the list. You can see from the command that, for a recipient to be visible in the address list, they must be located within the `Sales` OU in Active Directory and the recipient type must be `MailboxUsers`, which only applies to regular mailboxes and does not include other types, such as resource mailboxes, distribution groups, and so on.

There's more...

When you need to create an address list based on a more complex set of conditions, you'll need to use the `-RecipientFilter` parameter to specify an OPATH filter. For example, the following OPATH filter is not configurable when creating or modifying an address list in EAC/ECP:

```
New-AddressList -Name MobileUsers `
-RecipientContainer contoso.com `
-RecipientFilter {
   HasActiveSyncDevicePartnership -ne $false
}
```

You can see here that we're creating an address list for all the mobile users in the organization. We set the `RecipientContainer` parameter to the root domain, and within the recipient filter, we specified that all recipients with an ActiveSync device partnership should be included in the list.

A small reminder: update the address list after it's created, so that it applies and updates the list with accurate members. This is done using the `Update-AddressList` cmdlet.

[You can create global address lists using the `New-GlobalAddress list` cmdlet.]

You can combine multiple conditions in your recipient filters using PowerShell's logical operators. For instance, we can extend our previous example to add an additional requirement in the OPATH filter:

```
New-AddressList -Name MobileUsers `
-RecipientContainer contoso.com `
-RecipientFilter {
  (HasActiveSyncDevicePartnership -ne $false) -and
  (Phone -ne $null)
}
```

This time, in addition to having an ActiveSync device partnership, the user must also have a number defined within their Phone attribute in order for them to be included in the list.

> If you need to modify a recipient filter after an address list has already been created, use the Set-AddressList cmdlet.

Exchange supports a various number of both common and advanced properties that can be used to construct OPATH filters, as shown in the previous example. To view a list of common filterable properties that can be used with the -RecipientFilter parameter, see *Appendix A, Common Shell Information*, at the end of this book.

See also

▶ *Working with recipient filters* in Chapter 3, *Managing Recipients*
▶ *Exporting address list membership to a CSV file*

Exporting address list membership to a CSV file

When it comes to working with address lists, a common task is exporting the list of members to an external file. In this recipe, we'll take a look at the process of exporting the contents of an address list to a CSV file.

How to do it...

Let's start off with a simple example. The following commands will export the All Users address list to a CSV file:

```
$allusers = Get-AddressList "All Users"
Get-Recipient -RecipientPreviewFilter $allusers.RecipientFilter |
Select-Object DisplayName,Database |
Export-Csv -Path c:\allusers.csv -NoTypeInformation
```

When the command completes, a list of user display names and their associated mailbox databases will be exported to `c:\allusers.csv`.

How it works...

The first thing we will do in this example is create the `$allusers` variable that stores an instance of the `All Users` address list. We can then run the `Get-Recipient` cmdlet and specify the OPATH filter, using the `$allusers.RecipientFilter` object as the value for the `-RecipientPreviewFilter` parameter. The results are then piped to the `Select-Object` cmdlet that grabs the `DisplayName` and `Database` properties of the recipient. Finally, the data is exported to a CSV file.

Of course, the given example may not be that practical, as it does not provide the e-mail addresses for the user. We can also export this information, but it requires some special handling on our part. Let's export only the `DisplayName` and `EmailAddresses` properties for each user. To do this, use the following code:

```
$allusers = Get-AddressList "All Users"
Get-Recipient -RecipientPreviewFilter $allusers.RecipientFilter |
Select-Object DisplayName,
@{n="EmailAddresses";e={$_.EmailAddresses -join ";"}} |
Export-Csv -Path c:\allusers.csv -NoTypeInformation
```

Since each recipient can have multiple SMTP e-mail addresses, the `EmailAddresses` property of each recipient is a multivalued object. This means we can't simply export this value to an external file, since it is actually an object and not a simple string value. In the given command, we're using the `Select-Object` cmdlet to create a calculated property for the `EmailAddresses` collection. Using the `-Join` operator within the calculated property expression, we add each address in the collection to a single string that will be delimited with the semicolon (`;`) character.

There's more...

The given method will work for any of the address lists in your organization. For example, you can export the recipients of the **Global Address List** (**GAL**) using the following code:

```
$GAL = Get-GlobalAddressList "Default Global Address List"
Get-Recipient -RecipientPreviewFilter $GAL.RecipientFilter |
Select-Object DisplayName,
@{n="EmailAddresses";e={$_.EmailAddresses -join ";"}} |
Export-Csv -Path c:\GAL.csv -NoTypeInformation
```

As you can see here, the main difference is that this time, we are using the `Get-GlobalAddressList` cmdlet to export the default global address list. You can use this technique for any address list in your organization; just specify the name of the address list you want to export when using either the `Get-AddressList` or the `Get-GlobalAddressList` cmdlet. The exported CSV file will look similar to the following screenshot:

```
                    GAL.csv - Notepad                 _ □ X

File  Edit  Format  View  Help
"DisplayName","EmailAddresses"
"Administrator","SMTP:Administrator@testlabs.se"
"Jonas Andersson","SMTP:jonas.andersson@testlabs.se"
"Dave","smtp:dave@west.contoso.com;SMTP:dave@testlabs.se"
"Rob Jones","smtp:rjones@testlabs.se;SMTP:rob@fabrikam.com"
"John Davis","smtp:jdavis@testlabs.se;SMTP:jdavis@fabrikam.com"
"Conference Room 23","smtp:cr23@west.contoso.com;SMTP:cr23@testlat
"Pete Dickson","smtp:pdickson@west.contoso.com;SMTP:pdickson@test1
"Emanuel Moss","smtp:emoss@west.contoso.com;SMTP:emoss@testlabs.se
```

See also

▸ *Exporting reports to text and CSV files* in *Chapter 2, Exchange Management Shell Common Tasks*

▸ *Working with recipient filters* in *Chapter 3, Managing Recipients*

▸ *Creating address lists*

Configuring hierarchical address books

In Exchange 2010 SP1, the **hierarchical address book** (**HAB**) was introduced. This allows users with Outlook 2007 or later to browse for recipients using an organizational hierarchy. The idea is that you can give your users the ability to search for recipients based on your organization's structure, versus the Global Address List, which only provides a flat view. The configuration of a HAB can only be done using the Exchange Management Shell, and in this recipe, we'll take a look at an example of how you can configure this feature in your organization.

How to do it...

Let's see how to configure hierarchical address books using the following steps:

1. It is recommended that you create an OU in Active Directory to store the root HAB objects. You can create a new OU either by using your Active Directory administrations tools or by using PowerShell. The following code can be used to create an OU in the root of the `Contoso` domain called `HAB`:

```
$objDomain = [ADSI]''
$objOU = $objDomain.Create('organizationalUnit', 'ou=HAB')
$objOU.SetInfo()
```

2. Next, create a root distribution group for the HAB:

```
New-DistributionGroup -Name ContosoRoot `
-DisplayName ContosoRoot `
-Alias ContosoRoot `
-OrganizationalUnit contoso.com/HAB `
-SamAccountName ContosoRoot `
-Type Distribution `
-IgnoreNamingPolicy
```

3. Configure the `ContosoRoot` distribution group as the root organization for the HAB:

```
Set-OrganizationConfig -HierarchicalAddressBookRoot
ContosoRoot
```

4. At this point, you need to add subordinate groups to the root organization group. These can be existing groups or you can create new ones. In this example, we'll add three existing groups called `Executives`, `Finance`, and `Sales` to the root organization in the HAB:

```
Add-DistributionGroupMember -Identity ContosoRoot -Member
Executives

Add-DistributionGroupMember -Identity ContosoRoot -Member
Finance

Add-DistributionGroupMember -Identity ContosoRoot -Member
Sales
```

5. Finally, we'll designate each of the groups as hierarchical groups and set the seniority index for the subordinate groups:

```
Set-Group -Identity ContosoRoot -IsHierarchicalGroup $true

Set-Group Executives -IsHierarchicalGroup $true -
SeniorityIndex 100

Set-Group Finance -IsHierarchicalGroup $true -
SeniorityIndex 50

Set-Group Sales -IsHierarchicalGroup $true -SeniorityIndex
75
```

6. After this configuration has been completed, Outlook 2007+ users can click on the **Address Book** button and view a new tab called **Organization** that will list our HAB:

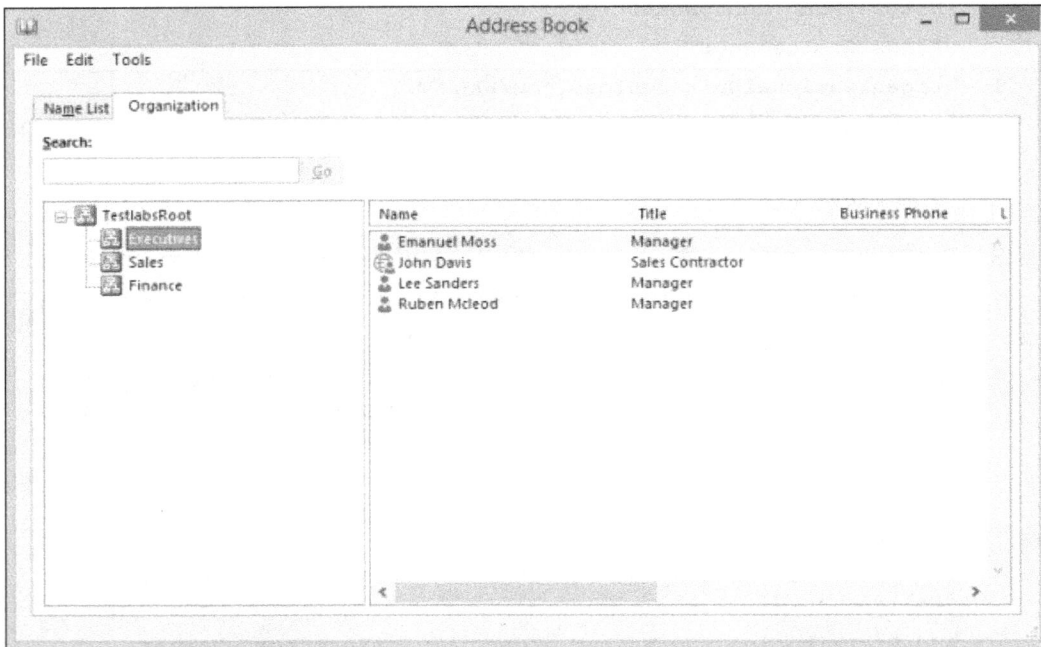

\How it works...

The root organization of a HAB is used as the top tier for the organization. Under the root, you can add multiple tiers by adding other distribution groups as members of this root tier and configure them as hierarchical groups. This allows you to create a HAB that is organized by a department, location, or any other structure that makes sense for your environment.

In order to control the structure of the HAB, you can set SeniorityIndex of each subgroup under the root organization. This index overrides the automatic sort order based on the DisplayName property, which would otherwise be used if no value was defined. This also works for individual recipients within each group. For example, you can set the SeniorityIndex value on each member of the Executives group using the Set-User cmdlet:

```
Set-User cmunoz -SeniorityIndex 100

Set-User awood -SeniorityIndex 90

Set-User ahunter -SeniorityIndex 80
```

The users will be displayed in an order, with the highest index number first. This allows you to further organize the HAB and override the default sort order, if needed.

There's more...

You may notice that, after configuring a HAB, Outlook 2007+ users are not seeing the **Organization** tab when viewing the **Address Book**. If this happens, double check the Active Directory schema attribute `ms-Exch-HAB-Root-Department-Link` using ADSIEdit. The `isMemberOfPartialAttributeSet` attribute should be set to `True`. If it is not, change this attribute to `True`, ensure that this has replicated to all DCs in the forest, and restart the Microsoft Exchange Active Directory Topology service on each Exchange server. Of course, this is something you'll want to do during out of hours to ensure that there is no disruption of service for end users. After this work has been completed, Outlook 2007+ users should be able to view the **Organization** tab in the **Address Book**.

We can make a basic script for the preceding tasks and save it to a file called `hab.ps1`:

```
$objDomain = [ADSI]''
$objOU = $objDomain.Create('organizationalUnit', 'ou=HAB')
$objOU.SetInfo()
$hab = Read-Host "Type a name for the HAB root"
New-DistributionGroup -Name $hab -DisplayName $hab `
-OrganizationalUnit "contoso.com/HAB" -SAMAccountName $hab `
-Type Distribution
Set-Group -Identity $hab —IsHierarchicalGroup $true
$File = Import-Csv ".\hab.csv"
$File | foreach {
  New-DistributionGroup -Name $_.GroupName -OrganizationalUnit `
  "contoso.com/HAB" -Type Distribution -SAMAccountName $_.GroupName
  Set-Group -Identity $_.GroupName -SeniorityIndex $_.Seniority `
  -IsHierarchicalGroup $true
  Add-DistributionGroupMember -Identity $hab -Member $_.GroupName
}
Set-OrganizationConfig -HierarchicalAddressBookRoot $hab
```

The script starts with creating an OU called HAB. A variable is created with the name `$hab`; the prompt will ask for a name for the HAB root. This name is used when creating the initial distribution group. A CSV file called `hab.csv` is imported to the `$File` variable. A `foreach` loop is used to process each row in the CSV file.

The CSV includes names of the distribution groups and the `SeniorityIndex` value they should be configured with. The script also makes sure that these groups are configured as hierarchical groups. Finally, the users need to be added to the corresponding groups to form the organization.

See also

  ▶ *Managing distribution groups* in *Chapter 3, Managing Recipients*

6

Mailbox Database Management

In this chapter, we will cover the following topics:

- ► Managing the mailbox databases
- ► Moving databases and logs to another location
- ► Configuring the mailbox database limits
- ► Reporting on the mailbox database size
- ► Finding the total number of mailboxes in a database
- ► Determining the average mailbox size per database
- ► Reporting on the database backup status
- ► Restoring data from a recovery database

Introduction

In this chapter, we will focus on several scenarios in which PowerShell scripting can be used to increase your efficiency when managing databases, which are the most critical resources in your Exchange environment. We will take a look at how you can add and remove mailbox databases, configure database settings, generate advanced reports on database statistics, and more from within the Shell.

Performing some basic steps

To work with the code samples in this chapter, follow these steps to launch the Exchange Management Shell:

1. Log on to a workstation or the server with the Exchange Management Tools installed.
2. Open the Exchange Management Shell by navigating to **Start | All Programs | Exchange Server 2013**.
3. Click on the **Exchange Management Shell** shortcut.

> Remember to start the Exchange Management Shell using **Run as administrator** to avoid permission problems.
>
> In the chapter, you might notice that in the examples of cmdlets, I have used the back tick (`` ` ``) character to break up long commands into multiple lines. The purpose of this is to make it easier to read. The back ticks are not required and should only be used if needed.

Managing the mailbox databases

The Exchange Management Shell provides a set of cmdlets for mailbox database management. In this recipe, we will take a look at how you can use these cmdlets to create, change, or delete mailbox databases. We will also take a look at how the automatic mailbox distribution works.

How to do it...

The process for managing mailbox databases is pretty straightforward. We'll start with creating a new mailbox database:

1. To create a mailbox database, use the `New-MailboxDatabase` cmdlet, as shown in the following example:

```
New-MailboxDatabase -Name DB4 `
-EdbFilePath E:\Databases\DB4\Database\DB4.edb `
-LogFolderPath E:\Databases\DB4\Logs `
-Server EX01
```

2. You can mount the database after it has been created using the `Mount-Database` cmdlet:

```
Mount-Database -Identity DB4
```

3. The name of a database can be changed using the `Set-MailboxDatabase` cmdlet:

   Set-MailboxDatabase -Identity DB4 -Name Database4

4. Finally, you can remove a mailbox database using the `Remove-MailboxDatabase` cmdlet:

   Remove-MailboxDatabase -Identity Database4 `

   -Confirm:$false

How it works...

The `New-MailboxDatabase` cmdlet requires that you provide a name for your database and specify the server name where it should be hosted. In the previous example, you can see that we created the `DB4` database on the `EX01` server. The `-EdbFilePath` parameter specifies the location for your database file; however, it is not required to use this for creating the database. Additionally, you can use the `-LogFolderPath` variable to identify the directory that should hold the transaction logs for this database. If no value is provided for either of these parameters, the database and log directories will be set to the default location within the Exchange installation directory.

Mounting a database is done as a separate step. If you want to create the database and mount it in one operation, pipe your `New-MailboxDatabase` command to the `Mount-Database` cmdlet, as shown in the following line of code:

New-MailboxDatabase -Name DB10 -Server EX01 | Mount-Database

The `Mount-Database` cmdlet can be used with mailbox databases. The same is true for its counterpart, `Dismount-Database`, which allows you to dismount a mailbox database.

As mentioned previously, to rename a mailbox database, we used the `Set-MailboxDatabase` cmdlet with the `-Name` parameter. It's important to note that while this will change the database name in the Active Directory and therefore in Exchange, it does not change the filename or path of the database.

Before running the `Remove-MailboxDatabase` cmdlet, you will need to move any regular mailboxes, archive mailboxes, or arbitration mailboxes to another database, using the `New-MoveRequest` or `New-MigrationBatch` cmdlet. The arbitration mailboxes can be found using the `Get-Mailbox -Arbitration` command; these can be found on the first created database.

Keep in mind that the removal of a database is only done logically in the Active Directory. Later on, you will need to manually delete the files and directories used by the database running the `Remove-MailboxDatabase` cmdlet.

[
There are only two required parameters for creating the mailbox database, which are `Name` and `Server`. However, the others such as `EdbFilePath` and `LogFolderPath` are good to use for specifying the configuration.
]

There's more...

Exchange 2010 implemented a new feature called automatic mailbox distribution. This allows you to omit the `-Database` parameter when creating or moving a mailbox, and an agent determines the most appropriate target database based on a number of factors.

The Mailbox Resources Management Agent, a cmdlet extension agent, is the application that runs in the background that handles this, and is enabled by default. The benefit of this application is that if you provision multiple mailboxes, or move multiple mailboxes at one time without specifying a target database, the mailboxes will be distributed across all of the available mailbox databases in the current Active Directory site from where you are running the commands.

Understanding the automatic mailbox distribution

Each mailbox database has three properties: `IsExcludedFromProvisioning`, `IsExcludedFromInitialProvisioning`, and `IsSuspendedFromProvisioning`. These control whether or not a database can be used for automatic mailbox distribution. By default, all are set to `$false`, which means that every mailbox database you create is available for automatic distribution out of the box. If you intend to create a mailbox database used strictly for archive mailboxes, or you don't want mailboxes to be placed in a particular database automatically, you can exclude the database from being automatically used. To do so, use the following command syntax after the database has been created:

```
Set-MailboxDatabase -Identity DB1 -IsExcludedFromProvisioning `
$true
```

When the `IsExcludedFromProvisioning` property is set to `$true`, you can still manually create mailboxes in the database, but it will not be used for automatic distribution.

Taking it a step further

Let's take a look at an example of creating mailbox databases in bulk. This can be helpful when creating many databases. The following code can be used for doing the job:

```
$data = Import-CSV .\DBs.csv
foreach($row in $data) {
  $DBName = $row.DBName
  $LogPath = 'E:\Databases\' + $DBName + '\Logs'
```

```
  $DBPath = 'E:\Databases\' + $DBName + '\Database\' + $DBName +
'.edb'
  $Server = $row.Server
  New-MailboxDatabase -Name $DBName -Server $Server -Edbfilepath `
  $DBPath -Logfolderpath $LogPath
}
foreach($row in $data) {
  $DBName = $row.DBName
Mount-Database $DBName
}
```

In this example, we create an array by importing a CSV file. We start looping through each row in the file, and also in the loop, we create new variables named DBName, LogPath, DBPath, and Server. These variables are then used in the New-MailboxDatabase cmdlet. Finally, with this small script, we'll loop through each row again and create a new variable named DBName, and try to mount each database in the CSV file.

> The resource called MSFT_xExchMailboxDatabase in the xExchange module for Desired State Configuration can be used for creating databases.
> When creating databases in larger environments, it can be impossible to mount the databases immediately; in these cases, let the Active Directory replication finish. When it's completed, the databases can be mounted.

See also

- *Reporting on mailbox database size*
- *Moving databases and logs to another location*

Moving databases and logs to another location

As your environment grows or changes over time, it may be necessary to move one or more databases and their log streams to another location. This is one of those tasks that's required to be done from the Exchange Management Shell. As an advantage, the Shell gives you some more flexibility. In this recipe, you will learn how to move the database and log files to another location.

How to do it...

To move the database file and log stream from the `DB1` database to a new location, use the following command syntax:

```
Move-DatabasePath -Identity DB1 `
-EdbFilePath F:\Databases\DB1\Database\DB1.edb `
-LogFolderPath F:\Databases\DB1\Logs `
-Confirm:$false `
-Force
```

After executing the preceding command, the `DB1` database and log files will be moved to the `F:\Databases\DB1\Database` directory, without prompting you for a confirmation.

How it works...

In this example, you can see that we are moving both the database file and the transaction logs to the same directory. You can use different directories or even separate disk spindles as the locations for the database and log folder paths if needed.

To remove the confirmation prompts, we need to set the `-Confirm` parameter to `$false` and also use the `-Force` switch parameter. This may be an important detail if you are running this cmdlet from an automated script. If not used, the cmdlet will not make any changes until an operator confirms it in the Shell.

Obviously, in order to move the database file or the logs, the database will need to be taken offline for the duration of the move. The `Move-DatabasePath` cmdlet will automatically dismount the database and remount it when the move process is complete. If the database is already dismounted at the time that you initiate a move, the database will not be automatically mounted upon completion of the command, and you will need to mount it manually using the `Mount-Database` cmdlet. Obviously, any users with a mailbox in a dismounted database will be unable to connect to their mailbox. If you need to move a database, ensure that this can be done during a time that will not impact end users.

Keep in mind that databases that are replicated within a **Database Availability Group** (**DAG**) cannot be moved. Each database copy in a DAG needs to use the same local path for the database and logs, so you cannot change this after copies have already been created. If you need to change the paths for a replicated database, you will need to remove all the database copies and perform the move. Once this process has been completed, you can create new database copies, that will use the new path.

There's more...

Before changing the `EdbfilePath` or the `LogFolderPath` locations for a database, you may want to check the existing configuration. To do so, use the `Get-MailboxDatabase` cmdlet, as shown in the following screenshot:

```
Machine: TLEX01.testlabs.se                        —  □  X
[PS] C:\Windows\system32>Get-MailboxDatabase | fl Name,EdbFilepath,Logfolde
rpath


Name          : DB01
EdbFilePath   : F:\Databases\DB01\DB01.edb
LogFolderPath : F:\Databases\DB01

Name          : DB02
EdbFilePath   : F:\Databases\DB02\DB02.edb
LogFolderPath : F:\Databases\DB02
```

Here, you can see that we are piping the `Get-MailboxDatabase` cmdlet to `Format-List` (using the `fl` alias) and selecting the `Name`, `EdbFilePath`, and `LogFolderPath` properties, which will display the relevant information for every database in the organization. You can retrieve this information for a single database by specifying the name of the database using the `-Identity` parameter.

Manually moving databases

In certain situations, you may prefer to manually copy or move the database and log files, instead of allowing the `Move-DatabasePath` cmdlet to move the data for you. In this case, you can use the following process:

1. Let's say that you need to move the DB2 database to the `F:\` drive. To do this manually, the first thing you will want to do is dismount the database:

    ```
    Dismount-Database -Identity DB2 -Confirm:$false
    ```

2. Next, use whatever method you prefer to copy the data to the new location on the `F:\` drive. After the data has been copied, use the `Move-DatabasePath` cmdlet to update the configuration information in Exchange, as shown next:

    ```
    Move-DatabasePath -Identity DB2 `
    -EdbFilePath F:\Databases\DB2\Database\DB2.edb `
    -LogFolderPath F:\Databases\DB2\Logs `
    -ConfigurationOnly `
    -Confirm:$false `
    -Force
    ```

3. The preceding command uses the `-ConfigurationOnly` switch parameter when running the `Move-DatabasePath` cmdlet. This ensures that only the configuration of the database paths is updated and there is no attempt made to copy the data files to the new location.

4. After the files are manually moved or copied and the configuration has been changed, you can remount the database, as shown in the following command:

```
Mount-Database -Identity DB2
```

At this point, the database will be brought online and the move operation will be complete.

Taking it a step further

Let's take a look at an example of how we can use the Shell to move databases in bulk. Let's say that we have added a new disk to the EX01 server using the S:\ drive letter, and all the databases need to be moved to this new disk under the Databases root directory. The following code can be used to perform the move:

```
foreach($i in Get-MailboxDatabase -Server EX01) {
  $DBName = $i.Name
  Move-DatabasePath -Identity $DBName `
  -EdbFilePath "S:\Databases\$DBName\Database\$DBName.edb" `
  -LogFolderPath "S:\Databases\$DBName\Logs" `
  -Confirm:$false `
  -Force
}
```

In this example, we use the `Get-MailboxDatabase` cmdlet to retrieve a list of all the mailbox databases on the EX01 server. As we loop through each mailbox database, we move the EDB file and log path under the S:\Database folder, in a subdirectory that matches the name of the database.

You can type the preceding code straight into the Shell, or save it in an external .ps1 file and execute it as a script.

See also

▶ *Looping through items* in *Chapter 1, PowerShell Key Concepts*
▶ *Working with variables and objects* in *Chapter 1, PowerShell Key Concepts*

Configuring the mailbox database limits

The Exchange Management Shell provides cmdlets that allow you to configure the storage limits for mailbox databases. This recipe will show you how to set these limits interactively in the shell or in bulk using an automated script.

How to do it...

To configure the storage limits for a mailbox database, use the `Set-MailboxDatabase` cmdlet, for example:

```
Set-MailboxDatabase -Identity DB1 `

-IssueWarningQuota 2gb `

-ProhibitSendQuota 2.5gb `

-ProhibitSendReceiveQuota 3gb
```

How it works...

In this example, we configured the `IssueWarningQuota`, `ProhibitSendQuota`, and `ProhibitSendRecieveQuota` limits for the `DB1` mailbox database. These are the storage limits that will be applied to each mailbox that is stored in this database. Based on the values used with the command, you can see that users will receive a warning once their mailbox reaches 2 GB in size. When their mailbox reaches 2.5 GB, they will be unable to send outbound e-mail messages, and when they hit the 3 GB limit, they will be unable to send or receive e-mail messages.

> You can override the database limits on a per mailbox basis using the `Set-Mailbox` cmdlet.

There's more...

Mailbox databases support the deleted item retention, which allows you to recover items that have been removed from the deleted items folder. By default, the retention period for the mailbox databases is set to 14 days, but this can be changed using the `-DeletedItemRetention` parameter, when using the appropriate cmdlet. For example, to increase the deleted item retention period for the `DB1` database, use the following command:

```
Set-MailboxDatabase -Identity DB1 -DeletedItemRetention 30
```

In this example, we have set the deleted item retention to 30 days. This parameter will also accept input in the form of a time span, and therefore can be specified using the `dd.hh:mm:ss` format. For example, we could have also used `30.00:00:00` as the parameter value, indicating that the deleted item retention should be 30 days, 0 hours, 0 minutes, and 0 seconds, but that would be pointless in this example. However, this format is useful when you need to be specific about hours or minutes; for instance, using `12:00:00` would indicate that the deleted items should only be retained for 12 hours.

In addition to the deleted item retention, mailbox databases also retain deleted mailboxes for 30 days by default. You can change this value using the `-MailboxRetention` parameter, as shown in the following command:

```
Set-MailboxDatabase -Identity DB1 -MailboxRetention 90
```

Like the value used for the `-DeletedItemRetention` parameter, you can specify a time span as the value for the `-MailboxRetention` parameter. Both of these parameters will accept a maximum of 24,855 days.

Finally, you can configure mailbox databases so that items will not be permanently deleted until a database backup has been performed. This is not enabled by default. To turn it on for a particular database, use the `-RetainDeletedItemsUntilBackup` parameter with the `Set-MailboxDatabase` cmdlet, for example:

```
Set-MailboxDatabase -Identity DB1 `
-RetainDeletedItemsUntilBackup $true
```

Taking it a step further

To configure these settings in bulk, we can make use of the pipeline to update the settings for a group of databases. For example, the following command will set the database limits for all mailboxes in the organization:

```
Get-MailboxDatabase | Set-MailboxDatabase `
-IssueWarningQuota 2gb `
-ProhibitSendQuota 2.5gb `
-ProhibitSendReceiveQuota 3gb `
-DeletedItemRetention 30 `
-MailboxRetention 90 `
-RetainDeletedItemsUntilBackup $true
```

In this command, we are piping the results of the `Get-MailboxDatabase` cmdlet to the `Set-MailboxDatabase` cmdlet and changing the default settings to the desired values for all databases in the organization.

▸   *Determining the average mailbox size per database*

Reporting on mailbox database size

It was quite difficult in Exchange 2007 to determine the size of a mailbox database using PowerShell. At that time, the `Get-MailboxDatabase` cmdlet did not return the size of the database, and instead, you had to use the cmdlet to determine the path to the EDB file and calculate the file size using the `Get-Item` cmdlet or WMI. With Exchange 2010, this was changed and determining the size information turned out to be very simple, and the information can easily be retrieved using the `Get-MailboxDatabase` cmdlet. In this recipe, we will take a look at how to report on the mailbox database size using the Exchange Management Shell for Exchange 2013.

How to do it...

To retrieve the total size of each mailbox database, use the following command:

```
Get-MailboxDatabase -Status | select-object Name,DatabaseSize
```

The output from this command might look something like this:

```
Machine: tlex01.testlabs.se                         _  □  X
[PS] C:\Scripts>Get-MailboxDatabase -Status | select-object Name,DatabaseSi
ze

Name                          DatabaseSize
----                          ------------
DB1                           896 MB (939,524,096 bytes)
DB2                           896 MB (939,524,096 bytes)
```

How it works...

When running the `Get-MailboxDatabase` cmdlet, we can use the `-Status` switch parameter to receive additional information about the database, such as the mount status, the backup status, and the total size of the database, as shown in the previous example. To generate a report with this information, simply pipe the command to the `Export-CSV` cmdlet and specify the path and filename, as shown in the following commands:

```
Get-MailboxDatabase -Status |
select-object Name,Server,DatabaseSize,Mounted |
Export-CSV -Path c:\databasereport.csv -NoTypeInformation
```

This time, we have added the server name, that the database is currently associated with, and the mount status for that database.

There's more...

When viewing the value of the database size, you might have noticed that we see the total size in megabytes, and in parenthesis, we see the value in bytes, rather than just seeing a single integer for the total size. The `DatabaseSize` property is of the type `ByteQuantifiedSize`, and we can use several methods provided by this type to convert the value if all we want to retrieve is a numeric representation of the database size.

For example, we can use the `ToKB`, `ToMB`, `ToGB`, and `ToTB` methods of the `DatabaseSize` object to convert the value to kilobytes, megabytes, gigabytes, or terabytes, as shown in the following command:

```
Get-MailboxDatabase -Status |
Select-Object Name,
@{n="DatabaseSize";e={$_.DatabaseSize.ToMb()}}
```

As you can see, this time, we have created a calculated property for the `DatabaseSize`, object and we are using the `ToMB` method to convert the value of the database. The output we get from the command would look something like this:

```
Machine: tlex01.testlabs.se                    _  □  X

[PS] C:\Scripts>Get-MailboxDatabase -Status | Select-Object Name,@{n="Datab
aseSize";e={$_.DatabaseSize.ToMb()}}

Name                                                          DatabaseSize
----                                                          ------------
DB1                                                                    896
DB2                                                                    896
```

This technique may be useful if you are looking to generate basic reports and you don't need all of the extra information that is returned by default. For instance, you may already know that your databases will always be in the range of hundreds of gigabytes. You can simply use a calculated property, as shown in the previous example, and call the `ToGB` method for each `DatabaseSize` object.

See also

▶ *Understanding the pipeline* in *Chapter 1, PowerShell Key Concepts*

Finding the total number of mailboxes in a database

You can retrieve all kinds of information about a mailbox database using the Exchange Management Shell cmdlets. Surprisingly, the total number of mailboxes in a given mailbox database is not one of those pieces of information. We need to retrieve this data manually. Luckily, PowerShell makes this easy, as you will see in this recipe.

How to do it...

Let's see how to find the total number of mailboxes in a database using the following steps:

1. There are two ways that you can retrieve the total number of mailboxes in a database. First, we can use the Count property of a collection of mailboxes:

    ```
    @(Get-Mailbox -Database DB1).count
    ```

2. Another way to retrieve this information is to use the Measure-Object cmdlet using the same collection from the preceding example:

    ```
    Get-Mailbox -Database DB1 | Measure-Object
    ```

How it works...

In both the steps, we use the Get-Mailbox cmdlet and specify the -Database parameter, which will retrieve all of the mailboxes in that particular database. In the first example, we wrapped the command inside the @() characters to ensure that PowerShell will always interpret the output as an array. The reason for this is that if the mailbox database contains only one mailbox, the resulting output object will not be a collection, and thus will not have a Count property.

> Remember, the default result size of Get-Mailbox is 1000. Set the -ResultSize parameter to Unlimited to override this.

The second step makes use of the `Measure-Object` cmdlet. You can see that, in addition to the `Count` property, we also get a number of other details. Consider the output, as shown in the following screenshot:

```
Machine: tlex01.testlabs.se                         _  □  x

[PS] C:\Scripts>Get-Mailbox -Database DB1 | Measure-Object


Count      :  3
Average    :
Sum        :
Maximum    :
Minimum    :
Property   :
```

To retrieve only the total number of mailboxes, we can extend this command further in two ways. First, we can enclose the entire command in parenthesis and access the `Count` property:

```
(Get-Mailbox -Database DB1 | Measure-Object).Count
```

In this case, the preceding command will return only the total number of mailboxes in the `DB1` database.

We can also pipe the command to `Select-Object`, and use the `-ExpandProperty` parameter to retrieve only the value of the `Count` property:

```
Get-Mailbox -Database DB1 |

Measure-Object |

Select-Object -ExpandProperty Count
```

This command will again only return the total number of mailboxes in the database.

One of the most common questions that comes up when people see both of these methods is, of course, which way is faster? Well, we can use the `Measure-Command` cmdlet to determine this information, but the truth is that your results will vary greatly and there probably won't be a huge difference in this case. The syntax to measure the time it takes to run a script or command is shown in the following command:

```
Measure-Command -Expression {@(Get-Mailbox -Database DB1).Count}
```

Simply, supply a script block containing the commands you want to measure, and assign it to the `-Expression` parameter, as shown previously. The `Measure-Command` cmdlet will return a `TimeSpan` object that reports on the total milliseconds, seconds, and minutes that it took to complete the command. You can then compare these values to other commands that produce the same result, but use alternate syntaxes or cmdlets.

[✎ To report on the total number of archive mailboxes, use `Get-Mailbox -Filter {ArchiveName -ne $null} | Measure-Object`.]

There's more...

We can easily determine the total number of mailboxes n each database using a single command. The key to this is using the `Select-Object` cmdlet to create a calculated property, as shown in the following example:

```
Get-MailboxDatabase |
Select-Object Name,
@{n="TotalMailboxes";e={@(Get-Mailbox -Database $_).count}}
```

This command will generate an output similar to the following screenshot:

```
Machine: tlex01.testlabs.se                    _  □  X

[PS] C:\Scripts>Get-MailboxDatabase | Select-Object Name,@{n="TotalMailboxe
s";e={@(Get-Mailbox -Database $_).count}}

Name                                                    TotalMailboxes
----                                                    --------------
DB1                                                                  3
DB2                                                                 29
```

This command pipes the output from `Get-MailboxDatabase` to the `Select-Object` cmdlet. For each database output by the command, we select the database name, and then, use the `$_` object when creating the calculated property to determine the total number of mailboxes, using the `Get-Mailbox` cmdlet. This command can be piped further down to the `Out-File` or `Export-CSV` cmdlets that will generate a report saved in an external file.

See also

▸ *Creating custom objects* in *Chapter 1, PowerShell Key Concepts*

Determining the average mailbox size per database

PowerShell is very flexible and gives you the ability to generate very detailed reports. When generating mailbox database statistics, we can utilize the data returned from multiple cmdlets provided by the Exchange Management Shell. This recipe will show you an example of this, and you will learn how to calculate the average mailbox size per database using PowerShell.

How to do it...

To determine the average mailbox size of a given database, use the following commands:

```
Get-MailboxStatistics -Database DB1 |
ForEach-Object {$_.TotalItemSize.value.ToMB()} |
Measure-Object -Average |
Select-Object -ExpandProperty Average
```

How it works...

Calculating an average is as simple as performing some basic math, but PowerShell gives us the ability to do this quickly with the `Measure-Object` cmdlet. The example uses the `Get-MailboxStatistics` cmdlet to retrieve all the mailboxes in the DB1 database. We then loop through each one, retrieving only the `TotalItemSize` property, and in the `ForEach-Object` script block, we convert the total item size to megabytes. The result from each mailbox can then be averaged using the `Measure-Object` cmdlet. At the end of the command, you can see that the `Select-Object` cmdlet is used to retrieve only the value of the `Average` property.

The number returned here will give us the average mailbox size in total for regular mailboxes, archive mailboxes, as well as any other types of mailboxes that have been disconnected. If you want to be more specific, you can filter out these mailboxes after running the `Get-MailboxStatistics` cmdlet:

```
Get-MailboxStatistics -Database DB1 |
Where-Object{!$_.DisconnectDate -and !$_.IsArchive} |
ForEach-Object {$_.TotalItemSize.value.ToMB()} |
Measure-Object -Average |
Select-Object -ExpandProperty Average
```

Notice that, in the preceding example, we added the `Where-Object` cmdlet to filter out any mailboxes that have a `DisconnectDate` object defined or where the `IsArchive` property is $true.

Another thing that you may want to do is round off the average. Let's say that the DB1 database contained 42 mailboxes and the total size of the database was around 392 megabytes. The value returned from the preceding command would roughly look something like 2.39393939393939. Rarely are all those extra decimal places of any use. Here are a couple of ways to make the output a little cleaner:

```
$MBAvg = Get-MailboxStatistics -Database DB1 |
ForEach-Object {$_.TotalItemSize.value.ToMB()} |
Measure-Object -Average |
Select-Object -ExpandProperty Average
[Math]::Round($MBAvg,2)
```

You can see that this time, we stored the result of the one-liner in the $MBAvg variable. We then use the Round method of the Math class in the .NET Framework to round off the value, specifying that the result should only contain two decimal places. Based on the previous information, the result of the preceding command would be 2.39.

We can also use string formatting to specify the number of decimal places to be used:

```
[PS] "{0:n2}" -f $MBAvg
2.39
```

> The -f (format) operator is documented in PowerShell's help system in about_operators.

Keep in mind that this command will return a string, so f you need to sort on this value, cast it to double:

```
[PS] [double]("{0:n2}" -f $MBAvg)
2.39
```

There's more...

The previous examples have only shown how to determine the average mailbox size of a single database. To determine this information for all mailbox databases, we can use the following code (save it to a file called size.ps1):

```
foreach($DB in Get-MailboxDatabase) {
  Get-MailboxStatistics -Database $DB |
  ForEach-Object{$_.TotalItemSize.value.ToMB()} |
  Measure-Object -Average |
  Select-Object @{n="Name";e={$DB.Name}},
  @{n="AvgMailboxSize";e={[Math]::Round($_.Average,2)}} |
  Sort-Object AvgMailboxSize -Desc
}
```

The result of this command would look something like the following screenshot:

```
Machine: tlex01.testlabs.se                                    _  □  x

[PS] C:\Scripts>.\size.ps1

Name                                                      AvgMailboxSize
----                                                      --------------
DB1                                                                14.97
DB2                                                                14.69
```

This example is very similar to the one we looked at previously. The difference is that, this time, we are running our one-liner using a `foreach` loop for every mailbox database in the organization. When each mailbox database has been processed, we sort the output based on the `AvgMailboxSize` property.

See also

▶ *Creating custom objects* in *Chapter 1, PowerShell Key Concepts*

Reporting on database backup status

Using the Exchange Management Shell, we can write scripts that will check on the last full backup time for a database that can be used for monitoring and reporting. In this recipe, you will learn how to check the last backup time for each database, and use this information to generate statistics and find databases that are not being backed up on a regular basis.

How to do it...

To check the last full backup time for a database, use the `Get-MailboxDatabase` cmdlet, as shown here:

```
Get-MailboxDatabase -Identity DB1 -Status | fl Name,LastFullBackup
```

How it works...

When you run the `Get-MailboxDatabase` cmdlet, you must remember to use the `-Status` switch parameter or else the `LastFullBackup` property will be `$null`. In the previous example, we checked the last full backup time for the `DB1` database and piped the output to the `Format-List` (using the `fl` alias) cmdlet. When viewing the `LastFullBackup` property for each database, you might find it helpful to pipe the output to the `Select-Object` cmdlet, as shown in the following screenshot:

```
Machine: tlex01.testlabs.se                    [_] [ロ] [X]

[PS] C:\Scripts>Get-MailboxDatabase -Status | Select-object Name,LastFullBa
ckup

Name                                   LastFullBackup
----                                   --------------
DB1                                    3/19/2015 7:50:02 PM
DB2                                    3/19/2015 7:50:02 PM
```

In addition to simply checking the date, it may be useful to schedule this script to run daily
and report on the databases that have not recently been backed up. For example, the
following command will only retrieve databases that have not had a successful full back
up in the last 24 hours:

```
Get-MailboxDatabase -Status |
?{$_.LastFullBackup -le (Get-Date).AddDays(-1)} |
Select-object Name,LastFullBackup
```

Here, you can see that the Get-MailboxDatabase output is piped to the Where-Object
cmdlet (using the ? alias), and we check the value of the LastFullBackup property for each
database. If the value is less than or equal to 24 hours ago, the database name and last full
backup time are retuned.

There's more...

Since the LastFullBackup property value is a DateTime object, not only can we use
comparison operators to find databases that have not been backed up within a certain time
frame, but we can also calculate the number of days since that time. This might be a useful
piece of information to add to a reporting or monitoring script. The following code will provide
this information:

```
Get-MailboxDatabase -Status | ForEach-Object {
  if(!$_.LastFullBackup) {
    $LastFull = "Never"
  }
  else {
    $LastFull = $_.LastFullBackup
  }
  New-Object PSObject -Property @{
    Name = $_.Name
    LastFullBackup = $LastFull
    DaysSinceBackup = if($LastFull-is [datetime]) {
      (New-TimeSpan $LastFull).Days
    }
```

```
    Else {
      $LastFull
    }
  }
}
```

When running this code in the Exchange Management Shell, you will see an output similar to the following screenshot:

```
Machine: tlex01.testlabs.se                                    _  □  X

[PS] C:\Scripts>.\lastbackup.ps1

   DaysSinceBackup  Name                          LastFullBackup
   ---------------  ----                          --------------
                 0  DB1                           3/19/2015 7:50:02 PM
                 0  DB2                           3/19/2015 7:50:02 PM
```

As you can see, we are simply looping through each mailbox database and retrieving the
`LastFullBackup` time. If a database has never been backed up, the value will be `$null`.
With this in mind, this code will return the string `Never` for those databases when reporting
on the status. If a value is present for `LastFullBackup`, we use the `New-TimeSpan` cmdlet
to determine the number of days since the last backup and include that in the data returned.

See also

▶ *Creating custom objects* in *Chapter 1, PowerShell Key Concepts*

Restoring data from a recovery database

When it comes to recovering data from a failed database, you have several options depending
on what kind of backup product you are using or how you have deployed Exchange 2013.
The ideal method for enabling redundancy is to use a DAG, which will replicate your mailbox
databases to one or more servers and provide automatic failover in the event of a disaster.
However, you may need to pull old data out of a database restored from a backup. In this
recipe, we will take a look at how you can create a recovery database and restore data from it
using the Exchange Management Shell.

How to do it...

First, restore the failed database using the steps required by your current backup solution. For
this example, let's say that we have restored the DB1 database file to `E:\Recovery\DB1` and
the database has been brought to a clean shutdown state. We can use the following steps to
create a recovery database and restore the mailbox data:

1. Create a recovery database using the `New-MailboxDatabase` cmdlet:

   ```
   New-MailboxDatabase -Name RecoveryDB `
   -EdbFilePath E:\Recovery\DB1\DB1.edb `
   -LogFolderPath E:\Recovery\DB01 `
   -Recovery `
   -Server MBX1
   ```

2. When you run the preceding command, you will see a warning that the recovery database was created using the existing database file. The next step is to check the state of the database, followed by mounting the database:

   ```
   Eseutil /mh .\DB1.edb
   Eseutil /R E02 /D
   Mount-Database -Identity RecoveryDB
   ```

3. Next, query the recovery database for all the mailboxes that reside in the database `RecoveryDB`:

   ```
   Get-MailboxStatistics -Database RecoveryDB | fl
   DisplayName,MailboxGUID,LegacyDN
   ```

4. Lastly, we will use the `New-MailboxRestoreRequest` cmdlet to restore the data from the recovery database for a single mailbox:

   ```
   New-MailboxRestoreRequest -SourceDatabase RecoveryDB `
   -SourceStoreMailbox "Joe Smith" `
   -TargetMailbox joe.smith
   ```

> When running the `eseutil` commands, make sure you are in the folder where the restored mailbox database and logs are placed.
> Also, make sure that the name of the recovery database is unique.

How it works...

When you restore the database file from your backup application, you may need to ensure that the database is in a clean shutdown state. For example, if you are using Windows Server Backup for your backup solution, you will need to use the `Eseutil.exe` database utility to play any uncommitted logs into the database to get it in a clean shutdown state.

Once the data is restored, we can create a recovery database using the
`New-MailboxDatabase` cmdlet, as shown in the first example. Notice that when
we ran the command, we used several parameters. First, we specified the path to the
EDB file and the log files, both of which are in the same location where we restored the
files. We also used the `-Recovery` switch parameter to specify that this is a special type
of database that will only be used to restore data and should not be used for production
mailboxes. Finally, we specified which mailbox server the database should be hosted on
using the `-Server` parameter. Make sure to run the `New-MailboxDatabase` cmdlet from
the mailbox server that you are specifying in the `-Server` parameter, and then mount the
database using the `Mount-Database` cmdlet.

The last step is to restore data from one or more mailboxes. As we saw in the previous
example, `New-MailboxRestoreRequest` is the tool that we can use for this task. This
cmdlet was introduced in Exchange 2010 SP1, so if you have used this process in the past,
the procedure is the same with Exchange 2013.

There's more...

When you run the `New-MailboxRestoreRequest` cmdlet, you need to specify the identity
of the mailbox you wish to restore using the `-SourceStoreMailbox` parameter. There are
three possible values you can use to provide this information: `DisplayName`, `MailboxGuid`,
and `LegacyDN`. To retrieve these values, you can use the `Get-MailboxStatistics` cmdlet
once the recovery database is online and mounted:

```
Get-MailboxStatistics -Database RecoveryDB | `
fl DisplayName,MailboxGUID,LegacyDN
```

Here, we have specified that we want to retrieve all the three of these values for each mailbox
in the `RecoveryDB` database.

Understanding target mailbox identity

When restoring data with the `New-MailboxRestoreRequest` cmdlet, you also need to
provide a value for the `-TargetMailbox` parameter. The mailbox needs to already exist
before running this command. If you are restoring data from a backup for an existing mailbox
that has not changed since the backup was done, you can simply provide the typical identity
values for a mailbox for this parameter.

If you want to restore data to a mailbox that is not the original source of the data, you need to
use the `-AllowLegacyDNMismatch` switch parameter. This will be useful if you are restoring
data to another user's mailbox, or if you've recreated the mailbox since the backup was taken.

Learning about other useful parameters

The `New-MailboxRestoreRequest` cmdlet can be used to granularly control how data is restored out of a mailbox. The following parameters may be useful to customize the behavior of your restores:

▶ `ConflictResolutionOption`: This parameter specifies the action to take if multiple matching messages exist in the target mailbox. The possible values are `KeepSourceItem`, `KeepLatestItem`, or `KeepAll`. If no value is specified, `KeepSourceItem` will be used by default.

▶ `ExcludeDumpster`: You can use this switch parameter to indicate that the dumpster should not be included in the restore.

▶ `SourceRootFolder`: You can use this parameter to restore data only from a root folder of a mailbox.

▶ `TargetIsArchive`: You can use this switch parameter to perform a mailbox restore to a mailbox archive.

▶ `TargetRootFolder`: This parameter can be used to restore data to a specific folder in the root of the target mailbox. If no value is provided, the data is restored and merged into the existing folders, and if they do not exist, they will be created in the target mailbox.

These are just a few of the useful parameters that can be used with this cmdlet, but there are more. For a complete list of all the available parameters, and full details on each one, run `Get-Help New-MailboxRestoreRequest -Detailed`.

Understanding the mailbox restore request cmdlets

There is an entire cmdlet set for the mailbox restore requests in addition to the `New-MailboxRestoreRequest` cmdlet. The remaining available cmdlets are outlined as follows:

▶ `Get-MailboxRestoreRequest`: This provides a detailed status of the mailbox restore requests

▶ `Remove-MailboxRestoreRequest`: This removes fully or partially completed restore requests

▶ `Resume-MailboxRestoreRequest`: This resumes a restore request that was suspended or failed

▶ `Set-MailboxRestoreRequest`: This can be used to change the restore request options after the request has been created

▶ `Suspend-MailboxRestoreRequest`: This suspends a restore request any time after the request was created, but before the request reaches the status of `Completed`

For complete details and examples of each of these cmdlets, use the `Get-Help` cmdlet with the appropriate cmdlet using the `-Full` switch parameter.

Taking it a step further

Let's say that you have restored your database from backup, you have created a recovery database, and now you need to restore each mailbox in the backup to the corresponding target mailboxes that are currently online. We can use the following script to accomplish this:

```
$mailboxes = Get-MailboxStatistics -Database RecoveryDB
foreach($mailbox in $mailboxes) {
  New-MailboxRestoreRequest -SourceDatabase RecoveryDB `
  -SourceStoreMailbox $mailbox.DisplayName `
  -TargetMailbox $mailbox.DisplayName
}
```

Here, you can see that first we use the `Get-MailboxStatistics` cmdlet to retrieve all the mailboxes in the recovery database and store the results in the `$mailboxes` variable. We then loop through each mailbox and restore the data to the original mailbox. You can track the status of these restores using the `Get-MailboxRestoreRequest` cmdlet and the `Get-MailboxRestoreRequestStatistics` cmdlet.

See also

- *Managing disconnected mailboxes* in *Chapter 4, Managing Mailboxes*
- *Importing and exporting mailboxes* in *Chapter 4, Managing Mailboxes*

7

Managing Client Access

In this chapter, we will cover the following topics:

- ▸ Managing ActiveSync, OWA, POP3, and IMAP4 mailbox settings
- ▸ Setting internal and external CAS URLs
- ▸ Managing the Outlook Anywhere settings
- ▸ Blocking Outlook clients from connecting to Exchange
- ▸ Reporting on active OWA and RPC connections
- ▸ Controlling the ActiveSync device access
- ▸ Reporting on ActiveSync devices

Introduction

The **Client Access Server** (**CAS**) role was introduced in Exchange 2007 to provide a dedicated access point to various services, such as **Outlook Web Access** (**OWA**), ActiveSync, POP3, and IMAP4 to clients. However, all MAPI clients connected directly to the mailbox server role. The CAS role was extended even further in Exchange 2010 and included some new features, including a functionality that will change the architecture of every Exchange deployment. At that time, the connections to public folders were still made by MAPI clients to the mailbox server role; connections from these clients to Exchange 2010 mailboxes were handled by the CAS role.

In this latest release, with Exchange 2013, Microsoft has simplified the CAS role. The CAS role is now stateless, which means that it does not save any data. Its job is more or less to help the clients to find a route to connect to the mailbox or any required service, such as ActiveSync; in short, a proxy server. This major architectural change reminds me a bit of the Exchange 2003 frontend and backend concept. Bear in mind that the role is not called frontend, the role names are still CAS and Mailbox.

Some benefits with this new architecture are as follows:

▸ The Layer 7 load balancer is not required anymore, which means cheaper deployment and investments.

▸ Another benefit would be that the CAS servers are not required to be on the same installation build/version, even though they need to be on Exchange 2013. This means that upgrades can be done more easily, and this would also help for troubleshooting and verifying that a new build is working in the way it should.

The CAS role and the Exchange Management Shell cmdlets used to manage it provide plenty of opportunities for automating repetitive tasks, from PowerShell one-liners, scripts, and functions.

In this chapter, we'll take a look at how you can control the access to the CAS services in your environment, customize their settings, and generate usage reports using the Exchange Management Shell.

Performing some basic steps

To work with the code samples in this chapter, follow these steps to launch the Exchange Management Shell:

1. Log on to a workstation or server with the Exchange Management tools installed.

2. Open the Exchange Management Shell by navigating to **Start | All Programs | Exchange Server 2013**.

3. Click on the **Exchange Management Shell** shortcut.

> Remember to start the Exchange Management Shell using **Run as administrator** to avoid permission problems.
>
> In this chapter, you might notice that in the examples of cmdlets, I have used the back tick (`) character to break up long commands into multiple lines. The purpose of this is to make it easier to read. The back ticks are not required and should only be used if needed.

Managing ActiveSync, OWA, POP3, and IMAP4 mailbox settings

You can use the Exchange Management Shell to configure a user's ability to access services, such as ActiveSync, OWA, POP3, and IMAP4. You can also allow or disallow MAPI connectivity and the ability to connect to Exchange using Outlook Anywhere. In this recipe, you'll learn the techniques used to control these settings, whether it is done interactively through the shell or using an automated script.

How to do it...

To control access to CAS services for a mailbox, use the `Set-CASMailbox` cmdlet. Here's an example of how you might use this cmdlet:

```
Set-CasMailbox -Identity 'Dave Smith' `
-OWAEnabled $false `
-ActiveSyncEnabled $false `
-PopEnabled $false `
-ImapEnabled $false
```

This command will disable OWA, ActiveSync, POP3, and IMAP4 for the mailbox that belongs to Dave Smith.

How it works...

When you create a mailbox, OWA, ActiveSync, POP3, IMAP4, and MAPI accesses are enabled by default. For most organizations, these default settings are acceptable, but if that is not the case for your environment, you can use the `Set-CASMailbox` cmdlet to enable or disable access to these services. This can be done for individual users as needed, or you can do this in bulk.

For example, let's say that all of the users in the `Sales` department should only be allowed to access Exchange internally through Outlook using MAPI, POP, and IMAP. We can use a simple pipeline command to make this change as follows:

```
Get-Mailbox -Filter {Office -eq 'Sales'} |
Set-CasMailbox -OWAEnabled $false `
-ActiveSyncEnabled $false `
-PopEnabled $true `
-ImapEnabled $true
```

As you can see, we use the `Get-Mailbox` cmdlet and specify a filter that limits the results to users that have their `Office` attribute in Active Directory set to `Sales`. The results are then piped to the `Set-CASMailbox` cmdlet and access to the CAS services is modified for each mailbox. Notice that this time, we've used additional parameters to allow POP and IMAP access.

Alternatively, you may want to block MAPI access and only allow users in your organization to connect through OWA. In this case, use the following command:

```
Get-Mailbox -RecipientTypeDetails UserMailbox |
Set-CasMailbox -OWAEnabled $true `
-ActiveSyncEnabled $false `
-PopEnabled $false `
-ImapEnabled $false `
-MAPIBlockOutlookRpcHttp $true
```

This time, we use `Get-Mailbox` to retrieve all the mailboxes in the organization. We're using the `-RecipientTypeDetails` parameter to specify that we want to find user mailboxes and exclude other types, such as discovery and resource mailboxes. The results are piped to the `Set-CASMailbox` cmdlet and access to CAS services is configured with the required settings. You'll notice that this time, we've included the `-MAPIBlockOutlookRpcHttp` parameter and set its value to `$true` so that users will only be able to access Exchange through OWA.

There's more...

If you are planning on provisioning all of your new mailboxes through an automated script, you may want to configure these settings at the time of mailbox creation. Consider the following script named `New-MailboxScript.ps1`:

```
param(
    $name,
    $password,
    $upn,
    $alias,
    $first,
    $last
)
$pass = ConvertTo-SecureString -AsPlainText $password -Force
$mailbox = New-Mailbox -UserPrincipalName $upn `
-Alias $alias `
-Name "$first $last" `
-Password $pass `
-FirstName $first `
-LastName $last
Set-CasMailbox -Identity $mailbox `
-OWAEnabled $false `
-ActiveSyncEnabled $false `
-PopEnabled $false `
-ImapEnabled $false
```

This script can be used to create a mailbox and configure the access to CAS services based on your requirements. If the script is saved in the root of the `C:` drive, the syntax would look like this:

```
[PS] C:\>.\New-MailboxScript.ps1 -first John -last Smith -alias
jsmith -password P@ssw0rd01 -upn jsmith@contoso.com
```

There are basically two phases to the script. First, the mailbox for the user is created using the `New-Mailbox` cmdlet. In this example, the result of `New-Mailbox` is saved in the `$mailbox` variable, and the mailbox is created using the parameters provided by the user running the script. Once the mailbox is created, the `Set-CASMailbox` cmdlet is used to configure the access to CAS services, and it uses the `$mailbox` variable to identify the mailbox to modify when the command executes.

See also

► *Adding, modifying, and removing mailboxes* in *Chapter 3, Managing Recipients*

Setting internal and external CAS URLs

Each CAS server has multiple virtual directories, some of which can only be modified through the Exchange Management Shell. Scripting the changes made to both the internal and external URLs can be a big time-saver, especially when deploying multiple servers. In this recipe, you will learn how to use the set of cmdlets that are needed to modify both the internal and external URLs for each CAS server virtual directory.

How to do it...

To change the external URL of the OWA virtual directory of a server named `cas1`, use the following command:

```
Set-OwaVirtualDirectory -Identity 'CAS1\owa (Default Web Site)' `
-ExternalUrl https://mail.contoso.com/owa
```

After the change has been made, we can view the configuration using the `Get-OwaVirtualDirectory` cmdlet:

```
[PS] C:\>Get-OwaVirtualDirectory -Server cas1 | fl ExternalUrl
ExternalUrl : https://mail.contoso.com/owa
```

Notice that if you change the URL for OWA, the ECP URL should be changed as well.

How it works...

Each CAS server hosts virtual directories in IIS that support OWA, **Exchange Control Panel (ECP)**, ActiveSync, **Offline Address Book (OAB)**, and **Exchange Web Services (EWS)**. Each of these services has an associated cmdlet set that can be used to manage the settings of each virtual directory. One of the most common configuration changes made during the deployment process is modifying the internal and external URLs for each of these services. The required configuration varies greatly depending on a number of factors in your environment, especially in larger multisite environments.

The following cmdlets can be used to modify several settings for each virtual directory, including the values for the internal and external URLs:

▶ `Set-ActiveSyncVirtualDirectory`: This is used to configure the internal and external URL values of the Microsoft-Server-ActiveSync virtual directory. Use the `InternalUrl` and `ExternalUrl` parameters to change the values.

▶ `Set-EcpVirtualDirectory`: This is used to configure the internal and external URL values of the ECP virtual directory. Use the `InternalUrl` and `ExternalUrl` parameters to change the values.

▶ `Set-OabVirtualDirectory`: This is used to configure the internal and external URL values of the OAB virtual directory. Use the `InternalUrl` and `ExternalUrl` parameters to change the values.

▶ `Set-OwaVirtualDirectory`: This is used to configure the internal and external URL values of the OWA virtual directory. Use the `InternalUrl` and `ExternalUrl` parameters to change the values.

▶ `Set-WebServicesVirtualDirectory`: This is used to configure the internal and external URL values of the EWS virtual directory. Use the `InternalUrl` and `ExternalUrl` parameters to change the values.

When running each of these cmdlets, you need to identify the virtual directory in question. For example, when modifying the external URL of the ECP virtual directory, the command might look similar to this:

```
Set-EcpVirtualDirectory -Identity 'CAS1\ecp (Default Web Site)' `
-ExternalUrl https://mail.contoso.com/ecp
```

The syntax here is similar to the first example where we modified the OWA virtual directory; the only difference is that the cmdlet name and the `ExternalUrl` value have changed. Notice that the identity of the virtual directory is in the format of `ServerName\VirtualDirectoryName (WebsiteName)`. The reason this needs to be done is because it's possible, but not very common, for a particular CAS server to be running more than one site in IIS, containing virtual directories for each of these CAS services.

If you are like most folks and have only the default website running in IIS, you can also take advantage of the pipeline if you forget the syntax needed to specify the identity of the virtual directory. For example, run the following command:

```
Get-EcpVirtualDirectory -Server cas1 |
Set-EcpVirtualDirectory -ExternalUrl https://mail.contoso.com/ecp
```

The preceding pipeline command makes the same change, as shown previously. This time, we're using the Get-EcpVirtualDirectory cmdlet, with the -Server parameter to identify the CAS server. We then pipe the resulting object to the Set-EcpVirtualDirectory cmdlet that makes the change to the ExternalUrl value.

> It is important to configure the URLs correctly, since this have an impact on end users. If they are not correctly configured and use a name that is not included in the certificate, then the end users will be prompted when they are trying to reach the services, or even worse, when the services are broken and not reachable.

There's more...

If you allow the access to Exchange through Outlook Anywhere, you'll need to configure the external URLs that will be handed to Outlook clients for services, such as ECP, OAB, and EWS. These URLs may need to point to an FQDN that resolves to a load balancer **Virtual IP Address** (**VIP**) or to your reverse proxy infrastructure, such as TMG or third-party solutions.

In addition, you'll probably want to configure your internal URLs to point to an FQDN that resolves to your internal load balancer VIP. In this situation, you want to make sure you do not modify the internal URL for both the OWA and ECP virtual directories in non-Internet-facing sites. This is because OWA and ECP connections from the Internet-facing CAS server will be proxied to the servers in the non-Internet-facing sites, and if the internal FQDN of the CAS server is not set on each these virtual directories, Kerberos authentication will fail and the user will not be able to access their mailbox.

Finally, for load balanced CAS servers, you'll want to configure the AutoDiscover internal URL so that it also points to an FQDN that resolves to your load balancer VIP. The syntax for this would look like the following:

```
Set-ClientAccessServer -Identity cas1 `
-AutoDiscoverServiceInternalUri `
https://mail.contoso.com/Autodiscover/Autodiscover.xml
```

Of course, you'll need to make all the changes to internal and external URLs on all the CAS servers.

Command syntax for the remaining virtual directories

We've already looked at the syntax for modifying both OWA and ECP and internal and external URLs; now, let's take a look at how we can do this for the remaining virtual directories. In these examples, we'll configure the external URL value using the `-ExternalUrl` parameter. If you need to modify the internal URL, simply use the `-InternalUrl` parameter.

To configure the external URL of the OAB, use the following syntax:

```
Set-OABVirtualDirectory -Identity "cas1\oab (Default Web Site)" `
-ExternalUrl https://mail.contoso.com/oab
```

To configure the external URL of the ActiveSync virtual directory, use the following syntax:

```
Set-ActivesyncVirtualDirectory -Identity `
"cas1\Microsoft-Server-ActiveSync (Default Web Site)" `
-ExternalURL https://mail.contoso.com/Microsoft-Server-Activesync
```

To configure the EWS virtual directory, use the following syntax:

```
Set-WebServicesVirtualDirectory -Identity `
"cas1\EWS (Default Web Site)" `
-ExternalUrl https://mail.contoso.com/ews/exchange.asmx
```

In each example, we're setting the value on the `cas1` server. When running these commands or using them in a script, replace the server name with the name of the appropriate CAS server.

Taking it one step further

In *Chapter 1*, *PowerShell Key Concepts,* we went through an introduction about **Desired State Configuration** (**DSC**), and we can now take the advantage of using the DSC server to push out a configuration to the Exchange server(s). We will utilize a module called xExchange module to configure the OWA URLs. Since we have used the pull mode before, notice the `-Force` parameter that is used.

The following example is a modified example from the xExchange module:

```
$configData = @{
  AllNodes = @(
    @{
      NodeName = '*'
      CertificateFile = 'C:\publickey.cer'
      Thumbprint = 'C72FA4F17DBE0C5F88522AA49DF86EB410B23A71'
    }
  @{
    NodeName = 'tlex01.testlabs.se'
```

```
        CASID = 'Site1CAS'
    }
  );
  Site1CAS = @(
    @{
        InternalNLBFqdn = 'mail.contoso.com'
        ExternalNLBFqdn = 'mail.contoso.com'
        AutoDiscoverSiteScope = 'Default-First-Site-Name'
        OABsToDistribute = 'Default Offline Address Book'
    }
  );
}
Configuration ConfigureVirtualDirectories
{
  param
    (
        [PSCredential]$ShellCreds
    )
  Import-DscResource -Module xExchange
  Node $AllNodes.NodeName
  {
    $casSettings = $ConfigurationData[$Node.CASId]
    #Thumbprint of the certificate used to decrypt credentials on the
target node
    LocalConfigurationManager
    {
      CertificateId = $Node.Thumbprint
    }
    xExchOwaVirtualDirectory OWAVdir
    {
      Identity = "$($Node.NodeName)\owa (Default Web Site)"
      Credential = $ShellCreds
      BasicAuthentication = $true
      ExternalAuthenticationMethods = 'Fba'
      ExternalUrl = "https://$($casSettings.ExternalNLBFqdn)/owa"
      FormsAuthentication = $true
      InternalUrl = "https://$($casSettings.InternalNLBFqdn)/owa"
      WindowsAuthentication = $false
      AllowServiceRestart = $true
    }
  }
}
if ($ShellCreds -eq $null)
{
```

```
    $ShellCreds = Get-Credential -Message 'Enter credentials for
establishing Remote Powershell sessions to Exchange'
}
ConfigureVirtualDirectories -ConfigurationData $configData - `
ShellCreds $ShellCreds
Set-DscLocalConfigurationManager -Path `
.\ConfigureVirtualDirectories `
-Verbose
Start-DscConfiguration -Path .\ConfigureVirtualDirectories - `
Verbose -Wait -Force
```

The preceding example is using a trusted certificate for encrypting and decrypting the password for creating a remote PowerShell session. When running this script, a similar result will be shown as follows:

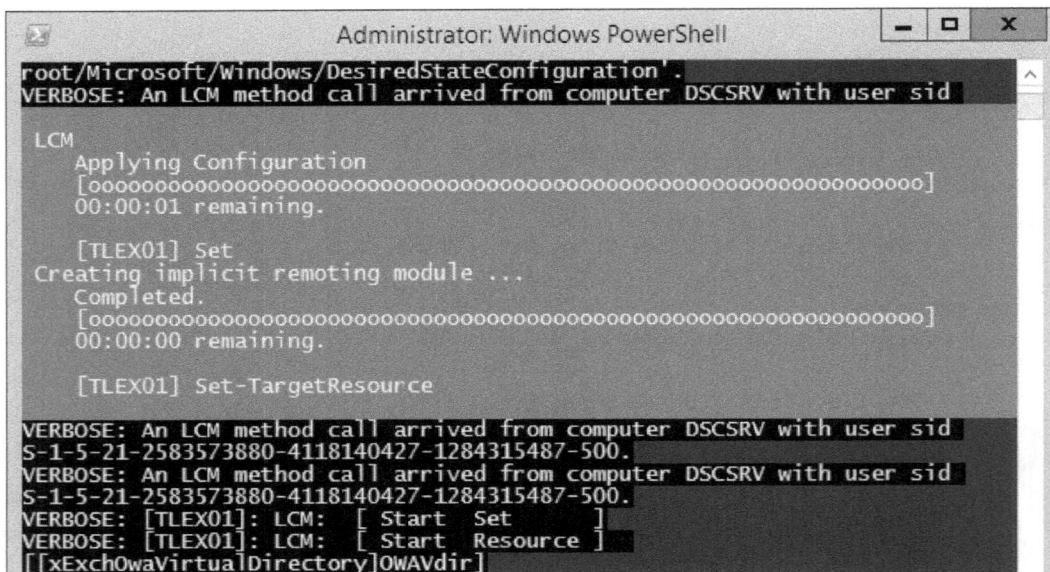

The three final rows in the example are explained as follows:

- `ConfigureVirtualDirectories`: This compiles the script
- `Set-DscLocalConfigurationManager`: This sets up the **Local Configuration Manager** (**LCM**) on the Exchange server to decrypt the credentials
- `Start-DscConfiguration`: This pushes the configuration to the Exchange server

The example using the Exchange module is just to show you an overview of how it can be used. The module can be used to configure all URLs, databases, Outlook Anywhere, and many more.

The module is updated over time at a pretty fast pace; to stay updated, I would recommend that you subscribe to the PowerShell team blog using RSS at `http://blogs.msdn.com/b/powershell/`.

See also

- ▸ *Generating a certificate request* in Chapter 10, *Exchange Security*
- ▸ *Installing certificates and enabling services* in Chapter 10, *Exchange Security*
- ▸ *Importing certificates on multiple Exchange servers* in Chapter 10, *Exchange Security*

Managing the Outlook Anywhere settings

With the new CAS architecture in place, Outlook Anywhere needs to be configured if Outlook is going to be used to access mailboxes and features. This feature allows Outlook clients to connect to Exchange through RPCs encapsulated into an HTTPS connection. This allows easy internal and external access to Exchange from Outlook, as there is no need to open RPC ports on firewalls. In this recipe, we'll take a look at how you can use the Exchange Management Shell to manage Outlook Anywhere settings.

How to do it...

By default, the Outlook Anywhere feature is enabled, but it needs to be configured with the correct hostname and authentication values. This is done using the `Set-OutlookAnywhere` cmdlet. See the following example:

```
Set-OutlookAnywhere -Identity 'CAS1\Rpc (Default Web Site)' `
-ExternalHostname mail.contoso.com `
-ExternalClientRequireSsl $true `
-InternalHostname mail.contoso.com `
-InternalClientRequireSsl $true `
-ExternalClientAuthenticationMethod Basic `
-InternalClientAuthenticationMethod Ntlm `
-SSLOffloading $false
```

In the preceding example, Outlook Anywhere is configured on the CAS1 server.

How it works...

Before enabling Outlook Anywhere, there are two prerequisites that need to be met. First, you need to ensure that your CAS server has a valid SSL certificate installed from a **certificate authority** (**CA**) that is trusted by your client machines. Exchange installs a self-signed certificate by default, but this will not be trusted by client workstations.

In addition, you'll need to make sure that the Microsoft Windows RPC over HTTP Proxy component is installed on the server. This is typically done before the installation of Exchange when all of the operating system prerequisites are installed.

When running the `Set-OutlookAnywhere` cmdlet, you can see that we specified the `ExternalHostname` property. This will be the FQDN that Outlook clients will use to connect to Exchange. You'll need to make sure that you have a DNS record created for this FQDN that resolves to your CAS server or to your reverse proxy infrastructure, such as ISA or TMG. A much appreciated feature in Exchange 2013 is that the `InternalHostname` property can be configured. This means that the `InternalUrl` parameter can be something else, which most likely is pointed to the internal load balancer VIP to spread the load.

When specifying a value for the `ExternalClientAuthenticationMethod` and `InternalClientAuthenticationMethod` parameters, you'll want to use either `Basic` or `NTLM`. This setting determines how users authenticate to Outlook Anywhere. When using the `Basic` authentication, the user's password is sent to the server in plain text, but the connection is secured by SSL. If you have workstations, which are not domain-joined, that will connect to Exchange through Outlook Anywhere, you'll need to use the `Basic` authentication.

If only domain-joined clients connect to Outlook Anywhere, such as roaming users with laptops that connect from home; using the `NTLM` authentication is a much more secure option for the `ClientAuthenticationMethod` property. When using `NTLM`, a user's password is not sent to the server; instead, `NTLM` sends a hashed value of the user's credentials to the server. Another benefit of using `NTLM` is that Outlook clients will not be prompted for their credentials when connecting to Outlook Anywhere. Keep in mind that if you are publishing Outlook Anywhere with a reverse proxy solution, such as TMG, you'll need to use **Kerberos Constrained Delegation** (**KCD**), which allows the TMG server to request a Kerberos service ticket from Active Directory on behalf of the user. Also, remember that the `NTLM` authentication may not work correctly with some firewalls; check with your firewall manufacturer's documentation for details.

Finally, `SSLOffloading` allows the CAS server to offload the encryption and decryption of the SSL connections to a third-party device. Unless you have an SSL offloading solution in place, set the `-SSLOffloading` parameter to `$false`. However, this parameter is not required if you don't use SSL offloading.

There's more...

In addition to enabling Outlook Anywhere from the shell, we can also perform some other routine tasks. For example, to view the Outlook Anywhere configuration, use the Get-OutlookAnywhere cmdlet, as follows:

```
[PS] C:\>Get-OutlookAnywhere | fl ServerName,ExternalHostname,
InternalHostname

ServerName : CAS1

ExternalHostname : mail.contoso.com

InternalHostname : mail.contoso.com
```

The Get-OutlookAnywhere cmdlet will return the configuration information for servers that have the Outlook Anywhere feature enabled.

If at any time you need to change the authentication method or external host name for Outlook Anywhere, you can use the Set-OutlookAnywhere cmdlet as follows:

```
Set-OutlookAnywhere -Identity 'CAS1\Rpc (Default Web Site)' `
-ExternalHostname 'outlook.contoso.com'
```

Notice that the identity of the server needs to be specified in the format of *ServerName\VirtualDirectoryName (WebsiteName)*.

See also

- ▸ *Generating a certificate request* in *Chapter 10, Exchange Security*
- ▸ *Installing certificates and enabling services* in *Chapter 10, Exchange Security*
- ▸ *Importing certificates on multiple Exchange servers* in *Chapter 10, Exchange Security*

Blocking Outlook clients from connecting to Exchange

Exchange gives you plenty of options to block clients from connecting to mailboxes, depending on the version of the Outlook client and the method used to access the mailbox. In this recipe, you'll learn how to configure these options using the Exchange Management Shell.

How to do it...

Let's take a look at how to block Outlook clients from connecting to Exchange using the following steps:

1. The `Set-CASMailbox` cmdlet can be used to block MAPI access to mailboxes based on several factors. For example, we can prevent an individual user from using Outlook to connect using Outlook Anywhere:

    ```
    Set-CASMailbox -Identity dsmith -MAPIBlockOutlookRpcHttp $true
    ```

2. In addition, we can also prevent a user whose Outlook is not configured in cached mode from connecting to their mailbox using the following command:

    ```
    Set-CASMailbox -Identity dsmith `
    -MAPIBlockOutlookNonCachedMode $true
    ```

    In both the cases, the user can still access their mailbox using OWA; as long as the `OWAEnabled` property is set to `$true`.

3. You can also block users from connecting to clients based on their Outlook version. The following command will block all versions of Outlook earlier than 2007 for every mailbox in the organization:

    ```
    Get-CASMailbox -Resultsize Unlimited |
    Set-CASMailbox -MAPIBlockOutlookVersions '-11.9.9'
    ```

4. To find all the mailboxes in an organization that have `MAPIBlockOutlookVersions` defined, run the following command:

    ```
    Get-CASMailbox -ResultSize Unlimited |
    ?{$_.MAPIBlockOutlookVersions}
    ```

5. To remove the restriction on a single mailbox, use the following command:

    ```
    Set-CASMailbox dsmith -MAPIBlockOutlookVersions $null
    ```

6. To remove the restriction on the entire organization, use the following command:

    ```
    Get-CASMailbox -ResultSize Unlimited |
    Set-CASMailbox -MAPIBlockOutlookVersions $null
    ```

How it works...

The `Set-CASMailbox` cmdlet allows you to configure which protocols and services a particular mailbox user can access. To determine the existing settings, we can use the `Get-CASMailbox` cmdlet. For instance, if you need to retrieve all the users that have been blocked from connecting to their mailboxes in non-cached mode, use the following command:

```
Get-CASMailbox | Where-Object{$_.MAPIBlockOutlookNonCachedMode}
```

To find all the mailboxes blocked from using Outlook Anywhere, the command is almost identical, just reference the correct property name:

```
Get-CASMailbox | Where-Object{$_.MAPIBlockOutlookRpcHttp}
```

In both the examples, we pipe the `Get-CASMailbox` cmdlet to the `Where-Object` cmdlet. Inside the filter, we will check to see whether the property values evaluate as `$true`. If that is the case, the command will return a list of users who have the corresponding setting enabled.

As always, we can use pipelining to enable or disable these settings for multiple users in a single command. Let's say that we want to block all of the users in the `Sales` OU from using Outlook Anywhere:

```
Get-CASMailbox -OrganizationalUnit contoso.com/Sales |
Set-CASMailbox -MAPIBlockOutlookRpcHttp $true
```

To remove this restriction, use the same command, but this time, set the parameter value to `$false`:

```
Get-CASMailbox -OrganizationalUnit contoso.com/Sales |
Set-CASMailbox -MAPIBlockOutlookRpcHttp $false
```

In both the cases, the `Get-CASMailbox` cmdlet retrieves every mailbox from the `Sales` OU and pipes the object's output by the command to the `Set-CASMailbox` cmdlet that then makes the change.

As we saw earlier, Outlook client versions can be blocked on a per-mailbox basis using the `Set-CASMailbox` cmdlet. This is done by specifying the client version using the `MAPIBlockOutlookVersions` parameter.

In Exchange 2007, you could check the `ClientVersion` property returned by the `Get-LogonStatistics` cmdlet to determine the version numbers used by Outlook clients in the organization. In Exchange 2013, the `ClientVersion` property will be reported based on the CAS server, making the connection to the mailbox server, not the actual Outlook client. If you need to determine the specific client versions in your environment, you can use the **Help | About** screen in Outlook to determine the exact version number.

A version number is made up of a major, minor, and build number. Here are a few version numbers for some commonly used versions of Outlook:

- ▸ Outlook 2003 SP2: 11.6568.6568
- ▸ Outlook 2007 RTM: 12.4518.1014
- ▸ Outlook 2010 RTM: 14.0.4760.1000
- ▸ Outlook 2013 RTM: 15.0.4420.1017

The major build numbers are consistent across the entire Office Suite, and never change. For example, for Office 2003, the build number is 11, for Office 2007, the build number is 12, for Office 2010, the build number is 14, and so on.

The minor and build numbers will change, depending on the hotfixes and service packs deployed to the clients. Therefore, the `-MAPIBlockOutlookVersions` parameter will accept a range of values that will allow you to be very specific about which versions should be blocked. You can even specify multiple version ranges and separate each one by a semicolon.

For example, the following command can be used to block access to Exchange for all versions of Outlook below 2007 and 2010:

```
Set-CASMailbox dsmith -MAPIBlockOutlookVersions '-5.9.9;7.0.0-11.9.9'
```

As you can see here, we've specified two values. The first value indicates that any client version below 5.9.9 will be unable to connect to this mailbox. The second value specifies a range from 7 to 11.9.9, which effectively blocks all access to any client versioned lower than 12.x.x, except for those versioned at 6.x.x. This allows only Outlook 2007 and 2010 clients to connect to this mailbox. It also allows Exchange server MAPI connections from other servers, identified using 6.x.x version numbers.

Keep in mind that when you are making these changes, they will not take effect right away. If you want to force this change so that it is effective immediately, restart the RPC CAS service on the Mailbox server used to access the mailbox. Make sure to do this outside the production hours, as it will knock every user connected to that CAS server offline.

There's more...

In addition to blocking Outlook versions at the mailbox level, we can also block them at the server level. Since the MAPI client endpoint is now at the Mailbox role again, we can use the `Set-RPCClientAccess` cmdlet to accomplish this:

```
Set-RpcClientAccess -Server cas1 `
-BlockedClientVersions '-5.9.9;7.0.0-13.9.9'
```

You can see here that we used the `BlockedClientVersions` parameter to define the client versions that should be blocked, and it works in exactly the same way as it does when using the `Set-CASMailbox` cmdlet. In this example, all client versions below Outlook 2010, with the exception of client versions 6.x.x, will be blocked at the CAS server level. Notice that the server name has been specified with this command, and you'll need to run it against each Mailbox server that should block specific Outlook versions.

Reporting on active OWA and RPC connections

One of the nice things about using PowerShell to manage Exchange is that you have a great deal of flexibility when it comes to solving problems. When the Exchange Management Shell does not provide a cmdlet that specifically meets your needs, you can often tap into other resources, which are accessible through PowerShell. This recipe provides a great example for this. In this section, we'll use PowerShell to query the performance counter data to determine the number of active OWA and HTTP/RPC (Outlook Anywhere) connections on one or more Mailbox servers.

How to do it...

Let's see how to report on active OWA and RPC connections using the following steps:

1. To determine the number of users currently logged into OWA on a Mailbox server, use the following command syntax:

   ```
   Get-Counter -Counter '\\tlex01\MSExchange OWA\Current Users'
   ```

   This retrieves the total number of users logged into OWA on the TLEX01 server. The output of this command will look similar to the following screenshot:

   In the preceding screenshot, we can see that two users are currently logged on to OWA.

2. To find the total number of HTTP/RPC (Outlook Anywhere) connections, we simply need to use another performance counter:

   ```
   Get-Counter '\\tlex01\MSExchange RpcClientAccess\User Count'
   ```

Similar to the previous example, the total number of HTTP/RPC connects will be reported, as shown in the following screenshot:

```
                          Machine: tlex01.testlabs.se              _  □  x
[PS] C:\Scripts>Get-Counter -Counter "\\tlex01\MSExchange RpcClientAccess\U
ser Count"

Timestamp                      CounterSamples
---------                      --------------
3/24/2015 8:56:59 PM           \\tlex01\msexchange rpcclientaccess\user count :
                               2
```

How it works...

The `Get-Counter` cmdlet can be used to retrieve the performance counter data from both local and remote machines. In the previous example, we collected the total number of current OWA users using the `\MSExchange OWA\Current Users` counter and the total number of HTTP/RPC connections using the `MSExchange RpcClientAccess\User Count` counter on the MBX1 server.

In both these examples, we've specified the computer name in the counter name assigned to the `-Counter` parameter. Another way to gather the performance counter data from a remote computer is to use the `-ComputerName` parameter, as shown in the following command:

```
Get-Counter 'MSExchange OWA\Current Unique Users' `
-ComputerName tlex01,tlex02
```

Notice that in the alternate syntax used previously, we've removed the computer name from the counter name, and we have assigned a list of server names using the `-ComputerName` parameter. This is a quick way to check the number of connections on multiple computers.

There are many Exchange-related performance counters on each Exchange server. You can also use the `Get-Counter` cmdlet to discover these counters:

```
Get-Counter -ListSet *owa* -ComputerName cas1 |
Select-Object -expand paths
```

This will do a wildcard search and return a list of counters on the specified server that have the letters `owa` in their name. You can use this syntax to quickly find the counter names that can be used with the `Get-Counter` cmdlet.

There's more...

To create more advanced and customizable reports, we can create a PowerShell function that returns a custom object with only the information we're interested in. Add the following function to your shell session:

```
function Get-ActiveUsers {
  [CmdletBinding()]
  param(
    [Parameter(Position=0,
    ValueFromPipelineByPropertyName=$true,
    Mandatory=$true)]
    [string[]]
    $Name
  )
  process {
    $Name | %{
      $RPC = Get-Counter "\MSExchange RpcClientAccess\User Count"
      -ComputerName $_
      $OWA = Get-Counter "\MSExchange OWA\Current Unique Users" `
      -ComputerName $_
      New-Object PSObject -Property @{
        Server = $_
        'RPC Client Access' = $RPC.CounterSamples[0].CookedValue
        'Outlook Web App' = $OWA.CounterSamples[0].CookedValue
      }
    }
  }
}
```

You can call the function and provide one or more Mailbox server names that you'd like to generate the report for, as shown in the following screenshot:

If you look closely at the code in the function, you'll notice that we've added some attributes to the $Name parameter. As you can see, in addition to being a mandatory parameter, it also accepts its value from the pipeline by a property name. This means that, instead of calling the function and providing a list of server names, we can leverage the objects that are returned by the Get-MailboxServer cmdlet to quickly generate a report using a pipeline command:

```
Machine: tlex01.testlabs.se                                    _  □  x

[PS] C:\Scripts>Get-MailboxServer | Get-ActiveUsers

        RPC Client Access Server                       Outlook Web App
        ------------------------                       ---------------
                        2 TLEX01                                      2
```

You can continue to pipe this command down to the Export-CSV or ConvertTo-Html cmdlet to generate an external report file that can be viewed outside the shell.

See also

▸   *Understanding the pipeline* in *Chapter 1, PowerShell Key Concepts*

Controlling ActiveSync device access

With the increase of smartphones being deployed, and the fact that ActiveSync can now be used pretty much on all mobile devices, Exchange 2010 introduced new functions that allowed you to control which devices are able to connect to your server. Using device access rules, you can define the specific devices or device types that can form an ActiveSync partnership with an Exchange server. This recipe will explore the options that can be used to allow, block, or quarantine ActiveSync devices using the Exchange Management Shell for Exchange 2013.

How to do it...

By default, there is an organization-wide configuration setting that will allow any ActiveSync device to connect to Exchange. You can modify this so that all devices are initially quarantined and need to be approved by an administrator before they can gain access. To implement this, use the following steps:

1.   First run the following command:

    ```
    Set-ActiveSyncOrganizationSettings -DefaultAccessLevel `
    Quarantine -AdminMailRecipients administrator@contoso.com
    ```

2. After the previous command completes, all the devices that attempt to form an ActiveSync device partnership will be quarantined. When a device is quarantined, the address provided by the `-AdminMailRecipients` parameter will be notified via e-mail. The user will also receive a message on their mobile device informing them that access needs to be granted by an administrator before they'll be able to access any content. Based on the information in the e-mail message, the administrator can choose to enable the device using the `Set-CASMailbox` cmdlet:

```
Set-CASMailbox -Identity dsmith -ActiveSyncAllowedDeviceIDs `
BAD73E6E02156460E800185977C03182
```

3. Once the command has been run, the user will be able to connect to your server.

How it works...

In Exchange 2013, you can manage the devices in the **Exchange Control Panel** (**ECP**), and, of course, the cmdlets can still be used if you want to do this work from the shell.

When configuring the ActiveSync organization settings, you have the option of adding a custom message that will be sent to the user when they receive the e-mail notification, explaining that their device has been quarantined. Use the `-UserMailInsert` parameter when running the `Set-ActiveSyncOrganizationSettings` cmdlet to configure this setting:

```
Set-ActiveSyncOrganizationSettings -DefaultAccessLevel `
Quarantine -AdminMailRecipients helpdesk@contoso.com `
-UserMailInsert 'Call the Help Desk for immediate assistance'
```

In addition to the administrative e-mail notifications, you can find all the devices that are currently in a quarantined state using the `Get-ActiveSync` device cmdlet:

```
Get-MobileDevice | ?{$_.DeviceAccessState -eq 'Quarantined'} |
fl UserDisplayName,DeviceAccessState,DeviceID
```

The output of the preceding command will be similar to the following screenshot:

This command retrieves ActiveSync devices and is filtered on the `DeviceAccessState` property. The output will provide the username, device access state, and the `DeviceID` that can be used to allow access using the `Set-CASMailbox` cmdlet.

There's more...

Manual approval of ActiveSync devices may not be something you want to take on as an administrative task. An alternative to this is to use device access rules. For instance, let's say that you want to block all ActiveSync devices that are not iPhone devices. You could set the `DefaultAccessLevel` property for the organization to `Block` and create a device access rule allowing only those devices:

```
New-ActiveSyncDeviceAccessRule -Characteristic DeviceType `
-QueryString iPhone -AccessLevel Allow
```

You can create multiple access rules for different types of devices if needed. To determine the device type, you can use the `Get-MobileDevice` cmdlet. The property values of `DeviceModel`, `DeviceType`, `DeviceOS`, `DeviceUserAgent`, and `XMSWLHeader` can be used with the `-QueryString` parameter to define the device type when creating a device access rule.

See also

- *Reporting on ActiveSync devices*
- *Managing ActiveSync, OWA, POP3, and IMAP4 mailbox settings*

Reporting on ActiveSync devices

The Exchange Management Shell provides several cmdlets that can be used for generating reports. We can obtain information about users and their devices, and we can also generate reports based on the end user activity and server usage. In this recipe, we'll take a look at how we can use these cmdlets to generate multiple ActiveSync reports from the Exchange Management Shell.

How to do it...

Let's see how to generate reports on ActiveSync devices using the following steps:

1. To generate a report for an individual user's device synchronization status, use the following command:

```
Get-MobileDeviceStatistics -Mailbox nate
```

2. This cmdlet will output a lot of information, some of which may not be very interesting. You can limit the data returned by selecting only the properties that provide useful information:

```
Get-MobileDeviceStatistics -Mailbox nate |
select LastSuccessSync,Status,DevicePhoneNumber,`
DeviceType
```

The output of the previous command will look similar to the following screenshot:

3. To export this information, you can pipe the command even further to the Export-CSV cmdlet:

```
Get-MobileDeviceStatistics -Mailbox nate |
select LastSuccessSync,Status,DevicePhoneNumber,`
DeviceType | Export-CSV -Path c:\report.csv -NoType
```

How it works...

Using the Get-MobileDeviceStatistics cmdlet, we can retrieve the mobile phones that are configured to synchronize with a particular user's mailbox. As you can see from the previous examples, it's quite easy to generate a report for an individual user. This cmdlet requires that you either specify the identity of the ActiveSync device or the mailbox of the owner. In order to generate reports based on statistics for multiple devices, we have a couple of options.

First, we can use the Get-MobileDevice cmdlet to retrieve a list of allowed devices and then pipe the results to the Get-MobileDeviceStatistics cmdlet:

```
$dev = Get-MobileDevice | ?{$_.DeviceAccessState -eq 'Allowed'}
$dev | ForEach-Object {
  $mailbox = $_.UserDisplayName
  $stats = Get-MobileDeviceStatistics -Identity $_
  $stats | Select-Object @{n="Mailbox";e={$mailbox}},
  LastSuccessSync,
  Status,
```

```
    DevicePhoneNumber,

    DeviceType

}
```

The preceding code retrieves all the ActiveSync devices with the `Allowed` access state. We loop through each device, retrieve the device statistics for each one, and return several properties that provide details about the user and the status of their device. Notice that, in the example, we're using a calculated property to return the mailbox name, since that information is not included in the output of the `Get-MobileDeviceStatistics` cmdlet.

The other method for obtaining this information is using the `Get-CASMailbox` cmdlet to find all the users with an ActiveSync device partnership, and then sending those objects down the pipeline to the `Get-MobileDeviceStatistics` cmdlet:

```
$mbx = Get-CASMailbox | ?{$_.HasActiveSyncDevicePartnership}

$mbx | ForEach-Object {

    $mailbox = $_.Name

    $stats = Get-MobileDeviceStatistics -Mailbox $mailbox

    $stats | Select-Object @{n="Mailbox";e={$mailbox}},

    LastSuccessSync,

    Status,

    DevicePhoneNumber,

    DeviceType

}
```

Similar to the previous example, we loop through each mailbox, retrieve the ActiveSync statistics, and then return the same properties as before. This version is considerably slower, since it has to first check every mailbox to determine whether a device partnership exists, but if you need specific filtering capabilities based on the properties returned by the `Get-CASMailbox` cmdlet, this may be a useful method. This will also filter out system mailboxes.

There's more...

The Exchange Management Shell also provides the `Export-ActiveSyncLog` cmdlet that can be used to generate reports based on ActiveSync usage. The cmdlet generates reports based on IIS log files and then outputs the following six separate CSV files that contain detailed information about the usage of ActiveSync devices:

- ▶ `Users.csv`: This provides details on ActiveSync usage for each user that includes the number of sent and received items

- ▶ `UserAgents.csv`: This provides details on the various user agents used by devices to access Exchange

- ▶ `StatusCodes.csv`: This provides the HTTP response code issued to ActiveSync clients

- ▶ `Servers.csv`: This provides details on the server usage, including total number of bytes sent and received

- ▶ `PolicyCompliance.csv`: This provides details on ActiveSync device compliance, such as the total number of compliant, noncompliant, and partially compliant devices

- ▶ `Hourly.csv`: This provides an hourly breakdown of the device synchronization activity

The cmdlet supports a number of parameters that can be used to generate reports. For example, the following command generates reports for ActiveSync activity taking place on March 24, 2015:

```
Export-ActiveSyncLog `
-Filename C:\inetpub\logs\LogFiles\W3SVC1\u_ex150324.log `
-OutputPath c:\report
```

When running this command, make sure that the directory specified for the output path has already been created. The given command generates the six CSV files discussed previously in the `c:\report` folder.

To generate reports for multiple log files, you'll need to do a little extra work. For example, run the following command:

```
$path = "C:\inetpub\logs\LogFiles\W3SVC1\"
Get-ChildItem -Path $path -Filter u_ex1503*.log | %{
  Export-ActiveSyncLog -Filename $_.fullname `
  -OutputPrefix $_.basename `
  -OutputPath c:\report
}
```

Here, we're using the `Get-ChildItem` cmdlet to retrieve a list of log files from March 2015. Each time we run the `Export-ActiveSyncLog` cmdlet for a log file, a new set of six CSV reports will be generated. Since we can only define one `OutputPath`, we use the log file base name as a prefix for each CSV report file generated. After the cmdlet has been run, six CSV reports for each day of the month will be located in the `c:\report` directory. You can read these reports in the shell using the `Import-CSV` cmdlet, or open them in Excel or Notepad for review.

See also

▶ *Creating custom objects* in *Chapter 1, PowerShell Key Concepts*

▶ *Controlling ActiveSync device access*

▶ *Managing ActiveSync, OWA, POP3, and IMAP4 mailbox settings*

8

Managing Transport Servers

In this chapter, we will cover the following topics:

- ▸ Managing connectors
- ▸ Configuring transport limits
- ▸ Allowing application servers to relay mail
- ▸ Working with custom DSN messages
- ▸ Managing connectivity and protocol logs
- ▸ Searching message tracking logs
- ▸ Working with messages in transport queues
- ▸ Searching anti-spam agent logs
- ▸ Implementing a header firewall
- ▸ Configuring the Edge Transport server role
- ▸ Managing the Edge Transport server role

Introduction

In Exchange 2013, SP1 (CU4) the Edge Transport was re ntroduced. We got the Edge Transport role in SP1 together with the CAS and Mailbox. In Exchange 2013, the CAS server is stateless, which means that by default it does not have any queue data; the queue is moved and placed on the Mailbox server, however, this can be changed. A benefit of the new architecture is that it is easier to manage and scale out the Exchange environment. The SMTP frontend service scales are based on a number of connections, which means if you need more servers, then you can scale out easily by adding more servers.

Exchange 2007 and 2010 Edge Transport server are supported to work together with an Exchange 2013 Mailbox server, for example, in EdgeSync.

In addition to routing messages, you can apply rules, configure settings, and enforce limits on messages as they pass through the servers in your environment. Transport agents can be used to provide basic anti-spam protection, and both roles implement detailed logging capabilities that can be leveraged from the shell. In this chapter, we'll take a look at several useful scripting techniques that include imposing limits and rules on messages and generating detailed reports on mail flow statistics.

Performing some basic steps

To work with the code samples in this chapter, follow these steps to launch the Exchange Management Shell:

1. Log on to a workstation or server with the Exchange Management tools installed.

2. You can connect using a remote PowerShell if you, for some reason, don't have Exchange Management tools installed. Use the following command:

```
$Session = New-PSSession -ConfigurationName `
Microsoft.Exchange -ConnectionUri `

http://tlex01/PowerShell/ -Authentication Kerberos

Import-PSSession $Session
```

3. Open the Exchange Management Shell by navigating to **Start | All Programs | Exchange Server 2013**.

4. Click on the **Exchange Management Shell** shortcut.

Remember to start the Exchange Management Shell using **Run as administrator** to avoid permission problems.

In this chapter, you might notice that in the examples of cmdlets I have used the back tick (`` ` ``) character to break up long commands into multiple lines. The purpose of this is to make it easier to read. The back ticks are not required and should only be used if needed.

Managing connectors

Exchange 2013 uses both send and receive connectors to transmit and accept messages from other servers. These connectors can be managed from within the **Exchange Admin Center** (**EAC**), but the addition, configuration, and removal of these connectors can also be completely managed from the Exchange Management Shell. In this recipe, we'll take a look at the various cmdlets that can be used to manage, send, and receive connectors. The receive connectors are maintained at the server level, while the send connectors are being maintained at an organization level.

How to do it...

Let's see how to create the send and receive connectors using the following steps:

1. To create a send connector, use the `New-SendConnector` cmdlet:

   ```
   New-SendConnector -Name Internet `
   -Usage Internet `
   -AddressSpaces 'SMTP:*;1' `
   -IsScopedConnector $false `
   -DNSRoutingEnabled $false `
   -SmartHosts smtp.contoso.com `
   -SmartHostAuthMechanism None `
   -UseExternalDNSServersEnabled $false `
   -SourceTransportServers mb1
   ```

2. Receive connectors can be created on each Exchange server using the `New-ReceiveConnector` cmdlet:

   ```
   New-ReceiveConnector -Name 'Inbound from DMZ' `
   -Usage 'Custom' `
   -Bindings '192.168.1.245:25' `
   -Fqdn mail.contoso.com `
   -RemoteIPRanges '172.16.23.0/24' `
   -PermissionGroups AnonymousUsers `
   -Server cas1
   ```

How it works...

By default, Exchange does not create send connectors used for routing messages to the Internet, and they need to be created manually using either EAC or the shell. However, there is a hidden implicit send connector that is used to send a mail between transport servers within the organization, and you don't need to worry about creating send connectors for internal mail flow.

In the previous example, we used the `New-SendConnector` cmdlet to create an Internet send connector on a Mailbox server. This cmdlet provides a number of options that control how the connector is configured. In this case, we've configured an address space of `SMTP:*;1`, which specifies that all messages addressed to recipients outside the organization will be sent through this connector. Instead of using DNS to route the messages, we're forwarding all messages to a smart host called `smtp.contoso.com`, which in this case, would be an SMTP gateway in the perimeter network. The source Mailbox server has been configured using the server name `mb1`, which means that any message destined for the Internet will be first routed through this server before being forwarded to the smart host. There are over 30 parameters available with this cmdlet, so you'll want to review the help file to determine how to configure the settings based on your needs. To do this, run `Get-Help New-SendConnector -Full`.

After a send connector has been created, its settings can be modified using the `Set-SendConnector` cmdlet. The following example will modify our previous Internet send connector by replacing the associated address spaces:

```
Set-SendConnector -Identity Internet `
-AddressSpaces 'SMTP:*.litwareinc.com;5',
'SMTP:corp.contoso.com;10'
```

To view all of the properties of a send connector, use the `Get-SendConnector` cmdlet and pipe the command to `Format-List`:

```
Get-SendConnector -Identity Internet | Format-List
```

To disable the connector, we can use the following syntax:

```
Set-SendConnector -Identity Internet -Enabled $false
```

Finally, the connector can be removed using the `Remove-SendConnector` cmdlet:

```
Remove-SendConnector -Identity Internet -Confirm:$false
```

Each Mailbox server will initially be configured during the installation of Exchange with five receive connectors: two for client connections named `Client Proxy <Server Name>` and `Client Frontend <Server Name>`, two for server connections called `Default <Server Name>` and `Default Frontend <Server Name>`, and finally, one for Outbound Proxy called `Frontend <Server Name>`. When installing an Exchange 2013 CAS and Mailbox server, you don't need to modify any of the default connectors for the internal mail flow to work. A design change regarding an inbound mail has been made in Exchange 2013; it now accepts mails from external senders by default, which is great. If you need to send mails from applications or servers, you probably want to configure the receive connector, so they aren't open for anyone to use them, or maybe just for specified IP addresses. You can read more about this in the *Allowing application servers to relay mail* recipe in this chapter,.

There's more...

Receive connectors are created on a per server basis. In step 2, we used the `New-ReceiveConnector` cmdlet to create a receive connector on the `cas1` server that will be used to accept messages from a remote SMTP server in the perimeter network. You can see that we configured the connector so that the `cas1` server is listening on the IP address 192.168.1.245 on TCP port 25 for incoming messages. Based on the `RemoteIPRanges` and `PermissionGroups` parameters, any host in the 172.16.23.0/24 subnet will be able to make an unauthenticated connection to `cas1` and submit messages to any recipient within the organization. Like the send connectors, there are a number of parameters that can be used to create a receive connector. Review the help file for this cmdlet using `Get-Help New-ReceiveConnector -Full` to determine all of the available options.

Similar to send connectors, receive connectors have the `Set-*` and `Remove-*` cmdlets that can be used to modify, disable, or remove a receive connector.

To change the settings of a receive connector, use the `Set-ReceiveConnector` cmdlet:

```
Set-ReceiveConnector -Identity 'cas1\Inbound from DMZ' `
-Banner '220 SMTP OK' `
-MaxInboundConnection 2500 `
-ConnectionInactivityTimeout '00:02:30'
```

Here, you can see that we've modified a number of properties on the receive connector. Each of the settings modified here can only be managed from the shell. To view all of the properties available, use the `Get-ReceiveConnector` cmdlet and pipe the command to `Format-List`:

```
Get-ReceiveConnector -Identity 'cas1\Inbound from DMZ' |
Format-List
```

To disable a receive connector, use the `Set-ReceiveConnector` cmdlet:

```
Set-ReceiveConnector -Identity 'cas1\Inbound from DMZ' `
-Enabled $false
```

You can remove a receive connector using the following command:

```
Remove-ReceiveConnector -Identity 'cas1\Inbound from DMZ' `
-Confirm:$false
```

See also

▸ *Configuring transport limits*

▸ *Allowing application servers to relay mail*

Configuring transport limits

Depending on your requirements, transport limits can be configured in multiple ways. We can configure limits on individual mailboxes, on specific connectors, and even at the organization level. In this recipe, you'll learn how to use the Exchange Management Shell to configure limits based on the total number of acceptable recipients for a message, and also the total maximum size of each message that passes through your organization.

How to do it...

To configure mail flow restrictions for an individual mailbox, use the `Set-Mailbox` cmdlet, as shown next:

```
Set-Mailbox -Identity dsmith `
-MaxSendSize 10mb `
-MaxReceiveSize 10mb `
-RecipientLimits 100
```

Here, you can see that we've set limits for Dave Smith so that the maximum send and receive size for messages sent to or from his mailbox is limited to 10 megabytes. In addition, the maximum number of recipients that can be addressed when he sends an e-mail message is limited to 100.

How it works...

All Exchange recipients provide some type of mail flow settings that can be applied on an individual basis. In the previous example, we applied limits on a mailbox, but you also have the option of applying the `MaxReceiveSize` property on distribution groups and contacts. You may want to implement individual mail flow limits on a subset of recipients, and to do this in bulk, we can take advantage of PowerShell's flexible pipelining capabilities.

For example, let's say that we'd like to configure the mail flow limits shown in the previous example for all the mailbox-enabled users in the `Marketing` OU. The following command would take care of this:

```
Get-Mailbox -OrganizationalUnit contoso.com/Marketing |
Set-Mailbox -MaxSendSize 10mb `
-MaxReceiveSize 20mb `
-RecipientLimits 100
```

Here, you can see that we're simply retrieving a list of mailboxes from the `Marketing` OU using the `Get-Mailbox` cmdlet. To configure the limits, we pipe those objects to the `Set-Mailbox` cmdlet, and each user is then updated with the new settings.

There's more...

In addition to setting limits on individual recipients, we have the option to configure limits organization-wide. To do this, we use the `Set-TransportConfig` cmdlet:

```
Set-TransportConfig -MaxReceiveSize 10mb `
-MaxRecipientEnvelopeLimit 1000 `
-MaxSendSize 10mb
```

This command will enforce a 10 megabyte send and receive limit for messages passing through all servers in the organization, as well as limit the total number of recipients per message to 1000.

Limits set on individual users will override these organization limits. For example, if the maximum send and receive size is set to 10 megabytes at the organization level, we can exclude specific users from these restrictions by configuring a higher maximum send and receive size on a per mailbox basis using the `Set-Mailbox` cmdlet.

Limits can also be set on a per connector basis. To set the limits on an Internet receive connector, the command might look something like this:

```
Set-ReceiveConnector -Identity CAS1\Internet `
-MaxMessageSize 20mb `
-MaxRecipientsPerMessage 100
```

Notice that the identity is referenced using the format of `ServerName\ConnectorName`. This command will update the `Internet` connector on the `cas1` server. If you have multiple CAS servers with this receive connector, you can update the settings for each server with one command:

```
Get-ReceiveConnector -Identity *\Internet |
Set-ReceiveConnector -MaxMessageSize 20mb `
-MaxRecipientsPerMessage 100
```

This time, we use the `Get-ReceiveConnector` cmdlet, using an asterisk (*) as a wildcard so that any connector in the organization named `Internet` will be retrieved. We pipe the output down to the `Set-ReceiveConnector` cmdlet and the change is made in bulk.

Modifying send connectors is a little easier because they are defined at the organization level, so you don't need to iterate through connectors on multiple servers. To modify the maximum message size limits on a send connector named `Internet`, you can run the following command:

```
Set-SendConnector -Identity Internet -MaxMessageSize 5mb
```

In this example, outbound messages through the `Internet` send connector are limited to 5 megabytes in size.

Implementing restrictions at the organization, user, and connector levels should give you plenty of options. However, you can also use transport rules to set a maximum attachment size per message, if needed.

See also

> ▸ *Managing transport rules*
> ▸ *Managing connectors*

Allowing application servers to relay mail

When you deploy Exchange 2013, you may be required to allow external devices to relay mail off of your servers. This may be an application server or a physical device, such as a copier or printer. In order to allow these external systems to anonymously relay mail, you'll need to configure receive connectors on your CAS or Mailbox servers that support this. In this recipe, we'll take a look at how you can do this with the Exchange Management Shell.

How to do it...

When implementing an unauthenticated relay, it is wise to use a dedicated receive connector for this purpose:

```
New-ReceiveConnector -Name Relay `
-Usage Custom `
-Bindings '192.168.1.245:25' `
-Fqdn mail.contoso.com `
-RemoteIPRanges 192.168.1.110 `
-Server CAS1 `
-PermissionGroups ExchangeServers `
-AuthMechanism TLS, ExternalAuthoritative
```

This command creates a receive connector on the CAS1 server named Relay. The settings used here specify that the connector listens on the server IP address of 192.168.1.245 on TCP Port 25, and will allow the host at 192.168.1.110 to relay mail, either internally or externally, without requiring authentication.

How it works...

When creating a relay connector using this technique, you want to ensure that only the hosts that are allowed to relay mail are allowed using the RemoteIPRanges property. If this connector was configured with a remote IP range of 0.0.0.0-255.255.255.255, this would effectively turn the Exchange server into an open relay. This is because the AuthMechanism parameter has been set to ExternalAuthoritative, which means that Exchange bypasses all security and fully trusts all messages received from hosts in the RemoteIPRanges list. Additionally, messages accepted through this connector will not be scanned by anti-spam agents or be restricted by any of the system-wide message size limits.

There's more...

If the devices or application servers in your environment only need to submit messages to the internal recipients and do not need to be completely trusted, creating a receive connector with the following settings is a better option:

```
New-ReceiveConnector -Name Relay `
-Usage Custom `
-Bindings '192.168.1.245:25' `
-Fqdn mail.contoso.com `
-RemoteIPRanges 192.168.1.110 `
-Server CAS1 `
-PermissionGroups AnonymousUsers
```

As you can see, we've removed the `AuthMechanism` parameter from the command and assigned `AnonymousUsers` to the permission groups. This is a more secure approach, since messages submitted from external devices or servers will now be subjected to anti-spam agents and message restrictions. If you need to allow these devices to route mails to external recipients through this connector, you'll also need to assign the anonymous users the extended right `ms-Exch-SMTP-Accept-Any-Recipient`:

```
Get-ReceiveConnector CAS1\Relay |
Add-ADPermission -User "NT AUTHORITY\ANONYMOUS LOGON" `
-ExtendedRights ms-Exch-SMTP-Accept-Any-Recipient
```

After the previous command has been executed, the `Relay` connector on the `CAS1` server will be updated and the host at `192.168.1.110` will be able to route messages through the server using an unauthenticated relay; it will still pass through the anti-spam agents and message restriction settings.

If you want to ensure that a single user or a domain is bypassing the anti-spam agents, you need to configure the content filtering. This can easily be accomplished by running the following command:

```
Set-ContentFilterConfig -BypassedSenders sending-user@contoso.com
Set-ContentFilterConfig -BypassedSenderDomains contoso.com
```

By running these commands, the user `sending-user@contoso.com` is bypassed by the anti-spam agents. The last command makes sure that the whole domain `contoso.com` is bypassed.

See also

- ▸ *Configuring transport limits*
- ▸ *Managing connectors*

Working with custom DSN messages

Delivery Status Notification (**DSN**) messages are system messages generated by the transport service that inform the sender of a message about its status. When a message cannot be delivered to a recipient, Exchange will respond to the sender with a message that is associated with a status message. Sometimes, these status messages may not be detailed enough for your liking. In those cases, you can create new messages associated with the DSN code to provide more details to the sender. This is something that has to be done from the Exchange Management Shell.

How to do it...

You can use the `New-SystemMessage` cmdlet to create a custom DSN message:

```
New-SystemMessage -DSNCode 5.1.1 `
-Text "The mailbox you tried to send an e-mail message to
does not exist. Please contact the Help Desk at extension
4112 for assistance." `
-Internal $true `
-Language En
```

In this example, a **Non Delivery Report** (**NDR**) with the custom DSN message will be delivered to senders that try to send messages to an invalid internal recipient.

How it works...

When creating a custom DSN message, you want to check whether it will be used for internal or external use. The previous example configured a custom message for `DSNCode 5.1.1` for internal use. In addition to this, you could create a separate custom DSN message for external users; just set the `-Internal` parameter to `$false`.

Custom DSN messages can also support basic HTML tags. This can be useful when creating an internal custom DSN that directs users to an internal help desk site. Here's another way we could have created the custom DSN message:

```
New-SystemMessage -DSNCode 5.1.1 `
-Text "The mailbox you tried to send an e-mail message to
does not exist. Please visit the
<a href='http://support.contoso.com'>help desk site</a>
for assistance" `
-Internal $true `
-Language En
```

In this example, we've included a hyperlink within the custom DSN message, so users can click on the link and visit an internal help desk website for additional assistance.

There's more...

To view custom DSN messages, use the `Get-SystemMessage` cmdlet:

```
Machine: tlex01.testlabs.se                          ─  □  x

[PS] C:\Scripts>Get-SystemMessage

Identity                        Text
--------                        ----
en\Internal\5.1.1               The mailbox you tried to send an e-mail messa...
```

You can also view the default system messages that were installed with Exchange. To do this, run the previous cmdlet with the `-Original` switch parameter:

```
Get-SystemMessage -Original
```

To modify a system message, use the `Set-SystemMessage` cmdlet:

```
Set-SystemMessage -Identity 'en\Internal\5.1.1' `
-Text "Sorry, but this recipient is no longer available
or does not exist."
```

As you can see here, we've modified the custom internal 5.1.1 message with a new message using the `-Text` parameter.

To remove a custom DSN message, use the `Remove-SystemMessage` cmdlet:

```
Remove-SystemMessage -Identity 'en\Internal\5.1.1' -Confirm:$false
```

The previous command removes the custom message created for the 5.1.1 DSN code without confirmation.

System-generated messages for mailbox and public folder quota warnings can also be customized:

```
New-SystemMessage -QuotaMessageType WarningMailbox `
-Text "Your mailbox is getting too large. Please
 delete some messages to free up space or call
 the help desk at extention 3391."`
-Language En
```

When creating a custom quota message, as shown previously, there is no need to specify a DSN code. The `-QuotaMessageType` parameter is used to modify the messages for the various warnings supported by the system. The `-QuotaMessageType` parameter accepts the following values that can be used to customize warning messages:

- `ProhibitSendReceiveMailBox`
- `ProhibitSendMailbox`
- `WarningMailbox`
- `WarningMailboxUnlimitedSize`
- `ProhibitPostPublicFolder`
- `WarningPublicFolder`
- `WarningPublicFolderUnlimitedSize`
- `ProhibitReceiveMailboxMessagesPerFolderCount`
- `WarningMailboxMessagesPerFolderCount`
- `WarningMailboxMessagesPerFolderUnlimitedCount`
- `ProhibitReceiveFolderHierarchyChildrenCountCount`
- `WarningFolderHierarchyChildrenCount`
- `WarningFolderHierarchyChildrenUnlimitedCount`
- `WarningFoldersCount`
- `ProhibitReceiveFoldersCount`
- `WarningFoldersCountUnlimited`
- `ProhibitReceiveFolderHierarchyDepth`
- `WarningFolderHierarchyDepth`
- `WarningFolderHierarchyDepthUnlimited`

When creating a custom quota message, you cannot use the `-Internal` parameter. This is not a problem since quota messages are only intended for internal recipients.

Managing connectivity and protocol logs

Every Exchange Mailbox server is capable of logging connection activities and SMTP conversations that take place between servers. You can configure the retention settings for these logs and then use them to diagnose mail flow issues within your environment. In this recipe, you'll learn how to configure the logging options on your servers, and how to examine the data when troubleshooting problems.

How to do it...

To view the connectivity logging configuration of a Mailbox server, use the
`Get-TransportService` cmdlet:

```
Get-TransportService -Identity tlex01 | fl ConnectivityLog*
```

The previous command retrieves the default connectivity logging settings for a Mailbox server
named `ex01`. The output returned will be similar to the following screenshot:

```
Machine: TLEX01.testlabs.se                                    _  □  x

[PS] C:\temp>Get-TransportService -Identity tlex01 | fl ConnectivityLog*


ConnectivityLogEnabled          : True
ConnectivityLogMaxAge           : 30.00:00:00
ConnectivityLogMaxDirectorySize : 1000 MB (1,048,576,000 bytes)
ConnectivityLogMaxFileSize      : 10 MB (10,485,760 bytes)
ConnectivityLogPath             : C:\Program Files\Microsoft\Exchange Serv
                                  er\V15\TransportRoles\Logs\Hub\Connectiv
                                  ity
```

How it works...

Connectivity logs record connection details about outbound message delivery queues on a
mailbox server. Connectivity logging is enabled by default on Exchange 2013 servers. Based
on the output of the `Get-TransportService` cmdlet in the previous example, we can see
that by default, the maximum age for connectivity log files is 30 days. Once a log file reaches
10 MB, a new log file will be created. The directory for connectivity logging will hold up to 1
GB of logs. Mailbox servers use circular logging for connectivity logs, so once the directory
reaches its maximum size, or the log files reach their maximum age, those log files will be
removed to make space for new log files.

You can control these settings using the `Set-TransportService` cmdlet. Here's an
example of modifying the connectivity log's maximum age and directory size on a Mailbox
server named `tlex01`:

```
Set-TransportService -Identity tlex01 `

-ConnectivityLogMaxAge 45 `

-ConnectivityLogMaxDirectorySize 5gb
```

If you change these settings on a mailbox server, it is recommended that you also update the
remaining Mailbox servers in your organization with a matching configuration.

To make this change to all the mailbox servers at once, use the following commands:

```
Get-TransportService |
Set-TransportService -ConnectivityLogMaxAge 45 `
-ConnectivityLogMaxDirectorySize 5gb
```

There's more...

You can configure protocol logging to record the SMTP conversations between your Mailbox servers and other mail servers. Protocol logging can be enabled on a per connector basis, but just like the connectivity logging options, the configuration of the protocol log file settings are made using the `Set-TransportService` cmdlet. The following screenshot shows these available properties:

```
Machine: TLEX01.testlabs.se                              _ □ X

[PS] C:\temp>Get-TransportService -Identity tlex01 | fl receiveprotocol*


ReceiveProtocolLogMaxAge              : 30.00:00:00
ReceiveProtocolLogMaxDirectorySize : 250 MB (262,144,000 bytes)
ReceiveProtocolLogMaxFileSize        : 10 MB (10,485,760 bytes)
ReceiveProtocolLogPath               : C:\Program Files\Microsoft\Exchange S
                                       erver\V15\TransportRoles\Logs\Hub\Pro
                                       tocolLog\SmtpReceive
```

Here, you can see that we've got protocol log settings for receive connectors. The settings shown here are the default values.

The send connectors will use the following protocol log configurations by default:

```
Machine: TLEX01.testlabs.se                              _ □ X

[PS] C:\temp>Get-TransportService -Identity tlex01 | fl sendprotocol*


SendProtocolLogMaxAge              : 30.00:00:00
SendProtocolLogMaxDirectorySize : 250 MB (262,144,000 bytes)
SendProtocolLogMaxFileSize        : 10 MB (10,485,760 bytes)
SendProtocolLogPath               : C:\Program Files\Microsoft\Exchange Serv
                                    er\V15\TransportRoles\Logs\Hub\ProtocolL
                                    og\SmtpSend
```

Just like connectivity logs, the send and receive protocol logs have a maximum age and directory size and are controlled by circular logging. The default settings can be changed with the `Set-TransportService` cmdlet:

```
Set-TransportService -Identity tlex01 `
-SendProtocolLogMaxAge 45 `
-ReceiveProtocolLogMaxAge 45
```

Again, if you plan on changing this setting, make sure you update all of the Mailbox servers in your organization with the same information.

Before you can capture protocol logging information, you need to enable verbose protocol logging on each connector that you want to report on:

```
Set-SendConnector -Identity Internet -ProtocolLoggingLevel Verbose
```

In the previous command, you can see that we've configured the `Internet` send connector for verbose protocol logging. You can do the same for a receive connector using the `Set-ReceiveConnector` cmdlet:

```
Get-ReceiveConnector -Identity *\Relay |
Set-ReceiveConnector -ProtocolLoggingLevel Verbose
```

Here, we are using an asterisk (*) as a wildcard to retrieve the `Relay` connector from each server in the organization. We can pipe the output to the `Set-ReceiveConnector` cmdlet to enable verbose protocol logging for the connector on each server.

All mailbox servers use an invisible intra-organization send connector that is used to transmit messages internally to other mailbox servers. You can configure verbose logging for this connector using the `Set-TransportService` cmdlet:

```
Set-TransportService -Identity tlex01 `
-IntraOrgConnectorProtocolLoggingLevel Verbose
```

The protocol log files for the intra-org connector will be saved in the send protocol log path.

The connectivity and protocol log files are stored in the CSV format and, by default, are organized in subdirectories under the following path:

```
<install path>\V15\TransportRoles\Logs\Hub\
```

The connectivity logs are stored in a sub directory called `Connectivity`, and the log file naming convention is in the format of `CONNECTLOGyyyymmdd-nnnn.log`, where `yyyymmdd` is the date that the log file was created, and where `nnnn` is an instance number, starting with 1 for each day. The instance number will be incremented by one as each log file reaches the default 10 MB limit, and a new log file is created.

The protocol logs are stored in subdirectories of this location in `ProtocolLog\SmtpReceive` and `ProtocolLog\SmtpSend`. The files in these folders use a naming convention in the format of `prefixyyyymmdd-nnnn.log`. The prefix for the log filename will be `SEND` for send connectors and `RECV` for receive connectors. Like connectivity logs, `yyyymmdd` is the date when the log file was created, and `nnnn` is the instance number that starts with 1 and is incremented as each new log file is created.

The connectivity logs store details about messages transmitted from local queues to the destination server. For example, a record in a connectivity log file will log the source queue, destination server, DNS resolution details, connection failures, and the total number of messages and bytes transferred.

The protocol logs store SMTP conversations that take place when either sending or receiving a message. The details logged will contain connector and session IDs, the local and remote endpoints of the servers involved, and the SMTP verbs used in the conversation.

Parsing log files

Even though connectivity and protocol logs are stored in a CSV format, each log file has a header information prepended to the file. The following screenshot shows an example of a connectivity log file in excel:

As you can see, the header information includes the Exchange version, the date, and the fields used in the log files. This header information, makes it impossible to read these files into the shell using the `Import-CSV` cmdlet. Luckily, PowerShell is so flexible that we can work around this with a little creativity.

Let's say that you are interested in finding all the errors in the connection log on a transport server named `tlex01`. Start the Exchange Management Shell on the `tlex01` server and run the following command:

```
$logpath = (Get-TransportService -Identity
tlex01).ConnectivityLogPath
```

This will store a reference to the connectivity log folder path that will make the following code easier to read and work with. Now let's say that you want to parse the connectivity logs from the past 24 hours for failures. We'll parse each log file in the directory and perform a wildcard search based on a keyword:

```
$logs = Get-ChildItem $logpath *.log |
?{$_.LastWriteTime -gt (Get-Date).AddDays(-1)}
$data = $logs | %{
  Get-Content $_.Fullname | %{
    $IsHeaderParsed = $false
    if($_ -like '#Fields: *' -and !$IsHeaderParsed) {
      $_ -replace '^#Fields: '
      $IsHeaderParsed = $true
    }
    else {
      $_
    }
  } | ConvertFrom-Csv
}
$data | Where-Object{$_.description -like '*fail*'}
```

This code will loop through each log file in the connectivity log folder that has been written to within the past 24 hours. For each log file, we'll read the content into the shell, excluding the header information, and convert the information to properly-formed CSV data using the `ConvertFrom-CSV` cmdlet. The result will be stored in the `$data` variable that can then be filtered on. In this example, any record in each of the log files where the description contains the word `fail` will be returned. You can adjust the `Where-Object` filter based on the information you are searching for.

Searching message tracking logs

The `Get-MessageTrackingLog` cmdlet is a versatile tool that can be used to search the message tracking logs on mailbox servers. In this recipe, you'll learn how to use this Exchange Management Shell cmdlet to generate detailed reports on various aspects of mail flow within your organization.

How to do it...

The `Get-MessageTrackingLog` cmdlet has a number of available parameters that can be used to perform a search. To retrieve all the messages sent from a Mailbox server during a specified time frame, use the following syntax:

```
Get-MessageTrackingLog -Server tlex01 `
-Start (Get-Date).AddDays(-1) `
-End (Get-Date) `
-EventId Send
```

Using this command, all the messages sent through SMTP from the `tlex01` server in the past 24 hours will be returned.

How it works...

Each mailbox server roles generates and collects message tracking logs. Message tracking is enabled by default, and the logs are stored in the `<install path>\V15\TransportRoles\Logs\MessageTracking` directory. Log files are limited to 10 megabytes, and when a log fi e reaches its maximum size, a new log file will be created. Log files are kept for either 30 days, or until the maximum size configured for the directory has been reached. Like connectivity and protocol logs, the message tracking logs are removed as needed using circular logging.

You can configure all of these options on mailbox servers using the `Set-TransportService` cmdlet.

In the previous example, we ran the `Get-MessageTrackingLog` cmdlet and specified a mailbox server to execute the search. Depending on your network topology, you may need to search several servers in order to get accurate results.

For instance, let's say that you've got multiple mailbox servers in your organization. You might want to generate a report for all the messages sent by a specific user within a certain time frame. You can search the logs on each mailbox server using the following syntax:

```
Get-TransportService |
Get-MessageTrackingLog -Start (Get-Date).AddDays(-1) `
-End (Get-Date) `
-EventId Send `
-Sender dmsith@contoso.com
```

Here, you can see that we're using the `Get-TransportService` cmdlet to retrieve a list of all the Mailbox servers in the organization. Those objects are piped to the `GetMessageTrackingLog` cmdlet where we specify the start and end time for the search, the event ID, and the sender. The records returned by the previous command will provide a number of useful properties, such as the sender and recipients of the message, the total size of the message, the IP address of the destination server, the subject of the message, and more. These records can be piped out to `Export-CSV` or `ConvertTo-Html` to generate an external report, or you can pipe the command to `Format-List` to view all of the properties for each log entry.

There's more...

The `-EventID` parameter can be used to specify the event category used to classify a tracking log entry when you perform a search. The following possible event categories can be used:

► `BadMail`: The message was submitted through the pickup or replay directories and cannot be delivered

► `Deliver`: The message delivery has been delayed

► `DSN`: A **Delivery Status Notification** (**DSN**) was generated

► `Expand`: Expansion of a distribution group

► `Fail`: Message delivery failed

► `PoisonMessage`: The message was added or removed from the poison message queue

► `Receive`: The message was received either through SMTP or by `StoreDriver`

► `Redirect`: The message was redirected to an alternate recipient

► `Resolve`: The recipients listed in the message were resolved to another e-mail address

► `Send`: The message was sent through SMTP to another mail server

- ▶ `Submit`: The message was logged by the mailbox submission service running on a mailbox server
- ▶ `Transfer`: The recipients were moved to a forked message because of content conversion, recipient limits, or agents

You can search message tracking logs based on the sender or recipient:

```
Get-MessageTrackingLog -Sender sales@litwareinc.com -EventId `
Receive
```

In this example, we're searching the message tracking logs for an external sender address and specifying `Receive` as the event category. This would allow us to track all inbound messages from this external sender.

In addition, you can use the `-Recipients` parameter to find messages sent to one or more e-mail addresses, as shown in the following command:

```
Get-MessageTrackingLog -Recipients `
dave@contoso.com,john@contoso.com
```

If you know the subject of the message you want to track, use the `-MessageSubject` parameter when running the command:

```
Get-TransportService |
Get-MessageTrackingLog -MessageSubject 'Financial Report for Q4'
```

When it comes to message tracking, you may need to generate reports based on the total number of messages sent or received. Let's say that your boss has asked you to determine the number of individual e-mail messages received by your mailbox servers from the Internet in the past week. Let's start with the following command:

```
Get-TransportService | Get-MessageTrackingLog -EventId Receive `
-Start (Get-Date).AddDays(-7) `
-End (Get-Date) `
-ResultSize Unlimited |
Where-Object {$_.ConnectorId -like '*\Internet'}
```

Here, we're specifying that the event category of the logs returned should be set to `Receive` with the `-EventID` parameter. Next, we specify the date 7 days ago as the start time for the search, and the current date for the end time. We set the `-ResultSize` parameter to `Unlimited` because, by default, this cmdlet will only return the first 1,000 results. Finally, we filter the output using the `Where-Object` cmdlet based on the connector. Since we have a dedicated receive connector for an inbound Internet e-mail, we filter the results so that only received messages through this connector are returned.

Now that we've got an idea of how to construct this command, let's take it a step further. Again, to ensure that we're getting all of the required information, we'll search the logs on each mailbox server and then output the total number of e-mail items and their total size for the past week:

```
$results = Get-TransportService |
Get-MessageTrackingLog -EventId Receive `
-Start (Get-Date).AddDays(-7) `
-End (Get-Date) `
-ResultSize Unlimited |
Where-Object {$_.ConnectorId -like '*\Internet'}
$results |
Measure-Object -Property TotalBytes -Sum |
Select-Object @{n="Total Items";e={$_.Count}},
@{n="Total Item Size (MB)";e={[math]::Round($_.Sum /1mb,2)}}
```

Although this could be done on one line, we've separated it out here into two phases for the sake of readability. First, we gather the message tracking logs on each mailbox server using the desired settings, and the output is stored in the `$results` variable.

Next, we pipe `$results` to the `Measure-Object` cmdlet that is used to sum up the `TotalBytes` for all the messages accepted from the `Internet` receive connector.

The command is piped further to the `Select-Object` cmdlet, where we create a custom object with calculated properties that display the total number of e-mail items and the total number of bytes represented in megabytes. The results from the previous code would look something like the following screenshot:

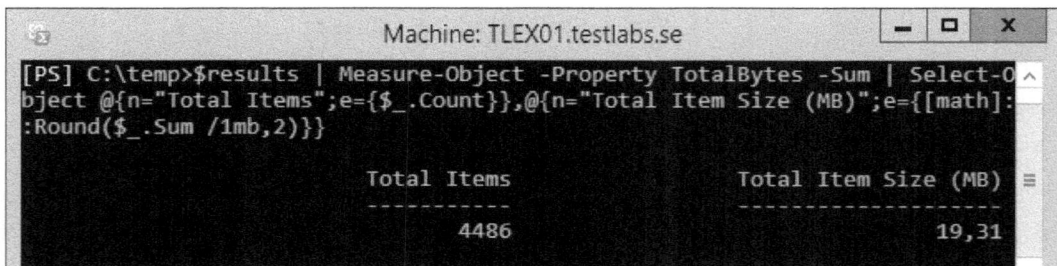

Taking it a step further

Message tracking logs can be used to create some pretty advanced reports. Let's say that you want to create a report that shows the total number of messages sent from your organization per external domain. This is possible using the following command:

```
$domain = @{}
$report = Get-TransportService |
Get-MessageTrackingLog -EventId Send `
-ResultSize Unlimited `
-Start (Get-Date).AddDays(-30) `
-End (Get-Date) |
Where-Object {$_.ConnectorId -eq 'Internet'}
if($report) {
  $domains = $report | %{$_.Recipients | %{$_.Split("@")[1]}}
  $domains | %{$domain[$_] = $domain[$_] + 1}
  Write-Output $domain
}
```

You can see here that first we create a hash table that will be used to keep track of each external domain. We then use the `Get-MessageTrackingLog` cmdlet to build a report for all of the messages sent in the past 30 days using a send connector named `Internet`. Next, we loop through the recipients and retrieve only the domain name from their e-mail addresses and store the results in the `$domains` array. Finally, we loop through each of the domains and add them to the hash table, incrementing the count by one for each matching result. Here's an example of the type of output you might get from the previous code:

```
Machine: TLEX01.testlabs.se                              _ □ X

Name                          Value
----                          -----
testlabs.se                   56
```

From the preceding output, we can see that, in this case, all the e-mails are sent to recipients at `testlabs.se`.

See also

- *Managing connectivity and protocol logs*
- *Working with messages in transport queues*

Working with messages in transport queues

Transport queues are a temporary storage location for messages that are in transit. Each mailbox server can have multiple queues at any given time, depending on the destination of the message. In this recipe, we'll cover several methods that can be used to view queued messages, remove messages from queues, and more.

How to do it...

To view the transport queues that are currently in use on a specific server, use the Get-Queue cmdlet:

```
Get-Queue -Server tlex01
```

In this example, the transport queues on the tlex01 server will be returned. The output might look similar to the following screenshot:

```
Machine: TLEX01.testlabs.se                      _  □  x

[PS] C:\temp>Get-Queue -Server tlex01

Identity         DeliveryType  Status MessageCount Velocity NextHopDomain
--------         ------------  ------ ------------ -------- -------------
TLEX01\1508      SmtpDeliv...  Ready  0            0        db02
TLEX01\1509      SmtpDeliv...  Ready  0            0,02     db01
TLEX01\Submis... Undefined     Ready  0            0        Submission
TLEX01\Shadow... ShadowRed...  Ready  3            0        tlex02.testl...
```

In this example, there is one message awaiting retry due to a DNS resolution problem for the destination domain.

How it works...

When running the Get-Queue cmdlet, the queues displayed will vary depending on what types of messages are currently awaiting delivery. The following queue types are used on the mailbox servers:

 ► **Submission queue**: All messages received by a mailbox server are first processed in the submission queue. After categorization, each message is moved to either a delivery queue or the retry queue. The queue identity will be listed as <ServerName>\Submission, for example, tlex01\Submission.

- ▶ **SMTP delivery to Mailbox queue**: All messages destined for direct delivery to a mailbox server using SMTP will go through this queue. This queue is used only on mailbox servers. The queue identity will be listed as `<ServerName>\Unique Number`, for example, `tlex01\15`.

- ▶ **Remote delivery queue**: All messages being routed to another server through SMTP will go through this queue. The queue identity will be listed as `<ServerName>\Unique Number`, for example, `tlex01\6`.

- ▶ **Poison message queue**: Messages that are determined to be potentially harmful will be placed in this queue. The queue identity will be listed as `<ServerName>\Poison`, for example, `tlex01\Poison`.

- ▶ **Unreachable queue**: Messages that cannot be routed to their destination server will be placed in this queue. The queue identity will be defined as `<ServerName>\Unreachable`, for example, `tlex01\Unreachable`.

In addition to viewing the queues on a single mailbox server, you can use the following command to view the queues on all the mailbox servers in the organization:

```
Get-TransportService | Get-Queue
```

If you work with busy mailbox servers, you may want to take advantage of the filtering capabilities of the `Get-Queue` cmdlet. For example, to filter by delivery type, you can use the following command:

```
Get-TransportService |
Get-Queue -Filter {DeliveryType -eq 'DnsConnectorDelivery'}
```

This example filters the results based on the `DeliveryType` parameter. The following values can be used with this filter:

- ▶ `DeliveryAgent`
- ▶ `DNSConnectorDelivery`
- ▶ `NonSMTPGatewayDelivery`
- ▶ `SmartHostConnectorDelivery`
- ▶ `SmtpDeliveryToMailbox`
- ▶ `SmtpRelayToConnectorSourceServers`
- ▶ `SmtpRelayToDag`
- ▶ `SmtpRelayToMailboxDeliveryGroup`
- ▶ `SmtpRelayToRemoteActiveDirectorySite`
- ▶ `SmtpRelayToServers`

- SmtpRelayWithinAdSitetoEdge
- Heartbeat
- ShadowRedundancy
- Undefined
- Unreachable

The `Get-Queue` cmdlet also supports several other properties that can be used to construct a filter:

- `Identity`: This specifies the queue identity in the format of server\destination, where destination is a remote domain, mailbox server, or queue name
- `LastError`: This is used to search by the last error message recorded for a queue
- `LastRetryTime`: This specifies the time when a connection was last tried for a queue
- `MessageCount`: This allows you to search by the total number of items in a queue
- `NextHopConnector`: This specifies the identity of the connector used to create a queue
- `NextHopDomain`: The next hop, such as an SMTP domain, server name, AD site, or mailbox database
- `NextRetryTime`: This is used to search by when a connection will next be tried by a queue
- `Status`: This shows the status of a queue, such as `Active`, `Ready`, `Retry`, or `Suspended`

For example, if you want to view queues that have a total message count of more than a certain number of messages, use the `MessageCount` property with the greater than (`-gt`) operator:

```
Get-Queue -Server tlex01 -Filter {MessageCount -gt 25}
```

Another useful method of finding backed up queues is to use the `Status` filter:

```
Get-Queue -Server tlex01 -Filter {Status -eq 'Retry'}
```

This example searches the queues on the `tlex01` server for queues that have messages with a status of `Retry`. Notice that this time, we've used the equals (`-eq`) comparison operator in the filter to specify the status type.

> To learn all about the available comparison operators supported by PowerShell, run the `Get-Help about_comparison_operators` command.

There's more...

To view messages that are queued for delivery, you can use the `Get-Message` cmdlet. If you want to view all of the messages that are sitting in queues with a status of `Retry`, use the following command:

```
Get-TransportService |
Get-Queue -Filter {Status -eq 'Retry'} |
Get-Message
```

The `Get-Message` cmdlet also provides a `-Filter` parameter that can be used to find messages that match a specific criteria:

```
Get-TransportService |
Get-Message -Filter {FromAddress -like '*contoso.com'}
```

The previous command returns all queued messages from every Mailbox server in the organization where the sender domain is `contoso.com`.

> To view the filterable properties of the `Get-Message` cmdlet, run the `Get-Help Get-Message -Parameter Filter` command.

If you know which server the message is queued on, and you just want to view the properties of the message, you can use the following syntax:

```
Get-Message -Server tlex01 -Filter {Subject -eq 'test'} |
Format-List
```

This example filters the `Subject` parameter of queued messages on the `tlex01` server. If you want to view all the messages queued on a server, you can simply remove the `-Filter` parameter and value.

To prevent the delivery of a message in a queue, you can use the `Suspend-Message` cmdlet:

```
Get-Message -Server tlex01 -Filter {Subject -eq 'test'} |
Suspend-Message -Confirm:$false
```

To suspend all messages in a particular queue, use the following command:

```
Get-Queue -Identity tlex01\7 |
Get-Message |
Suspend-Message -Confirm:$false
```

Keep in mind that messages in the submission or poison message queue cannot be suspended. When the time comes to allow delivery, you can use the `Resume-Message` cmdlet:

```
Get-Message -Server tlex01 -Filter {Subject -eq 'test'} |
Resume-Message
```

Or, we can resume all the messages in a particular queue using the following command:

```
Get-Queue -Identity tlex01\7 |
Get-Message |
Resume-Message
```

When you need to force a retry for a queue, you can use the `Retry-Queue` cmdlet:

```
Get-Queue -Identity tlex01\7 | Retry-Queue
```

The `Retry-Queue` cmdlet can also be used to resubmit messages to the submission queue, which will allow the categorizer to reprocess the messages. You can resubmit messages with a status of `Retry` in the mailbox or remote delivery queues, or messages that are stored in the unreachable or poison message queues.

For example, to resubmit all the messages in queues with a `Retry` status on all Mailbox servers in the organization, use the following command:

```
Get-TransportService |
Get-Queue -Filter {Status -eq 'Retry'} |
Retry-Queue -Resubmit $true
```

Or, to resubmit messages in the unreachable queue on a specific server, use the following command:

```
Retry-Queue -Identity tlex01\Unreachable -Resubmit $true
```

> Messages with a suspended status cannot be resubmitted using the `Retry-Queue` cmdlet.

You can purge messages from transport queues using the `Remove-Message` cmdlet:

```
Get-TransportService |
Get-Queue -Filter {DeliveryType -eq 'DnsConnectorDelivery'} |
Get-Message | Remove-Message -Confirm:$false
```

The preceding command retrieves queued messages on all Mailbox servers with a specified delivery type and removes them without confirmation. An NDR will be generated and sent to the originator of the message advising them that they'll need to resend the message.

The `Remove-Message` cmdlet provides multiple parameters that can be used to either identify the message based on the message identity, or using a filter with the `-Filter` parameter when you only want to remove a single message:

```
Remove-Message -Identity tlex01\10\13 -WithNDR $false `
-Confirm:$false
```

The previous command removes a single message based on its `MessageIdentity` value. Notice that this time, we've set the `-WithNDR` parameter to `$false`, and the sender will not be notified that the message will not be delivered.

See also

- ▸ *Configure the Edge Transport role*
- ▸ *Implementing a header firewall*

Searching anti-spam agent logs

Exchange 2013 Mailbox servers are capable of using several anti-spam agents to reduce the amount of unwanted e-mail messages that enter your organization. All anti-spam activity is logged by Mailbox servers, and this data can be used to troubleshoot issues and generate reports. In this recipe, you'll learn how to search the anti-spam agent logs using the Exchange Management Shell. Notice that these anti-spam agents are not installed by default.

How to do it...

The `Get-AgentLog` cmdlet can be used to parse the anti-spam agent logs. To find all the log entries for a particular agent, filter the output based on the `Agent` property:

```
Get-AgentLog | ?{$_.Agent -eq 'Content Filter Agent'}
```

When running this command in a busy environment, you may get back a large number of results, and you may want to consider refining your filter and perhaps limiting the date range to a specific period of time.

How it works...

All of the anti-spam agents use a series of log files on each Mailbox server with the anti-spam agents installed. By default, Mailbox servers do not have the anti-spam agents installed, but you can install them manually using the following commands:

```
cd $exscripts
.\Install-AntiSpamAgents.ps1
Restart-Service MSExchangeTransport
```

After performing the preceding commands, the agents will be installed, and the transport service needs to be restarted.

By default, the agent log file directory is set to a maximum size of 250 megabytes. Each individual log file is limited to 10 megabytes in size and will be kept for a maximum of 7 days, or until the directory reaches its maximum size. These values can be adjusted using the `Set-TransportService` cmdlet along with the `AgentLogMaxAge`, `AgentLogMaxDirectorySize`, and `AgentLogMaxFileSize` parameters.

The following anti-spam filters are available for Exchange Mailbox servers:

- **Content filtering**: This uses the Microsoft SmartScreen technology to process the contents of each message and determine whether or not the content of the message is appropriate.

- **Sender ID**: This determines the action to be taken based on whether or not the sender of a message is transmitting the message from a mail server associated with the sender's domain. This is used to combat domain spoofing.

- **Sender filtering**: This allows you to configure one or more blocked senders and the action that should be taken if a message is received from a specific address.

- **Recipient filtering**: This determines the action to be taken based on the recipients of an e-mail message.

- **Protocol analysis**: This is the underlying agent for sender reputation functionality.

When viewing agent log entries in the shell, several properties are available that can be used to determine the status of the message, as shown in the following screenshot:

```
Machine: TLEX01.testlabs.se                          _  □  X

[PS] C:\temp>Get-AgentLog | ?{$_.Agent -eq 'Sender Filter Agent'}


RunspaceId        : 3c99c8d9-52e8-4985-b66a-ce16fe7701a1
Timestamp         : 2015-04-07 16:36:40
SessionId         : 08D001B4111A0783
IPAddress         : 172.16.1.21
MessageId         :
P1FromAddress     : spammer@litwareinc.com
P2FromAddresses   : {}
Recipients        : {}
Agent             : Sender Filter Agent
Event             : OnMailCommand
Action            : RejectCommand
SmtpResponse      : 554 5.1.0 Sender denied
Reason            : ExactMatch
ReasonData        : spammer@litwareinc.com
Diagnostics       :
NetworkMsgID      : 00000000-0000-0000-0000-000000000000
TenantID          : 00000000-0000-0000-0000-000000000000
Directionality    : Undefined
```

In this example, you can see that the message was blocked because the `P1FromAddress` property was configured as a blocked sender on `Sender Filtering Agent` with the action set to `RejectCommand`.

There's more...

When you run the `Get-AgentLog` cmdlet, every entry in the log file will be returned. In an environment that receives a lot of e-mails, this can be a little overwhelming and slow. To narrow your searches, you can specify a time frame using the `-StartDate` and `-EndDate` parameters:

```
Get-AgentLog -StartDate (Get-Date).AddDays(-7) -EndDate (Get-Date)
```

The previous command retrieves the agent logs for the past 7 days. In this example, the start and end dates are specified using the `Get-Date` cmdlet, but if needed, you can manually type the date and time for the search, as shown in the following command:

```
Get-AgentLog -StartDate "1/4/2015 9:00 AM" -EndDate `
"1/9/2015 11:00 PM"
```

You can also create searches based on the agent, as shown in the first example of this recipe. You can combine this technique with a time frame as well to refine your searches, as shown in the following command:

```
Get-AgentLog -StartDate (Get-Date).AddDays(-7) -EndDate `
(Get-Date) |  ?{$_.Agent -eq 'Sender Filter Agent'}
```

This command pulls the agent logs from the past 7 days. The output is piped to the `Where-Object` cmdlet (using the `?` alias) to filter based on the `Agent` property of the log entry. In this example, only the logs for `Sender Filter Agent` are retrieved.

The agent logs provide properties that identify both the sender and recipient addresses for the message. To search based on the sender, use the following command:

```
Get-AgentLog |
?{$_.P1FromAddress -or $_.P2FromAddress -eq `
'sales@litwareinc.com'}
```

This command checks both the `P1FromAddress` and `P2FromAddress` properties, and only returns the log entries where the sender address is `sales@litwareinc.com`.

You can use a similar filter using the `-Like` comparison operator and a wild card to find all the messages in the log from a particular sending domain:

```
Get-AgentLog |
?{$_.P1FromAddress -or $_.P2FromAddress -like '*@litwareinc.com'}
```

To retrieve the logs for specific recipients, filter on the `Recipients` property:

```
Get-AgentLog | ?{$_.Recipients -eq 'dsmith@contoso.com}
```

You can export the agent logs to a CSV file that can be used in another application, such as Excel. To do this, pipe the desired logs to the `Export-CSV` cmdlet:

```
Get-AgentLog -StartDate (Get-Date).AddDays(-3) -EndDate (Get-Date)
|
?{$_.Agent -eq 'Content Filter Agent' -and $_.ReasonData -gt 4} |
Export-CSV c:\contentfilter.csv -NoType
```

In this example, agent logs from the past 3 days processed by the `Content Filter Agent` and with an SCL rating of `4` or higher are exported to a CSV file.

You can use the `-Location` parameter to search agent log files that are located in an alternate directory. This may be useful when you have specific retention requirements and still need to report on old data that is no longer on your production servers. When using this parameter, specify the full path to the directory containing the log files:

```
Get-AgentLog -Location e:\logs
```

Keep in mind that this parameter requires a local path, so a UNC path to a shared network folder will not work.

See also

▸ *Exporting reports to text and CSV files* in *Chapter 2, Exchange Management Shell Common Tasks*

Implementing a header firewall

When messages are passed from one server to another through SMTP, Exchange Edge, and Mailbox servers, add custom `X-Header` fields to the message header. These headers can contain a variety of information, such as mail server IP addresses, **spam confidence levels** (**SCL**), content filtering results, and rule processing statuses. Header firewalls are used to remove these custom `X-Header` fields so that unauthorized sources cannot obtain detailed information about your messaging environment. In this recipe, you'll learn how to use the Exchange Management Shell to implement a header firewall that prevents the disclosure of the internal information sent to an external source.

How to do it...

One of the most common uses of a header firewall is to remove the internal server infrastructure details from SMTP e-mail message headers destined for an external recipient. To do this, on an Edge Transport server, you need to modify the permissions for the Internet send connector using the `Remove-ADPermission` cmdlet:

```
Remove-ADPermission -Identity "EdgeSync - Litware to Internet" `
-User "MS Exchange\Edge Transport Servers" `
-ExtendedRights Ms-Exch-Send-Headers-Routing `
-Confirm:$false
```

In this example, the Edge server's Internet send connector, named `EdgeSync - Litware to Internet`, is modified. The `Ms-Exch-Accept-Headers-Routing` permission is removed from the Internet send connector for the `MS Exchange\Edge Transport Servers` account.

How it works...

By default, all connectors are configured to include routing headers in SMTP e-mail messages. This can be a security concern for many organizations, as it exposes the Exchange version in the message header. In addition, for Mailbox servers that are configured to send messages directly to the Internet, the internal IP addresses of the servers that handle the messages are included in the headers.

When viewing the headers of a message received from the `contoso.com` mail server, the following information is available:

```
Received: from tlex01.contoso.com ([x.x.x.x]) by tlex01.c
([10.100.100.20]) with mapi id 15.00.1044.021; Wed, 8 Apr
```

Here, we can see the internal IP address of the contoso mail server at `10.100.100.20` and the version number is `15.00.1044.021`, which tells us that the server is running Exchange 2013 CU7. When implementing a header firewall for routing headers, this information will not be sent to external recipients.

There's more...

If you do not use an Edge Transport server to send Internet e-mails, and instead send messages to the Internet directly from the Mailbox server, then you'll need to specify a different user when running the `Remove-ADPermission` cmdlet:

```
Remove-ADPermission -Identity Internet `
-User "NT Authority\Anonymous Logon" `
-ExtendedRights Ms-Exch-Send-Headers-Routing `
-Confirm:$false
```

Again, you'll need to specify the name of the send connector that is used to send outbound Internet e-mails. When dealing with Mailbox servers, you can remove the permission for the `NT Authority\Anonymous Logon` account, since the `MS Exchange\Edge Transport Servers` user is specific only to Edge Transport servers.

See also

- *Configure the Edge Transport server role*
- *Working with messages in transport queues*

Configure the Edge Transport server role

The Exchange Edge Transport role is responsible for handling mail flow from and to your organization and can be used to secure messages sent to and received from the Internet. In addition to routing messages, you can apply rules, configure settings, and enforce limits on messages as they pass through the servers in your environment. Transport agents can be used to provide basic anti-spam protection, and both the roles implement detailed logging capabilities that can be leveraged from the shell.

The Edge Transport role was reintroduced in Exchange 2013 Service Pack 1 (CU4). In this recipe, we will take a look on how to install the Edge Transport role and how to configure the Edge subscription.

The Edge subscription is the procedure for exporting the information from the Edge transport server(s) and importing it into the Mailbox server(s). This is to allow them to use the EdgeSync service.

EdgeSync is a scheduled synchronization where it's synchronized; for example, the available e-mail addresses from Active Directory into the ADLDS directory instance of the Edge server(s). The replication of data is performed in only one way, from Mailbox to Edge. The information that's being synchronized is used in order to allow the Edge servers to filter and secure e-mails based on, for example, recipient filtering, which means it drops e-mails that are being sent to non-existing mailboxes.

[📝 It is fully supported to use Exchange 2007 and 2010 Edge Transport together with Exchange 2013. In future, this may change.]

How to do it...

For being able to install the Edge Transport role on Windows 2012 Server and Windows 2012 R2 Server, there is a technical prerequisite, which is to install the Windows feature called **Active Directory Lightweight Directory Services (ADLDS)**.

Another thing to consider and solve prior to starting the installation is to make sure that the Exchange 2013 Mailbox servers can resolve the names of the Edge servers and vice versa. Since the Edge servers are placed in DMZ, they are probably not joined to the domain, and most customers don't have any DNS servers in DMZ for doing name lookups to internal resources. If this is the case, you can easily go ahead and use the hosts file by just adding each Mailbox server with its corresponding IP address

The DNS suffix should be added to the Edge servers for the internal domain; so for example, if contoso.com is the internal domain name, then add `contoso.com` as the DNS suffix to the Edge servers.

Last but not least, verify that the traffic is allowed between Mailbox servers and the Edge servers. It's using TCP/25 (SMTP), TCP/50389 (ADLDS), and TCP/50636 (ADLDS).

Also make sure that the traffic for sending and receiving e-mails are allowed from external (Internet) to the Edge servers, and also that the Edge servers are allowed to send e-mails externally.

Installing the prerequisite is done through Windows PowerShell by running the following cmdlet:

```
Install-WindowsFeature ADLDS
```

Once the prerequisite is installed, proceed with installing the Edge Transport role on the server; this is done by using the following command:

```
Setup.exe /mode:Install /role:EdgeTransport `
/IAcceptExchangeServerLicenseTerms
```

After the installation is completed successfully, it's time for creating the Edge subscription. This is done from the Edge server, by creating the XML file:

```
New-EdgeSubscription -FileName C:\Edge.xml
```

Once the subscription file is exported, copy it to the Mailbox servers, and run the following cmdlet for completing the subscription:

```
New-EdgeSubscription -FileData ([byte[]]$(Get-Content `
-Path "C:\temp\Edge.xml" -Encoding Byte -ReadCount 0)) -Site `
"Default-First-Site-Name"
```

When the subscription is configured, two send connectors are being created: `EdgeSync - Default-First-Site-Name to Internet` and `EdgeSync - Inbound to Default-First-Site-Name`. If you had any send connectors for sending e-mails to external recipients created prior to configuring Edge subscription, make sure to remove these to only allow the Edge servers to send e-mails to external recipients. Verify your send connectors by running the following cmdlet:

```
Get-SendConnector | ft -AutoSize
```

The output will look similar to the following screenshot:

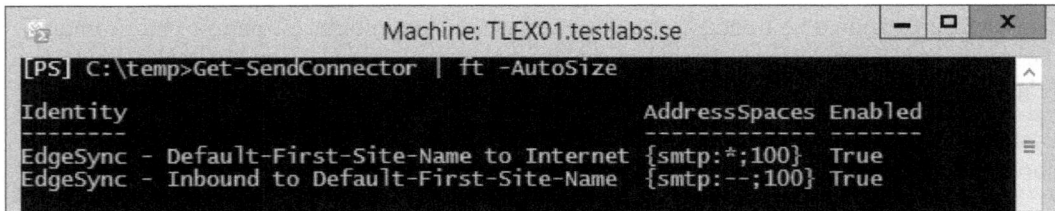

How it works...

Most of the preceding information is described during the steps; some information can be added.

When creating the initial Edge subscription, the `Site` parameter is used for specifying the site where the Mailbox server is placed. In the preceding example, I've used the default value called `Default-First-Site-Name`, which is the initial created Active Directory site.

If you have multiple Edge servers, which is recommended for high availability, you do have to create multiple Edge subscriptions, one per Edge server.

When a new Mailbox server is added to the messaging environment, it needs to be added to the subscription by running the same procedure for it.

There's more...

Once you have created the subscription and you want to see whether everything works as expected, you can run the following cmdlets:

```
Start-EdgeSynchronization
Test-EdgeSynchronization
```

The first cmdlet will start the synchronization of the recipient information and the result will be shown once it's completed.

Running the second cmdlet will show `SyncStatus`, which should be stated as `Normal`. It will also show you at what time the synchronization was last run and when it's scheduled to run the next time.

If you, for any reason, want to force a full synchronization, once the synchronization is set up and running, you can use the following cmdlet:

```
Start-EdgeSynchronization -ForceFullSync
```

> A Telnet client and network monitoring of your choice are both great tools when the Edge role is being implemented but also during troubleshooting.

See also

- ▶ *Implementing a header firewall*
- ▶ *Working with messages in transport queues*

9
High Availability

In this chapter, we will cover the following topics:

- ▶ Building a Windows NLB cluster for CAS servers
- ▶ Creating a Database Availability Group
- ▶ Adding mailbox servers to a Database Availability Group
- ▶ Configuring Database Availability Group network settings
- ▶ Adding mailbox copies to a Database Availability Group
- ▶ Activating mailbox database copies
- ▶ Working with lagged database copies
- ▶ Reseeding a database copy
- ▶ Using the automatic reseed feature
- ▶ Performing maintenance on Database Availability Group members
- ▶ Reporting on database status, redundancy, and replication

Introduction

If you have worked with previous versions of Exchange, you may have been involved in implementing or supporting a high-availability solution that required a shared storage model. This allowed multiple server nodes to access the same physical storage, and in the event of an active server node failure, another node in the cluster could take control of the cluster resources, since it had local access to the databases and log files. This was a good model for server availability, but did not provide any protection for data redundancy.

With the release of Exchange 2007, Microsoft still supported this clustering model, re-branded as **Single Copy Clusters** (**SCC**), but they also introduced a new feature known as continuous replication. Among the three types of continuous replication options provided, **Cluster Continuous Replication** (**CCR**) was the high-availability solution for Exchange 2007 that eliminated the potential risk of a single point of failure at the storage level. With CCR, there were no requirements for shared storage, and database changes were replicated to a passive cluster node using asynchronous log shipping after an initial database seed. Although CCR provided some compelling advantages, there were several limitations. First, you were limited to only two nodes in a CCR cluster. In addition, implementing and managing this configuration required that administrators understand the intricacies of Windows failover clustering.

Microsoft improved on their continuous replication technology and introduced **Database Availability Groups** (**DAGs**) in Exchange 2010. Limitations imposed by CCR in Exchange 2007 were removed by allowing up to 16 nodes to participate within a DAG, while also giving you the option of hosting active copies of individual databases on every server. The reliance on Windows failover clustering administration expertise has been reduced, and you can completely manage all aspects of mailbox server high availability from the Exchange Management Tools.

In Exchange 2013, there are a couple of great new features introduced, such as Managed Store, which in short means that every mailbox database has its own Windows process (`Microsoft.Exchange.Store.Worker.exe`). Another feature, Managed Availability, is an internal health check which tries to start up services that have been stopped for some reason. Microsoft has made some great developments regarding the lagged copy feature; it now only requires half the amount of IOPS than the active server/disk requires. The lagged copy can also start to play down the logs if the server is running out of disk, which is a great feature. These examples are just a few of the newly-introduced features.

In this chapter, we'll cover several aspects of managing Exchange high availability using the shell. You'll learn how to create DAGs, manage database copies, perform maintenance on DAG members, use the new feature called automatic reseed, and generate reports on mailbox database copies.

In addition to providing high availability for the mailbox server role through DAGs, we can eliminate a single point of failure for servers hosting the CAS role using Network Load Balancing, which we'll cover first.

Performing some basic steps

To make use of all the examples in this chapter, we'll reed to use the Exchange Management Shell, and for one recipe, we have the option of using a standard PowerShell console.

You can launch the Exchange Management Shell using the following steps:

1. Log on to a workstation or server with the Exchange Management Tools installed.

2. You can connect using a remote PowerShell if you, for some reason, don't have the Exchange Management Tools installed. Use the following command:

   ```
   $Session = New-PSSession -ConfigurationName '
   Microsoft.Exchange -ConnectionUri '
   http://tlex01/PowerShell/ -Authentication Kerberos
   Import-PSSession $Session
   ```

3. Open the Exchange Management Shell by navigating to **Start | All Programs | Exchange Server 2013**.

4. Click on the **Exchange Management Shell** shortcut.

To launch a standard PowerShell console, open a standard PowerShell console by navigating to **Start | All Programs | Accessories**, click on the `Windows PowerShell` folder, and then click on the **Windows PowerShell** shortcut.

Unless specified otherwise in the *Getting ready* section, all of the recipes in this chapter will require the use of the Exchange Management Shell.

> Remember to start the Exchange Management Shell using **Run as administrator** to avoid permission problems.
>
> In this chapter, you might notice that, in the examples of cmdlets, I have used the back tick (') character to break up long commands into multiple lines. The purpose of this is to make it easier to read. The back ticks are not required and should only be used if needed.

Building a Windows NLB cluster for CAS servers

High availability for servers running the CAS role is achieved using **Network Load Balancing** (**NLB**) and CAS arrays. While it is recommended that you use a **hardware load balancing** (**HLB**) solution. Windows NLB is still supported and may be appropriate for small or medium sized organizations. In this recipe, you'll learn how to create a Windows NLB cluster using PowerShell for servers running Windows Server 2008 R2, Windows Server 2012, or Windows Server 2012 R2.

Getting ready

For this example, you'll need to run some commands against each of your CAS servers that will be a part of the NLB cluster. You must run these commands from at least one of the CAS servers, and each server in the cluster will need to be running Windows Server 2008 R2, Windows Server 2012, or Windows Server 2012 R2 for this to work.

To complete the steps in this recipe, you can use a standard Windows PowerShell console or use the Exchange Management Shell from the server. The cmdlets in this recipe are based on Windows Server 2012 R2.

How to do it...

Let's see how to build a Windows NLB cluster for CAS servers using the following steps:

1. The first step is to install Windows NLB and its tools on each CAS server. You can run these commands on each server to install the required components:

   ```
   Add-WindowsFeature NLB, RSAT-NLB
   ```

   If you have PowerShell remoting enabled on all of your CAS servers, you can install the required components on every server at once using the `Invoke-Command` cmdlet:

   ```
   $servers = 'cas1','cas2','cas3','cas4'
   Invoke-Command -ScriptBlock {
      Add-WindowsFeature NLB,RSAT-NLB
   } -ComputerName $servers
   ```

2. Once each of the CAS servers has the required NLB components installed, make sure to restart each server. Then, import the `NetworkLoadBalancingClusters` module and create the `NLB` cluster on the first node. The following command assumes that the network interface name on the server has been renamed to `NLB`. Your server might be using the default interface name, which would be `Local Area Connection`:

```
Import-Module NetworkLoadBalancingClusters
New-NlbCluster -InterfaceName NLB '
-ClusterName CASLB '
-HostName CAS1 '
-ClusterPrimaryIP 172.16.23.200
```

3. Remove the default port rules that are created for the cluster:

```
Get-NlbClusterPortRule | Remove-NlbClusterPortRule -Force
```

4. Next, create the port rules for the required services:

```
Get-NlbCluster |
Add-NlbClusterPortRule -StartPort 80 '
-EndPort 80 '
-Protocol TCP '
-Affinity Single
Get-NlbCluster |
Add-NlbClusterPortRule -StartPort 443 '
-EndPort 443 '
-Protocol TCP '
-Affinity Single
Get-NlbCluster |
Add-NlbClusterPortRule -StartPort 25 '
-EndPort 25 '
-Protocol TCP '
-Affinity Single
```

5. At this point, you can add the remaining nodes to the cluster. In this example, we'll add the `cas2` server to the cluster:

```
Get-NlbCluster |
Add-NlbClusterNode -NewNodeName cas2 '
-NewNodeInterface NLB
```

How it works...

Windows Server 2008 R2, Windows Server 2012, and Windows Server 2012 R2 include the Server Manager PowerShell module, which is a replacement for the `ServerManagerCmd.exe` utility. Using the Server Manager module, we can install various roles and features on the server. In addition, Windows Server 2008 R2, Windows Server 2012, and Windows Server 2012 R2 also include the `NetworkLoadBalancingClusters` module that can be used to install and configure Windows NLB, and as you've seen, we can use both the modules to install and configure an NLB cluster for Exchange CAS servers.

Installing the components is fairly straightforward. When installing the NLB and RSAT-NLB features, you need to install the features using the `Add-WindowsFeature` cmdlet. Once the RSAT-NLB tools are installed, we can use the `NetworkLoadBalancingClusters` module, which is loaded using the `Import-Module` cmdlet.

When you initially create the NLB cluster, you use the `New-NLBCluster` cmdlet. In the previous example, we created an NLB cluster using the name `CASLB`, which is assigned using the `-ClusterName` parameter. This name can be anything you like, as it will not be used by clients to access the nodes in the cluster. The `-InterfaceName` and `-ClusterPrimaryIP` parameters are very important. You need to specify the network interface name on the server as the value for the `-InterfaceName` parameter. The cluster primary IP address is the shared IP address that will be used to balance the traffic between the CAS servers. You'll need to create a host (A) record in the DNS that resolves to this IP address.

There's more...

In the previous example, we created port rules for several TCP ports, which are described as follows:

- ▸ 25: SMTP connections
- ▸ 80: HTTP connections
- ▸ 443: HTTPS connections

Since the load balancing has been simplified with Exchange 2013, load balancing this set of ports will take care of the web services offered by the CAS role, such as Outlook Web App, Exchange ActiveSync, Exchange Web Services, and so on. If you need to provide access to other services, such as POP or IMAP, you can use the `Add-NLBPortRule` cmdlet to add additional port rules for those protocols.

As a best practice, you should explicitly define the TCP ports that need to be load balanced on each node, and with the new architecture, there is no requirement for having the affinity configured. It's recommended that you have the affinity set to `None`, since the new CAS server is actually just proxying the connections to the Mailbox server.

Taking it a step further

In step 5 of this recipe, we looked at an example of adding a CAS server to the Windows NLB cluster. You can automate this process when adding multiple servers using a simple pipeline command. As long as the servers have matching network interface names (which is recommended), you can use the following command:

```
'cas2','cas3','cas4' | ForEach-Object{
  Get-NlbCluster |
  Add-NlbClusterNode -NewNodeName $_ '
  -NewNodeInterface NLB
}
```

You can see here that we're simply pipelining an array of server names to the `Foreach-Object` cmdlet. For every server in the collection, we add the computer to the `NLB` cluster.

Since Windows NLB doesn't scale well over eight nodes and doesn't provide service awareness or any affinity options other than a single affinity (requests coming from the same client IP), most organizations that are serious about load balancing will implement a hardware-based load balancing solution.

See also

- *Managing the Outlook Anywhere settings* in *Chapter 7, Managing Client Access*
- *Setting internal and external CAS URLs* in *Chapter 7, Managing Client Access*

Creating a Database Availability Group

The initial setup and configuration of a Database Availability Group is done using a single cmdlet named `New-DatabaseAvailabilityGroup`. In this recipe, we'll take a look at how you can automate the creation of a DAG using the Exchange Management Shell.

How to do it...

To create a DAG, use the `New-DatabaseAvailabilityGroup` cmdlet:

```
New-DatabaseAvailabilityGroup -Name DAG '
-WitnessServer CAS1 '
-WitnessDirectory C:\FSW '
-DatabaseAvailabilityGroupIPAddresses 192.168.1.55
```

The previous command creates a new Database Availability Group named DAG. The file share witness server is set to a Client Access server named CAS1, and the path for the directory is also specified, along with an IP address that will be used only by the DAG cluster resources.

How it works...

When you run the New-DatabaseAvailabilityGroup cmdlet, the only requirement is that you use a unique name for the DAG. In the previous example, we specified the information for the file share witness and IP address, but these values are optional.

> The witness server is a quorum resource used by Windows failover clustering as a tie breaker in DAGs with an even number of nodes.

If you do not provide a value for the witness server or witness server directory, Exchange will attempt to locate a Client Access server in the current Active Directory site. One will be selected automatically and the configuration of the witness server and its directory will be taken care of by Exchange.

Keep in mind that, if you do not provide an IP address for the DAG, Exchange will attempt to obtain an address for the DAG using DHCP, but it is recommend that you set the IP address statically.

There's more...

If you create a DAG using the minimum amount of information, you can always come back later and modify the configuration. For instance, say we first issue the following command:

```
New-DatabaseAvailabilityGroup -Name DAG
```

At this point, the DAG will attempt to automatically configure the witness server details and will try to obtain an IP address using DHCP. You can review the settings of the DAG using the Get-DatabaseAvailabilityGroup cmdlet:

```
Get-DatabaseAvailabilityGroup -Identity DAG
```

We can update the DAG using the Set-DatabaseAvailabilityGroup cmdlet to modify the settings:

```
Set-DatabaseAvailabilityGroup -Identity DAG '

-WitnessServer CAS1 '

-WitnessDirectory C:\FSW '

-DatabaseAvailabilityGroupIPAddresses 192.168.1.55
```

You do not have to place the witness directory on another Exchange server. For example, it's quite common for small and medium size organizations to utilize two Exchange servers, both running the Mailbox and Client Access server roles, as a two-node DAG, along with a hardware load balancer to provide high availability for the CAS role. In this case, you could use a member server in the domain as the witness server; just make sure that the Exchange Trusted Subsystem security group in Active Directory is a member of the local administrator group on that server.

When you are planning on adding servers that are located in separate IP subnets, you'll need to specify an IP address that can be used by the DAG in each of the corresponding networks. For example, run the following command:

```
New-DatabaseAvailabilityGroup -Name DAG '
-DatabaseAvailabilityGroupIPAddresses 10.1.1.10,192.168.1.10
```

In this example, one of the DAG members is in the `10.1.1.0/24` subnet and the other is located in the `192.168.1.0/24` subnet. This will allow the cluster IP address to be brought online by a server in either site.

If you have already created the DAG and need to change the addresses, use the `Set-DatabaseAvailabilityGroup` cmdlet:

```
Set-DatabaseAvailabilityGroup -Identity DAG '
-DatabaseAvailabilityGroupIPAddresses 10.1.1.25,192.168.1.25
```

In Exchange 2013 SP1, a new enhancement was introduced called IP less DAG. It generally means that IP addresses are not required anymore for the cluster name object, the network name resource, and for the database availability group. This functionality requires that Windows Server 2012 R2 is being used.

To create a DAG, use the `New-DatabaseAvailabilityGroup` cmdlet:

```
New-DatabaseAvailabilityGroup -Name DAG '
-WitnessServer FSW -WitnessDirectory C:\FSW '
-DatabaseAvailabilityGroupIpAddresses '
([System.Net.IPAddress])::None
```

The previous command creates a new Database Availability Group named DAG using the new functionality.

See also

▶ *Adding mailbox servers to a Database Availability Group*

Adding mailbox servers to a Database Availability Group

Once you've created a Database Availability Group, you'll need to add DAG members, which are servers running the Mailbox server role. In this recipe, you'll learn how to add mailbox servers to a DAG using the Exchange Management Shell.

How to do it...

To add a mailbox server to a DAG, use the `Add-DatabaseAvailabilityGroupServer` cmdlet:

```
Add-DatabaseAvailabilityGroupServer -Identity DAG '
-MailboxServer MBX1
```

In this example, the `MBX1` server is added to a database availability group named `DAG`.

How it works...

In order to run the `Add-DatabaseAvailabilityGroupServer` cmdlet, the servers being added to the DAG must be running an Enterprise Edition of either Windows Server 2008 R2, Windows Server 2012 Standard Edition, or Windows Server 2012 R2 Standard Edition. This is due to the requirement of the Windows failover clustering component, which is required by the DAG. Additionally, the servers must not be a member of an existing DAG for you to successfully run this command.

If you use this cmdlet to add a mailbox server to a DAG, the Windows failover clustering feature will automatically be installed if it has not been already.

When the first mailbox server is added to the DAG, a computer account known as a **Cluster Network Object** (**CNO**) is added to the Active Directory. The name of the computer account will be created using the same name as the DAG. For this cmdlet to complete successfully, when the first mailbox server is added to the DAG, the **Exchange Trusted Subsystem** (**ETS**) universal security group must have the appropriate permissions in the Active Directory to create the account. In many cases, this should not be an issue, but if you work in an environment where Active Directory security permissions have been modified to restrict access, you may need to pre-stage this CNO object and ensure that the Exchange Trusted Subsystem group has been granted full control permissions on the object. If you need to pre-stage the CNO, you can refer to an official link available at `http://technet.microsoft.com/en-us/library/ff367878(v=exchg.150).aspx`.

There's more...

The `Add-DatabaseAvailabilityGroupServer` cmdlet will need to be run for each mailbox server that will be included in the DAG. If you want to automate this process, you have a couple of options.

First, if you simply need to add all of the mailbox servers in the organization to the DAG, use the following code:

```
Get-MailboxServer |

Add-DatabaseAvailabilityGroupServer -Identity DAG
```

If you are working in a more complex environment with multiple Active Directory sites, you'll need to do a little more work. When adding servers to a DAG, you'll probably need to limit this to all of the mailbox servers in a particular AD site. The following code will allow you to accomplish this:

```
$mbx = Get-ExchangeServer | Where-Object{
  $_.Site -match 'Default-First-Site-Name' '
  -and $_.ServerRole -match 'Mailbox'
}
$mbx | ForEach-Object{
  Add-DatabaseAvailabilityGroupServer -Identity DAG '
  -MailboxServer $_
}
```

Here, you can see that we're using the `Get-ExchangeServer` cmdlet to retrieve all the mailbox servers in the default Active Directory site and store the results in the `$mbx` variable. We then pipe this variable to the `Add-DatabaseAvailabilityGroupServer` cmdlet and add each server to the DAG in the site.

See also

- ▶ *Adding mailbox copies to a Database Availability Group*

Configuring Database Availability Group network settings

The Exchange Management Shell includes several cmdlets that allow you to configure the network connections used by servers in a DAG. After you have created DAG networks, or after they've been added automatically by DAG network discovery, you can view the DAG networks and their settings, modify the replication configuration, or remove them completely. This recipe provides multiple examples of how you can perform all of these tasks from the shell.

How to do it...

To view the configuration settings of your existing DAG networks, use the `Get-DatabaseAvailabilityGroupNetwork` cmdlet:

```
Machine: TLEX01.testlabs.se                    _  □  x

[PS] C:\temp>Get-DatabaseAvailabilityGroupNetwork

Identity                ReplicationEnabled      Subnets
--------                ------------------      -------
DAG\MapiDagNetwork      True                    {{172.16.1.0/24,Up}}
DAG\ReplicationDagNet... True                   {{10.0.0.0/8,Up}}
```

The output of the preceding cmdlet shows that there are currently two DAG networks in an organization with a single DAG. The identity of the network, the replication state, and the associated subnets are provided.

How it works...

When you create a DAG, Exchange will automatically discover the existing network connections on each server and create a DAG network for the corresponding IP subnet. Although there is a cmdlet called `New-DatabaseAvailabilityGroupNetwork`, you would rarely need to use it, as this is generally done automatically.

If you need to force Exchange to rediscover the DAG network configuration after changes have been made, you can use the `Set-DatabaseAvailabilityGroup` cmdlet:

Set-DatabaseAvailabilityGroup -Identity DAG –DiscoverNetworks

Simply provide the name of the DAG using the `-Identity` parameter and use the `-DiscoverNetworks` switch parameter to indicate that Exchange should search for changes in the network configuration.

There's more...

By default, all DAG networks are used for log shipping and seeding. If you do not want to allow replication on a specific network, use the `Set-DatabaseAvailabilityGroup` cmdlet:

```
Set-DatabaseAvailabilityGroup -Identity DAG '
-ManualDagNetworkConfiguration $True
Set-DatabaseAvailabilityGroupNetwork -Identity '
DAG\MapiDagNetwork -ReplicationEnabled $false
```

You may consider doing this if you want dedicated DAG networks for replication and heart beating.

Additionally, you may have other network connections on your mailbox servers that should not be used by the DAG at all. This is commonly seen with iSCSI network adapters that are used only for connecting to a storage area network. Since Exchange will attempt to discover all network interfaces and add a DAG network for each one, you'll need to completely disable those DAG networks if they are not be used:

```
Set-DatabaseAvailabilityGroupNetwork -Identity DAG\DAGNetwork04 '
-IgnoreNetwork $true
```

In this example, `DAGNetwork04` will be ignored by the DAG. To remove this restriction, use the same cmdlet and set the `-IgnoreNetwork` parameter to `$false` for the required DAG network.

Renaming and removing DAG networks

When making modifications to DAG networks, you may need to rename or remove one or more networks. This can be easily done in the Exchange Management Console, but if you like to work in the shell, you can do this quickly with the built-in cmdlets. For example, assume that the output of `Get-DatabaseAvailabilityGroupNetwork` shows the following:

```
Machine: TLEX01.testlabs.se                          _  □  x

[PS] C:\Program Files\Microsoft\Exchange Server\V15\scripts>Get-DatabaseAva
ilabilityGroupNetwork

Identity              ReplicationEnabled     Subnets
--------              ------------------     -------
DAG\Mapi              True                   {{172.16.1.0/24,Up}}
DAG\Replication       True                   {{10.0.0.0/24,Up}}
DAG\ReplicationDagNet...  True               {{10.110.0.0/24,Misco...
```

In the preceding screenshot, you can see here that `DAG\ReplicationDagNet...` is listed as `Misconfigured`. In this case, this was an automatically-generated DAG network that is no longer in use by any of the servers in the DAG. Use the `Remove-DatabaseAvailabilityGroupNetwork` cmdlet to delete the network:

```
Remove-DatabaseAvailabilityGroupNetwork -Identity '
DAG\ReplicationDagNetwork -Confirm:$false
```

If, for any reason, you need or want to rename a network, then this can be done using the following cmdlet:

```
Set-DatabaseAvailabilityGroupNetwork -Identity '
DAG\ReplicationDagNetwork03 -Name Replication
```

You can run the `Get-DatabaseAvailabilityGroupNetwork` cmdlet again to view the DAG network configuration and verify that the changes have been made.

Adding mailbox copies to a Database Availability Group

Once your Database Availability Group has been created and configured, the next step is to set up database replication by adding new mailbox database copies of existing databases. In this recipe, we'll take a look at how to add mailbox database copies using the Exchange Management Shell.

How to do it...

Use the `Add-MailboxDatabaseCopy` cmdlet to create a copy of an existing database:

```
Add-MailboxDatabaseCopy -Identity DB01 '
-MailboxServer MBX2 '
-ActivationPreference 2
```

When running this command, a copy of the `DB01` database is created on the `MBX2` server.

How it works...

When creating a copy of a database on another mailbox server, you need to ensure that the server is in the same DAG as the mailbox server hosting the source mailbox database. In addition, a mailbox server can only hold one copy of a given database, and the database path must be identical on every server in the DAG, so make sure that the disk path exists on the server you are adding a copy to.

[🖊 You can remove a database copy using the
Remove-MailboxDatabaseCopy cmdlet. Run Get-Help
Remove-MailboxDatabaseCopy -Full for details.]

When running the Add-MailboxDatabaseCopy cmdlet, you need to specify the identity
of the database and the destination mailbox server that will be hosting the database copy.
The activation preference for a database can optionally be set when you create the database
copy. The value of the activation preference is one of the criteria used by the Active Manager
during a failover event to determine the best replicated database copy to activate.

There's more...

In order to create and mount mailbox databases and add database copies to multiple servers
in a DAG, several commands must be run from within the shell. If you do deployments on a
regular basis or if you build up and tear down lab environments frequently, this is a process
that can easily be automated with PowerShell.

The PowerShell function New-DAGMailboxDatabase creates new mailbox databases from
scratch, mounts them, and then adds passive copies of each database to the remaining
servers you specify. The code for this function is as follows:

```
function New-DAGMailboxDatabase {
param(
    $ActiveServer,
    $PassiveServer,
    $DatabasePrefix,
    $DatabaseCount,
    $EdbFolderPath,
    $LogFolderPath
  )
For ($i=1; $i -le $DatabaseCount; $i++)
{
    $DBName = $DatabasePrefix + $i
    New-MailboxDatabase -Name $DBName '
    -EdbFilePath "$EdbFolderPath\$DBName\$DBName.edb" '
    -LogFolderPath "$LogFolderPath\$DBName" '
    -Server $ActiveServer
    Mount-Database -Identity $DBName
    $PassiveServer | Foreach-Object {
      Add-MailboxDatabaseCopy -Identity SDBName '
      -MailboxServer $_
    }
  }
}
```

Once you've added this function to your shell session, you can run it using a syntax similar to the following:

```
New-DAGMailboxDatabase -ActiveServer mbx1 '
-PassiveServer mbx2,mbx3,mbx4,mbx5 '
-DatabaseCount 3 '
-DatabasePrefix MDB '
-EdbFolderPath E:\Database '
-LogFolderPath E:\Database
```

Running this function with the given parameters will do a number of things. First, you can see, by looking at the function parameter values, that three new databases will be created using a prefix of MDB. This function will create each database using the same prefix, and then number them in order. In this example, the active server, MBX1, will have three new databases created, called MDB1, MDB2, and MDB3. The -PassiveServer parameter needs to have one or more servers defined. In this case, you can see that we'll add database copies of the three new databases on each of the passive servers specified. All databases and log files on each server will be located in a folder under E:\Database in a subdirectory that matches the database name.

In some environments, you might find that trying to mount a database immediately after it was created will fail. What it boils down to is that the mount operation is happening too quickly. If you run into this, you can add a delay before the mount operation; use something, such as Start-Sleep 10, before calling the Mount-Database cmdlet. This will suspend the script for 10 seconds, giving Exchange time to catch up and realize that the database has been created before trying to mount it.

See also

▶ *Reporting on database status, redundancy, and replication*

Activating mailbox database copies

After you've created a Database Availability Group and have added multiple database copies to the servers in your organization, you'll need to be able to move the active copies to other servers. In this recipe, you'll learn how to do this using the Exchange Management Shell.

How to do it...

Manually moving the active mailbox database to another server in a DAG is a process known as a database switchover. In order to activate passive mailbox database copies on another server, you'll need to use the `Move-ActiveMailboxDatabase` cmdlet:

```
Move-ActiveMailboxDatabase DB01 '
-ActivateOnServer MBX2 '
-Confirm:$false
```

In this example, the passive mailbox database copy of `DB01` is activated on the `MBX2` server.

How it works...

When activating a database copy, you can optionally set the `-MoveComment` parameter to a string value of your choice that will be recorded in the event log entry for the move operation.

You can choose to activate one mailbox database copy at a time or you can move all the active databases on a particular server to one or more servers in the DAG, as shown in the following command:

```
Move-ActiveMailboxDatabase -Server MBX2 '
-ActivateOnServer MBX1 '
-Confirm:$false
```

As you can see here, all the active databases on `MBX2` will be moved to `MBX1`. Obviously, this requires that you have the database copies located on `MBX1` for every mailbox database on `MBX2`.

When moving mailbox database copies, you can also override the auto mount dial settings for the target server by specifying one of the following values for the mount dial override settings:

- ▶ `None`: When using `None`, the currently configured mount dial setting on the target server will be used.
- ▶ `Lossless`: This is the default value for the `-MountDialOverride` parameter. When performing a lossless mount, all log files from the active copy must be fully replicated to the passive copy.
- ▶ `GoodAvailability`: This specifies that the copy queue length must be less than or equal to six log files in order to activate the passive copy.
- ▶ `BestEffort`: This mounts the database regardless of the copy queue length and could result in data loss.
- ▶ `BestAvailability`: This specifies that the copy queue length must be less than or equal to 12 log files in order to activate the passive copy.

For example, to move the active database of DB01 from MBX2 to MBX1 with good availability, use the `-MountDialOverride` parameter when running the cmdlet:

```
Move-ActiveMailboxDatabase DB01 '
-ActivateOnServer MBX1 '
-MountDialOverride GoodAvailability '
-Confirm:$false
```

There's more...

If you want to forcefully activate an unhealthy database copy, there are a few parameters available with the `Move-ActiveMailboxDatabase` cmdlet that can be used, depending on the situation.

For example, if you have a database copy with a corrupt content index state, you can force activation of the database using the `-SkipClientExperienceChecks` parameter:

```
Move-ActiveMailboxDatabase DB01 '
-ActivateOnServer MBX1 '
-SkipClientExperienceChecks '
-Confirm:$false
```

At this point, the search catalog on DB01 will need to be recrawled or reseeded.

You also have the option of skipping database health checks when attempting to move an active database. It is recommended that you only do this when an initial activation attempt has failed:

```
Move-ActiveMailboxDatabase DB01 '
-ActivateOnServer MBX1 '
-SkipHealthChecks '
-Confirm:$false
```

Finally, you can use the `-SkipLagChecks` parameter to allow activation of a database copy that has copy and replay queue lengths outside their required thresholds, as shown in the following command:

```
Move-ActiveMailboxDatabase DB01 '
-ActivateOnServer MBX1 '
-SkipLagChecks '
-Confirm:$false
```

It's important to point out here that activating databases that are missing log files will result in data loss and unhappy users.

See also

▸ *Reporting on database status, redundancy, and replication*

Working with lagged database copies

The concept of a lagged database copy is based on functionality introduced with Exchange 2007 that was included with **Standby Continuous Replication** (**SCR**). Using lagged database copies, we can configure a replay lag time in which log files that are replicated to database copies are not played into the database file, therefore lagging behind the active database for a given period of time. The benefit of this is that it gives you the ability to recover point in time data in the event of a logical database corruption. In this recipe, you'll learn how to use the Exchange Management Shell to work with lagged database copies.

How to do it...

Let's see how to work with lagged database copies using the following steps:

1. To create a lagged database copy, specify a replay lag time value when adding a mailbox database copy:

    ```
    Add-MailboxDatabaseCopy -Identity DB03 '

    -MailboxServer MBX2 '

    -ReplayLagTime 3.00:00:00
    ```

    In this example, a new lagged database copy is added to the MBX2 mailbox server with a three day replay lag time.

2. You can also change a regular database copy to a lagged copy:

    ```
    Set-MailboxDatabaseCopy -Identity DB01\MBX2 '

    -ReplayLagTime 12:00:00
    ```

    This time, the passive database copy of DB01 on the MBX2 server is configured with a lag replay time of 12 hours. Notice that the -Identity parameter is specified in the format of <Database Name>\<Server Name>.

How it works...

When creating lagged database copies, the maximum replay time that can be set is 14 days. In addition to the -ReplayLagTime parameter, both cmdlets shown in the previous example provide a -TruncationLagTime parameter. Setting the truncation lag time on a lagged database copy allows you to configure the amount of time that Exchange will hold on to any log files that have been played into the database before deleting them.

When using either the -ReplayLagTime or -TruncationLagTime parameters, you need to specify the amount of time in the format of Days.Hours:Minutes:Seconds. Alternatively, you can pass a TimeSpan object to either of these parameters:

```
Set-MailboxDatabaseCopy -Identity DB01\MBX2 '

-ReplayLagTime (New-TimeSpan -Hours 12)
```

The New-TimeSpan cmdlet is a PowerShell core cmdlet and has parameters that can be used to create a TimeSpan object defined in days, hours, minutes, and seconds.

One of the things you need to keep in mind is that you don't want lagged database copies to be automatically activated in the event of a database failover. The first reason for this is that you lose your point in time data recovery options. Secondly, if you have several days of log files that still need to be replayed into a database, the mount time for a lagged database can be very long and can take several hours.

Based on these reasons, you'll want to block activation of your lagged copies after they have been configured. To do this, use the Suspend-MailboxDatabaseCopy cmdlet:

```
Suspend-MailboxDatabaseCopy -Identity DB01\MBX2 '

-ActivationOnly '

-Confirm:$false
```

Make sure you use the -ActivationOnly switch parameter when running the cmdlet, as shown previously, otherwise it will be suspended indefinitely.

There's more...

Unfortunately, to replay the log files up to a specific point in time, you need to follow a process that cannot be done entirely using the shell. First, you need to suspend the lagged database copy. Next, you have to figure out which log files are required to meet your point in time backup requirements, and move any log files that aren't needed out of the log file path to another location. Finally, you delete the checkpoint file for the database and replay any outstanding log files into the database using the Eseutil command-line utility.

At this point, the database should be clean, and you should be able to resume and activate the database copy. Fortunately, database logical corruption is an extremely rare occurrence, but if you need to recover from a specific point in time, you may want to consider using Windows Server Backup or a third-party backup solution, or become familiar with the process of recovering from a lagged database copy.

Reseeding a database copy

There may be times when database replication issues arise in your environment. These issues could be caused by hardware failures, network issues, or, in extremely rare cases, log file corruption, and leave you with failed database copies that need to be reseeded. This recipe outlines the process of reseeding database copies using the Exchange Management Shell.

How to do it...

Let's see how to reseed a database copy using the following steps:

1. To reseed a database copy, suspend the replication using the following command syntax:

    ```
    Suspend-MailboxDatabaseCopy -Identity DB01\MBX2 '
    -Confirm:$false
    ```

2. Next, you're ready to reseed the database. Use the `Update-MailboxDatabaseCopy` cmdlet, as shown in the following command:

    ```
    Update-MailboxDatabaseCopy -Identity DB01\MBX2 '
    -DeleteExistingFiles
    ```

How it works...

When using the `Update-MailboxDatabaseCopy` cmdlet to reseed a database copy, you can use the `-DeleteExistingFiles` switch parameter to remove the passive database and log files. Depending on the size of the database, it may take a long time to perform the reseed. Once the reseed is complete, replication for the database will automatically be resumed.

If you don't want replication to resume automatically after a reseed, you can configure it for manual resume:

```
Update-MailboxDatabaseCopy -Identity DB01\MBX2 '
-DeleteExistingFiles '
-ManualResume
```

In this example, we've added the `-ManualResume` switch parameter. After the reseed, we can manually resume replication:

```
Resume-MailboxDatabaseCopy -Identity DB01\MBX2
```

There's more...

One of the things that you may run into is a database with a corrupt content index state. In this situation, it's not necessary to reseed the entire database, and you can reseed the content index catalog independently:

```
Update-MailboxDatabaseCopy -Identity DB01\MBX2 -CatalogOnly
```

The `-CatalogOnly` switch parameter, as shown previously, will allow you to reseed the content index catalog without reseeding the database.

Alternatively, you also have the option of reseeding only the database:

```
Update-MailboxDatabaseCopy -Identity DB01\MBX2 -DatabaseOnly
```

In this example, the `DB01` database on the `MBX2` server is reseeded, without having to seed a copy of the content index catalog.

See also

▶ *Reporting on database status, redundancy, and replication*

▶ *Using the automatic reseed feature*

Using the automatic reseed feature

One of the new features in Exchange 2013 is automatic reseed, or in short, auto reseed. This feature is one of my personal favorites of the new ones, as it minimizes the amount of work an administrator needs to do if a disk is broken and needs to be replaced and if the database needs to be reseeded. However, be aware of the fact that the administrator needs to replace the broken disk(s).

We will walk you through a simple setup using one mailbox database using this feature.

How to do it...

Let's see how to use the automatic reseed feature using the following steps:

1. We'll start with configuring the DAG with the folder structure using the following command:

```
Set-DatabaseAvailabilityGroup DAG '
-AutoDagDatabasesRootFolderPath "C:\ExDbs"
Set-DatabaseAvailabilityGroup DAG '
-AutoDagVolumesRootFolderPath "C:\ExVols"
Set-DatabaseAvailabilityGroup DAG '
-AutoDagDatabaseCopiesPerVolume 1
```

2. Next, verify the changes. Use the `Get-DatabaseAvailabilityGroup` cmdlet, as shown here:

```
Get-DatabaseAvailabilityGroup DAG | Format-List *auto*
```

3. Create the folder structure; this can be done either using Explorer or the Command Prompt:

```
md C:\ExDBs
md C:\ExDBs\DB01
md C:\ExVols
md C:\ExVols\Volume1
md C:\ExVols\Volume2
```

4. Verify the folder structure using the following command:

```
dir C:\ExDBs /s
dir C:\ExVols /s
```

5. Next, add two disks per Mailbox server, one to hold the database and one to act as a spare disk. These two disks should be mounted and used as volumes. The result will be similar to the following screenshot:

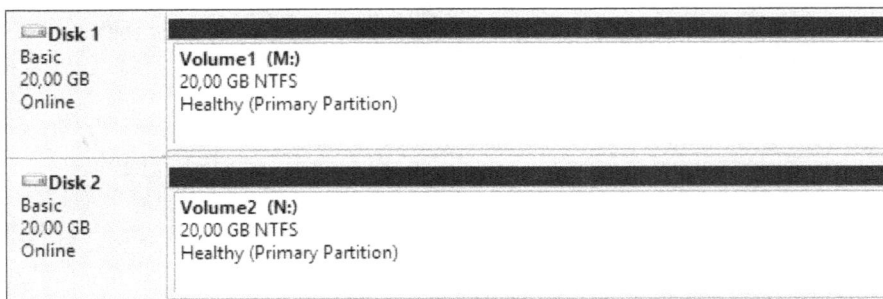

Disk 1	
Basic	**Volume1 (M:)**
20,00 GB	20,00 GB NTFS
Online	Healthy (Primary Partition)

Disk 2	
Basic	**Volume2 (N:)**
20,00 GB	20,00 GB NTFS
Online	Healthy (Primary Partition)

6. When the disks have been formatted and added, it is time to mount them into the folder structure that was created in step 3.

This is done using either disk management or the `mountvol` command:

```
Mountvol.exe C:\ExDBs\DB01 \\?\Volume{43895ac2-a485-11e2-93f5`-
000c2997a8b3}\
```

```
Mountvol.exe C:\ExVols\Volume01 \\?\Volume{43895ac2-a485-11e2-`
93f5-000c2997a8b3}\
```

```
Mountvol.exe C:\ExVols\Volume02 \\?\Volume{43895ad2-a485-11e2-`
93f5-000c2997a8b3}\
```

`Volume02` will be used as a spare disk in the preceding example. When the volumes have been mounted into each folder, they will look similar to the following screenshot in Explorer:

Name ▲	Date modified	Type	Size
Volume1	2015-04-14 19:16	File folder	20 968 444 ...
Volume2	2015-04-14 19:17	File folder	20 968 444 ...

7. Verify that the correct volume was mounted into the correct database folder, which can be done using the `Mountvol.exe` command in Command Prompt:

```
Mountvol.exe C:\ExDBs\DB01 /L
```

```
Mountvol.exe C:\ExVols\Volume01 /L
```

```
Mountvol.exe C:\ExVols\Volume02 /L
```

8. Next, the database folder structure needs to be created and this can be done either using Explorer or the Command Prompt:

```
md C:\ExVols\Volume01\DB01.db
md C:\ExVols\Volume01\DB01.log
```

9. Make sure you verify that the database and log structure was created successfully according to the naming standard, since this s important. You must use the following format for the folder structure:

```
C:\<DatabaseFolderName>\VolumeX\<dbname>.db
C:\<DatabaseFolderName>\VolumeX\<dbname>.log
```

Verify that the folders are named correctly; these folders can be listed using the following command:

```
dir C:\ExDBs /s
dir C:\ExVols /s
```

10. One of the final steps will be to create the mailbox database. This task will be accomplished by running the following command:

```
New-MailboxDatabase -Name DB01 -Server TLEX01 '
-EdbFilePath C:\ExDBs\DB01\DB01.db\DB01.edb '
-LogFolderPath C:\ExDBs\DB01\DB01.log
```

11. Finally, add a mailbox database copy to the second server. This is done by running the following command:

```
Add-MailboxDatabaseCopy -Identity DB01 -MailboxServer TLEX02 -`
ActivationPreference 2
```

How it works...

To start with, we configured the DAG to use the `C:\ExDBs` and `C:\ExVols` folders. These can be changed to the names that suit your environment. The default folder values can also be used, which are `C:\ExchangeDatabases` and `C:\ExchangeVolumes`. We changed them for illustrating a basic example of how it can be done.

When the folders were in place, we configured the DAG using the `-AutoDagDatabaseCopiesPerVolume` parameter and set it to 1. This is because we have one database per volume in our example. This means that this parameter should be set to the number of databases that each volume will host.

One of the most important things to remember when configuring is that the database and log folder structure needs to follow a certain name structure. The database and log folder should be the same as the database name followed by a dot and `db` or `log` depending on if they should contain the database or the log files.

Refer to the following example of a folder structure for the mailbox database called `DB01`:

```
C:\ExDBs\DB01\DB01.db\
C:\ExDBs\DB01\DB01.log\
```

The mailbox database is then created and a copy is also added to the second server.

When the configuration is in place, we are ready to check whether it is working like it should. This can simply be done by disconnecting a physical disk or putting the active volume offline if using a virtual machine and disks.

In the preceding example, I will put the disk offline for the server that holds the active database. This means the database will failover and then the spare volume should replace the broken drive and the database should receive the database and log files from the other Mailbox server, which now holds the active copy of the mailbox database.

In the earlier example scenario, it took about 30 seconds before Exchange detected that the database was broken because the disk was offline. Then, the database was activated on the second Mailbox server, and it took an additional 2 minutes before the automatic reseed took place.

The information about the automatic reseed can be found in the event viewer by navigating to **Application and Services logs | Microsoft Exchange | HighAvailability | Seeding**. The following is a screenshot showing when the auto reseed was completed:

Reseed	Number of events: 4			
Level	Date and Time	Source	Event ID	Task Category
(i) Information	2015-04-14 15:55:34	HighAvailability	826	Seeding Target
(i) Information	2015-04-14 15:55:30	HighAvailability	1110	Auto Reseed Manager
(i) Information	2015-04-14 15:55:30	HighAvailability	825	Seeding Target
(i) Information	2015-04-14 15:55:29	HighAvailability	1109	Auto Reseed Manager

The **Event ID 825** and **1109** means that the reseed progress was started. The **Event ID 826** and **1110** means that the automatic reseed was successfully completed.

> However, there is no guarantee that you will have the same time in your environment, as the result shown in the preceding screenshot, so you need to verify the function before deploying it into production. I would recommend that you check how long the whole procedure takes and document every step in detail.

See also

▶ *Reporting on database status, redundancy, and replication*

▶ *Reseeding a database copy*

▶ *Working with lagged database copies*

Performing maintenance on Database Availability Group members

When it comes to performing maintenance on servers that are part of a DAG, you'll need to move any active databases off to another member in the DAG. This will allow you to install patches or take the server down for hardware repairs or upgrades, without affecting database availability. This recipe will show you how to use some of the built-in PowerShell scripts installed by Exchange 2013 that can be used to place a server in and out of the maintenance mode.

How to do it...

Let's see how to perform maintenance on a DAG using the following steps:

1. First, switch to the `$exscripts` directory:

   ```
   Set-Location $exscripts
   ```

2. Next, run the `StartDagServerMaintenance.ps1` script and specify the server name that should be put into maintenance mode:

   ```
   .\StartDagServerMaintenance.ps1 -ServerName MBX1
   ```

How it works...

When you run the `StartDagMaintenance.ps1` script, it moves all the active databases that are running on the specified server to other members of the DAG. The script will then pause the server node in the cluster and set the `DatabaseCopyAutoActivationPolicy` mailbox server setting to `Blocked`. The `Suspend-MailboxDatabaseCopy` cmdlet is run for each database hosted by the DAG member, and the cluster core resources are moved to another server in the DAG, if needed.

After the maintenance is complete, run the `StopDagServerMaintenance.ps1` script to take the server out of maintenance mode:

`.\StopDagServerMaintenance.ps1 -ServerName MBX1`

This will run the `Resume-MailboxDatabaseCopy` cmdlet for each database located on the specified server and resume the node in the cluster. The auto activation policy for the mailbox server will then be set back to `Unrestricted` and the server will be back online, ready for production use.

There's more...

After you've performed maintenance on your DAG members, the databases that were previously active are not moved back, even after running the stop DAG maintenance script.

If you are performing maintenance on multiple servers at the same time, you might end up with an uneven distribution of active databases running on other servers in the DAG.

To correct this, the `RedistributeActiveDatabases.ps1` script located in the `$exscripts` folder can be used to rebalance the active database copies across the DAG. There are two options for balancing active database copies within a DAG: by activation preference and by site and activation preference.

When using the `-BalanceDbsByActivationPreference` parameter, the script tries to move the databases to their most preferred copy based on the activation preference, regardless of the Active Directory site. If you use the `-BalanceDbsBySiteAndActivationPreference` parameter, the script will attempt to activate the most preferred copy and try to balance them within each Active Directory site.

When running the script, specify the name of the DAG and the preferred method used to rebalance the databases:

```
.\RedistributeActiveDatabases.ps1 -DagName DAG '

-BalanceDbsByActivationPreference '

-ShowFinalDatabaseDistribution '

-Confirm:$false
```

Notice that the `-ShowFinalDatabaseDistribution` parameter was also used when we ran this script. This will provide a report that displays the actions that were taken to balance the databases, as shown in the following screenshot:

Here, you can see that several key pieces of information are returned, including the success or failure of the moves and the total duration.

> The steps for placing a server into maintenance mode are documented and can be found at https://technet.microsoft.com/en-us/library/dd298065(v=exchg.150).aspx.

Reporting on database status, redundancy, and replication

When dealing with servers and database copies in a DAG, you need to keep a close eye on your database status, including replication health, as well as operational events, such as database mounts, moves, and failovers. In this recipe, you'll learn how to use the Exchange Management Shell, along with some built-in PowerShell scripts to proactively monitor your servers and databases configured for high availability.

How to do it...

To view the status information about databases that have been configured with database copies, use the `Get-MailboxDatabaseCopyStatus` cmdlet:

```
Get-MailboxDatabase |

Get-MailboxDatabaseCopyStatus |

select Name,Status,ContentIndexState
```

In this example, we're viewing all the database copies to determine the health and status of the databases. The output of the previous command will look similar to the following screenshot:

```
Machine: tlex01.testlabs.se                         _ □ X

[PS] C:\Databases>Get-MailboxDatabase | Get-MailboxDatabaseCopyStatus | sel
ect Name,Status,ContentIndexState

Name                                    Status          ContentIndexState
----                                    ------          -----------------
DB1\TLEX01                              Mounted         Healthy
DB1\TLEX02                              Healthy         Healthy
DB2\TLEX01                              Mounted         Healthy
DB2\TLEX02                              Healthy         Healthy
DB3\TLEX01                              Healthy         Healthy
DB3\TLEX02                              Mounted         Healthy
```

In the preceding screenshot, you can see which server is currently hosting active mailbox databases that are reported with a status of `Mounted`. The passive database copies hosted on the servers are reported as `Healthy`.

How it works...

In our previous example, we selected only a few of the available properties returned by the `Get-MailboxDatabaseCopyStatus` cmdlet to get an idea of the health of the databases. The default output of the `Get-MailboxDatabaseCopyStatus` cmdlet will also provide details about the status of your mailbox database copies and show you the `CopyQueueLength` and `ReplayQueueLength` values. Keeping an eye on this information is critical to ensure that the database replication is working properly.

If you need to retrieve more detailed information about the database copies on a server, you can pipe this cmdlet to `Format-List` and review several properties that provide details about the copy and replay queue length, log generation and inspection, activation status, and more:

```
Get-MailboxDatabaseCopyStatus -Server MBX1 | Format-List
```

To view the details of a particular database copy, use the `-Identity` parameter and specify the database and server name in the format of `<Database Name>\<Server Name>`, as shown in the following command:

```
Get-MailboxDatabaseCopyStatus -Identity DB01\MBX1
```

You can review the status of networks being used for log shipping and seeding using the `-ConnectionStatus` switch parameter:

```
Get-MailboxDatabaseCopyStatus -Identity DB01\MBX2 '
-ConnectionStatus | Format-List
```

When using this parameter, the `IncomingLogCopyingNetwork` and `SeedingNetwork` properties returned in the output will provide the replication networks being used for these operations.

There's more...

Another way to get a quick overview of the replication status of your mailbox database copies is to use the `Test-ReplicationHealth` cmdlet.

When you run this cmdlet, use the `-Identity` parameter to specify the mailbox server that should be tested, as shown in the following screenshot:

```
Machine: TLEX01.testlabs.se                                      _ □ x

[PS] C:\Program Files\Microsoft\Exchange Server\V15\scripts>Test-Replicatio
nHealth -Identity TLEX02

Server        Check                        Result      Error
------        -----                        ------      -----
TLEX02        ClusterService               Passed
TLEX02        ReplayService                Passed
TLEX02        ActiveManager                Passed
TLEX02        TasksRpcListener             Passed
TLEX02        TcpListener                  Passed
TLEX02        ServerLocatorService         Passed
TLEX02        DagMembersUp                 Passed
TLEX02        ClusterNetwork               Passed
TLEX02        QuorumGroup                  Passed
TLEX02        FileShareQuorum              Passed
TLEX02        DatabaseRedundancyCheck      Passed
TLEX02        DatabaseAvailabilityCheck    Passed
TLEX02        DBCopySuspended              Passed
TLEX02        DBCopyFailed                 Passed
TLEX02        DBInitializing               Passed
```

As you can see from the output, all of the cluster services and resources are tested. In addition, several aspects of database copy health will be checked, including log replay, log copy queues and the status of the database and whether it is suspended, disconnected, or initializing.

To proactively monitor replication health on an on-going basis, you can schedule the following script to run every hour or so. It will send a message to a specified e-mail address with any errors that are being reported:

```
param(
  $To,
  $From,
  $SMTPServer
)

$DAGs = Get-DatabaseAvailabilityGroup
$DAGs | Foreach-Object{
  $_.Servers | Foreach-Object {
    $test = Test-ReplicationHealth -Identity $_.Name
    $errors = $test | Where-Object{$_.Error}
    if($errors) {
      $errors | Foreach-Object {
```

```
      Send-MailMessage -To $To '
      -From $From '
     -Subject "Replication Health Error" '
     -Body $_.Error '
     -SmtpServer $SMTPServer
    }
   }
  }
 }
```

This script iterates though every DAG in your environment and every mailbox server that is a member of a DAG. The `Test-ReplicationHealth` cmdlet is run for each server, and any errors reported will be e-mailed to the specified recipient.

To use this script, save the previous code to a file, such as `ReplicationHealth.ps1`. When you schedule the script to run, call the script and provide values for the recipient e-mail address, the sender address, and the SMTP server used to send the message:

```
c:\ReplicationHealth.ps1 -To administrator@contoso.com '
-From sysadmin@contoso.com '
-SMTPServer cas1.contoso.com
```

Remember, depending on where your script is running from, if you are using one of your Client Access Servers as the SMTP server, you may need to configure your receive connectors to allow SMTP relay.

Understanding switchover and failover metrics

The `CollectOverMetrics.ps1` script can be used to read the event logs from the mailbox servers that are configured in a DAG, and it gathers information about database mounts, moves, and failovers. This script is installed with Exchange 2013 and is located in the `$exscripts` directory.

To run the script, switch to the `$exscripts` directory:

```
Set-Location $exscripts
```

Next, run the script and specify the name of the DAG you want to to receive a report for, and the location where the report should be saved:

```
.\CollectOverMetrics.ps1 -DatabaseAvailabilityGroup DAG '
-ReportPath c:\temp\Reports
```

When running this command, you'll see an output similar to the following screenshot:

```
Machine: TLEX01.testlabs.se                             - □ x
[PS] C:\Program Files\Microsoft\Exchange Server\V15\scripts>.\CollectOverMe
trics.ps1 -DatabaseAvailabilityGroup DAG -ReportPath C:\temp\Report
Get statistics from TLEX02
Get statistics from TLEX01
Found total of 44 entries
Searching for ACLL loss reports on TLEX02.
Searching for ACLL loss reports on TLEX01.

Generated the following per-DAG reports:
C:\temp\Report\FailoverReport.DAG.2015_04_14_20_06_27.csv
```

As you can see, each server in the DAG will be processed and a CSV file will be generated in the specified report path. At this point, you can read the CSV file into the shell using the `Import-CSV` cmdlet:

Import-Csv '

c:\temp\Reports\FailoverReport.DAG.2015_04_14_20_06_27.csv

You can then view details about switchover or failover events in each database, which will be similar to the following screenshot:

```
Machine: TLEX01.testlabs.se                             - □ x
[PS] C:\Program Files\Microsoft\Exchange Server\V15\scripts>Import-Csv C:\t
emp\Report\FailoverReport.DAG.2015_04_14_20_06_27.csv

DatabaseName         : DB02
TimeRecoveryStarted  : 2015-04-14 18:48:42
TimeRecoveryEnded    : 2015-04-14 18:50:06
ActionInitiator      : Automatic
ActionCategory       : Move
ActionReason         : NodeDown
Result               : Failed
DurationOutage       : 83,755204
DurationDismount     : 83,4997556
DurationBcs          : 0,1567969
DurationAcll         : 0.0
DurationMount        : 0.0
DurationOther        : 0,255448399999992
ActiveOnStart        : TLEX01.testlabs.se
ActiveOnFinish       : TLEX01.testlabs.se
```

You can limit the reports to specific databases when running the script and also specify a start and end time so that you can limit the information returned to meet your requirements.

The `CollectReplicationMetrics.ps1` file also has the ability to create the report in an HTML format; it's done by adding the `-GenerateHtmlReport` parameter.

Understanding replication metrics

The CollectReplicationMetrics.ps1 file is also included in the $exscripts directory on Exchange 2013 servers. This script can be used to collect data from performance counters related to database replication, and it needs to be run for a period of time for it to gather information. Similar to the CollectOverMetrics.ps1 script, you need to specify a DAG name and a path used to save the report in the CSV or HTML format. When running CollectReplicationMetrics.ps1, you need to specify a duration that defines the amount of time for which the script will run. You also need to specify a frequency interval for which metrics will be collected.

To run the script, switch to the $exscripts directory:

```
Set-Location $exscripts
```

Next, run the script and specify the DAG name, duration, frequency, and report path that should be used using the following command:

```
.\CollectReplicationMetrics.ps1 -DagName DAG '
-Duration '01:00:00' '
-Frequency '00:01:00' '
-ReportPath c:\temp\reports
```

Using the given parameter values, the script will run for one hour, and collect replication metrics every minute. When the script completes, you can read the CSV files that were generated into the shell using the Import-CSV cmdlet, or open them up in Excel for review.

See also

▶ *Scheduling scripts to run at a later time* in *Chapter 2, Exchange Management Shell Common Tasks*

10
Exchange Security

In this chapter, we will cover the following topics:

- ► Granting users full access permissions to mailboxes
- ► Finding users with full access to mailboxes
- ► Sending e-mail messages as another user or group
- ► Working with Role Based Access Control
- ► Creating a custom RBAC role for administrators
- ► Creating a custom RBAC role for end users
- ► Troubleshooting RBAC
- ► Generating a certificate request
- ► Installing certificates and enabling services
- ► Importing certificates on multiple Exchange servers

Introduction

When it comes to managing security in Exchange 2013, you have several options, depending on the resources that you're dealing with. For example, you can allow multiple users to open a mailbox by assigning them full access permissions to a mailbox object, but granting administrators the ability to create recipient objects needs to be done through **Role Based Access Control** (**RBAC**). Obviously, since the security for both of these components is handled differently, we have unrelated sets of cmdlets that need to be used to get the job done, and managing each of them through the shell will require a unique approach.

In this chapter, we'll take a look at several solutions implemented through the Exchange Management Shell that address each of the components described previously, as well as some additional techniques that can be used to improve your efficiency when dealing with Exchange security.

Performing some basic steps

To work with the code samples in this chapter, follow these steps to launch the Exchange Management Shell:

1. Log on to a workstation or server with the Exchange Management Tools installed.
2. You can connect using a remote PowerShell. If you, for some reason, don't have the Exchange Management tools installed, use the following command:

    ```
    $Session = New-PSSession -ConfigurationName '

    Microsoft.Exchange -ConnectionUri '

    http://tlex01/PowerShell/ -Authentication Kerberos

    Import-PSSession $Session
    ```

3. Open the Exchange Management Shell by navigating to **Start | All Programs | Exchange Server 2013.**
4. Click on the **Exchange Management Shell** shortcut.

To launch a standard PowerShell console, open a standard PowerShell console by navigating to **Start | All Programs | Accessories**, and then click on the Windows PowerShell folder and then on the **Windows PowerShell** shortcut.

Unless specified otherwise in the *Getting ready* section, all of the recipes in this chapter will require the use of the Exchange Management Shell.

> Remember to start the Exchange Management Shell using **Run as administrator** to avoid permission problems.
>
> In this chapter, you might notice that, in the examples of cmdlets, I have used the back tick (') character to break up long commands into multiple lines. The purpose of this is to make it easier to read. The back ticks are not required and should only be used if needed.

Granting users full access permissions to mailboxes

One of the most common administrative tasks that Exchange administrators need to perform is to manage the access rights to one or more mailboxes. For example, you may have several users that share access to an individual mailbox, or you may have administrators and help desk staff that need to be able to open end users mailboxes when troubleshooting a problem or providing technical support. In this recipe, you'll learn how to assign the permissions required to perform these tasks through the Exchange Management Shell.

How to do it...

To assign full access rights for an individual user to a specific mailbox, use the `Add-MailboxPermission` cmdlet:

```
Add-MailboxPermission -Identity dsmith '
-User hlawson '
-AccessRights FullAccess '
-AutoMapping $false
```

After running this command, the user `hlawson` will be able to open the mailbox that belongs to `dsmith` and read or modify the data within the mailbox, without having the mailbox automatically added and mapped in Outlook.

How it works...

When you assign full access rights to a mailbox, you may notice that the change does not take effect immediately, and the user that has been granted permissions to a mailbox still cannot access that resource. This is because the Information Store service uses a cached mailbox configuration that, by default, is only refreshed every two hours. You can force the cache to refresh by restarting the Information Store service on the mailbox server that is hosting the active database where the mailbox resides. Obviously, this is not something that should be done during business hours on production servers, as it will disrupt mailbox access for end users.

Since we can grant permissions to a mailbox using the `Add-MailboxPermission` cmdlet, you would be correct when assuming that this change can also be reversed if needed. To remove the permissions assigned in the previous example, use the `Remove-MailboxPermission` cmdlet:

```
Remove-MailboxPermission -Identity dsmith '
-User hlawson '
-AccessRights FullAccess '
-Confirm:$false
```

In addition to assigning full access permissions to individual users, you can also assign this right to a group:

```
Add-MailboxPermission -Identity dsmith '
-User "IT Help Desk" '
-AccessRights FullAccess
```

In this example, the `IT Help Desk` is a mail-enabled universal security group, and it has been granted full access to the `dsmith` mailbox. All users who are members of this group will be able to open the mailbox and access its contents through Outlook or OWA.

Of course, you may need to do this for multiple users, and doing so for one mailbox at a time is not very efficient. To make this a little easier, we can make use of a simple pipeline command. For example, let's say that you want to grant full access rights to all the mailboxes in the organization:

```
Get-Mailbox -ResultSize Unlimited -RecipientTypeDetails UserMailbox |
Add-MailboxPermission -User "IT Help Desk" '
-AccessRights FullAccess
```

The given command retrieves all the user mailboxes in the organization, and sends them down the pipeline to the `Add-MailboxPermission` cmdlet, where full access rights are assigned to the `IT Help Desk` group.

There's more...

If you need to assign access permissions to all the mailboxes in your organization, you probably should consider doing this at the database level, rather than on an individual mailbox basis. In the previous example, we used a pipeline operation to apply the permissions to all mailboxes with a command. The limitation with this is that the command only sets the permissions on the existing mailboxes; any new mailbox created afterwards will not inherit these permissions. You can solve this problem by assigning the `Generic-All` extended right to a user or group on a particular database.

For example, if all of our mailboxes are located in the DB01 database, we can allow user access to every mailbox in the database using the following command:

```
Add-ADPermission -Identity DB01 '
-User support '
-AccessRights GenericAll
```

After running this command, the support account will be able to log on to every mailbox in the DB01 database, as well as any mailboxes created in that database in the future.

Of course, you'll likely have more than one database in your organization. If you want to apply this setting to every mailbox database in the organization, pipe the output from the Get-MailboxDatabase cmdlet to the Add-ADPermission cmdlet using the appropriate parameters:

```
Get-MailboxDatabase |
Add-ADPermission -User support '
-AccessRights GenericAll
```

Once this command has been run, the user account support will be able to connect to any mailbox in the Exchange organization.

See also

▶ *Sending e-mail messages as another user or group*

Finding users with full access to mailboxes

One of the issues with assigning full mailbox access to users and support personnel is that things change over time. People change roles, move to other departments, or even leave the organization. Keeping track of all of this and removing full access permissions when required can be challenging in a fast-paced environment. This recipe will allow you to solve these issues using the Exchange Management Shell to find out exactly who has full access permissions to the mailboxes in your environment.

How to do it...

To find all of the users or groups who have been assigned full access rights to a mailbox, use the `Get-MailboxPermission` cmdlet:

```
Get-MailboxPermission -Identity administrator |
Where-Object {$_.AccessRights -like "*FullAccess*"}
```

You can see here that we are limiting the results using a filter by piping the output to the `Where-Object` cmdlet. Only the users with the `FullAccess` access rights will be returned.

How it works...

The previous command is useful for quickly viewing the permissions for a single mailbox while working interactively in the shell. The first problem with this approach is that it also returns a lot of information that we're probably not interested in. Consider the truncated output from our previous command:

```
Machine: tlex01.testlabs.se                                    _  □  X

[PS] C:\Scripts>Get-MailboxPermission -Identity admins | Where-Object {$_.A
ccessRights -like "*FullAccess*"}

Identity              User               AccessRights    IsInherited Deny
--------              ----               ------------    ----------- ----
testlabs.se/Users...  NT AUTHORITY\SELF  {FullAccess...  False       False
testlabs.se/Users...  TESTLABS\sysadmin  {FullAccess}    False       False
testlabs.se/Users...  TESTLABS\IT Help   {FullAccess}    False       False
testlabs.se/Users...  TESTLABS\admins    {FullAccess}    True        True
testlabs.se/Users...  TESTLABS\Domain A...{FullAccess}   True        True
testlabs.se/Users...  TESTLABS\Enterpri..{FullAccess}    True        True
testlabs.se/Users...  TESTLABS\Organiza..{FullAccess}    True        True
```

Notice that both the `IT Help Desk` and `sysadmin` user have full access permissions to the administrator mailbox. This is useful because we know that someone assigned these permissions to the mailbox, as this is not something Exchange is going to do on its own. What is not so useful is that we also see all of the built-in full access permissions that apply to every mailbox, such as the `NT AUTHORITY\SELF` user and other default permissions. To filter out this information, we can use a more complex filter:

```
Get-MailboxPermission administrator |
Where-Object {
  ($_.AccessRights -like "*FullAccess*") '
  -and ($_.User -notlike "NT AUTHORITY\SELF") '
  -and ($_.IsInherited -eq $false)
}
```

You can see that we're still filtering based on the `AccessRights` property, but now we're excluding the `SELF` account and any other accounts that receive their permissions through inheritance. The output now gives us something that's a little easier to work with when reviewing a report:

```
Machine: tlex01.testlabs.se                                    _ □ x

[PS] C:\Scripts>Get-MailboxPermission admins | Where-Object {($_.AccessRigh
ts -like "*FullAccess*") -and ($_.User -notlike "NT AUTHORITY\SELF") -and (
$_.IsInherited -eq $false)}

Identity              User                 AccessRights    IsInherited Deny
--------              ----                 ------------    ----------- ----
testlabs.se/Users...  TESTLABS\sysadmin    {FullAccess}    False       False
testlabs.se/Users...  TESTLABS\IT Help ... {FullAccess}    False       False
```

This is an easy way to figure out which accounts have been assigned full access to a mailbox via the `Add-MailboxPermission` cmdlet. Keep in mind that users who have been assigned these permissions at the database level receive their permissions through inheritance, so you may need to adjust the filter to meet your specific needs.

There's more...

Finding out which users have full access rights to an individual mailbox can be useful for quick troubleshooting, but chances are that you're going to need to figure this out for all the mailboxes in your organization. The following code will generate the output that provides this information:

```
foreach($mailbox in Get-Mailbox -ResultSize Unlimited) {
  Get-MailboxPermission $mailbox |
  Where-Object {
    ($_.AccessRights -like "*FullAccess*") '
    -and ($_.User -notlike "NT AUTHORITY\SELF") '
    -and ($_.IsInherited -eq $false)
  }
}
```

As you can see here, we use a `foreach` loop to process all of the mailboxes in the organization. Inside the loop, we're using the same filter from the previous example to determine which users have full access rights to each mailbox.

Sending e-mail messages as another user or group

In some environments, it may be required to allow users to send e-mail messages from a mailbox as if the owner of that mailbox had actually sent this message. This can be accomplished by granting the `Send-As` permissions to a user on a particular mailbox. In addition, you can also allow a user to send e-mail messages that are sent using the identity of a distribution group. This recipe explains how you can manage these permissions from the Exchange Management Shell.

How to do it...

To assign the `Send-As` permissions to a mailbox, we use the `Add-ADPermission` cmdlet:

```
Add-ADPermission -Identity "Frank Howe" `
-User "Eric Cook" `
-ExtendedRights Send-As
```

After running the previous command, `Eric Cook` can send messages from the mailbox of `Frank Howe`.

How it works...

The `Add-ADPermission` cmdlet uses the `-Identity` parameter to classify the object to which you will assign the permissions. Unlike many of the Exchange cmdlets, you cannot use the alias of the mailbox when assigning a value to the `-Identity` parameter. You can use the user's display name, as shown previously, as long as it is unique, or you can use the distinguished name of the object. If you do not know a user's full name, you can use the `Get-Mailbox` cmdlet and pipe the object to the `Add-ADPermission` cmdlet:

```
Get-Mailbox fhowe |
Add-ADPermission -User ecook -ExtendedRights Send-As
```

You might find this syntax useful when assigning the `Send-As` right in bulk. For example, to grant a user `Send-As` permission for all users in a particular OU, use the following syntax:

```
Get-Mailbox -OrganizationalUnit contoso.com/Sales |
Add-ADPermission -User ecook -ExtendedRights Send-As
```

If you ever need to remove these settings, simply use the `Remove-ADPermission` cmdlet. This command will remove the permissions assigned n the first example:

```
Remove-ADPermission -Identity "Frank Howe" '
-User ecook '
-ExtendedRights Send-As '
-Confirm:$false
```

There's more...

To assign the `Send-As` permissions to a distribution group, the process is exactly the same as for a mailbox. Use the `Add-ADPermission` cmdlet, as shown in the following command:

```
Add-ADPermission -Identity Marketing '
-User ecook '
-ExtendedRights Send-As
```

You can also provide the identity of the group to the `Add-ADPermission` cmdlet via a pipeline command, just as we saw earlier with the `Get-Mailbox` cmdlet. To do this with a distribution group, use the `Get-DistributionGroup` cmdlet:

```
Get-DistributionGroup -ResultSize Unlimited |
Add-ADPermission -User ecook -ExtendedRights Send-As
```

In the given example, the user `ecook` is given the `Send-As` right for all the distribution groups in the organization.

Working with Role Based Access Control

The security model that was introduced in Exchange 2C10 is still present in Exchange 2013. With the introduction of the RBAC permissions model, you can essentially determine which cmdlets administrators and end users are allowed to change settings within the system. This recipe will show you how to work with the predefined RBAC permissions in Exchange 2013.

How to do it...

Let's say that you need to allow a member of your staff to manage the settings of the Exchange servers in your organization. This administrator only needs to manage server settings and should not be allowed to perform ary other tasks, such as recipient management.

Exchange 2013 provides a large set of predefined permissions that can be used to address common tasks such as these. In this case, we can use the `Server Management` role group that allows administrators to manage the servers in the organization.

All we need to do to assign the permission is to add the required user account to this role group:

```
Add-RoleGroupMember -Identity "Server Management" -Member bwelch
```

At this point, the user can use the Exchange Management Console or the Exchange Management Shell to perform server-related management tasks.

How it works...

Exchange 2013 implements RBAC by grouping sets of cmdlets used to perform specific tasks in management roles. Think of a management role simply as a list of cmdlets. For example, one of the roles assigned via the `Server Management` role group is called Exchange Servers. This role allows an assigned user the ability to use over 30 separate cmdlets that are specifically related to managing servers, such as `Get-ExchangeServer`, `Set-ExchangeServer`, and more.

There are a number of built-in role groups that you can use to delegate typical management tasks to the administrators in your environment. You can view all of the built-in role groups using the `Get-RoleGroup` cmdlet.

Role groups can assign many different management roles to a user. In the previous example, we were working with the `Server Management` role group, which assigns a number of different management roles to any user that is added to this group. To view a list of these roles, we can use the `Get-ManagementRoleAssignment` cmdlet:

```
Get-ManagementRoleAssignment -RoleAssignee 'Server Management' |
Select-Object Role
```

The output of this command is shown in the following screenshot:

As you can see, each management role assigned through this role group is returned. To determine which cmdlets are made available by each of these roles, we can run the `Get-ManagementRoleEntry` cmdlet against each of them individually. An example of this can be seen in the following screenshot:

Management role entries are listed in the format of `<Role Name>\<Cmdlet Name>`. The `Get-ManagementRoleEntry` cmdlet can be used with wildcards, as shown in the previous command. The output of the `Get-ManagementRoleEntry` command in the previous example is truncated for readability, but as you can see, there are several cmdlets that are part of the `Exchange Servers` management role, which can be assigned via the `Server Management` role group. If only this role is assigned to a user, they are given access to these specific cmdlets and will not see other cmdlets, such as `New-Mailbox`, as that is part of another management role.

To view all of the management roles that exist in the organization, use the `Get-ManagementRole` cmdlet. You can then use the `Get-ManagementRoleEntry` cmdlet to determine which cmdlets belong to that role.

There's more...

Many of the management roles installed with Exchange 2013 can be assigned to users by adding them to a role group. Role groups are associated with management roles through something called role assignments. Although the recommended method of assigning permissions is through the use of role groups, you can still directly assign a management role to a user with the `New-ManagementRoleAssignment` cmdlet:

New-ManagementRoleAssignment -Role 'Mailbox Import Export' '

-User administrator

In this example, the administrator is assigned the `Mailbox Import Export` role, which is not associated with any of the built-in role groups. In this case, we can create a direct assignment as shown previously, or use the `-SecurityGroup` parameter to assign this role to an existing role group or a custom role group created with the `New-RoleGroup` cmdlet.

RBAC for end users

Everything we've discussed so far is related to RBAC for administrators, but end users need to be able to run cmdlets too. Now, this doesn't mean that they need to fire up EMS and start executing commands, but the other things that they can change will require the use of PowerShell cmdlets behind the scenes.

A good example of this is the **Exchange Control Panel** (**ECP**). When a user logs into ECP, the very first thing they see is the **Account Information** screen, which allows them to change various settings that apply to their user account, such as their address, city, state, zip code, and phone numbers. When users change this information in ECP, these changes are carried out in the background with the Exchange Management Shell cmdlets.

Here's the confusing part. End users are also assigned permissions from management roles, but not through role groups or role assignments, as they are applied to administrators. Instead, end users are assigned their management roles through something called a role assignment policy.

When you install Exchange, a single role assignment policy is created. Mailboxes that are created or moved over to Exchange 2013 will use the `Default Role Assignment Policy` property which gives users some basic rights, such as modifying their contact information, creating inbox rules through ECP, and more.

To determine which management roles are applied to the `Default Role Assignment Policy`, use the following command:

```
Get-RoleAssignmentPolicy "Default Role Assignment Policy" |
Format-List AssignedRoles
```

See also

 ▸ *Creating a custom RBAC role for administrators*
 ▸ *Creating a custom RBAC role for end users*
 ▸ *Troubleshooting RBAC*

Creating a custom RBAC role for administrators

Sometimes, the management roles that are installed by Exchange are not specific enough to meet your needs. When you are faced with this issue, the solution is to create a custom RBAC role. The process can be a little tricky, but the level of granular control that you can achieve is quite astounding. This recipe will show you how to create a custom RBAC role that can be assigned to administrators based on a very specific set of requirements.

How to do it...

Let's say that your company has decided that a group of support personnel should be responsible for the creation of all new Exchange recipents. You want to be very specific about what type of access this group will be granted, and you plan on implementing a custom management role based on the following requirements:

► Support personnel should be able to create Exchange recipients in the Employees OU in the Active Directory

► Support personnel should not be able to create Exchange recipients in any other OU in the Active Directory

► Support personnel should not be able to remove recipients in the Employees OU, or any other OU in the Active Directory

Use the following steps to implement a custom RBAC role for the support group based on the previous requirements:

1. First, we need to create a new custom management role:

    ```
    New-ManagementRole -Name "Employee Recipient Creation" '
    -Parent "Mail Recipient Creation"
    ```

2. Next, we need to modify the role so that the support staff cannot remove recipients from the organization:

    ```
    Get-ManagementRoleEntry "Employee Recipient Creation\*" |
    Where-Object {$_.name -like "remove-*"} |
    Remove-ManagementRoleEntry -Confirm:$false
    ```

3. Now we need to scope this role to a specific location in the Active Directory:

    ```
    New-ManagementScope -Name Employees '
    -RecipientRoot contoso.com/Employees '
    -RecipientRestrictionFilter {
       (RecipientType -eq "UserMailbox") -or
       (RecipientType -eq "MailUser") -or
       (RecipientType -eq "MailContact")
    }
    ```

4. Finally, we can create a custom role group and add the support staff as members:

```
New-RoleGroup -Name Support '
-Roles "Employee Recipient Creation" '
-CustomRecipientWriteScope Employees '
-Members bjacobs,dgreen,jgordon
```

How it works...

The built-in management roles cannot be modified, so when we want to customize an existing role to meet our needs, we need to create a new custom role based on an existing parent role. Since we know that the built-in `Mail Recipient Creation` role provides the cmdlets that our support group will need, the first thing we must do is create a new role as a child of the `Mail Recipient Creation` role, called `Employee Recipient Creation`.

One of the requirements in our scenario was that support personnel should not be able to remove recipients from the organization, so we edited our custom role to get rid of any cmdlets that could be used to remove recipients from the `Employees` OU, or from any other location in the Active Directory. We used the `Remove-ManagementRoleEntry` cmdlet to delete all of the `Remove-*` cmdlets from our custom role, and therefore, this will prevent users assigned to the custom role from removing recipient objects.

Next, we created a management scope that defines what the support group can access. We used the `New-ManagementScope` cmdlet to create the `Employees` management scope. As you can see from the command, we specified the recipient root as the `Employees` OU, as per the requirements in our scenario. When specifying `RecipientRoot`, we are also required to specify `RecipientRestrictionFilter`, which will be limited to the `UserMailbox`, `MailUser`, and `MailContact` recipient types.

Finally, we created our management role group using the `New-RoleGroup` cmdlet. The command used created a role group named `Support`, which created a universal security group in the Microsoft Exchange Security Groups OU in Active Directory. The role group was created using the `Employees` management scope, limiting the access to the `Employees` OU. Also, notice that we added three users to the group using the `-Members` parameter. Doing it this way automatically creates the management role assignment for us. You can view the management role assignments using the `Get-ManagementRoleAssignment` cmdlet.

There's more...

One of the things that make custom RBAC role assignments so powerful is the use of the management scope. When we created the `Employees` management scope, we used the `-RecipientRestrictionFilter` parameter to limit the types of recipients that would apply to that scope. When creating the role group, we specified this scope using the `-CustomRecipientWriteScope` parameter. This locks the administrator down to only writing to recipient objects that match the scope's filter and recipient root.

Keep in mind that scopes can be created with a `ServerRestrictionFilter` parameter and role groups and role assignments can be configured to use these scopes by assigning them to the `CustomConfigWriteScope` parameter. This can be useful when assigning custom RBAC roles for administrators who will be working on servers, as opposed to recipients. For example, instead of limiting your staff to working with recipient objects in a specific OU, you could create a custom role that only applies to specific servers in your organization, such as ones that are located in another city or another Active Directory site.

See also

▶ *Working with Role Based Access Control*
▶ *Creating a custom RBAC role for end users*
▶ *Troubleshooting RBAC*

Creating a custom RBAC role for end users

Like custom RBAC roles for administrators, you can also create custom roles that apply to your end users. This may be useful when you need to allow them to modify additional configuration settings that apply to their own accounts through the ECP. This recipe will provide a real-world example of how you might implement a custom RBAC role for end users in your Exchange organization.

How to do it...

When users log on to ECP, they have the ability to modify their work phone number, fax number, home phone number, and mobile phone number, among other things. Let's say that we need to limit this so that they can only update their home phone number, as their work, fax, and mobile numbers will be managed by the administrators in your organization.

Since built-in roles cannot be modified, we need to create a custom role based on one of the existing built-in roles. Use the following steps to implement a custom RBAC role for end users based on the previous requirements:

1. The `MyContactInformation` role allows end users to modify their contact information, so we'll create a new custom role based on this parent role:

    ```
    New-ManagementRole -Name MyContactInfo '
    -Parent MyContactInformation
    ```

2. The `Set-User` cmdlet is what executes in the background when users modify their contact information. This is done using several parameters made available through this cmdlet. We'll create an array that contains all of these parameters so that we can modify them later:

    ```
    $parameters = Get-ManagementRoleEntry "MyContactInfo\Set-User" |
    Select-Object -
    ExpandProperty parameters
    ```

3. Next, we'll create a new array that excludes the parameters that allow the end users to change their business-related phone numbers:

    ```
    $parameters = $parameters |
    Where-Object{
        ($_ -ne "Phone") -and '
        ($_ -ne "MobilePhone") -and '
        ($_ -ne "Fax")
    }
    ```

4. Now we'll modify the Set-User cmdlet so that it only provides our custom list of parameters:

    ```
    Set-ManagementRoleEntry -Identity "MyContactInfo\Set-User" '
    -Parameters $parameters
    ```

5. The `MyContactInformation` role is assigned to end users through the default role assignment policy, so we need to remove that assignment from the policy:

    ```
    Remove-ManagementRoleAssignment -Identity '
    "MyContactInformation-Default Role Assignment Policy" '
    -Confirm:$false
    ```

6. Finally, we can add our custom RBAC role to the default role assignment policy:

    ```
    New-ManagementRoleAssignment -Role MyContactInfo
    -Policy "Default Role Assignment Policy"
    ```

When users log in to ECP, they'll only be able to modify their home phone numbers.

How it works...

As you can see from these steps, not only do management roles provide users with access to cmdlets, but also to specific parameters available on those cmdlets. We're able to limit the use of the Set-User cmdlet by removing the access to the parameters that allow users to modify properties of their account that we do not want them to change.

End user management roles are assigned through a role assignment policy. By default, only one role assignment policy is created when you deploy Exchange 2013, called the Default Role Assignment Policy. In the first example, we created a custom role based on the existing MyContactInformation role, which allows end users to update their personal contact details.

One of the questions that you may ask at this point is how did we determine that the MyContactInformation role was the one that needed to be modified? Well, we can come to this conclusion by first checking which roles assign the Set-User cmdlet with the -Phone parameter:

```
Machine: TLEX01.testlabs.se

[PS] C:\>Get-ManagementRole -Cmdlet Set-User -CmdletParameters Phone

Name                    RoleType

----                    --------
Mail Recipients         MailRecipients
User Options            UserOptions
MyContactInformation    MyContactInformation
MyAddressInformation    MyContactInformation
```

All of the built-in end user management roles are prefixed with My, and as you can see from the preceding screenshot, the only two roles that apply here are listed at the bottom. Now we need to check the default role assignment policy:

```
Machine: TLEX01.testlabs.se

[PS] C:\>Get-RoleAssignmentPolicy "Default Role Assignment Policy" | Format
-List AssignedRoles


AssignedRoles : {MyTeamMailboxes, MyDistributionGroupMembership, My Market
                place Apps, MyBaseOptions, MyContactInformation, MyTextMes
                saging, MyVoiceMail}
```

As you can clearly see from the preceding screenshot, the only roles assigned to the end users that contain the Set-User cmdlet are assigned by the MyContactInformation role, and we know that this is the role that needs to be replaced with a custom role.

There's more...

If you don't want to modify the existing role assignment policy, you can create a new role assignment policy that can be applied to individual users. This may be useful if you need to test things without affecting other users. To do this, use the `New-RoleAssignmentPolicy` cmdlet and specify a name for the policy and all the roles that should be applied via this role assignment policy:

```
New-RoleAssignmentPolicy -Name MyCustomPolicy '
-Roles MyDistributionGroupMembership,
MyBaseOptions,
MyTeamMailboxes,
MyTextMessaging,
MyVoiceMail,
MyContactInfo
```

Once this is complete, you can assign the role assignment policy to an individual user with the `Set-Mailbox` cmdlet:

```
Set-Mailbox -Identity "Ramon Shaffer" '
-RoleAssignmentPolicy MyCustomPolicy
```

If you later decide that this new policy should be used for all of your end users, you'll need to do two things. First, you'll need to set this role assignment policy as the default policy for new mailboxes:

```
Set-RoleAssignmentPolicy MyCustomPolicy -IsDefault
```

Then, you'll need to modify the existing users so that they'll be assigned the new role assignment policy:

```
Get-Mailbox -ResultSize Unlimited |
Set-Mailbox -RoleAssignmentPolicy MyCustomPolicy
```

See also

- ▶ *Working with Role Based Access Control*
- ▶ *Creating a custom RBAC role for administrators*
- ▶ *Troubleshooting RBAC*

Troubleshooting RBAC

Troubleshooting permission issues can be challenging, especially if you've implemented custom RBAC roles. In this recipe, we'll take a look at some useful troubleshooting techniques that can be used to troubleshoot issues related to RBAC.

How to do it...

There are several scenarios in which you can use the Exchange Management Shell cmdlets to solve problems with RBAC, and there are a couple of cmdlets that you'll need to use to do this. The following steps outline the solutions for some common troubleshooting situations:

1. To determine which management roles have been assigned to a user, use the following command syntax:

    ```
    Get-ManagementRoleAssignment -GetEffectiveUsers |
    Where-Object {$_.EffectiveUserName -eq 'sysadmin'}
    ```

2. To retrieve a list of users that have been assigned a specific management role, run the following command and specify a role name, such as the Legal Hold role:

    ```
    Get-ManagementRoleAssignment -Role 'Legal Hold' `
    -GetEffectiveUsers
    ```

3. You can determine whether a user has write access to a recipient, server, or database. For example, use the following syntax to determine whether the sysadmin account has the ability to modify the Dave Jones mailbox:

    ```
    Get-ManagementRoleAssignment -WritableRecipient djones `
    -GetEffectiveUsers |
    Where-Object{$_.EffectiveUserName -eq 'sysadmin'}
    ```

After running the previous command, any roles that give the sysadmin write access to the specified recipient will be returned.

How it works...

The Get-ManagementRoleAssignment cmdlet is a useful tool when it comes to troubleshooting RBAC issues. If an administrator is unable to modify a recipient or make a change against a server, it is possible that the role assignment is either incorrect or it might not exist at all. In each step shown previously, we used the -GetEffectiveUsers parameter with this cmdlet, which provides a quick way to find out if certain roles have been assigned to a specific user.

In addition to the `-WritableRecipient` parameter, you have the option of using either the `-WritableServer` or `-WritableDatabase` parameters. These can be used to determine whether an administrator has write access to a server or database object. This can be useful to determine whether a role assignment has not been made for an administrator that should be able to modify one of these objects. You can also use this as a method to determine whether some administrators have been granted too much control in your environment.

There's more...

If someone is not receiving the permissions you think they should, they may not be a member of the required role group. The steps outlined previously should help you make this determination, but it may be as simple as making sure the administrator has been added to the right role group that will assign the appropriate roles. You can retrieve the members of a role group in the shell using the `Get-RoleGroupMember` cmdlet. This command will return all the members of the `Organization Management` role group:

`Get-RoleGroup 'Organization Management' | Get-RoleGroupMember`

You can also use these cmdlets to generate a report of all the members of each role group. For example, the following code will display the member of each role group in the shell:

```
foreach($rg in Get-RoleGroup) {
  Get-RoleGroupMember $rg |
  Select-Object Name,@{n="RoleGroup";e={$rg.Name}}
}
```

See also

▶ *Working with Role Based Access Control*

▶ *Creating a custom RBAC role for administrators*

▶ *Creating a custom RBAC role for end users*

Generating a certificate request

In order to create a new certificate, you need to generate a certificate request using either the Exchange Admin Center, or through the shell using the `New-ExchangeCertificate` cmdlet. Once you have a certificate request generated, you can obtain a certificate from an internal Certificate Authority or a third-party external **Certificate Authority** (**CA**). In this recipe, we'll take a look at the process of generating a certificate request from the Exchange Management Shell.

How to do it...

Let's see how to generate a certificate request using the following steps:

1. In this example, we'll generate a request using two **Subject Alternative Names** (**SANs**). This will allow us to support multiple URLs with one certificate:

```
$cert = New-ExchangeCertificate -GenerateRequest '
-SubjectName "c=US, o=Contoso, cn=mail.contoso.com" '
-DomainName autodiscover.contoso.com,mail.contoso.com '
-PrivateKeyExportable $true
```

2. After the request has been generated, we can export it to a file that can be used to submit a request to a CA:

```
$cert | Out-File c:\cert_request.txt
```

How it works...

When you install Exchange 2013, self-signed certificates are automatically generated and installed to encrypt data passed between servers. Since these self-signed certificates will not be trusted by your client machines when accessing the CAS role, it is recommended that you replace these certificates with new certificates issued from a trusted CA. If you do not replace these certificates, clients such as Outlook 2013 and Outlook Web App users will receive certificate warnings informing them that the certificates are not issued from a trusted source. This can create some confusion for end users and could generate calls to your help desk.

You can get around these certificate warnings by installing the server's self-signed certificates in the **Trusted Root Certificate Authorities** store on the client machines, but even in a small environment, this can become an administrative headache. That's why it is recommended that you replace the self-signed certificates before placing your Exchange 2013 servers into production.

When using the `New-ExchangeCertificate` cmdlet to generate a certificate request, you can use the `-SubjectName` parameter to specify the common name of the certificate. This value is set using an X.500 distinguished name, and as you saw in step 2, the common name for the certificate was set to `mail.contoso.com`. If you do not provide a value for the `-SubjectName` parameter, the hostname of the server where the cmdlet is run to generate the request will be used.

The `-DomainName` parameter is used to define one or more FQDNs that will be listed in the **Subject Alternative Name** field of the certificate. This allows you to generate certificates that support multiple FQDNs that can be installed on multiple Exchange servers. For example, you may have several CAS servers in your environment, and instead of generating multiple certificates for each one, you can simply add **Subject Alternative Name** to cover all of the possible FQDNs that users will need to access, and then install a single certificate on multiple CAS servers.

The `New-ExchangeCertificate` cmdlet outputs a certificate request in Base64 format. In the previous example, we saved the output of the command in a variable so that we could simply output the data to a text file. Once the request is generated, you'll need to supply the data from this request to the issuing CA. This is usually done through a web form hosted by the CA where you submit the certificate request. You can simply open the request file in Notepad, copy the data, and paste it into the submission form on the CA website. Once the information is submitted, the CA will generate a certificate that can be downloaded and installed on your servers. Refer to the next recipe in this chapter titled *Installing certificates and enabling services* for steps on how to complete this process.

There's more...

It's recommended as a best practice that you limit the number of Subject Alternative Names on your certificates, so your name space design should be completely defined before creating your certificates. For example, let's say that you've got four CAS servers in a CAS array and all of your servers are located in a single Active Directory site. Even though you have multiple servers, you only need to include the FQDNs that your end users will use to access these servers. If you configure your CAS URLs appropriately, there's no need to include the server's FQDN or hostname as a Subject Alternative Name in this scenario.

If you plan on installing a certificate on multiple servers, make sure that you mark the certificate as exportable by setting the `-PrivateKeyExportable` parameter to `$true`. This will allow you to export the certificate and install it on the remaining servers in your environment.

> It's recommended that you use either the Exchange Management Shell or the Exchange Admin Center for generating the certificate, and not the MMC snap-in or IIS management console.

See also

- *Installing certificates and enabling services*
- *Importing certificates on multiple Exchange servers*

Installing certificates and enabling services

After you've generated a certificate request and have obtained a certificate from a CA, you will need to install the certificate on your server using the `Import-ExchangeCertificate` cmdlet. This recipe will show you how to install certificates issued from a certificate authority and how to assign services to the certificate using the Exchange Management Shell.

How to do it...

Let's see how to install and enable services using the following steps:

1. Let's say that you have requested and downloaded a certificate from an Active Directory Enterprise CA and downloaded the file to the root of the `c:\` drive. First, read the certificate data into a variable in the shell using the following command:

   ```
   $certificate = Get-Content -Path c:\certnew.cer '
   -Encoding Byte '
   -ReadCount 0
   ```

2. Next, we can import the certificate and complete the pending request:

   ```
   Import-ExchangeCertificate -FileData $certificate
   ```

3. Now that the certificate is installed, we can enable it for specific services:

   ```
   Get-ExchangeCertificate -DomainName mail.contoso.com |
   Enable-ExchangeCertificate -Services IIS,SMTP
   ```

At this point, the certificate has been installed and will now be used for Client Access services, such as Outlook Web App and the Exchange Control Panel, and also for securing SMTP.

How it works...

Since the Exchange Management Shell uses remote PowerShell sessions, the `Import-ExchangeCertificate` cmdlet cannot use a local file path to import a certificate file. This is because the cmdlet could be running on any server within your organization and a local file path may not exist. This is why we need to use the `-FileData` parameter to provide the actual data of the certificate. In step 1, we read the certificate data into a byte array using the `Get-Content` cmdlet, which is a PowerShell core cmdlet, and is not run through the remote PowerShell on the Exchange server. The content of the certificate is stored as a byte array in the `$certificate` variable, and we can assign this data to the `-FileData` parameter of the `Import-ExchangeCertificate` cmdlet, which allows us to import the certificate to any Exchange server through the remote PowerShell.

> Use the `-Server` parameter with the `Get-ExchangeCertificate` cmdlet to target a specific server. Otherwise, the cmdlet will run against the server you are currently connected to.

There's more...

As shown previously, once the certificate has been imported, it needs to have one or more services assigned before it can be used by an Exchange server. After importing a certificate, you can use the `Get-ExchangeCertificate` cmdlet to view it:

```
Machine: TLEX01.testlabs.se

[PS] C:\>Get-ExchangeCertificate

Thumbprint                                Services   Subject
----------                                --------   -------
B52588F73B3288C6D59128F3AB57D4B1B6537373  ....S..    CN=Microsoft Excha...
C4589B60CEA545A01672B2093D87F63A1D9A7362  IP.WS..    CN=TLEX01
1058AFC8BDC4276CDC6EF5A5BA6D68CFD5E7BB75  .......    CN=WMSvc-TLEX01
```

You can see that we have two certificates installed. When assigning services to a certificate, we need to be specific about which one needs to be modified. We can do this either by specifying the thumbprint of the certificate when running the `Enable-ExchangeCertificate` cmdlet, or using the method shown previously, where we used the `Get-ExchangeCertificate` cmdlet with the `-DomainName` parameter to retrieve a particular certificate, and send it down the pipeline to the `Enable-ExchangeCertificate` cmdlet.

Let's say that we're connected to a server named `TLEX01`. We've imported a certificate, and now we need to view all of the installed certificates so that we can figure out which one needs to be enabled and assigned the appropriate services. We can do this by viewing a few key properties of each certificate using the `Get-ExchangeCertificate` cmdlet:

```
Machine: TLEX01.testlabs.se

[PS] C:\>Get-ExchangeCertificate | Format-List Thumbprint,CertificateDomain
s,Services,IsSelfSigned


Thumbprint          : B52588F73B3288C6D59128F3AB57D4B1B6537373
CertificateDomains  : {}
Services            : SMTP
IsSelfSigned        : True

Thumbprint          : C4589B60CEA545A01672B2093D87F63A1D9A7362
CertificateDomains  : {TLEX01, TLEX01.testlabs.se}
Services            : IMAP, POP, IIS, SMTP
IsSelfSigned        : True
```

Here, you can see that we've retrieved the `Thumbprint`, `CertificateDomains`, and assigned `Services` for each installed Exchange certificate in the list format. We also selected the `IsSelfSigned` property that will tell us whether or not the certificate was issued from a CA or installed by Exchange as a self-signed certificate. It's pretty clear from the output that the second certificate in the list is the one that was issued from a certificate authority, since the `IsSelfSigned` property is set to `$false`. At this point, we can use the certificate thumbprint to assign services to this certificate using the following command:

```
Enable-ExchangeCertificate '
-Thumbprint CF61E66A6BE1A286471B30DFCEA1126F6BC7DCBB '
-Services IIS,SMTP
```

If you have multiple certificates installed, especially with duplicate domain names, use the method shown here to assign services based on the certificate thumbprint. Otherwise, you may find it easier to enable certificates based on the domain name, as shown in the first example.

See also

▶ *Importing certificates on multiple Exchange servers*

▶ *Generating a certificate request*

Importing certificates on multiple Exchange servers

If your environment contains multiple Exchange servers, you'll likely want to use the same certificate on multiple servers. If you have a large amount of servers, importing certificates one at a time, even with the Exchange Management Shell it, could end up being quite time-consuming. This recipe will provide a method to automate this process using the Exchange Management Shell.

How to do it...

Once you've gone through the process of generating a certificate request, installing a certificate and assigning the services on one server, you can export that certificate and deploy it to your remaining servers.

The following steps outline the process of exporting an installed certificate on a server named `TLEX01` and importing that certificate on a server named `TLEX02`:

1. In order to export a certificate, we'll first need to assign a password to secure the private key that will be exported with the certificate:

    ```
    $password = ConvertTo-SecureString -String P@ssword '
    -AsPlainText '
    -Force
    ```

2. Now we can export the certificate data with the `Export-ExchangeCertificate` cmdlet. We'll retrieve the certificate from the `TLEX01` server and export the data to a binary-encoded value stored in a variable:

    ```
    $cert = Get-ExchangeCertificate '
    -DomainName mail.contoso.com -Server TLEX01 |
    Export-ExchangeCertificate -BinaryEncoded:$true '
    -Password $password
    ```

3. Next, we can import the certificate file data into the `TLEX02` server as a certificate:

    ```
    Import-ExchangeCertificate -FileData $cert.FileData '
    -Password $password '
    -Server TLEX02
    ```

4. Finally, we can assign the services to the certificate that was recently imported on the `TLEX02` server:

    ```
    Get-ExchangeCertificate '
    -DomainName mail.contoso.com -Server TLEX02 |
    Enable-ExchangeCertificate -Services IIS,SMTP
    ```

How it works...

As you can see from these steps, exporting a certificate from one server and importing it on an additional server is rather complex and would be even more so if you want to do this on 5 or 10 servers. If this is a common task that needs to be done frequently, then it makes sense to automate it even further. The following PowerShell function will automate the process of exporting a certificate from a source server and will import the certificate on one or more target servers:

```
function Deploy-ExchangeCertificate {
  param(
    $SourceServer,
```

```
        $Thumbprint,
        $TargetServer,
        $Password,
        $Services
    )
    $password = ConvertTo-SecureString -String $Password '
    -AsPlainText '
    -Force
    $cert = Get-ExchangeCertificate -Thumbprint $Thumbprint '
    -Server $SourceServer |
        Export-ExchangeCertificate –BinaryEncoded:$true '
        -Password $Password
    foreach($Server in $TargetServer) {
        Import-ExchangeCertificate -FileData $cert.FileData '
        -Password $Password '
        -Server $Server
        Enable-ExchangeCertificate -Thumbprint $Thumbprint '
        -Server $Server '
        -Services $Services '
        -Confirm:$false '
        -Force
    }
}
```

This function allows you to specify a certificate that has been properly set up and installed on a source server, and then deploy that certificate and enable a specified list of services on one or more servers. The function accepts a number of parameters and requires that you specify the thumbprint of the certificate that you want to deploy.

Let's say that you've got a Client Access server array that contains six CAS servers. You've gone through the certificate generation process, obtained the certificate from a trusted certificate authority, and installed the certificate on the first CAS server. Now you can add the Deploy-ExchangeCertificate function to your PowerShell session and deploy the certificate to the remaining servers in the array.

First, you need to determine the thumbprint on the source server you want to deploy, and you can do this using the Get-ExchangeCertificate cmdlet. The next step is to run the function with the following syntax:

```
Deploy-ExchangeCertificate -SourceServer cas1 '
-TargetServer TLEX02,TLEX03,TLEX04,TLEX05,TLEX06 '
-Thumbprint DE4382508E325D27D2D48033509EE5F9C621A07B '
-Services IIS,SMTP '
-Password P@ssw0rd
```

The function will export the certificate on the TLEX01 server with the thumbprint value assigned to the -Thumbprint parameter. The value assigned to the -Password parameter will be used to secure the private key when the certificate data is exported. The certificate will then be installed on the five remaining CAS servers in the array and will have the IIS and SMTP services assigned.

There's more...

You may want to export your certificates to an external file that can be used to import the certificate on another server at a later time. To do this, use the following command:

```
$password = ConvertTo-SecureString '
-String P@ssword '
-AsPlainText '
-Force
$file = Get-ExchangeCertificate '
-Thumbprint DE4382508E325D27D2D48033509EE5F9C621A07B -Server '
TLEX01 | Export-ExchangeCertificate -BinaryEncoded:$true '
-Password $password
Set-Content -Path c:\cert.pfx -Value $file.FileData -Encoding Byte
```

This is similar to the previous examples, except that this time we're exporting the certificate data to an external .pfx file.

You can use the following commands to import this certificate at a later time on another server in your environment:

```
$password = ConvertTo-SecureString '
-String P@ssword '
-AsPlainText '
-Force
$filedata = Get-Content -Path c:\cert.pfx -Encoding Byte -`
ReadCount 0
Import-ExchangeCertificate -FileData ([Byte[]]$filedata) '
-Password $password '
-Server TLEX02
```

This will import the certificate from the external .pfx file to the TLEX02 server. Once this is complete, you can use the Enable-ExchangeCertificate cmdlet to assign the required services to the certificate.

See also

▶ *Generating a certificate request*

▶ *Installing certificates and enabling services*

11
Compliance and Audit Logging

In this chapter, we will cover the following topics:

- ▶ Managing archive mailboxes
- ▶ Configuring archive mailbox quotas
- ▶ Creating retention tags and policies
- ▶ Applying retention policies to mailboxes
- ▶ Placing mailboxes on Retention Hold
- ▶ Placing mailboxes on In-Place Hold
- ▶ Performing a discovery search
- ▶ Configuring administrator audit logging
- ▶ Searching the administrator audit logs
- ▶ Configuring S/MIME for OWA

Introduction

One of the significant changes introduced in Exchange 2013 was the development of the feature called litigation hold; this was developed and ended up in a feature called In-Place Hold. Regarding retention policies, there is now support to handle the calendar and tasks folders. One more welcomed feature is that it's possible to archive the contents from Lync into the mailbox. This comes together with a new search engine called FAST, which makes the search across platforms available (Exchange, SharePoint, and Lync). It also makes the search faster, which is good from an end user's perspective.

The compliance and audit logging features that were introduced in Exchange 2010 still apply to Exchange 2013. Over the years, many organizations have relied on third-party products for archiving and retaining e-mail messages for legal protection and regulatory compliance. Fortunately, this function is now built into the product, along with some very powerful auditing capabilities that can track which users are accessing and modifying items in mailboxes and which administrators are making changes throughout the Exchange organization.

In this chapter, we'll take a look at some of the most common tasks related to compliance and audit logging that can be automated through the Exchange Management Shell. This includes managing retention polices, performing legal searches, and restoring items from mailboxes, along with generating detailed reports based on mailbox and administrator audit logs. We will also take a look at implementing S/MIME, since this feature was brought back in Service Pack 1 (CU4).

Performing some basic steps

To work with the code samples in this chapter, follow these steps to launch the Exchange Management Shell:

1. Log on to a workstation or server with the Exchange Management Tools installed.

2. You can connect using a remote PowerShell if, for some reason, you don't have the Exchange Management tools installed. To do so, use the following command:

```
$Session = New-PSSession -ConfigurationName
' Microsoft.Exchange -ConnectionUri '
http://tlex01/PowerShell/ -Authentication Kerberos
Import-PSSession $Session
```

3. Open the Exchange Management Shell by navigating to **Start | All Programs | Exchange Server 2013**.

4. Click on the **Exchange Management Shell** shortcut.

5. To launch a standard PowerShell console, open a standard PowerShell console by navigating to **Start | All Programs | Accessories**, click on the Windows PowerShell folder, and then click on the Windows PowerShell shortcut.

6. Unless specified otherwise in the *Getting ready* section, all of the recipes in this chapter will require the use of the Exchange Management Shell.

Remember to start the Exchange Management Shell using **Run as administrator** to avoid permission problems.

In this chapter, you might notice that, in the examples of cmdlets, I have used the back tick (') character to break up long commands into multiple lines. The purpose of this is to make it easier to read. The back ticks are not required and should only be used if needed.

Managing archive mailboxes

In Exchange 2010, a new personal storage concept was introduced, which still remains in Exchange 2013, called an archive mailbox. The idea is that you can give one or more users a secondary mailbox that can be accessed from anywhere, just like their regular mailbox, and it can be used to store older mailbox data thus, eliminating the need for a PST file. The benefit of this is that the archive mailboxes can now be located on a database separate from the primary mailbox, allowing administrators to put low-priority, archived mailbox data on an inexpensive lower tier of storage. In this chapter, we'll take a look at how you can manage archive mailboxes for your users through the Exchange Management Shell.

How to do it...

To create an archive mailbox for an existing mailbox, use the `Enable-Mailbox` cmdlet, as shown in the following command:

```
Enable-Mailbox -Identity administrator -Archive
```

How it works...

When you create an archive mailbox for a user, they can access their personal archive when connecting to Outlook 2007, 2010, and 2013, or the Outlook Web App. In the previous example, we created an archive mailbox for an existing user. Using a command, we can easily do this in bulk for multiple users. For example, to create an archive mailbox for all users in the `DB01` database, you could use the following command:

```
Get-Mailbox -Database DB01 |
Enable-Mailbox -Archive -ArchiveDatabase ARCHIVE01
```

As you can see, we're making use of the pipeline here to perform a bulk operation on all of the mailboxes in the DB01 database. The result of the Get-Mailbox command is piped to the Enable-Mailbox cmdlet. The -Archive switch parameter tells the cmdlet that we know this user already has a mailbox, and we just want to create a personal archive for the user. In addition, we've specified the -ArchiveDatabase parameter so that the archives for each mailbox will not be created in the same database as the primary mailbox, but instead in the ARCHIVE01 database.

When creating the archive mailboxes, they will receive the default size limitation for an archive mailbox, which have a warning quota limit set to 90 GB and the archive quota limit set to 100 GB.

In addition to creating an archive for an existing user, we can enable a personal archive for a mailbox as it is created. For example, the following commands will create a mailbox and a personal archive for a new user:

```
$password = ConvertTo-SecureString P@ssword -AsPlainText -Force

New-Mailbox -Name "Dave Smith" -alias dsmith '

-UserPrincipalName dave@contoso.com '

-Database DB01 '

-Archive '

-ArchiveDatabase ARCHIVE01 '

-Password $password
```

In this command, we've created the primary mailbox in the DB01 database, and again, we've made use of the -Archive and -ArchiveDatabase parameters so that the archive is created in the ARCHIVE01 database.

There's more...

If you need to turn off an archive mailbox for a user, you can use the Disable-Mailbox cmdlet with the -Archive switch parameter. The command to disable the personal archive for Dave Smith is as simple as this:

```
Disable-Mailbox -Identity dsmith -Archive –Confirm:$false
```

When you run this command, the archive mailbox for the user goes into a disconnected state, but the user can still access their primary mailbox. The disconnected archive mailbox is retained in the database until the deleted mailbox retention period for the database has elapsed.

[🖎 Be aware, as enabling the in-place archive requires Enterprise CAL for the enabled users.]

See also

▸ *Adding, modifying, and removing mailboxes* in *Chapter 3*, *Managing Recipients*

▸ *Configuring archive mailbox quotas*

Configuring archive mailbox quotas

As you enable archive mailboxes for end users and set up retention policies, you may find that the default limitations configured for archive mailboxes do not meet your needs. In this recipe, you'll learn how to modify archive mailbox quotas using the Exchange Management Shell.

How to do it...

Let's see how to configure archive mailbox quotas using the following steps:

1. To modify the archive quota settings for a single mailbox, use the `Set-Mailbox` cmdlet:

   ```
   Set-Mailbox dsmith -ArchiveQuota 10gb -ArchiveWarningQuota 8gb
   ```

2. To do this in bulk, use the `Get-Mailbox` cmdlet to retrieve the mailboxes that need to be updated and pipe the results to the `Set-Mailbox` cmdlet. For example, this command would update all the users in the DB01 database:

   ```
   Get-Mailbox -Database DB01 |
   Where-Object {$_.ArchiveName} |
   Set-Mailbox -ArchiveQuota 10gb -ArchiveWarningQuota 8gb
   ```

As you can see here, we're filtering the results of the `Get-Mailbox` cmdlet based on the `ArchiveName` property. If this property is defined, then we know that the user has an archive mailbox enabled.

How it works...

There are two settings that can be used to configure quotas for archive mailboxes:

- ▶ `ArchiveWarningQuota`: When an archive mailbox exceeds the size set for the archive warning quota, a warning message is sent to the mailbox owner and an event is logged on the mailbox server that hosts the archive mailbox

- ▶ `ArchiveQuota`: When an archive mailbox exceeds the size set for the archive quota, a warning message is sent to the mailbox owner and items can no longer be moved to the archive mailbox

In Exchange 2013, archive mailboxes are configured with default limitations. The archive warning quota is set to 90 GB and the archive quota is set to 100 GB. These settings can only be applied on a per-mailbox basis, unlike regular mailboxes, which can receive their limits from the parent database.

If you implement custom archive quotas, you may need to run a script on a regular basis in order to update any new archives that have been recently created. For example, let's say that you've decided that archive mailboxes should not be larger than 5 GB. You can run a script regularly, either manually or through a scheduled task, that will update any new users that have been added to the organization:

```
Get-Mailbox -ResultSize Unlimited |
Where-Object {$_.ArchiveName -and $_.ArchiveQuota -ge 100gb} |
Set-Mailbox -ArchiveQuota 5gb -ArchiveWarningQuota 4gb
```

Again, we're using the `Where-Object` cmdlet to filter on the `ArchiveName` property, but we've added another filter to check whether the `ArchiveQuota` value is greater than or equal to 100 GB. If so, we send those mailboxes down the pipeline to the `Set-Mailbox` cmdlet and modify the archive quota settings.

There's more...

You can view the current settings for these values using the `Get-Mailbox` cmdlet. For example, to check the values for a specific user, run the following command:

```
Get-Mailbox -Identity dave | Format-List *archive*
```

You will be presented with the following screenshot:

```
Machine: tlex01.testlabs.se                    [_] [□] [x]
[PS] C:\Scripts>Get-Mailbox -Identity dave | Format-List *archive*

ArchiveDatabase            : Archive01
ArchiveGuid                : 094c6c54-4f09-4d83-8f1a-353a4a009c0d
ArchiveName                : {In-Place Archive - Dave Jones}
JournalArchiveAddress      :
ArchiveQuota               : 10 GB (10,737,418,240 bytes)
ArchiveWarningQuota        : 8 GB (8,589,934,592 bytes)
ArchiveDomain              :
ArchiveStatus              : None
ArchiveState               : Local
DisabledArchiveDatabase    :
DisabledArchiveGuid        : 00000000-0000-0000-0000-000000000000
ArchiveRelease             :
```

The preceding command uses a wildcard to display all the properties of a mailbox that contain the word `archive`. This will provide the quota settings, as well as the database location for the archive mailbox, which may be different from that of the user's primary mailbox.

See also

► *Managing archive mailboxes*

Creating retention tags and policies

Retention policies are the recommended methods for implementing messaging records management in Exchange 2013. Retention policies use retention tags to apply settings to mailbox folders and individual items. Retention tags are configured with a retention action that can be taken when an item reaches its retention age limit. In this recipe, you'll learn how to create retention tags and policies in the Exchange Management Shell.

How to do it...

There are three types of retention tags that can be used to apply retention settings to a mailbox through a retention policy. The following steps outline the process of creating custom retention tags based on these types and assigning them to a new retention policy:

1. The following command will create a retention policy tag for the `Inbox` folder, specifying that items older than 90 days should be deleted permanently:

```
New-RetentionPolicyTag -Name AllUsers-Inbox '
-Type Inbox '
-Comment "Items older than 90 days are deleted" '
```

```
-RetentionEnabled $true '
-AgeLimitForRetention 90 '
-RetentionAction PermanentlyDelete
```

2. In addition, we can create a default policy tag for the entire mailbox. To do this, we need to set the type to `All`. A default retention policy tag of `Type All` will apply to any item that does not have a retention tag applied:

```
New-RetentionPolicyTag -Name AllUsers-Default '
-Type All '
-Comment "Items older than 120 days are permanently deleted" '
-RetentionEnabled $true '
-AgeLimitForRetention 120 '
-RetentionAction PermanentlyDelete
```

3. We can also create personal tags that can be used by end users for personal items:

```
New-RetentionPolicyTag -Name Critical '
-Type Personal '
-Comment "Use this tag for all critical items" '
-RetentionEnabled $true '
-AgeLimitForRetention 730 '
-RetentionAction DeleteAndAllowRecovery
```

4. After creating these tags, we can create a new retention policy and add the previously created tags:

```
New-RetentionPolicy -Name AllUsers '
-RetentionPolicyTagLinks AllUsers-Inbox,'
AllUsers-Default,Critical
```

At this point, the `AllUsers` retention policy can be assigned to one or more mailboxes, and the settings defined by the retention tags will be applied.

How it works...

The management of retention tags and policies can be done both from the Exchange Admin Center and using the shell. You might find it easier to manage the policies through the GUI, but in either case, the cmdlets used to create and manage tags and policies can still be used if automation or command-line administration is required.

As we saw from the previous example, there are three types of retention tags that can be used to apply retention settings to mailbox folders and messages. These types are outlined in detail as follows:

- **Retention policy tags**: These are used to apply settings to default folders, such as Inbox and Sent Items.

- **Default policy tags**: These apply to any item that does not have a retention tag set. A retention policy can contain only one default policy tag.

- **Personal tags**: These can be applied by users who access their mailboxes from Outlook 2010, Outlook 2013, or the Outlook Web App. Personal tags can be applied to custom folders and individual items.

When you create one or more retention tags to be applied to a policy, you'll need to define the type using one of these settings. Additionally, retention tags have actions that will be used when the age limit for retention is met. The available retention actions are outlined as follows:

- MarkAsPastRetentionLimit: This action will mark an item as past the retention limit, displaying the message using strikethrough text in Outlook 2007, 2010, or 2013 or the Outlook Web App.

- DeleteAndAllowRecovery: This action will perform a hard delete, sending the message to the dumpster. The user will be able to recover the item using the **Recover Deleted Items** dialog box in Outlook 2010 and Outlook 2013 or the Outlook Web App.

- PermanentlyDelete: This action will permarently delete the message. It cannot be restored using the **Recover Deleted Items** dialog box.

- MoveToArchive: This action moves the message to the user's archive mailbox.

When working with retention tags and policies, there are a few things you should keep in mind. First, mailboxes can only be assigned one policy at a time, and you cannot have multiple retention policy tags for a single default folder in the same retention policy. For example, you can't have two retention policy tags for the Inbox default folder in the same retention policy.

Retention policies can contain one default policy tag of type All. You can assign multiple personal tags to a policy, but be careful not to go overboard, as this can be confusing for users. Also, keep in mind that retention tags are not applied to mailboxes until they have een linked to an enabled retention policy and the managed folder assistant has run against each mailbox.

> Keep in mind that the managed folder assistant is throttle-based in Exchange 2013, which means that it will run whenever there are resources available. It can, however, be forced to start using the Start-ManagedFolderAssistant cmdlet.

There's more...

You can create a retention policy without initially linking any retention tags to it. You can also go back and add retention tags to a policy later if needed. If you need to add or remove tags to an existing policy, you can use the `Set-RetentionPolicy` cmdlet. For example, to add the `Sales-Inbox` and `Sales-DeletedItems` retention policy tags to the `Sales-Users` retention policy, your command would look like the following:

```
Set-RetentionPolicy -Identity Sales-Users '
-RetentionPolicyTagLinks Sales-Inbox,Sales-DeletedItems
```

The thing to note here is that this command will overwrite the policy's current tag list. If you need to add tags and keep the policy's existing tags, you will need to use a special syntax. For example, run the following command:

```
$Tags = (Get-RetentionPolicy Sales-Users).RetentionPolicyTagLinks

$NewTags = Get-RetentionPolicyTag Sales-Critical

$Tags += $NewTags

Set-RetentionPolicy Sales-Users -RetentionPolicyTagLinks $Tags
```

What we're doing here is saving the existing tag list applied to the `Sales-Users` policy in the `$Tags` variable. We then add a new tag to the list and store that result in the `$NewTags` variable. Finally, we add the `$NewTags` variable to the existing `$Tags` collection and assign that back to the retention policy when running the `Set-RetentionPolicy` cmdlet.

Understanding default tags

When you install Exchange 2013, several retention tags are created by default. These may be specific enough to meet your needs, so you might want to take a look at these before creating any custom tags. To view the current list of available retention tags, use the `Get-RetentionPolicyTag` cmdlet:

```
Machine: tlex01.testlabs.se

[PS] C:\Scripts>Get-RetentionPolicyTag | Select-Object Name,Type,RetentionA
ction

Name                              Type             RetentionAction
----                              ----             ---------------
Personal 1 year move ...          Personal         MoveToArchive
Default 2 year move t...           All             MoveToArchive
Personal 5 year move ...          Personal         MoveToArchive
Personal never move t...          Personal         MoveToArchive
1 Week Delete                     Personal         DeleteAndAllowRecovery
1 Month Delete                    Personal         DeleteAndAllowRecovery
6 Month Delete                    Personal         DeleteAndAllowRecovery
1 Year Delete                     Personal         DeleteAndAllowRecovery
5 Year Delete                     Personal         DeleteAndAllowRecovery
Never Delete                      Personal         DeleteAndAllowRecovery
Recoverable Items 14 ...       RecoverableItems    MoveToArchive
```

In addition, Exchange automatically creates retention policies for use with personal archives and arbitration mailboxes. In Exchange 2013, by default, only one retention policy is created, that is, Default MRM policy. This policy can be applied to mailboxes that contain a personal archive and it provides a built-in set of retention tags.

Some of the retention tags used within these policies are considered system tags and, by default, are not visible when running the `Get-RetentionPolicyTag` cmdlet. You can view the tags included with these policies using the `-IncludeSystemTags` switch parameter:

```
Get-RetentionPolicyTag -IncludeSystemTags
```

See also

▶ *Applying retention policies to mailboxes*

Applying retention policies to mailboxes

Retention policies are not automatically applied to end user mailboxes and must be set manually using either the Exchange Admin Center or the Exchange Management Shell. In this recipe, you'll learn how to apply retention policies to mailboxes from the command line, which will be useful when performing a retention policy assignment on a large number of mailboxes, or on a regular basis as new mailboxes are created.

How to do it...

Let's see how to apply retention policies to mailboxes using the following steps:

1. To apply a retention policy to a mailbox, you use the `Set-Mailbox` cmdlet, specifying the retention policy name using the `-RetentionPolicy` parameter. For example, to do this for one user, the command would look something like this :

   ```
   Set-Mailbox dsmith -RetentionPolicy AllUsers
   ```

2. In addition, you may need to perform this operation on all mailboxes at once. In this case, you could use the following command:

   ```
   Get-Mailbox -RecipientTypeDetails UserMailbox |
   Set-Mailbox -RetentionPolicy AllUsers
   ```

How it works...

Retention policies are set on a per-mailbox basis. Unfortunately, there is no default setting that allows you to apply retention policies for new mailboxes. This can become a problem if your organization regularly creates new mailboxes and administrators forget to assign a retention policy during the provisioning process.

To get around this, you can schedule the following command to run on a regular basis:

```
Get-Mailbox -RecipientTypeDetails UserMailbox |
Where-Object {$_.RetentionPolicy -eq $null} |
Set-Mailbox -RetentionPolicy AllUsers
```

The preceding command will retrieve all of the user mailboxes in the organization that do not have a retention policy setting. This is done by piping the results of the `Get-Mailbox` cmdlet to a filter that checks whether the `RetentionPolicy` property is `$null`. Any mailboxes retrieved based on this filter will be piped down to the `Set-Mailbox` cmdlet, where a retention policy will be applied.

Another option would be to set the retention policy as mailboxes are created using the scripting agent. See the *Automating tasks with the scripting agent* recipe in *Chapter 2, Exchange Management Shell Common Tasks,* for more details.

There's more...

Once a retention policy is set on a mailbox, the retention settings defined by the policy's retention tags will be applied to each mailbox by the Managed Folder Assistant. The Managed Folder Assistant is a service that runs on each mailbox server and, by default, it is set to process every mailbox on the server within one day.

The Managed Folder Assistant is now throttle-based, which means that the tasks will be running all time and it will do its work when there are resources available. Having said that, it is possible to force the Managed Folder Assistant to run immediately, but keep in mind that it could impact the performance of the mailbox server.

To force the Managed Folder Assistant to process a particular mailbox, use the `Start-ManagedFolderAssistant` cmdlet:

```
Start-ManagedFolderAssistant -Identity dsmith@contoso.com
```

To force the Managed Folder Assistant to run against all mailboxes in a particular database, use the following command:

```
Get-Mailbox -Database DB01 | Start-ManagedFolderAssistant
```

See also

- ▸ *Placing mailboxes on Retention Hold*
- ▸ *Scheduling scripts to run at a later time* in *Chapter 2, Exchange Management Shell Common Tasks*
- ▸ *Automating tasks with the scripting agent* in *Chapter 2, Exchange Management Shell Common Tasks*

Placing mailboxes on Retention Hold

When a user goes on vacation or will be out of the office for an extended period of time, you may need to suspend the processing of the retention policy applied to their mailbox. This recipe will show you how to use the Exchange Management Shell to place mailboxes on Retention Hold, as well as how to remove the Retention Hold and discover which mailboxes are currently configured for Retention Hold.

How to do it...

Let's see how to place a mailbox on Retention Hold using the following steps:

1. To place a mailbox on Retention Hold, use the Set-Mailbox cmdlet:

   ```
   Set-Mailbox -Identity dsmith -RetentionHoldEnabled $true
   ```

2. To remove the Retention Hold setting from the mailbox, use the same command, but set the `-RetentionHoldEnabled` parameter to `$false`:

   ```
   Set-Mailbox -Identity dsmith -RetentionHoldEnabled $false
   ```

How it works...

When Retention Hold is enabled for a mailbox, the user who owns that mailbox can still open their mailbox, send and receive messages, delete items, and so on. The only difference is that any items that are past the retention period for any assigned tags will not be processed.

You can include a retention comment when placing a user on Retention Hold. Users running supported versions of Outlook will see the retention comments in the backstage area of Outlook. To add a comment, use the same command used previously, but supply a message using the `-RetentionComment` parameter:

```
Set-Mailbox -Identity dsmith '
-RetentionHoldEnabled $true '
-RetentionComment "You are currently on retention hold"
```

Since the Retention Hold setting is enabled using the `Set-Mailbox` cmdlet, you can easily apply this setting to many mailboxes at once with a simple command. Let's say that you need to do this for all users in the `Marketing` distribution group:

```
Get-DistributionGroupMember -Identity Marketing |
Set-Mailbox -RetentionHoldEnabled $true
```

Or, maybe you need to do this for all users in a particular database:

```
Get-Mailbox -Database DB01 |
Set-Mailbox -RetentionHoldEnabled $true
```

In addition to simply enabling this setting, you also have the option of configuring a start and end date for the Retention Hold period using the following command:

```
Set-Mailbox -Identity dsmith -RetentionHoldEnabled $true '
-StartDateForRetentionHold '5/1/2015 8:00:00 AM' '
-EndDateForRetentionHold '5/30/2015 5:00:00 PM'
```

This command will preconfigure the start date for the Retention Hold period and remove that setting when the end date elapses.

There's more...

If you are not sure which users are currently configured with the Retention Hold setting, you can use the following command to retrieve all mailboxes that have Retention Hold enabled:

```
Get-Mailbox -ResultSize Unlimited |
Where-Object{$_.RetentionHoldEnabled}
```

Any mailboxes with the `RetentionHoldEnabled` property set to `$true` will be retrieved using the preceding command.

See also

► *Placing mailboxes on In-Place Hold*

Placing mailboxes on In-Place Hold

When an organization is dealing with the possibility of a legal action, data such as documents and e-mail messages related to the case will usually need to be reviewed, and an effort to preserve this information must be made. Exchange 2013 allows you to protect and maintain this data by placing mailboxes on In-Place Hold. This prevents users or retention policies from modifying or removing any messages that may be required during the legal discovery process. In this recipe, you'll learn how to manage In-Place Hold settings for mailboxes from the Exchange Management Shell.

> Litigation hold was introduced in Exchange 2010, and it still remains in Exchange 2013. However, it's recommended that you use the In-Place Hold feature instead, which is more developed than litigation hold.

How to do it...

Let's see how to place a mailbox on In-Place Hold using the following steps:

1. To place a mailbox on In-Place Hold, use the `New-MailboxSearch` cmdlet:

   ```
   New-MailboxSearch -Name "InPlace-Hold-dsmith" '
   -SourceMailboxes "dsmith@contoso.com" '
   -InPlaceHoldEnabled $true
   ```

2. To remove the In-Place Hold setting from the mailbox, we need to disable the In-Place Hold and remove the mailbox search using the following cmdlet:

   ```
   Set-MailboxSearch -Identity "InPlace-Hold-dsmith" '
   -InPlaceHoldEnabled $false
   Remove-MailboxSearch -Identity "InPlace-Hold-dsmith"
   ```

How it works...

At first glance, it may seem that In-Place Hold and Retention Hold are essentially the same, but the truth is that they are quite different. When you place a mailbox on In-Place Hold, retention policies are not suspended, which gives the end user the impression that the policies are still in place and that data can be removed from the mailbox.

When a user empties their `Deleted Items` folder or performs a *Shift+Delete* on messages, these items are moved to the `Recoverable Items` folder. Users can recover these items by default for up to 14 days, but they can also delete items from the `Recoverable Items` folder using the Recover Deleted Items tool in an attempt to permanently purge the data from their mailbox. Deleting items for the `Recoverable Items` folder places the data in the `Purges` sub folder, which is hidden from the user. When a mailbox is on In-Place Hold, an administrator can access the items in a folder called `DiscoveryHold` using discovery search, and the mailbox assistant does not purge the items in this folder when the database's deleted item retention period elapses. During the In-Place Hold period, each object version is saved, and when a user or process changes an item, each version is saved to a new version and placed in a folder called `Versions`.

Messages located in the `Recoverable Items` folder do not count against a user's mailbox storage quota, but each mailbox does have a `RecoverableItemsQuota` property that is set to 30 GB by default. This property can be changed at the database level using the `Set-MailboxDatabase` cmdlet, or at the mailbox level using the `Set-Mailbox` cmdlet.

> Keep in mind that when you place a mailbox on In-Place Hold, it may take up to 60 minutes to take effect. You'll receive a warning message in the Shell explaining this when you enable the setting for a mailbox.

Like the Retention Hold, you can include a retention comment when placing a user on In-Place Hold, as some organizations are required to inform users of this for legal purposes. Users running Outlook 2010 will see retention comments in the backstage area of Outlook. To add a comment, provide a message using the `-RetentionComment` parameter together with the `-RetentionUrl` parameter when placing the mailbox on In-Place Hold:

```
Set-Mailbox -Identity dsmith '

-RetentionComment "You are currently on in-place hold, please visit the provided URL" '

-RetentionUrl http://intranet.contoso.com/in-place-hold/
```

After this setting has been configured, it might take a while before it takes effect; it will show up in Outlook when you click on the **File** button, and it will look something similar to the following screenshot:

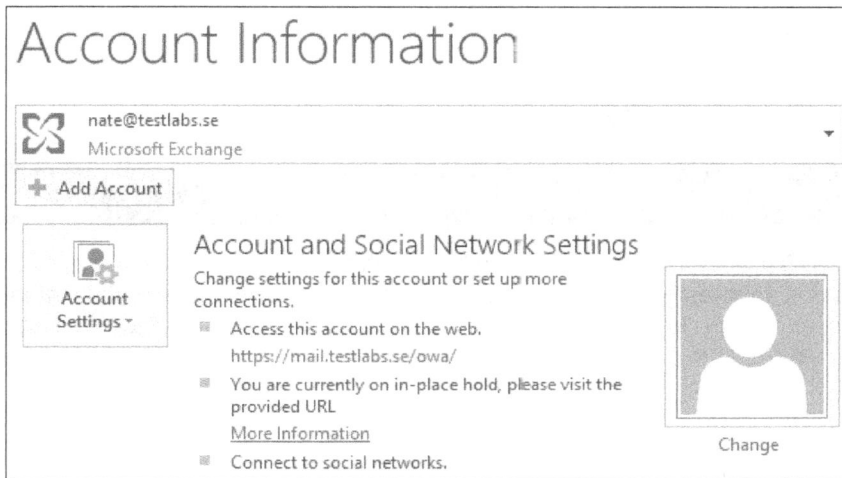

There's more...

To determine which users are currently on In-Place Hold, use the `Get-Mailbox` cmdlet and retrieve the mailboxes that have a value configured in the `InPlaceHolds` field using the following cmdlet:

```
Get-Mailbox -ResultSize Unlimited | Where {$_.InPlaceHolds -ne ""}
```

When a mailbox has been placed on In-Place Hold, you can view the date it was placed on hold and which user enabled the setting by viewing the properties of the `Get-MailboxSearch` cmdlet:

> The use of POP and IMAP protocols by clients doesn't get captured by In-Place Hold.

See also

▸ *Performing a discovery search*

Performing a discovery search

Exchange 2013 provides the ability to search through mailboxes for content that might be required during an investigation, such as a violation of organizational policy or regulatory compliance, or due to a lawsuit. Although this can be done through the Exchange Admin Center, you may need to do this from the command line. In this recipe, you'll learn how to perform discovery searches from the Exchange Management Shell.

How to do it...

In order to perform a discovery search, you'll need special permissions. By default, no one, not even the user who installed Exchange 2013, is assigned the right to perform searches. Using an account that is a member of the Organization Management role group, you can assign the required permissions in one of the two ways, and then perform a discovery search. These tasks are outlined in the following steps:

1. For example, if you are using the administrator account that is already a part of the Organization Management role group, you can assign yourself the permission to perform discovery searches by adding your account to the Discovery Management role group:

   ```
   Add-RoleGroupMember -Identity "Discovery Management" '
   -Member administrator
   ```

2. As an alternative, you can also give yourself or another user a direct role assignment to the Mailbox Search role:

   ```
   New-ManagementRoleAssignment -Role "Mailbox Search" '
   -User administrator
   ```

3. After you have been assigned permissions, you'll need to restart the Exchange Management Shell so that the cmdlets required to perform the search will be loaded. Then, you can use the `New-MailboxSearch` cmdlet to create a new search:

```
New-MailboxSearch -Name Case1 '
-TargetMailbox "Discovery Search Mailbox" '
-SearchQuery 'Subject:"Corporate Secrets"' '
-StartDate "1/1/2015" '
-EndDate "12/31/2015" '
-MessageTypes Email '
-IncludeUnsearchableItems '
-LogLevel Full
```

The previous command will search all the mailboxes in the organization for messages sent or received in the year 2015 with a subject of `Corporate Secrets`. Any messages found matching this criterion will be copied to the `Discovery Search Mailbox`.

How it works...

One of the benefits of using the shell instead of the EAC when performing a discovery search is that you can specify the target mailbox. The EAC requires that you use a Discovery Search Mailbox to store the results. With the `New-MailboxSearch` cmdlet, you can provide a value for the `-TargetMailbox` parameter and specify another mailbox.

If you perform a search without specifying any source mailboxes, all of the mailboxes in the organization will be searched, as in our previous example. One thing to keep in mind is that, in order to successfully perform a search, you need to have healthy database indexes, and indexing needs to be enabled (it is, by default) for each database that contains the mailboxes you are searching.

Let's take a look at another example. This time, we'll search a specific mailbox and store the results in an alternate mailbox using the following command:

```
New-MailboxSearch -Name Case2 '
-SourceMailboxes dsmith,jjones '
-TargetMailbox administrator '
-SearchQuery 'Subject:"Corporate Secrets"' '
-MessageTypes Email '
-StatusMailRecipients legal@contoso.com
```

This time, we've specified two source mailboxes to search, and the results will be stored in the administrator mailbox. The `-StatusMailRecipients` parameter is also used to send an e-mail notification to the legal department when the search is complete. Also notice that, this time, we did not specify a start or end date, so the search will be performed against all items in each source mailbox.

The key to performing a precise search is using the `-SearchQuery` parameter. This allows you to use keywords and specific property values when searching for messages with **Advanced Query Syntax** (**AQS**). See *Appendix B, Query Syntaxes,* at the end of this book, for details on creating an AQS query.

Once a discovery search has been completed, you can export the items captured by the search by accessing the target mailbox. Whether it is the Discovery Search Mailbox or an alternate mailbox that you specified when running the command, you can give your account full access permissions to the mailbox and access the items using Outlook or OWA.

There's more...

Once you start a discovery search, it may take some time to complete, depending on the size and number of mailboxes you are working with. These searches can be completely managed from the shell. For example, if you want to remove a search before it completes, you can use the `Remove-MailboxSearch` cmdlet. You can also stop a search, modify its properties, and then restart the search. Let's say that we've just created a new search; we can check its status with the `Get-MailboxSearch` cmdlet:

```
Get-MailboxSearch | Select-Object Name,Status,Percentcomplete
```

If needed, we can stop the search before it is completed, modify the properties, and then restart the search using the mailbox search cmdlets:

```
Stop-MailboxSearch -Identity Case2
Set-MailboxSearch -Identity Case2 -SourceMailboxes Finance,HR
Start-MailboxSearch -Identity Case2
```

As you can see in these commands, we first stop the `Case2` search, then modify the source mailboxes it is configured to run against, and finally restart the search.

See also

▶ *Deleting messages from mailboxes* in *Chapter 4, Managing Mailboxes*

Configuring administrator audit logging

Administrator audit logging allows you to track the cmdlets that are being run within your Exchange organization. The log entries provide details about the cmdlets and parameters used, such as when a command was executed, which objects were affected by the command, and the user who ran the cmdlet. In this recipe, you'll learn how to configure the options used to define the administrator audit logging settings in your environment.

How to do it...

For new installations of Exchange 2013, administrator audit logging is enabled by default. Let's perform the following steps to configure administrator audit logging:

1. To determine the current configuration, use the `Get-AdminAuditLogConfig` cmdlet, as shown in the following screenshot:

2. You can review the output and check the `AdminAuditLogEnabled` property. If this is set to `False`, use the `Set-AdminAuditLogConfig` cmdlet to enable administrator audit logging:

```
Set-AdminAuditLogConfig -AdminAuditLogEnabled $true
```

The administrator audit log settings are an organization-wide setting. The previous command only needs to be run once from a server within the Exchange organization.

How it works...

Once administrator audit logging has been enabled, the default settings are configured so that all cmdlets are audited. Cmdlets running through the Exchange Management Shell or the Exchange Admin Center are all subject to the administrator audit log settings.

If you take another look at the output of the `Get-AdminAuditLogConfig` cmdlet, you'll notice that `AdminAuditLogCmdlets` is set to the asterisk (*) character, which means that all cmdlets by default are configured for auditing. This is true only with cmdlets that make changes to the environment. Any `Get-*` cmdlets are not subject to auditing, since they do not make any changes and would generate a large number of logs.

You can override this setting using the `Set-AdminAuditLogConfig` cmdlet. For example, if you only want to audit one or two specific cmdlets, you can assign each cmdlet name, separated by a comma, to the `-AdminAuditLogCmdlets` parameter:

```
Set-AdminAuditLogConfig '
-AdminAuditLogCmdlets Set-Mailbox,Set-CASMailbox
```

The same goes for cmdlet parameters. If you want to limit which parameters are audited for each cmdlet, specify a list of parameter names using the `–AdminAuditLogParameters` parameter.

> When making changes to the `Set-AdminAuditLogConfig` cmdlet, you'll receive a warning message that it may take up to 1 hour for the change to take effect. To apply the changes immediately, simply close and reopen the shell.

You can also exclude specific cmdlets from being audited. To do so, use the following command:

```
Set-AdminAuditLogConfig -AdminAuditLogExcludedCmdlets New-Mailbox
```

In this example, the `New-Mailbox` cmdlet will not be audited. You can exclude multiple cmdlets by supplying a list of cmdlet names separated by a comma.

By default, the administrator audit log will keep up to 90 days of log entries. This setting can also be modified using the `Set-AdminAuditLogConfig` cmdlet. Audit log entries are stored in a hidden, dedicated arbitration mailbox.

There's more...

The Exchange Management Shell provides a number of troubleshooting cmdlets that use the verb `Test`. By default, these cmdlets are not audited because they can generate a significant amount of data in a short amount of time. If you need to enable logging of the `Test-*` cmdlets, use the `Set-AdminAuditLogConfig` cmdlet:

```
Set-AdminAuditLogConfig -TestCmdletLoggingEnabled $true
```

It is recommended that you only leave test cmdlet logging enabled for short periods of time. Once you are done, you can disable the setting by setting the value back to $false:

```
Set-AdminAuditLogConfig -TestCmdletLoggingEnabled $false
```

See also

▸ *Searching administrator audit logs*

Searching the administrator audit logs

You can use the Exchange Management Shell to search the administrator audit logs and generate reports based on the cmdlets and parameters used to modify objects within your Exchange environment. Like mailbox audit log reports, we have two ways in which we can view the audit logs from the Exchange Management Shell, and in this recipe, we'll take a look at both the methods.

How to do it...

Let's see how to perform administrator audit log search using the following steps:

1. To perform a synchronous administrator audit log search in the shell, we can use the Search-AdminAuditLog cmdlet. For example, after executing the following command, the following results will be displayed in the shell:

```
Search-AdminAuditLog -Cmdlets Set-Mailbox '
-StartDate 5/1/2015 '
-EndDate 5/30/2015 '
-IsSuccess $true
```

This command will return all of the log entries for the Set-Mailbox cmdlet for the month of May. Only the log entries from successful commands will be returned.

2. To perform an asynchronous search, use the `New-AdminAuditLogSearch` cmdlet:

```
New-AdminAuditLogSearch -Name "AdminAuditLogSearch01" '
-Cmdlets Set-Mailbox '
-StartDate 5/1/2015 '
-EndDate 5/30/2015 '
-StatusMailRecipients admin@contoso.com
```

Based on the parameters used here, the results of the search will be the same, the difference is that the search will take place in the background, and instead of displaying the results in the shell, a message will be e-mailed to a recipient and the report will be attached in the XML format.

How it works...

The administrator audit log entries provide the complete details of every cmdlet that was used to make a change in your environment. When using the `Search-AdminAuditLog` cmdlet, we can limit the results based on a specific time frame and by the name of the cmdlet or the parameters that were used. If you run the cmdlet without any parameters, all of the entries in the administrator audit log will be returned.

One of the most useful things about this cmdlet is that you can quickly determine how and why something has recently been changed. For example, the user named Nate Davis reports that his primary e-mail address has been changed, since one of his customers noticed and told him. You could consult the administrator audit logs to determine what might have happened to his account:

```
Machine: tlex01.testlabs.se                               _  □  X

[PS] C:\Scripts>Search-AdminAuditLog | ?{$_.ObjectModified -like '*nate*'}

RunspaceId          : 01cc65fc-8544-4f22-be0a-dabe8efdb730
ObjectModified      : testlabs.se/Sales/Nate Davis
CmdletName          : Set-Mailbox
CmdletParameters    : {Identity, PrimarySmtpAddress}
ModifiedProperties  : {EmailAddresses, UMDtmfMap, WindowsEmailAddress,
                      Extensions, PrimarySmtpAddress, IndexedPhoneNumbers,
                      OriginalPrimarySmtpAddress,
                      OriginalWindowsEmailAddress}
Caller              : testlabs.se/Users/admins
ExternalAccess      : False
Succeeded           : True
Error               : None
RunDate             : 5/9/2015 12:22:43 PM
OriginatingServer   : TLEX01 (15.00.1044.021)
Identity            : AAMkADk4MzQzYWY5LTUzM2ItNDVmNC1iM2YzLTUzOGQzYTkxNTgwM
                      gBGAAAAAArcN7C98iKTqHRlfX2VVlEBwCParIYYdUYT55PHtJbDJ
                      o3AAAAAAEYAACParIYYdUYT55PHtJbDJo3AABTFcyuAAA=
IsValid             : True
```

Using the previous command, we search the administrator audit log and pipe the results to the `Where-Object` cmdlet, filtering on the `ObjectModified` property, where the object contains the user's last name. The most recent command used to modify this object will be returned first. In the preceding screenshot, we can see that the `Set-Mailbox` cmdlet was run against this object by the administrator account, and the `Identity` and `PrimarySmtpAddress` parameters were used for setting a new primary e-mail address to the mailbox.

There's more...

The default view of each administrator audit log entry provides a lot of detailed information, but we can work with the properties of each log entry to gain even more insight into what was changed. One good example of this is the ability to view the new and old values that have been set on an object.

For example, let's say that we want to review the audit logs to determine the changes made by the ten most recent commands. First, we can save the results in a variable:

```
$logs = Search-AdminAuditLog | Select-Object -First 10
```

Each of the log entries are now stored in the `$logs` variable, which at this point is an array of audit log entries. To view the first entry in the list, we can access the zero element of the array:

```
Machine: tlex01.testlabs.se                           _  □  x

[PS] C:\Scripts>$logs[0]

RunspaceId          : 01cc65fc-8544-4f22-be0a-dabe8efdb730
ObjectModified      : testlabs.se/Sales/Nate Davis
CmdletName          : Set-Mailbox
CmdletParameters    : {Identity, PrimarySmtpAddress}
ModifiedProperties  : {EmailAddresses, UMDtmfMap, WindowsEmailAddress,
                       Extensions, PrimarySmtpAddress, IndexedPhoneNumbers,
                       OriginalPrimarySmtpAddress,
                       OriginalWindowsEmailAddress}
Caller              : testlabs.se/Users/admins
ExternalAccess      : False
Succeeded           : True
Error               : None
RunDate             : 5/9/2015 12:22:43 PM
```

After reviewing the details, we can see that the `Set-Mailbox` cmdlet modified a couple of properties of an account. To determine these values, we can view the `ModifiedProperties` property of the current array element:

```
Machine: tlex01.testlabs.se                          _  □  x

[PS] C:\Scripts>$logs[0].ModifiedProperties | Format-List


Name      : EmailAddresses
NewValue  : SMTP:nate.davis@testlabs.se;smtp:nate@testlabs.se;smtp:nate@tes
            tlabstrial.onmicrosoft.com;smtp:nate@testlabstrial.mail.onmicro
            soft.com;x500:/o=ExchangeLabs/ou=Exchange Administrative Group
            (FYDIBOHF23SPDLT)/cn=Recipients/cn=305ad7a6fed84850a3c164155a9d
            fa21-Nate
OldValue  : smtp:nate.davis@testlabs.se;SMTP:nate@testlabs.se;smtp:nate@tes
            tlabstrial.onmicrosoft.com;smtp:nate@testlabstrial.mail.onmicro
            soft.com;x500:/o=ExchangeLabs/ou=Exchange Administrative Group
            (FYDIBOHF23SPDLT)/cn=Recipients/cn=305ad7a6fed84850a3c164155a9d
            fa21-Nate
```

By viewing the output in a list format, we can see that the users previously had different SMTP addresses configured for their account. When the cmdlet was executed, it changed the SMTP address. Here, in the preceding screenshot, we can see both the new value and the old value of the mailbox. There are additional attributes that change when the `PrimarySmtpAddress` value gets changed. These have been removed in the previous screenshot for the reason that it took too much space, but they can be viewed in your own messaging environment.

See also

▸ *Configuring administrator audit logging*

Configuring S/MIME for OWA

For those of you who might not be aware of what **S/MIME (Secure/Multipurpose Internet Mail Extensions)** is, this short description might be helpful.

As most of you are aware, messages or e-mails, in general, are mostly insecure if they are not digitally signed and their transport isn't encrypted. With S/MIME, the messages can be digitally signed, which can be seen as a guarantee that the sender is the person they claim to be and not anyone else. With the use of S/MIME, the contents and attachments of messages can be encrypted.

In Exchange 2013 RTM, the support for S/MIME was removed for OWA, but it was brought back when Service Pack 1 was released, which was great.

For this recipe, I've decided to use an internal PKI solution based on Windows Server 2012 R2 for issuing certificates to users for securing their e-mails and ensuring their identities. The important thing to keep in mind, when implementing this in production, is that it's recommended that you use certificates from a third-party trusted root issuer. However, the internal PKI solution is great in lab or training environments. The reason behind this, it being not recommended to use the internal PKI solution in production, is that the root certificate created for the PKI infrastructure is not known by anyone outside the domain, which means that the recipients of our encrypted messages don't know about the trusted root certificate, so they cannot decrypt the contents of the messages.

So let's start with the configuration and take a look at the results in this recipe.

How to do it...

To verify the current configuration, we can easily run the following cmdlet:

```
Get-SMIMEConfig
```

In this example, I've configured my environment to give the user the option to select the user certificate themselves. For the encryption algorithm, I've used the option of RC2 with 128-bit encryption. These options are configured using the following cmdlet:

```
Set-SmimeConfig -OWAAllowUserChoiceOfSigningCertificate $true '

-OWAEncryptionAlgorithms 6602:128
```

Once this configuration is in place, the root certificate of the internal PKI solution needs to be exported and configured as a S/MIME, issuing CA; this is done by running the following cmdlet:

```
Get-ChildItem -Path '

"Cert:\LocalMachine\CA\175AC872CA60AAD30FBBC66228A706CDA8E4B787" '

| Export-Certificate -Type SST '

-FilePath C:\Media\SMIME\testlabsca.sst

Set-SmimeConfig -SMIMECertificateIssuingCA (Get-Content `
C:\Media\SMIME\testlabsca.sst -Encoding Byte)
```

With the configuration in place, I proceeded with the Windows 8.1 client and logged in using two of the users called Dave Jones and Nate Davis, requested the certificate for securing messages, which in my environment is based on a template called S/MIME.

This was easily done with the following command:

```
Certreq -Enroll S-MIME
```

With the certificate in place, it should look similar to the following screenshot:

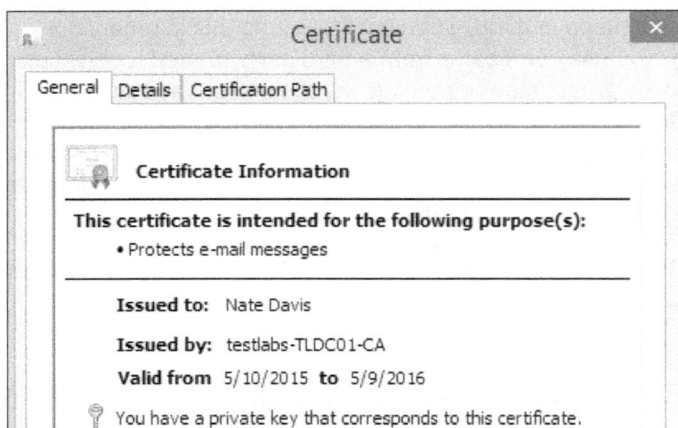

When using the OWA, the S/MIME control needs to be deployed to the clients; this can also be downloaded and installed by the end users, but it's recommended to get this deployed using any existing deployment solution or using a group policy for getting it installed.

> This recipe is just an example of how S/MIME can be used in Exchange 2013 together with OWA. The security is not the focus of this recipe, so when deploying this in your lab and production environments, make sure to investigate all the requirements and make decision based on them.

How it works...

Currently, when this book was written, for using S/MIME, there were four options of using S/MIME for its purpose: Outlook 2010 or 2013, Outlook Web App, and Exchange ActiveSync.

When the user certificate is issued, their certificate gets published to their Active Directory user object under the `userSMIMECertificate` and `userCertificate` attributes.

When you get the option to send a digitally signed message without encrypting the content(s), the signing itself happens in Outlook at the sender, where the information is retrieved and validated against the certificate and the signature is added to the message. Once this is done, the message is sent. With the information being retrieved, this information is unique, and it can be proved that this message has come from the sender.

When the recipient receives and opens the message, a procedure for verifying the digital signature starts. The sender's information is retrieved from the Active Directory and verified against the added signature. The digital signature is included in the message, if the signature and information matches, the signature is validated, which means that the sender is identified and unique.

> TechNet has an overview of S/MIME and the procedures that take place, which can be found at `https://technet.microsoft.com/library/aa995740(v=exchg.65).aspx`.

The difference between only using digital signature and encryption is that when the message is not encrypted, the contents are being sent in clear text. However, the digital signature ensures the unique identity of the sender.

When sending confidential contents, it's recommended that you encrypt the message together with digitally signing it. If anyone comes across an encrypted message, it cannot be read or opened.

When receiving a digitally signed and encrypted message, it will look similar to the following screenshot:

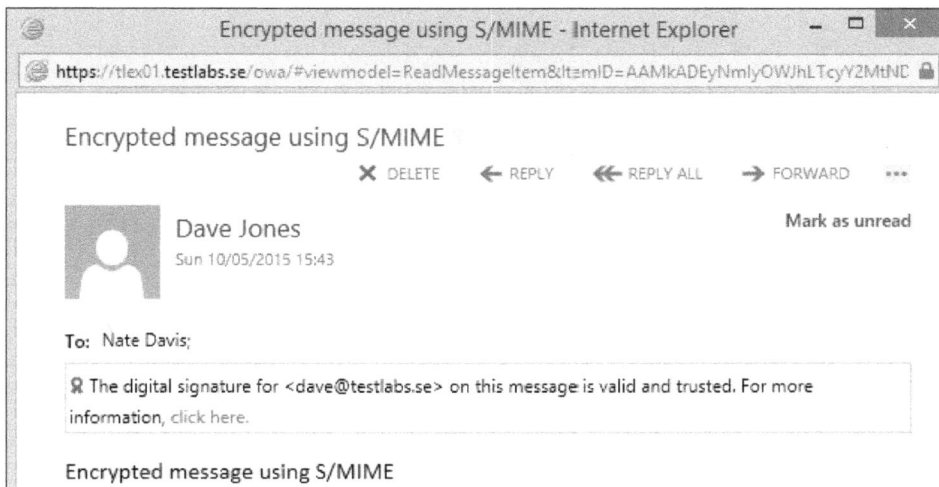

This book is based on the on-premises version of Exchange 2013. However, the option of using S/MIME can also be found in Exchange Online, which is part of Office 365.

> S/MIME can also be used in Exchange Online, and it can be configured by following the article on *Exchange Team Blog* at `http://blogs.technet.com/b/exchange/archive/2014/12/15/how-to-configure-s-mime-in-office-365.aspx`.

See also

▶ *Searching message tracking logs* in Chapter 8, *Managing Transport Servers*
▶ *Managing connectivity and protocol logs* in Chapter 8, *Managing Transport Servers*

12

Scripting with the Exchange Web Services Managed API

In this chapter, we will cover the following topics:

- ▶ Getting connected to EWS
- ▶ Sending e-mail messages with EWS
- ▶ Working with impersonation
- ▶ Searching mailboxes
- ▶ Retrieving the headers of an e-mail message
- ▶ Deleting e-mail items from a mailbox
- ▶ Creating calendar items
- ▶ Exporting attachments from a mailbox

Introduction

Exchange Web Services (**EWS**) was introduced with Exchange 2007. It gave developers the ability to write applications that previously required the use of multiple APIs, such as CDOEx, Exchange OLEDB, WebDAV and more. Today, developers can call the Exchange Management Shell cmdlets from .NET-managed applications to perform administrative tasks programmatically. When it comes to manipulating the contents of a mailbox, such as creating or modifying calendar items, e-mail messages, contacts, or tasks, developers now use EWS.

Working with EWS requires formatting and sending an XML request over HTTP and parsing the XML response from an Exchange server. Initially, developers used either raw XML or auto-generated proxy classes in Visual Studio to do this, and it required some very verbose code that was difficult to read and debug. Fortunately, the EWS team developed and released the EWS Managed API in April 2009. The EWS Managed API is a fully object-oriented .NET wrapper for the EWS XML protocol that makes life much easier for application developers.

Applications written using the Managed API require a fraction of the code that developers previously had to write when working with raw XML or auto-generated proxy classes. This makes for a huge increase in productivity because the code is easier to read and troubleshoot, and the learning curve for new developers is much lower. The good news is that this is also true for Exchange administrators who want to write advanced PowerShell scripts that utilize EWS. The EWS Managed API can be used to do things in PowerShell that are not possible with the Exchange Management Shell cmdlets. The EWS Managed API assembly can be loaded into the shell, and with the right permissions, you can immediately start building scripts that can access and manipulate the data within any mailbox inside the organization.

In this chapter, we will cover some of the key concepts of using EWS in your PowerShell scripts, such as connecting to EWS, sending e-mail messages, and working with items in one or more mailboxes. The end goal is to give you a basic understanding of the EWS Managed API so that you can start to build some basic scripts or decipher the code samples you come across on the Internet or within the TechNet documentation.

Performing some basic steps

To work with the code samples in this chapter, perform the following steps to download the EWS Managed API:

1. Download the EWS Managed API from `http://www.microsoft.com/en-us/download/details.aspx?id=42951`.

2. Download and run `EwsManagedApi.msi`.

3. During the installation, select a destination folder, such as `C:\EWS`, or choose the default directory `C:\Program Files\Microsoft\Exchange\Web Services\2.2`. You will need to note the location so that you can import the `Microsoft.Exchange.WebServices.dll` assembly into the shell.

You can use either a standard PowerShell console or the Exchange Management Shell to run the code for each recipe in this chapter.

Getting connected to EWS

When working with EWS, you first need to create an instance of the `ExchangeService` class that can be used to send SOAP messages to an Exchange server. This class has several properties and methods that can be used to specify explicit credentials, set the web service's end-point URL, or make a connection using the built-in AutoDiscover client. In this recipe, you'll learn how to make a connection to EWS that can be used to run custom scripts against the web service.

How to do it...

Let's see how to get connected to EWS using the following steps:

1. The first thing we need to do is load the EWS Managed API assembly into the shell:

   ```
   Add-Type -Path C:\EWS\Microsoft.Exchange.WebServices.dll
   ```

2. Now we can create an instance of the `ExchangeService` class:

   ```
   $svc = New-Object `
   Microsoft.Exchange.WebServices.Data.ExchangeService
   ```

3. At this point, we can use the `AutoDiscoverUrl` method to determine the EWS end point on the closest Client Access Server for the mailbox with a particular SMTP address:

   ```
   $svc.AutoDiscoverUrl("jonand@testlabs.se")
   ```

Now that we have an Exchange service connection created, we can send e-mail messages, create and modify items within a mailbox, and perform other tasks. The output will look similar to the following screenshot:

```
Administrator: Windows PowerShell                          _  □  ×
PS C:\EWS> Add-Type -Path C:\EWS\Microsoft.Exchange.WebServices.dll
PS C:\EWS> $svc = New-Object Microsoft.Exchange.WebServices.Data.ExchangeSe
rvice
PS C:\EWS> $svc.AutoDiscoverUrl("jonand@testlabs.se")
PS C:\EWS>
```

How it works...

Before we can start working with the classes in the EWS Managed API, the assembly must be loaded so that the .NET Framework types are available when running scripts that utilize the API. This is only valid for the current shell session, and if you want to create scripts, you'll want to make sure that this is always the first thing that is done before invoking any code. We used the `Add-Type` cmdlet in the previous example to load the assembly, but the following command is also valid:

```
[System.Reflection.Assembly]::LoadFile(
  "C:\ews\Microsoft.Exchange.WebServices.dll"
)
```

This is basically the longhand method of doing the same thing we did before; loading an unreferenced assembly into the shell environment. Notice that in both the examples, we are using the path `C:\EWS`. This is not the default path where the assembly is installed, but you can copy it to any folder of your choice. For example, let's take a look at the following screenshot:

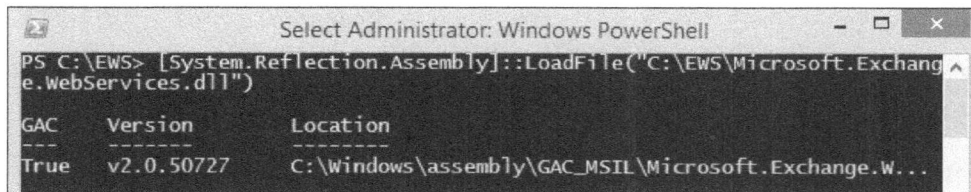

When creating an instance of the `ExchangeService` class, we have the option of versioning the connection. For example, run the following command:

```
$svc=New-Object
Microsoft.Exchange.WebServices.Data.ExchangeService `
-ArgumentList "Exchange2013_SP1"
```

Here, we are passing the Exchange version to the `ExchangeService` class constructor. When you do not provide a value, the most recent version of Exchange will be used, which in this case would be Exchange 2013 SP1, since we're using the 2.2 Version of the API. The values that can be used for Exchange are `Exchange2007_SP1`, `Exchange2010`, `Exchange2010_SP1`, `Exchange2010_SP2`, `Exchange2013`, and `Exchange2013_SP1`.

Since we didn't specify any credentials when creating the `ExchangeService` object, we need to provide the SMTP address associated with the mailbox of the currently logged on user when calling the `AutoDiscoverUrl` method.

There's more...

If you want to use explicit credentials when creating your `ExchangeService` object, rather than using the credentials of the currently logged on user, you need to do a couple of things differently. The following code will create an instance of the `ExchangeService` class using an alternate set of credentials:

```
[System.Reflection.Assembly]::LoadFile(
  "C:\ews\Microsoft.Exchange.WebServices.dll"
)
$svc = New-Object Microsoft.Exchange.WebServices.Data.ExchangeService
$svc.Credentials = New-Object '
Microsoft.Exchange.WebServices.Data.WebCredentials '
-ArgumentList "jonand","P@ssw0rd01","testlabs.se"
```

In addition, you also have the option of setting the EWS URL manually:

```
$url = "https://autodiscover.testlabs.se/EWS/Exchange.asmx"
$svc.Url = New-Object System.Uri -ArgumentList $url
```

Although it is possible to set the URL manually, developers use `AutoDiscover` as a best practice, as it allows the API to determine the best Client Access Server that should be used as the web service's URL. A hard-coded URL value could potentially mean a broken script if things change later on in your environment. The output of the preceding cmdlets will look similar to the following screenshot:

Certificates matter

Just like the Outlook Web App, the EWS virtual directory is secured with an SSL certificate. If you are still using the self-signed certificates that are installed by default on Client Access Servers you'll need to override a security check done by the API to validate the certificate, otherwise you will be unable to connect. To do this, we can use the `ServicePointManager` class in the `System.Net` namespace.

This class can be used to hook up a certificate validation callback method, and as long as that method returns `$true`, the API will consider the self-signed certificate to be trusted:

```
$svc = New-Object
Microsoft.Exchange.WebServices.Data.ExchangeService

$spm = [System.Net.ServicePointManager]

$spm::ServerCertificateValidationCallback = {$true}

$svc.AutoDiscoverUrl("jonand@testlabs.se")
```

Certificate validation callback methods are written to perform additional checks on a certificate. These callback methods return a Boolean value that indicates whether or not a certificate can be trusted. Instead of writing a callback method, we're assigning a script block that returns `$true` to the `ServerCertificateValidationCallback` property. This forces the API to consider any EWS end-point to be secure, regardless of the status of the certificate used to secure it. Keep in mind that self-signed certificates are considered to be a bootstrap security configuration, so connections to Exchange can be secured out of the box. The best practice is to replace these certificates with trusted commercial or enterprise PKI certificates. For example, refer to the following screenshot regarding the URL override:

Sending e-mail messages with EWS

As we saw in *Chapter 2, Exchange Management Shell Common Tasks*, we can use the PowerShell's built-in `Send-MailMessage` cmdlet to send e-mail messages. This can be a useful tool when writing scripts that need to send notifications, but the EWS Managed API has several distinct advantages over this approach. In this recipe, we'll take a look at how to send e-mail messages through EWS and why this might be a better option for organizations that have an Exchange infrastructure in place.

How to do it...

Let's see how to send e-mail messages with EWS using the following steps:

1. First, we'll import the EWS Managed API assembly, create an instance of the `ExchangeService` class, and set the EWS erd point using AutoDiscover:

    ```
    Add-Type -Path C:\EWS\Microsoft.Exchange.WebServices.dll

    $svc = New-Object '

    -TypeName Microsoft.Exchange.WebServices.Data.ExchangeService

    $svc.AutoDiscoverUrl("administrator@contoso.com")
    ```

2. Next, we'll create an instance of the `EmailMessage` class:

    ```
    $msg = New-Object '

    -TypeName Microsoft.Exchange.WebServices.Data.EmailMessage '

    -ArgumentList $svc
    ```

3. At this point, we can set specific properties on the `$msg` object, such as the subject, body, and one or more recipients:

    ```
    $msg.Subject = "Test E-Mail"

    $msg.Body = "This is a test"

    $msg.From = "administrator@contoso.com"

    $msg.ToRecipients.Add("sysadmin@contoso.com")

    $msg.SendAndSaveCopy()
    ```

Once this code has been executed, the message is sent to `sysadmin@contoso.com`.

How it works...

When we send e-mail messages through EWS, we don't have to worry about specifying an SMTP server, as the message is transmitted through the web service. This allows our code to run on any machine that has PowerShell installed, and we don't need to modify the receive connectors on the Client Access Server to allow a specific host to relay e-mail. Additionally, EWS will allow us to use AutoDiscover to automatically find the correct end point, which prevents the need to hardcode server names into our scripts.

Setting the `Subject`, `Body`, and `From` properties of an `EmailMessage` object is pretty straightforward. We simply need to assign a value as we would with any other object. Adding recipients requires that we use the `Add` method of the `ToRecipients` property. If you have multiple recipients that must be addressed, you can call this method for each one, or you can loop through a collection using the `ForEach-Object` cmdlet:

```
$to = "sysadmin@contoso.com","IT@contoso.com","help@contoso.com"
$to | ForEach-Object {$msg.ToRecipients.Add($_)}
```

When you call the `Add` method, you'll notice that the `ToRecipients` property will be returned for each address added to the message. For example, referring to the following screenshot, maybe you noticed that I used the `Out-Null` command; it is used to have a proper screenshot size:

If you want to simply call this method, without having anything returned to the screen, pipe the command to `Out-Null`, as shown in the following command:

```
$msg.ToRecipients.Add("sales@contoso.com") | Out-Null
```

In addition, we can also carbon copy and blind copy recipients on the message:

```
$msg.CcRecipients.Add("sales@contoso.com") | Out-Null
```

```
$msg.BccRecipients.Add("dmsith@contoso.com") | Out-Null
```

Finally, if you do not want to save a copy of the message in the Sent Items folder, you can simply use the Send method:

$msg.Send()

Keep in mind that, since we did not provide any credentials when connecting to EWS, the user running this code will need to have a mailbox on the server that corresponds to the From address being used. Since we are connecting with our currently logged on credentials, the message must be sent from the mailbox of the user running the code.

There's more...

Instead of typing all of the commands required to instantiate the ExchangeService object, it makes much more sense to put this code into a reusable function. Call AutoDiscover, create the e-mail message object, and set all of the required properties. Consider the following code:

```
function Send-EWSMailMessage {
  param(
  [Parameter(
    Position=0,
    Mandatory=$true,
    ValueFromPipelineByPropertyName=$true
  )]
  [String[]]
  $PrimarySmtpAddress,
  [Parameter(
    Position=1, Mandatory=$true
  )]
  [String]
  $From,
  [Parameter(
    Position=2, Mandatory=$true
  )]
  [String]
  $Subject,
  [Parameter(
    Position=3, Mandatory=$true
  )]
  [String]
  $Body,
  [Parameter(
    Position=4, Mandatory=$false
  )]
```

```
        [String[]]
        $Cc,
        [Parameter(
          Position=5, Mandatory=$false
        )]
        [String[]]
        $Bcc
        )
        begin {
          Add-Type -Path C:\EWS\Microsoft.Exchange.WebServices.dll
        }
        process {
          $svc = New-Object '
          -TypeName Microsoft.Exchange.WebServices.Data.ExchangeService
          $svc.AutodiscoverUrl($From)
          $msg = New-Object '
          -TypeName Microsoft.Exchange.WebServices.Data.EmailMessage '
          -ArgumentList $svc
          $msg.Subject = $Subject
          $msg.Body = $Body
          $PrimarySmtpAddress | %{
            $msg.ToRecipients.Add($_) | Out-Null
          }
          if ($Cc -ne $null)
          {
            $msg.CcRecipients.Add($Cc) | Out-Null
          }
          if ($Bcc -ne $null)
          {
            $msg.BccRecipients.Add($Bcc) | Out-Null
          }
          $msg.SendAndSaveCopy()
        }
      }
```

This is an advanced function that can be run in a couple of different ways. Notice that the first parameter is called `PrimarySmtpAddress`, and it accepts a value from the pipeline by a property name. This will allow us to add the function to the Exchange Management Shell and take advantage of the pipeline to send e-mail messages. For example, once this function has been loaded into EMS, we can do something like this:

```
Get-Mailbox -OrganizationalUnit contoso.com/sales |
Send-EWSMailMessage -From administrator@contoso.com '
```

```
-Subject 'Sales Meeting' '
-Body 'Tomorrows sales meeting has been cancelled' '
-Cc administrator@contoso.com '
-Bcc manager@contoso.com
```

Here you can see that we're retrieving all the users from the `Sales` OU and piping those objects to our `Send-EWSMailMessage` function. One message will be addressed and sent to each recipient because the `PrimarySmtpAddress` parameter receives its value from each object that comes across the pipeline. Notice that a carbon copy e-mail will be sent to the specified mailbox when using the `Cc` parameter, and a blind carbon copy e-mail will be sent to the specified mailbox using the `Bcc` parameter.

Since the `PrimarySmtpAddress` parameter also accepts an array of string objects, we can run the function and specify a list of recipients, as shown in the following command:

```
Send-EWSMailMessage -From admins@testlabs.se '
-PrimarySmtpAddress helpdesk@testlabs.se,lsanders@testlabs.se '
-Subject 'Critical alert on TLEX01' '
-Body 'TLEX01 Server is low on disk space' '
-Cc itmanager@testlabs.se
```

Also, notice that the e-mail will be sent as a carbon copy to the specified mailbox using the `Cc` parameter. This can be helpful if the function is used for sending out important e-mails that might be of interest to the manager too. Both the `Cc` and `Bcc` parameters can be used and they both accept an array of string objects. The following screenshot shows you an example of how the PowerShell function can be used:

See also

▶ *Sending SMTP e-mails through PowerShell* in *Chapter 2, Exchange Management Shell Common Tasks*

Working with impersonation

When building PowerShell scripts that leverage the EWS Managed API, we can use impersonation to access a user's mailbox on their behalf, without having to provide their credentials. In order to utilize impersonation, we need permissions inside the Exchange organization, and then we need to configure the `ExchangeService` connection object with the impersonated user ID. In this recipe, you'll learn how to assign the permissions and write a script that uses EWS impersonation.

Getting ready

In this recipe, you will need to use the Exchange Management Shell in order to assign permissions for `ApplicationImpersonation`.

How to do it...

Let's see how to work with impersonation using the following steps:

1. The first thing you need to do is assign your account in the `ApplicationImpersonation` RBAC role from the Exchange Management Shell:

   ```
   New-ManagementRoleAssignment -Role ApplicationImpersonation '
   -User administrator
   ```

2. After we've been granted the permissions, we need to import the EWS Managed API assembly and configure the `ExchangeService` connection object:

   ```
   Add-Type -Path C:\EWS\Microsoft.Exchange.WebServices.dll
   $svc = New-Object -TypeName '
   Microsoft.Exchange.WebServices.Data.ExchangeService
   $id = New-Object -TypeName '
   Microsoft.Exchange.WebServices.Data.ImpersonatedUserId '
   -ArgumentList "SmtpAddress","dsmith@contoso.com"
   $svc.ImpersonatedUserId = $id
   $svc.AutoDiscoverUrl("dsmith@contoso.com")
   ```

We now have an `ExchangeService` connection to EWS as the impersonated user `dsmith`.

How it works...

In order to access a mailbox using the permissions of an impersonated user, we use RBAC to create a management role assignment for the user that will be calling the code. Like any other management role assignment, this can be done directly for one user or to a group. Keep in mind that you can also associate scopes when assigning the `ApplicationImpersonation` role. The command shown in our example will give the administrator account impersonation rights to any mailbox in the organization.

Once we have the impersonation rights, we load the EWS Managed API assembly and create an instance of the `ExchangeService` class to bind to the EWS end point.

Notice that when we create the `$id` object, we're creating an instance of the `ImpersonatedUserId` class and passing two values to the constructor. First, we specify that we want to identify the user to impersonate, using a data type of `SmtpAddress`. The next value passed to the constructor is the actual e-mail address of the impersonated user. The final step is to assign this object to the `$svc.ImpersonatedUserId` property.

Now that our `ExchangeService` connection is configured for impersonation, we can do things, such as send e-mails, modify calendar items, or search the mailbox of the impersonated user.

There's more...

Let's take a look at how we can use impersonation using a modified version of the `Send-EwsMailMessage` function, which was included in the *Sending e-mail messages with EWS* recipe earlier in this chapter. Add the following function to your shell session:

```
function Send-EWSMailMessage {
  param(
    [Parameter(
      Position=0,
      Mandatory=$true,
      ValueFromPipelineByPropertyName=$true
      )]
    [String[]]
    $PrimarySmtpAddress,
    [Parameter(
      Position=1, Mandatory=$true
    )]
    [String]
```

```
      $From,
      [Parameter(
        Position=2, Mandatory=$true
      )]
      [String]
      $Subject,
      [Parameter(
        Position=3, Mandatory=$true
      )]
      [String]
      $Body,
      [Parameter(
        Position=4, Mandatory=$false
      )]
      [String[]]
      $Cc,
      [Parameter(
        Position=5, Mandatory=$false
      )]
      [String[]]
      $Bcc
    )
    begin {
      Add-Type -Path C:\EWS\Microsoft.Exchange.WebServices.dll
    }
    process {
      $svc = New-Object '
      -TypeName Microsoft.Exchange.WebServices.Data.ExchangeService
      $id = New-Object -TypeName '
      Microsoft.Exchange.WebServices.Data.ImpersonatedUserId '
      -ArgumentList "SmtpAddress",$From
      $svc.ImpersonatedUserId = $id
      $svc.AutodiscoverUrl($From)
      $msg = New-Object '
      -TypeName Microsoft.Exchange.WebServices.Data.EmailMessage '
      -ArgumentList $svc
      $msg.Subject = $Subject
      $msg.Body = $Body
      $PrimarySmtpAddress | %{
        $msg.ToRecipients.Add($_) | Out-Null
      }
```

```
    if ($Cc -ne $null)
    {
       $msg.CcRecipients.Add($Cc) | Out-Null
    }
    if ($Bcc -ne $null)
    {
       $msg.BccRecipients.Add($Bcc) | Out-Null
    }
    $msg.SendAndSaveCopy()
  }
}
```

As you can see, we've modified this version of the function so that the SMTP address specified using the -From parameter is used as the impersonated user ID. Let's say that you are logged in to Windows using the domain administrator account, which has been assigned the ApplicationImpersonation RBAC role. Once the function has been loaded into the shell, you can execute the following command:

```
Send-EWSMailMessage -From sysadmin@testlabs.se '

-PrimarySmtpAddress helpdesk@testlabs.se '

-Subject 'Critical alert on TLEX04' '

-Body 'TLEX04 Server is low on disk space' '

-Cc admins@testlabs.se '

-Bcc itmanager@testlabs.se
```

Using this command, the e-mail message is sent through EWS from the sysadmin mailbox. The message appears to the recipient as if the sysadmin account had sent it. The following screenshot shows an illustrative example of how it could be used:

Searching mailboxes

The EWS Managed API can be used to search one or more folders within an Exchange mailbox. The latest version of the API supports searches using Advanced Query Syntax, allowing us to search folders using the indexes created by the Exchange Search service. This makes searching a mailbox folder very fast and less resource-intensive than methods that were used with previous versions of the API. In this recipe, you'll learn how to search the contents of a mailbox through PowerShell and the EWS Managed API.

How to do it...

Let's see how to search the contents of a mailbox using the following steps:

1. First, load the assembly, create the `ExchangeService` object, and connect to EWS:

   ```
   Add-Type -Path C:\EWS\Microsoft.Exchange.WebServices.dll

   $svc = New-Object
   Microsoft.Exchange.WebServices.Data.ExchangeService

   $svc.AutoDiscoverUrl("jonand@testlabs.se")
   ```

2. Next, create a view of the total number of items that should be returned from the search:

   ```
   $view = New-Object -TypeName '

   Microsoft.Exchange.WebServices.Data.ItemView '

   -ArgumentList 100
   ```

3. The next step is to create a property set that contains all the properties of each message we want to be returned, and then associate that property set with the `$view` object created in the preceding step:

   ```
   $propertyset = New-Object Microsoft.Exchange.WebServices.Data. `
   PropertySet (

   [Microsoft.Exchange.WebServices.Data.BasePropertySet]::IdOnly,

   [Microsoft.Exchange.WebServices.Data.ItemSchema]::Subject,

   [Microsoft.Exchange.WebServices.Data.ItemSchema]::HasAttachments,

   [Microsoft.Exchange.WebServices.Data.ItemSchema]::DisplayTo,

   [Microsoft.Exchange.WebServices.Data.ItemSchema]::DisplayCc,

   [Microsoft.Exchange.WebServices.Data.ItemSchema]::DateTimeSent,

   [Microsoft.Exchange.WebServices.Data.ItemSchema]::DateTimeReceived
   )

   $view.PropertySet = $propertyset
   ```

4. Next, define a search query using the AQS syntax:

```
$query = "Subject:sales"
```

5. We can then perform the search using the `FindItems` method of our `ExchangeService` object:

```
$items = $svc.FindItems("Inbox",$query,$view)
```

6. Finally, loop through each item and return a custom object that contains the properties for each message:

```
$items | Foreach-Object{
  New-Object PSObject -Property @{
    Id = $_.Id.ToString()
    Subject = $_.Subject
    To = $_.DisplayTo
    Cc = $_.DisplayCc
    HasAttachments = [bool]$_.HasAttachments
    Sent = $_.DateTimeSent
    Received = $_.DateTimeReceived
  }
}
```

When executing this code, any of the last 100 items in the administrator inbox that have the word `sales` in the subject line will be returned.

How it works...

Since we are not supplying any credentials when creating the `ExchangeService` object and we're not using impersonation, the search will be performed in the administrator mailbox, as this is the logged-on user. You may have noticed that the property set only contains a few key properties of each message. Although there are many more available properties that can be returned, as a best practice, we should only retrieve the properties that interest us. This way, if we are executing the code over and over, perhaps even against multiple mailboxes, we are not burdening the Exchange servers by requesting unnecessary data.

The key to a successful search is to construct the appropriate AQS query. You can use an AQS query for specific properties of a message using word phrase restriction, date range restriction, or message type restriction. For example, instead of querying using the `Subject` property, we can search for messages retrieved within a certain time frame:

```
$svc.FindItems(
  "Inbox",
  "Sent:05/01/2015..05/30/2015",
  $view
)
```

Notice that the first value passed in the call to `FindItems` is the folder that we want to search, next is the AQS query that specifies that we only want to retrieve items that were sent between specific dates in May. And finally, we pass in the `$view` object that specifies the total number of items to return with a defined property set.

There are a number of well-known mailbox folders that can be searched using the `FindItems` method:

- `ArchiveDeletedItems`: The `Deleted Items` folder in the archive mailbox
- `ArchiveMsgFolderRoot`: The root of the message folder hierarchy in the archive mailbox
- `ArchiveRecoverableItemsDeletions`: The root of the folder hierarchy of recoverable items that have been soft-deleted from the `Deleted Items` folder of the archive mailbox
- `ArchiveRecoverableItemsPurges`: The root of the hierarchy of recoverable items that have been hard-deleted from the `Deleted Items` folder of the archive mailbox
- `ArchiveRecoverableItemsRoot`: The root of the `Recoverable Items` folder hierarchy in the archive mailbox
- `ArchiveRecoverableItemsVersions`: The root of the `Recoverable Items versions` folder hierarchy in the archive mailbox
- `ArchiveRoot`: The root of the folder hierarchy in the archive mailbox
- `Calendar`: The `Calendar` folder
- `Contacts`: The `Contacts` folder
- `DeletedItems`: The `Deleted Items` folder
- `Drafts`: The `Drafts` folder
- `Inbox`: The `Inbox` folder

- ► JunkEmail: The Junk E-mail folder

- ► RecoverableItemsDeletions: The root of the folder hierarchy of recoverable items that have been soft-deleted from the Deleted Items folder

- ► RecoverableItemsPurges: The root of the folder hierarchy of recoverable items that have been hard-deleted from the Deleted Items folder

- ► RecoverableItemsRoot: The root of the Recoverable Items folder hierarchy

- ► RecoverableItemsVersions: The root of the Recoverable Items versions folder hierarchy in the archive mailbox

- ► SearchFolders: The Search Folders folder, also known as the Finder folder

- ► SentItems: The Sent Items folder

For details, see the complete list of members for the *WellKnownFolderName enumeration* in the Exchange Web Services Managed API 2.0 SDK documentation on MSDN at http://msdn.microsoft.com/en-us/library/microsoft.exchange.webservices.data.wellknownfoldername(v=exchg.80).aspx and http://msdn.microsoft.com/en-us/library/jj536567(v=exchg.150).aspx.

There's more...

One piece of interesting information that is not returned by the code in the previous example is the body of the message. This is because there are a number of properties that the FindItems method will not return, one of which is the message body. In order to retrieve the message body, we can bind to the message after the search has been performed using the ID of the message.

Let's extend the previous code so that we can retrieve the body of the message and add the ability to impersonate the target mailbox. Add the following code to a file called MailboxSearch.ps1:

```
Param($query,$mailbox)
Add-Type -Path C:\EWS\Microsoft.Exchange.WebServices.dll
$svc = New-Object
Microsoft.Exchange.WebServices.Data.ExchangeService
$id = New-Object -TypeName '
Microsoft.Exchange.WebServices.Data.ImpersonatedUserId '
-ArgumentList "SmtpAddress",$mailbox
$svc.ImpersonatedUserId = $id
$svc.AutoDiscoverUrl($mailbox)
$view = New-Object -TypeName '
Microsoft.Exchange.WebServices.Data.ItemView '
-ArgumentList 100
```

```
$propertyset = New-Object
Microsoft.Exchange.WebServices.Data.PropertySet (
    [Microsoft.Exchange.WebServices.Data.BasePropertySet]::IdOnly,
    [Microsoft.Exchange.WebServices.Data.ItemSchema]::Subject,
    [Microsoft.Exchange.WebServices.Data.ItemSchema]::HasAttachments,
    [Microsoft.Exchange.WebServices.Data.ItemSchema]::DisplayTo,
    [Microsoft.Exchange.WebServices.Data.ItemSchema]::DisplayCc,
    [Microsoft.Exchange.WebServices.Data.ItemSchema]::DateTimeSent,
    [Microsoft.Exchange.WebServices.Data.ItemSchema]::DateTimeReceived
)
$view.PropertySet = $propertyset
$items = $svc.FindItems("Inbox",$query,$view)
$items | Foreach-Object{
  $emailProps = New-Object -TypeName '
  Microsoft.Exchange.WebServices.Data.PropertySet(
      [Microsoft.Exchange.WebServices.Data.BasePropertySet]::IdOnly,
      [Microsoft.Exchange.WebServices.Data.ItemSchema]::Body
  )
  $emailProps.RequestedBodyType = "Text"
  $email =
[Microsoft.Exchange.WebServices.Data.EmailMessage]::Bind(
    $svc, $_.Id, $emailProps
  )
  New-Object PSObject -Property @{
    Id = $_.Id.ToString()
    Subject = $_.Subject
    To = $_.DisplayTo
    Cc = $_.DisplayCc
    HasAttachments = [bool]$_.HasAttachments
    Sent = $_.DateTimeSent
    Received = $_.DateTimeReceived
    Body = $email.Body
  }
}
```

When running the script, provide values for the -Query and -Mailbox parameters:

```
c:\MailboxSearch.ps1 -query "Sent:05/01/2015..05/30/2015" '
-mailbox sysadmin@testlabs.se
```

When the script gets executed, the first 100 items in the `sysadmin` mailbox that were sent between May 1 and 30 will be returned. The script will output a custom object for each item that contains the `Id`, `Subject`, `To`, `Cc`, `HasAttachments`, `Sent`, `Received`, and `Body` properties. Notice that, even though the body might be composed as HTML, we've only requested the text type for the body in the property set used when binding to the message. Look at the following screenshot:

Notice that the date format is changed due to the regional settings in my lab environment: use the date format that applies to your environment.

See also

▶ *Exporting attachments from a mailbox*

Retrieving the headers of an e-mail message

When troubleshooting mail flow issues, you may need to take a look at the headers of an e-mail message. This is easy to do through Outlook for items in your own mailbox, but if you want to do this on behalf of another user, it requires you to have permission to access their mailbox, and then you need to open their mailbox in Outlook to view the headers. In this recipe, we'll take a look at how you can retrieve the headers of a message in your own mailbox, as well as another user's mailbox, using the EWS Managed API and PowerShell.

How to do it...

Let's see how to retrieve the headers of an e-mail message using the following steps:

1. First, load the assembly, create the `ExchangeService` object, and connect to EWS:

```
Add-Type -Path C:\EWS\Microsoft.Exchange.WebServices.dll
$svc = New-Object
Microsoft.Exchange.WebServices.Data.ExchangeService
$svc.AutoDiscoverUrl("jonand@testlabs.se")
```

2. Next, create a view of the total number of items that should be returned from the search:

```
$view = New-Object -TypeName '
Microsoft.Exchange.WebServices.Data.ItemView '
-ArgumentList 100
```

3. The next step is to create a property set that will include the message ID. We then need to associate that property set with the `$view` object created in the previous step:

```
$schema = [Microsoft.Exchange.WebServices.Data.ItemSchema]
$propertyset = New-Object -TypeName '
Microsoft.Exchange.WebServices.Data.PropertySet (
   $schema::IdOnly
)
$view.PropertySet = $propertyset
```

4. Next, define a search query using the AQS syntax:

```
$query = "Subject:'Sales'"
```

5. We can then perform the search using the `FindItems` method of our `ExchangeService` object:

```
$items = $svc.FindItems("Inbox",$query,$view)
```

6. Loop through each item returned by the search and retrieve the message header information:

```
$items | Foreach-Object{
  $headerview = New-Object -TypeName '
  Microsoft.Exchange.WebServices.Data.ItemView '
  -ArgumentList 1
```

```
    $headerprops = New-Object -TypeName '
      Microsoft.Exchange.WebServices.Data.PropertySet (
      $schema::InternetMessageHeaders
    )
    $headerview.PropertySet = $headerprops
    $message = `
[Microsoft.Exchange.WebServices.Data.Item]::Bind(
      $svc, $_.Id, $headerview.PropertySet
    )
    $message.InternetMessageHeaders
}
```

How it works...

The code in this example is very similar to what we used in the *Searching mailboxes* recipe. Again, since we are not supplying any credentials when creating the `ExchangeService` object, and we're not using impersonation, the search will be performed in the administrator mailbox. When calling the `FindItems` method, we're specifying the folder to be searched, the AQS search query to be used, and the item view.

For each item returned by the search, we need to create a new view and property set for the single instance of the message that returns only the message headers. We then bind to the message and return the header information.

The header information returned will provide details of which server received the message, the content type of the message, the subject and date, and all of the X-Headers included with the message.

There are a number of well-known mailbox folders that can be searched using the `FindItems` method. For details, see the *Searching mailboxes* recipe.

There's more...

Of course, we'll primarily need to retrieve the message headers for an item in another user's mailbox. Here is an extended version of our previous code that implements EWS impersonation and provides parameters for the mailbox and folder to be searched. Add the following code to a script called `GetMessageHeaders.ps1`:

```
Param($query, $mailbox, $folder)
Add-Type -Path C:\EWS\Microsoft.Exchange.WebServices.dll
$svc = New-Object
Microsoft.Exchange.WebServices.Data.ExchangeService
$id = New-Object -TypeName '
```

```
Microsoft.Exchange.WebServices.Data.ImpersonatedUserId '
-ArgumentList "SmtpAddress",$mailbox
$svc.ImpersonatedUserId = $id
$svc.AutoDiscoverUrl($mailbox)
$view = New-Object -TypeName '
Microsoft.Exchange.WebServices.Data.ItemView '
-ArgumentList 100
$schema = [Microsoft.Exchange.WebServices.Data.ItemSchema]
$propertyset = New-Object -TypeName '
Microsoft.Exchange.WebServices.Data.PropertySet (
  $schema::IdOnly
)
$view.PropertySet = $propertyset
$query = $query
$items = $svc.FindItems($folder,$query,$view)
$items | Foreach-Object{
  $headerview = New-Object -TypeName '
  Microsoft.Exchange.WebServices.Data.ItemView '
  -ArgumentList 1
  $headerprops = New-Object -TypeName '
    Microsoft.Exchange.WebServices.Data.PropertySet (
    $schema::InternetMessageHeaders
  )
  $headerview.PropertySet = $headerprops
  $message = [Microsoft.Exchange.WebServices.Data.Item]::Bind(
    $svc, $_.Id, $headerview.PropertySet
  )
  $message.InternetMessageHeaders
}
```

To run the script against an alternate mailbox, provide the query and the SMTP address associated with the mailbox:

```
c:\GetMessageHeaders.ps1 -query "Subject:'Sales Meeting'" '
-mailbox dave@testlabs.se '
-folder Inbox
```

When the script gets executed, the headers for each message that match the AQS query will be returned, and the output will look similar to the following screenshot:

```
Administrator: Windows PowerShell                          –  □   ×

PS C:\Script> .\GetMessageHeaders.ps1 -query "Subject:'Sales Meeting'" -mai
lbox dave@testlabs.se -folder Inbox

Name                               Value
----                               -----
Received                           from tlex01.testlabs.se (192.168....
Received                           from tlex01.testlabs.se (192.168....
Received                           from tlex01.testlabs.se ([fe80::f...
Content-Type                       application/ms-tnef
Content-Transfer-Encoding          binary
Subject                            Sales Meeting
Thread-Topic                       Sales Meeting
Thread-Index                       AQHQjjenlRUAyMS6s06eVf+axFt3xA==
Date                               Thu, 14 May 2015 13:18:07 +0200
Message-ID                         <9570c060422249508a0e671d4860aefc...
Accept-Language                    en-US
Content-Language                   en-US
X-MS-Exchange-Organization-SCL     -1
X-MS-TNEF-Correlator               <9570c060422249508a0e671d4860aefc...
MIME-Version                       1.0
X-MS-Exchange-Transport-FromEntity... Hosted
X-MS-Exchange-Organization-Message... Originating
X-MS-Exchange-Organization-AuthSource tlex01.testlabs.se
X-MS-Exchange-Organization-AuthAs  Internal
X-MS-Exchange-Organization-AuthMec... 04
X-Originating-IP                   [192.168.0.5]
X-MS-Exchange-Organization-Network... de23e2a8-3749-47e9-0758-08d25c4eca18
Return-Path                        admins@testlabs.se
X-MS-Exchange-Organization-AVStamp... 1.0
```

See also

▶ *Working with impersonation*

Deleting e-mail items from a mailbox

The Exchange Management Shell provides cmdlets that allow you to delete items from one or more mailboxes. This can also be done with the EWS Managed API, and you can get a little more control over how the items are deleted compared to what the built-in cmdlets provide. In this recipe, you'll learn how to use the EWS Managed API to delete items from one or more mailboxes using PowerShell.

How to do it...

Let's see how to delete e-mail items from a mailbox using the following steps:

1. First, load the assembly, create the `ExchangeService` object, and connect to EWS:

```
Add-Type -Path C:\EWS\Microsoft.Exchange.WebServices.dll

$svc = New-Object Microsoft.Exchange.WebServices.Data. `
ExchangeService

$svc.AutoDiscoverUrl("admins@testlabs.se")
```

2. Next, create a view of the total number of items that should be returned from the search:

```
$view = New-Object -TypeName '

Microsoft.Exchange.WebServices.Data.ItemView '

-ArgumentList 100
```

3. Create a property set that will include the message ID. We then need to associate this property set with the `$view` object created in the previous step:

```
$propertyset = New-Object Microsoft.Exchange.WebServices.Data. `
PropertySet (

    [Microsoft.Exchange.WebServices.Data.BasePropertySet]::IdOnly

)

$view.PropertySet = $propertyset
```

4. Next, define a search query using the AQS syntax:

```
$query = "body:'Inappropriate content'"
```

5. We can then perform the search using the `FindItems` method of our Exchange Service object:

```
$items = $svc.FindItems("Inbox",$query,$view)
```

6. For each item returned by the search, bind to the message and call the `Delete` method, specifying the delete mode that should be used:

```
$items | Foreach-Object{
  $message =
[Microsoft.Exchange.WebServices.Data.Item]::Bind(
    $svc, $_.Id
  )
  $message.Delete("SoftDelete")
}
```

How it works...

The code in this example is very similar to the one we used in the *Searching mailboxes* recipe. Again, since we are not supplying any credentials when creating the `ExchangeService` object, and we're not using impersonation, the search will be performed in the administrator mailbox. When calling the `FindItems` method, we're specifying the folder to be searched, the AQS search query to be used, and the item view.

Notice that this time, we only need to specify the ID of the message in the property set. This is because we only want to call the `Delete` method on the item class, and we don't need to retrieve any other data from the message. In this example, we've defined a string of inappropriate content that should be found in the body of the message.

We loop through each item returned by the search, and create an instance of the message using the item class `Bind` method. At this point, we call the `Delete` method, which accepts one of the three values from the `DeleteMode` enumeration. The valid values for this method are defined as follows:

- ▶ `HardDelete`: This permanently deletes the item
- ▶ `MoveToDeletedItems`: This moves the item to the `Deleted Items` folder of the target mailbox
- ▶ `SoftDelete`: This moves the item to the dumpster and can be recovered by the mailbox owner using the `Recoverable Items` feature of Outlook and OWA

Having the ability to specify the delete mode gives you a little more control when deleting items in a mailbox than the built-in Exchange Management Shell cmdlets.

There are a number of well-known mailbox folders that can be searched for using the `FindItems` method. For details, see the *Searching mailboxes* recipe.

There's more...

Whenever you are executing a code that can perform a destructive operation, it makes sense to implement the `ShouldProcess` method introduced with PowerShell v2 advanced functions. Implementing `ShouldProcess` in an advanced function gives you the ability to add the common risk mitigation parameters, such as `-Whatif` and `-Confirm`. The following function takes our previous code up a notch, as it is written as an advanced function that implements `ShouldProcess`. Add the following function to your Exchange Management Shell session:

```
function Remove-MailboxItem {
  [CmdletBinding(
```

```
    SupportsShouldProcess = $true, ConfirmImpact = "High"
)]
param(
  [Parameter(
    Position=0,
    Mandatory=$true,
    ValueFromPipelineByPropertyName=$true
  )]
  [String]
  $PrimarySmtpAddress,
  [Parameter(
    Position = 1, Mandatory = $true
  )]
  [String]
  $SearchQuery,
  [Parameter(
    Position = 2, Mandatory = $false
  )]
  [int]
  $ResultSize = 100,
  [Parameter(
    Position = 3, Mandatory = $false
  )]
  [string]
  $Folder = "Inbox",
  [Parameter(
    Position = 4, Mandatory = $false
  )]
  [ValidateSet(
   'HardDelete',
   'SoftDelete',
   'MoveToDeletedItems'
  )]
  $DeleteMode = "MoveToDeletedItems"
)
begin {
  Add-Type -Path C:\EWS\Microsoft.Exchange.WebServices.dll
}
process {
  $svc = New-Object -TypeName '
```

```
        Microsoft.Exchange.WebServices.Data.ExchangeService `
        $id = New-Object -TypeName '
        Microsoft.Exchange.WebServices.Data.ImpersonatedUserId '
        -ArgumentList "SmtpAddress",$PrimarySmtpAddress
        $svc.ImpersonatedUserId = $id
        $svc.AutoDiscoverUrl($PrimarySmtpAddress)
        $view = New-Object -TypeName '
        Microsoft.Exchange.WebServices.Data.ItemView '
        -ArgumentList 100
        $propertyset = New-Object -TypeName '
        Microsoft.Exchange.WebServices.Data.PropertySet (
            [Microsoft.Exchange.WebServices.Data.BasePropertySet]::IdOnly
        )
        $view.PropertySet = $propertyset
        $items = $svc.FindItems($Folder,$SearchQuery,$view)
        $items | %{
            $message =
    [Microsoft.Exchange.WebServices.Data.Item]::Bind(
            $svc, $_.Id
            )
            if ($pscmdlet.ShouldProcess($message.Subject)) {
            $message.Delete($DeleteMode)
            }
        }
    }
  }
}
```

We now have a `Remove-MailboxItem` function that supports impersonation, allowing the code to execute against one or more mailboxes. In addition, it supports pipeline input by the property name, so you can utilize the `Get-Mailbox` cmdlet to delete items from multiple mailboxes using a simple command. Consider the following command:

```
Get-Mailbox -ResultSize Unlimited |
Remove-MailboxItem -SearchQuery "Body:'Free Surface Pro'" '
-DeleteMode HardDelete
```

In this example, we pipe every mailbox in the organization down to the `Remove-MailboxItem` function, which will perform a hard delete on each message that matches the AQS query. Since the `ConfirmImpact` property is set to `High`, you'll be prompted for confirmation before each message is deleted.

To force a delete operation without confirmation, you can set the `-Confirm` parameter to `$false`. To do this on a single mailbox, you can use the following command:

```
Remove-MailboxItem -PrimarySmtpAddress sysadmin@contoso.com '
-SearchQuery "Body:'Buy cheap drugs'" '
-DeleteMode HardDelete '
-Confirm:$false
```

You can also use the `-Whatif` parameter here to test the command to ensure that the correct messages will be deleted:

```
Remove-MailboxItem -PrimarySmtpAddress sysadmin@contoso.com '
-SearchQuery "Body:'Buy cheap drugs'" '
-DeleteMode HardDelete '
-Whatif
```

To illustrate an example, we use the `Get-Mailbox` cmdlet and pipe the result to the created function together with a search query that searches for all the mails with a subject that has the word `Sales` included. The function will soft delete the e-mails that are returned, which means they will end up in the dumpster.

Refer to the following screenshot for an example of a similar output using the created function:

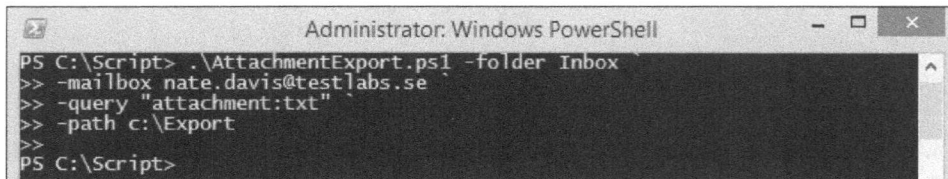

See also

▸ *Searching mailboxes*

Creating calendar items

Imagine that you have a monitoring script written in PowerShell that checks the memory, CPU, or disk utilization on all of your Exchange servers. In addition to alerting your team to any critical problems via e-mail, it might also be nice to schedule a reminder in the future for noncritical issues by creating a calendar item in one or more mailboxes. The EWS Managed API makes it easy to create a calendar item through PowerShell using just a few commands.

How to do it...

Let's see how to create calendar items using the following steps:

1. First, load the assembly, create the `ExchangeService` object, and connect to EWS:

   ```
   Add-Type -Path C:\EWS\Microsoft.Exchange.WebServices.dll
   $svc = New-Object
   Microsoft.Exchange.WebServices.Data.ExchangeService
   $svc.AutoDiscoverUrl("admins@testlabs.se")
   ```

2. Next, create a new appointment object:

   ```
   $appt = New-Object -TypeName '
   Microsoft.Exchange.WebServices.Data.Appointment '
   -ArgumentList $svc
   ```

3. Fill out the subject and body for the appointment:

   ```
   $appt.Subject = "Review Disk Space Utilization on Server(s)"
   $appt.Body = "TLEX01 has only 40% free disk space on drive C:"
   ```

4. Set the start and end time for the appointment:

   ```
   $start = (Get-Date).AddDays(1)
   $appt.Start = $start
   $appt.End = $start.AddHours(1)
   ```

5. Add one or more required attendees to the appointment:

   ```
   $appt.RequiredAttendees.Add("helpdesk@testlabs.se")
   $appt.RequiredAttendees.Add("sysadmin@testlabs.se")
   ```

6. Finally, save the appointment and send a copy to all attendees:

   ```
   $mode =
   [Microsoft.Exchange.WebServices.Data.SendInvitationsMode]
   $appt.Save($mode::SendToAllAndSaveCopy)
   ```

How it works...

By using the code in this example, we are creating the calendar item in the mailbox of the user calling the code. The `Appointment` class is used to create the item, and after we've created an instance of this class, we set the details of the appointment using the `Subject` and `Body` properties.

The `Start` and `End` properties need to be assigned a `DateTime` object. In our example, we're using the `AddDays` method of the current date and time to set the start time for the meeting in exactly 24 hours. We then use the same object to increment the time by one hour, and we assign that to the `End` property for the appointment.

When adding attendees to the appointment, we use the `RequiredAttendees.Add` method. When you call the `Add` method, you'll notice that the `RequiredAttendees` property will be returned for each required attendee added to the appointment. If you want to simply call this method, without having anything returned to the screen, there are a few ways you can accomplish this. First, you can pipe the command to `Out-Null`:

```
$appt.RequiredAttendees.Add("helpdesk@testlabs.se") | Out-Null
$appt.RequiredAttendees.Add("sysadmin@testlabs.se") | Out-Null
```

You'll see this written in another way by casting the commands to `[void]`:

```
[void]$appt.RequiredAttendees.Add("helpdesk@testlabs.se")
[void]$appt.RequiredAttendees.Add("sysadmin@testlabs.se")
```

Finally, you can assign the commands to `$null`, which is said to be the fastest method:

```
$null = $appt.RequiredAttendees.Add("helpdesk@testlabs.se")
$null = $appt.RequiredAttendees.Add("sysadmin@testlabs.se")
```

In addition to adding the required attendees, we can also add one or more optional attendees to the item:

```
$null = $appt.OptionalAttendees.Add("IT@testlabs.se")
```

Finally, when calling the `Save` method for the appointment, you need to pass in a value from the `SendInvitationsMode` enumeration. The valid values that can be used are `SendOnlyToAll`, `SendToAllAndSaveCopy`, and `SendToNone`.

There's more...

Let's make this easier by wrapping all of the code up into a reusable function. Add the following code to your PowerShell session:

```
function New-CalendarItem {
  [CmdletBinding()]
  param(
  [Parameter(
    Position=1, Mandatory=$true
  )]
  [String]
  $Subject,
  [Parameter(
    Position=2, Mandatory=$true
  )]
  [String]
  $Body,
  [Parameter(
    Position=3, Mandatory=$true
  )]
  [String]
  $Start,
  [Parameter(
    Position=4, Mandatory=$true
  )]
  [String]
  $End,
  [Parameter(
    Position=5
  )]
  [String[]]
  $RequiredAttendees,
  [Parameter(
    Position=8
  )]
  [String]
  $Mailbox
  )
  begin{
```

```
      Add-Type -Path C:\EWS\Microsoft.Exchange.WebServices.dll
  }
  process {
    $svc = New-Object -TypeName '
   Microsoft.Exchange.WebServices.Data.ExchangeService '
    $id = New-Object -TypeName '
   Microsoft.Exchange.WebServices.Data.ImpersonatedUserId '
    -ArgumentList "SmtpAddress",$Mailbox

    $svc.ImpersonatedUserId = $id
    $svc.AutodiscoverUrl($Mailbox)
    $appt = New-Object -TypeName '
   Microsoft.Exchange.WebServices.Data.Appointment '
    -ArgumentList $svc
    $appt.Subject = $Subject
    $appt.Body = $Body
    $appt.Start = $Start
    $appt.End = $End
    if($RequiredAttendees) {
      $RequiredAttendees | Foreach-Object{
        $null = $appt.RequiredAttendees.Add($_)
      }
    }
    $mode = `
[Microsoft.Exchange.WebServices.Data.SendInvitationsMode]
    $appt.Save($mode::SendToAllAndSaveCopy)
  }
}
```

This function can be used to create a calendar item in the mailbox of another user. For this
to work, you'll need to be assigned the ApplicationImpersonation RBAC role. To run the
function, you might have to do something like this:

```
New-CalendarItem -Subject "Reboot Server" '
-Body "Reboot EXCH-SRV01 server after 5PM today" '
-Start (Get-Date).AddHours(6) '
-End (Get-Date).AddHours(7) '
-Mailbox sysadmin@testlabs.se '
-RequiredAttendees helpdesk@testlabs.se,admins@testlabs.se
```

In this example, the calendar item is created in the sysadmin mailbox. Multiple attendees will be added to the item and will receive an invitation for the meeting when it is saved. Notice that the meeting is scheduled for 6 hours in the future, with a total duration of 1 hour. For example, refer to the following screenshot:

If you want to create calendar items in multiple mailboxes, loop through a collection with the Foreach-Object cmdlet and run the function for each user:

```
$start = Get-Date "Friday, May 15, 2015 5:00:00 PM"
$end = $start.AddHours(1)
Get-DistributionGroupMember ITSupport | Foreach-Object{
  New-CalendarItem -Subject "Install Hotfixes" '
  -Body "Start patching servers after 5PM today" '
  -Start $start '
  -End $end '
  -Mailbox $_.PrimarySMTPAddress
}
```

In this example, each member of the IT Support distribution group will have a calendar item created in their mailbox that will serve as a reminder; no attendees will be added to the item.

See also

▸ *Sending e-mail messages with EWS*

Exporting attachments from a mailbox

The Exchange Management Shell provides cmdlets that allow you to export e-mail messages from one mailbox to another. These e-mails can then be exported to a PST file, or you can open an alternate mailbox and access the data. The only limitation is that this provides no option to export only the message attachments. The EWS Managed API has this built-in functionality. In this recipe, you'll learn how to export e-mail attachments from an Exchange mailbox using PowerShell.

How to do it...

Let's see how to export attachments from a mailbox using the following steps:

1. First, load the assembly, create the `ExchangeService` object, and connect to EWS:

   ```
   Add-Type -Path C:\EWS\Microsoft.Exchange.WebServices.dll
   $svc = New-Object
   Microsoft.Exchange.WebServices.Data.ExchangeService
   $svc.AutoDiscoverUrl("admins@testlabs.se")
   ```

2. Next, create a view of the total number of items that should be returned from the search:

   ```
   $view = New-Object -TypeName '
   Microsoft.Exchange.WebServices.Data.ItemView '
   -ArgumentList 100
   ```

3. Next, create a property set, and then associate this property set with the `$view` object:

   ```
   $base = [Microsoft.Exchange.WebServices.Data.BasePropertySet]
   $propertyset = New-Object -TypeName '
   Microsoft.Exchange.WebServices.Data.PropertySet (
      $base::FirstClassProperties
   )
   $view.PropertySet = $propertyset
   ```

4. Define a query for the type of attachments you are looking for. For example, if you are looking for attachments in Microsoft Word format, use the following command:

   ```
   $query = "Attachment:docx"
   ```

5. We can then perform the search using the `FindItems` method of our `ExchangeService` object:

   ```
   $items = $svc.FindItems("Inbox",$query,$view)
   ```

6. Finally, we loop through each item returned and export the attachments to the specified folder on the filesystem, such as `c:\export`:

   ```
   $items | ForEach-Object{
     if($_.HasAttachments  ) {
       $_.Load()
       $_.Attachments | ForEach-Object {
   ```

```
    $_.Load()
    $filename = $_.Name
    Set-Content -Path c:\export\$filename '
    -Value $_.Content '
    -Encoding Byte '
    -Force
  }
 }
}
```

How it works...

The code in this example is very similar to the one we used in the *Searching mailboxes* recipe. Again, since we are not supplying any credentials when creating the `ExchangeService` object and we're not using impersonation, the search will be performed in the administrator mailbox. When calling the `FindItems` method, we're specifying the folder to be searched, the AQS search query to be used, and the item view.

As you can see, we're using the `Attachment` property in the AQS query. This allows us to search for a string within the filename or inside the file itself. When the results are returned, we loop through each message and use the `Load` method to load the attachment, which allows us to access the `Content` property of each attachment. The `Content` property stores the message attachment as a byte array, which can be easily used to recreate the file using the `Set-Content` cmdlet by specifying the encoding as `Byte`.

There are a number of well-known mailbox folders that can be searched using the `FindItems` method. For details, see the *Searching mailboxes* recipe.

There's more...

Like many of our previous examples, reusability is key. Let's take this code and add a few enhancements so that it can be run via a PowerShell script. Add the following code to a file called `AttachmentExport.ps1`:

```
Param($folder, $query, $path, $mailbox)
Add-Type -Path C:\EWS\Microsoft.Exchange.WebServices.dll
$svc = New-Object
Microsoft.Exchange.WebServices.Data.ExchangeService
$id = New-Object -TypeName '
Microsoft.Exchange.WebServices.Data.ImpersonatedUserId '
-ArgumentList "SmtpAddress",$mailbox
```

```
$svc.ImpersonatedUserId = $id
$svc.AutoDiscoverUrl($mailbox)
$view = New-Object -TypeName '
Microsoft.Exchange.WebServices.Data.ItemView '
-ArgumentList 100
$base = [Microsoft.Exchange.WebServices.Data.BasePropertySet]
$propertyset = New-Object -TypeName '
Microsoft.Exchange.WebServices.Data.PropertySet (
  $base::FirstClassProperties
)
$view.PropertySet = $propertyset
$items = $svc.FindItems($folder,$query,$view)
$items | Foreach-Object{
  if($_.HasAttachments) {
    $_.Load()
    $_.Attachments | ForEach-Object {
      $_.Load()
      $filename = $_.Name
      Set-Content -Path $path\$filename '
      -Value $_.Content '
      -Encoding Byte '
      -Force
    }
  }
}
```

Using this script, we can export the attachments from one or more mailboxes since we've included the code to support impersonation. Just make sure your account has been assigned the `ApplicationImpersonation` RBAC role when running this script against another mailbox. Let's say that we want to export all of the Excel files that are attached to messages in the `sysadmin` mailbox. Run this script with the following syntax:

```
c:\AttachmentExport.ps1 -folder Inbox '
-mailbox nate.davis@testlabs.se '
-query "attachment:docx" '
-path c:\Export
```

You can also export all the attachments simply using a wildcard in the search query:

```
c:\AttachmentExport.ps1 -folder Inbox '
-mailbox nate.davis@testlabs.se '
-query "attachment:txt" '
-path c:\Export
```

Keep in mind that, since our item view is set to 100, we may need to increase the number if we want to search through mailbox folders with a higher item count. Refer to the following screenshot for an example of how the script is used, and the result:

See also

▶ *Searching mailboxes*

A

Common Shell Information

This appendix provides additional information related to the **Exchange Management Shell** (**EMS**). You can use this section as a reference to find commonly-used automatic shell variables and type accelerators, along with a list of commonly-used EMS scripts that are installed with Exchange 2013. Additionally, common filterable properties supported by EMS cmdlets that include filter parameters are outlined in detail.

Commonly-used shell variables

PowerShell and the Exchange Management Shell provide several automatic variables. The following table provides a list of commonly-used automatic variables with a description for each one:

Variable Name	Description
$$	This contains the last token in the last command received.
$?	This contains the execution status of the last command.
$^	This contains the first token in the last command received.
$_	This contains the current object being processed within a pipeline.
$Args	This contains an array of undeclared arguments received by a function, script, or script block.

Variable Name	Description
$Error	This contains an array of error objects recorded in the current shell session. The latest error can be accessed using the zero index of the array, that is, $error[0].
$Exbin	This references the full path to the Exchange Server\ Bin directory. This variable is only present when starting the shell using the Exchange Management Shell shortcut on a machine with the Exchange tools installed.
$ExScripts	This references the full path to the Exchange scripts directory. This variable is only present when starting the shell using the Exchange Management Shell shortcut on a machine with the Exchange tools installed.
$False	This provides a Boolean false value when used in commands and scripts.
$ForEach	This contains the enumerator inside a ForEach-Object loop.
$Home	This contains the full path to the user's home directory.
$Host	This contains an object that represents the current PowerShell host application.
$Input	This contains the enumerator for items passed to a function. The $Input variable can access the current object being processed within a pipeline.
$MaximumHistoryCount	This specifies the maximum number of entries that can be saved in the command history in the current Shell session.
$Null	This provides a null or empty value when used in commands and scripts.
$Profile	This contains the full path to the PowerShell profile for the current user and the current host application.
$PSHome	This contains the full path to the installation directory of Windows PowerShell.
$Pwd	This contains the path to the current location.
$True	This provides a Boolean true value.

To view the variables currently defined in your shell session, run `Get-Variable`. You can also read more about PowerShell variables by running the `Get-Help <TopicName>` cmdlet on the following topics:

▸ `about_Automatic_Variables`

▸ `about_Environment_Variables`

▸ `about_Preference_Variables`

[
The preceding topics only reference PowerShell-specific variables, and not the shell variables that are specific to the Exchange Management Shell.
]

Commonly-used type accelerators

Type accelerators, also referred to as type shortcuts, allow you to create an object of a specific .NET Framework type, without having to enter the entire type name. This is a feature that is supported by both PowerShell and the Exchange Management Shell, and allows you to reduce the amount of typing required when creating an object or explicitly typing a variable. The following table lists some of the most commonly-used type shortcuts:

Type shortcut	.NET framework type
`[int]`	`System.Int32`
`[long]`	`System.Int64`
`[string]`	`System.String`
`[bool]`	`System.Boolean`
`[byte]`	`System.Byte`
`[double]`	`System.Double`
`[decimal]`	`System.Decimal`
`[datetime]`	`System.DateTime`
`[array]`	`System.Array`
`[hashtable]`	`System.Collections.HashTable`
`[switch]`	`System.Management.Automation.SwitchParameter`
`[adsi]`	`System.DirectoryServices.DirectoryEntry`

Scripts available in the $Exscripts directory

The following table lists some of the most commonly-used EMS PowerShell scripts that are installed with Exchange 2013:

Name	Description
AddUsersToPFRecursive.ps1	This adds a user and their permissions to the client permissions list for a public folder and all the folders beneath it in the hierarchy.
AntispamCommon.ps1	This script is referenced by other anti-spam scripts in Exchange 2007 and is not intended to be used directly.
CheckDatabaseRedundancy.ps1	This monitors the redundancy of replicated mailbox databases.
CheckInvalidRecipients.ps1	This fixes recipient objects that have multiple primary SMTP addresses defined.
CITSConstants.ps1	This file contains global constants used by CI Troubleshooter library.
CITSLibrary.ps1	This file contains the Content Index Troubleshooter functions.
CITSTypes.ps1	This file contains additional types used by CI troubleshooter library.
CollectOverMetrics.ps1	This reports on the database availability group, switchover, and failover metrics.
CollectReplicationMetrics.ps1	This reports on the replication status and statistics for databases.
ConfigureAdam.ps1	This is used to modify the default configuration of the **Active Directory Application Mode** (**ADAM**) directory service on the Edge Transport server.
ConfigureCafeResponseHeaders.ps1	This possibly modifies the OWA response header. CAFE is an abbreviation for **Client Access Front End**.
Configure-EnterprisePartnerApplication.ps1	This configures a Partner Application that uses the OAuth protocol to authenticate to Exchange.

Name	Description
`ConfigureNetworkProtocolParameters.ps1`	This configures a Global Catalog running on the machine on which the script is run to listen on the standard NSPI Rpc-over-Http port 6004. This would enable Rpc-over-Http connections from Outlook clients to a GC, RpcProxy by CAS server role.
`Configure-SMBIPsec.ps1`	This script is to be used to help you add the necessary IPsec configuration to protect SMB (File Share) communication.
`ConvertOABVDir.ps1`	This converts the OAB virtual directory to an IIS web application/application pool.
`ConvertTo-MessageLatency.ps1`	This provides end-to-end latency information gathered from message tracking logs.
`DagCommonLibrary.ps1`	This contains a collection of DAG-related functions for use by other scripts.
`DatabaseMaintSchedule.ps1`	This generates the maintenance and quota notification schedule time based on a set of input values.
`DiagnosticScriptCommonLibrary.ps1`	This script is a library of functions for common diagnostic script executions. Diagnostic scripts to dot source file to invoke the functions.
`Disable-AntimalwareScanning.ps1`	This disables anti-malware scanning.
`Disable-InMemoryTracing.ps1`	This is used to undo the changes made by the `Enable-InMemoryTracing.ps1` script.
`Disable-OutsideIn.ps1`	This disables Oracle Outside In Technology (c) for text extraction.
`Enable-AntimalwareScanning.ps1`	This enables antimalware scanning.

Name	Description
`Enable-CrossForestConnector.ps1`	This configures a send connector for cross-forest trust for anonymous users.
`Enable-InMemoryTracing.ps1`	This enables In Memory Tracing.
`Enable-OutlookCertificateAuthentication.ps1`	This configures virtual directories to allow Outlook for smart card authentication.
`Enable-OutsideIn.ps1`	This enables Oracle Outside In Technology (c) for text extraction.
`ExchUCUtil.ps1`	This configures Exchange Unified Messaging for the use of Office Communications Server.
`Export-MailPublicFoldersForMigration.ps1`	This exports the properties of all the mail- enabled public folders to a CSV file.
`Export-OutlookClassification.ps1`	This generates the `Classifications.xml` file for Outlook.
`Export-PublicFolderStatistics.ps1`	This generates a CSV file with lists of public folders and the individual sizes.
`Export-RetentionTags.ps1`	This exports retention tags to an external file.
`FilteringConfigurationCommands.ps1`	This finds and backs up the FIPS configuration file, returns the full path to the FIPS configuration file, and returns null on failure.
`get-AntispamFilteringReport.ps1`	This generates a report on anti-spam filtering.
`get-AntispamSCLHistogram.ps1`	This reports on all the entries for the Content Filter and groups by SCL values.
`get-AntispamTopBlockedSenderDomains.ps1`	This reports on the top 10 (unless specified otherwise) sender domains blocked by anti-spam agents.
`get-AntispamTopBlockedSenderIPs.ps1`	This reports on the top 10 (unless specified otherwise) sender IPs blocked by anti-spam agents.
`get-AntispamTopBlockedSenders.ps1`	This reports on the top 10 (unless specified otherwise) senders blocked by anti-spam agents.

Name	Description
`get-AntispamTopRBLProviders.ps1`	This reports on the top 10 (unless specified otherwise) reasons for rejection by blocklist providers.
`get-AntispamTopRecipients.ps1`	This reports on the top 10 (unless specified otherwise) recipients rejected by anti-spam agents.
`Get-PublicFolderMailboxSize.ps1`	This retrieves the size of the public folder mailbox, excluding the size of deleted folders.
`Get-StoreTrace.ps1`	This troubleshoots Store Traces.
`Get-UCPool.ps1`	This reports on the UC Pools created by OCS/Lync.
`GetValidEngines.ps1`	This returns a list of engines being used by the forefront filtering agent.
`Import-MailPublicFoldersForMigration.ps1`	This imports the mail-enabled public folders from a CSV file and calls the `Enable-MailPublicFolder` cmdlet.
`Import-RetentionTags.ps1`	This imports retention tags from an external file.
`Install-AntispamAgents.ps1`	This installs the anti-spam agents on a mailbox server.
`MailboxDatabaseReseedUsingSpares.ps1`	This validates the safety of the environment, before swapping fails to copy database to a spare disk and reseeding.
`ManagedStoreDiagnosticFunctions.ps1`	This runs a query against a managed store mailbox database.
`ManageScheduledTask.ps1`	This manages scheduled tasks in PowerShell.
`Merge-PublicFolderMailbox.ps1`	This merges the contents of the given public folder mailbox with the target public folder mailbox.
`MigrateUMCustomPrompts.ps1`	This migrates a copy of all Unified Messaging custom prompts.
`MoveMailbox.ps1`	This works like the `Move-Mailbox` cmdlet in Exchange 2007 and performs synchronous mailbox moves.
`Move-PublicFolderBranch.ps1`	This moves the contents of folders that reside along with the given folder to the target public folder mailbox.

Name	Description
`Move-TransportDatabase.ps1`	This moves the queue database to an alternate disk on a transport server.
`new-TestCasConnectivityUser.ps1`	This creates a test user that can be used when testing connectivity on CAS servers.
`Prepare-MoveRequest.ps1`	This prepares mailboxes for cross-forest mailbox moves.
`PublicFolderToMailboxMapGenerator.ps1`	This generates a CSV mapping file that contains the public folder to the mailbox structure.
`RedistributeActiveDatabases.ps1`	This attempts to redistribute active databases evenly across a number of mailbox servers within a DAG.
`ReinstallDefaultTransportAgents.ps1`	This reinstalls default transport agents on servers.
`RemoveUserFromPFRecursive.ps1`	This removes a user from the client permissions list for a public folder and all the folders beneath it in the hierarchy.
`ReplaceUserPermissionOnPFRecursive.ps1`	This replaces the permissions of a user for a public folder with a new set of permissions and applies it to all the folders beneath it in the hierarchy.
`ReplaceUserWithUserOnPFRecursive.ps1`	This replaces a user for a new user on the client permissions list for a public folder and applies it to all the folders beneath it in the hierarchy.
`Reset-AntispamUpdates.ps1`	This removes the anti-spam agents from a transport server.
`ResetAttachmentFilterEntry.ps1`	This resets the list of attachment types for attachment-filtering to factory set defaults.
`ResetCasService.ps1`	This resets the virtual directory on CAS.
`ResumeMailboxDatabaseCopy.ps1`	This resumes activation and log file replication for specified mailbox databases.
`RollAlternateServiceAccountPassword.ps1`	This is used to update the service account credentials and distributes the update to specified CAS servers.

Name	Description
`SearchDiagnosticInfo.ps1`	This prints the result of `Get-SearchDiagnosticInfo`.
`Split-PublicFolderMailbox.ps1`	This splits the given public folder mailbox based on the size of the folders.
`StartDagServerMaintenance.ps1`	This initiates the DAG server maintenance.
`StopDagServerMaintenance.ps1`	This stops the DAG server maintenance and resumes mailbox database copies.
`StoreTSConstants.ps1`	This file contains global constants used by the Store Database Troubleshooters.
`StoreTSLibrary.ps1`	This is a collection of Store Troubleshooting on **Content Index** (**CI**) catalogs.
`Troubleshoot-CI.ps1`	This performs troubleshooting on Content Index catalogs.
`Troubleshoot-DatabaseLatency.ps1`	This diagnoses disk subsystem issues (used by SCOM).
`Troubleshoot-DatabaseSpace.ps1`	This troubleshoots log growth (used by SCOM).
`Uninstall-AntispamAgents.ps1`	This uninstalls the anti-spam agents.
`Update-AppPoolManagedFrameworkVersion.ps1`	This is used during the installation and updates the procedure for updating the Application Pool.
`Update-MalwareFilteringServer.ps1`	This updates the malware filter definitions.

Scripts may be added to this directory as you install roll up updates and service packs, and some of them will only be present when a specific server role is installed. For example, the anti-spam scripts will only be available on mailbox servers. To view all the scripts in the `$ExScripts` folder, run `Get-ChildItem $exscripts -Filter *.ps1`.

Properties that can be used with the -Filter parameter

There are a number of EMS cmdlets that provide a -Filter parameter that can be used to narrow searches based on the value of an OPath property. These properties can also map to a particular LDAP attribute.

The following table lists some of the commonly used properties and the cmdlets that can be used to query their values using the -Filter parameter:

Property Name	Attribute	Cmdlets Supported	Input Value
Alias	mailNickname	Get-DistributionGroup Get-DynamicDistributionGroup Get-Mailbox Get-MailContact Get-MailPublicFolder Get-MailUser Get-Recipient Get-RemoteMailbox	String/ Wildcard
City	L	Get-Contact Get-Recipient Get-User	String/ Wildcard
Company	Company	Get-Contact Get-Recipient Get-User	String/ Wildcard
Database	homeMDB	Get-Mailbox Get-Recipient	DN
Department	department	Get-Contact Get-Recipient Get-User	String/ Wildcard

Property Name	Attribute	Cmdlets Supported	Input Value
DisplayName	displayName	Get-CASMailbox Get-Contact Get-DistributionGroup Get-DynamicDistributionGroup Get-Group Get-Mailbox Get-MailboxStatistics Get-MailContact Get-MailPublicFolder Get-MailUser Get-Recipient Get-RemoteMailbox Get-UMMailbox Get-User	String/ Wildcard
Distinguished Name	distinguished Name	Get-CASMailbox Get-Contact Get-DistributionGroup Get-DynamicDistributionGroup Get-Group Get-Mailbox Get-MailContact Get-MailPublicFolder Get-MailUser Get-Recipient Get-RemoteMailbox Get-UMMailbox Get-User	DN
EmailAddresses	proxy Addresses	Get-CASMailbox Get-DistributionGroup Get-DynamicDistributionGroup Get-Mailbox Get-MailContact Get-MailPublicFolder Get-MailUser Get-Recipient Get-RemoteMailbox Get-UMMailbox	E-mail Address (wildcard)

Property Name	Attribute	Cmdlets Supported	Input Value
FirstName	givenName	Get-Contact Get-Recipient Get-User	String/ Wildcard
HiddenFrom Address ListsEnabled	msExchHideFrom AddressLists	Get-DistributionGroup Get-DynamicDistribution Group Get-Mailbox Get-MailContact Get-MailPublicFolder Get-MailUser Get-Recipient Get-RemoteMailbox	$true $false
HomePhone	homePhone	Get-Contact Get-User	String/ Wildcard
LastName	sn	Get-Contact Get-Recipient Get-User	String/ Wildcard
Manager	manager	Get-Contact Get-Recipient Get-User	String/ Wildcard
Name	name	Get-CASMailbox Get-Contact Get-DistributionGroup Get-DynamicDistributionGroup Get-Group Get-Mailbox Get-MailContact Get-MailPublicFolder Get-MailUser Get-Recipient Get-RemoteMailbox Get-UMMailbox Get-User	String
Phone	telephone Number	Get-Contact Get-Recipient Get-User	String/ Wildcard

Property Name	Attribute	Cmdlets Supported	Input Value
PrimarySmtp Address	N/A	Get-CASMailbox Get-DistributionGroup Get-DynamicDistributionGroup Get-Mailbox Get-MailContact Get-MailPublicFolder Get-MailUser Get-Recipient Get-RemoteMailbox Get-UMMailbox	SMTP Address
SamAccount Name	SamAccount Name	Get-CASMailbox Get-DistributionGroup Get-Group Get-Mailbox Get-MailUser Get-Recipient Get-RemoteMailbox Get-UMMailbox Get-User	String
StateOr Province	st	Get-Contact Get-Recipient Get-User	String/ Wildcard
Street Address	street Address	Get-Contact Get-User	String
Title	title	Get-Contact Get-Recipient Get-User	String
UserPrincipal Name	userPrincipal Name	Get-Mailbox Get-MailUser Get-Recipient Get-RemoteMailbox Get-User	User logon name User principal name/ Wildcard

The preceding table only includes a list of commonly used filterable properties that can be used with the `-Filter` parameter. In addition to this list, there are several other properties that can be filtered. Refer to the article in the TechNet documentation for a complete list at `http://technet.microsoft.com/en-us/library/bb738155(v=exchg.150).aspx`.

Properties that can be used with the -RecipientFilter parameter

There are a number of EMS cmdlets that provide a `-RecipientFilter` parameter and can be used to define the criteria used for dynamic distribution groups, e-mail address policies, and address lists. The following cmdlets support this parameter:

- `New-AddressList`
- `New-DynamicDistributionGroup`
- `New-EmailAddressPolicy`
- `New-GlobalAddressList`
- `Set-AddressList`
- `Set-DynamicDistributionGroup`
- `Set-EmailAddressPolicy`
- `Set-GlobalAddressList`

The following table lists some of the common properties used when creating a recipient filter using the `-RecipientFilter` parameter:

Property Name	LDAP Attribute	Input Value
`Alias`	`mailNickname`	String/Wildcard
`City`	`L`	String/Wildcard
`Company`	`Company`	String/Wildcard
`Database`	`homeMDB`	Mailbox database Identity DN
`DisplayName`	`displayName`	String/Wildcard
`EmailAddresses`	`proxyAddresses`	E-mail address (wildcard)
`ExternalEmailAddress`	`targetAddress`	E-mail address (wildcard)
`FirstName`	`givenName`	String/Wildcard

HiddenFromAddress ListsEnabled	msExchHideFrom AddressLists	$true $false
LastName	Sn	String/Wildcard
Manager	Manager	String/Wildcard
Name	Name	String
Office	physicalDelivery OfficeName	String
SamAccountName	SamAccountName	String/Wildcard
StateOrProvince	St	String/Wildcard
StreetAddress	streetAddress	String
Title	Title	String
UserPrincipalName	userPrincipalName	User logon name User principal name/ Wildcard

The preceding table only includes a list of commonly used filterable properties that can be used with the `-RecipientFilter` parameter. In addition to this list, there are several other properties that can be filtered. Refer to the article in the TechNet documentation for a complete list at `http://technet.microsoft.com/en-us/library/bb738157(v=exchg.150).aspx`.

B

Query Syntaxes

Advanced Query Syntax

This appendix provides additional information related to working with **Advanced Query Syntax** (**AQS**) when performing queries with Exchange Search. AQS can be used to perform searches with the Exchange Web Services Managed API.

The following Exchange Management Shell cmdlets provide a `-SearchQuery` parameter that can be used to define an AQS query:

- `New-MailboxSearch`
- `Search-Mailbox`
- `Set-MailboxSearch`

The tables in this appendix outline the AQS keywords that can be used with these cmdlets to perform queries in Exchange Search, along with the EWS Managed API.

Using the word phrase search

The following table outlines the properties that can be used to define an AQS query using a word phrase restriction:

Property	Examples	Description

`Attachments`	`attachment:report.xlsx`
	
	`attachment:salesreport.docx`
	
	`attachment:pptx`
	
	`attachment:*`
		This searches for items that have an attachment with a specific name, such as `report.xlsx` or `salesreport.docx`. You can include partial filenames, as shown in the third example, to find all messages with a certain extension. The file body of any attachments will also be searched. The last example finds all messages that have an attachment.

`Cc`	`Cc:administrator`
	
	`Cc:sales@contoso.com`
		This searches for items where `administrator` or `sales@contoso.com` is included in the carbon copy line.

`From`	`From:Bob`
	
	`From:Bob Smith`
		This searches for items sent from `Bob` or `Bob Smith`.

`To`	`To:Bob`
	
	`To:Bob Smith`
		This searches for items sent to `Bob` or `Bob Smith`.

`Bcc`	`Bcc:Bob`
	
	`Bcc:Bob Smith`
		This searches for items where `Bob` was included in the blind carbon copy line.

`Subject`	`Subject:sales`	This searches for items with the word `sales` in the subject line.
	`Subject:(Sales Meeting)`	This searches for items with the words `Sales` or `Meeting` in the subject line.

Property	Examples	Description
Body	`Body:financial` `Content:financial`	This searches for items where the word `financial` appears in the message body.
Participants	`Participants:Bob Smith`	This searches for items with `Bob Smith` in the To, Cc, or Bcc fields.
RetentionPolicy	`Retentionpolicy:critical`	This searches for items that have the `critical` retention tag applied.
Not Defined	`Financial Report`	This searches for items that contain both `Financial` and `Report` in all word phrase properties.

When performing a word phrase search, the property names and search terms are case insensitive. If you want an exact match, enclose the search query in double quotes, otherwise the search will default to a prefix match. For example, searching for the term *report* would match the word *reporting* unless enclosed in double quotes, indicating an exact search.

Examples

If you want to delete all the messages in the administrator mailbox where the sender's e-mail address is `sales@contoso.com`, use the following commands:

```
Search-Mailbox -Identity administrator '
-SearchQuery "from:sales@contoso.com" '
-DeleteContent '
-Force
```

If you want to create a discovery search based on messages that contain the phrase `Employee Salary` in every mailbox, use the following code:

```
New-MailboxSearch -Name MySearch '
-TargetMailbox "Discovery Search Mailbox" '
-SearchQuery 'Body:"Employee Salary"' '
-MessageTypes Email '
-IncludeUnsearchableItems '
-LogLevel Full
```

Using a date range search

The following table outlines the properties that can be used to define an AQS query using a date range restriction:

Property	Example	Description
Received	Received:today	This searches for items received today
	Received:05/15/2015	This searches for items received on May 15
	Received:05/01/2015..05/30/2015	This searches for items received between May 1 and May 30
Sent	Sent:today	This searches for items sent today
	Sent:05/15/2015	This searches for items sent on May 15

You can use relative dates when performing a date range restricted search. For example, today, tomorrow, or yesterday can be used with the Received or Sent keywords.

You can use a specific day of the week: (Sunday, Monday, Tuesday, Wednesday, Thursday, Friday, or Saturday) with the Received or Sent keywords.

You can also use a specific month: (January, February, March, April, May, June, July, August, September, October, November, or December) with the Received or Sent keywords.

Examples

If you want to delete all messages in the administrator mailbox that were received today, use the following command:

```
Search-Mailbox -Identity administrator '
-SearchQuery "Received:today" '
-DeleteContent '
-Force
```

If you want to delete all messages in the administrator mailbox that have been received between March and July, use the following command:

```
Search-Mailbox -Identity administrator '
-SearchQuery "Received:03/01/2015..07/01/2015" '
-DeleteContent '
-Force
```

Using the message type search

The following table outlines the properties that can be used to define an AQS query using a message type restriction:

Property	Example	Description
Kind	Kind:email	This searches all e-mail items
	Kind:meetings	This searches all meeting items
	Kind:tasks	This searches all task items
	Kind:notes	This searches all note items
	Kind:docs	This searches all doc items
	Kind:journals	This searches all journal items
	Kind:contacts	This searches all contact items
	Kind:im	This searches all im items

Examples

If you want to delete all contacts from a mailbox, use the following command:

```
Search-Mailbox -Identity administrator '
-SearchQuery "Kind:Contacts" '
-DeleteContent '
-Force
```

If you want to delete all the notes from a mailbox, use the following code:

```
Search-Mailbox -Identity administrator '
-SearchQuery "Kind:Notes" '
-DeleteContent '
-Force
```

Using the logical connector search

The following table outlines the properties that can be used to define an AQS query using a logical connector between two keywords:

Connector	Example	Description
AND	Subject:sales AND Subject:report	This searches for items with both `sales` and `report` in the subject line
OR	Subject:sales OR Subject:report	This searches for items with the word `sales` or `report` in the subject line
NOT	NOT Body:sales Body:(NOT sales)	This searches for items without the word `sales` in the body

Examples

If you want to delete meeting items that have specific content in the body, such as the phrase `Social Security Number`, use the following commands:

```
Search-Mailbox -Identity administrator '
-SearchQuery 'Body:"Social Security Number" AND Kind:Meeting' '
-DeleteContent '
-Force
```

If you want to perform a discovery search based on keywords used in either the body or subject of the message in a particular mailbox, use the following commands:

```
New-MailboxSearch -Name MyTestSearch '
-SourceMailboxes administrator '
-TargetMailbox "Discovery Search Mailbox" '
-SearchQuery 'Body:"Social Security Number" OR Subject:"SSN"' '
-MessageTypes Email '
-IncludeUnsearchableItems '
-LogLevel Full
```

Index

Symbols

$Exscripts directory
scripts 412-417
-AccessRights parameter, values
CreateItems 111
CreateSubfolders 111
DeleteAllItems 111
DeleteOwnedItems 111
EditAllItems 111
EditOwnedItems 111
FolderContact 111
FolderOwner 111
FolderVisible 111
ReadItems 111
-CorruptionType parameter, values
AggregateCounts 145
FolderView 145
ProvisionedFolder 145
SearchFolder 145
-EventID parameter 254
-MemberDepartRestriction parameter
Closed value 176
Open value 176
-MemberJoinRestriction parameter
ApprovalRequired value 176
Closed value 176
Open value 175
-SearchQuery parameter 134, 148

A

Active Directory
user photos, importing into 113-116
**Active Directory Lightweight Directory
Services (ADLDS) 269**

active OWA and RPC connections
reporting on 225-228
ActiveSync device
access, controlling 228-230
reporting on 230-233
ActiveSync mailbox settings
managing 210-213
administrator audit logging
configuring 359, 360
administrator audit logs
searching 361-364
**Advanced Query Syntax
(AQS) 134, 148, 358, 425**
anti-spam agent logs
searching 263-265
anti-spam filters
content filtering 264
protocol analysis 264
recipient filtering 264
sender filtering 264
Sender ID 264
application servers
allowing, to relay mail 242, 243
archive mailboxes
managing 341, 342
archive mailbox quotas
configuring 343, 344
ArchiveQuota 344
ArchiveWarningQuota 344
arrays
working with 20-24
attachments
exporting, from mailbox 403-406
automatic mailbox distribution 188, 189
automatic replies and Out of Office settings
managing 105, 106

[PACKT] PUBLISHING   enterprise
professional expertise distilled

Thank you for buying
Microsoft Exchange Server
PowerShell Cookbook
Third Edition

About Packt Publishing

Packt, pronounced 'packed', published its first book, *Mastering phpMyAdmin for Effective MySQL Management*, in April 2004, and subsequently continued to specialize in publishing highly focused books on specific technologies and solutions.

Our books and publications share the experiences of your fellow IT professionals in adapting and customizing today's systems, applications, and frameworks. Our solution-based books give you the knowledge and power to customize the software and technologies you're using to get the job done. Packt books are more specific and less general than the IT books you have seen in the past. Our unique business model allows us to bring you more focused information, giving you more of what you need to know, and less of what you don't.

Packt is a modern yet unique publishing company that focuses on producing quality, cutting-edge books for communities of developers, administrators, and newbies alike. For more information, please visit our website at www.PacktPub.com.

About Packt Enterprise

In 2010, Packt launched two new brands, Packt Enterprise and Packt Open Source, in order to continue its focus on specialization. This book is part of the Packt Enterprise brand, home to books published on enterprise software – software created by major vendors, including (but not limited to) IBM, Microsoft, and Oracle, often for use in other corporations. Its titles will offer information relevant to a range of users of this software, including administrators, developers, architects, and end users.

Writing for Packt

We welcome all inquiries from people who are interested in authoring. Book proposals should be sent to author@packtpub.com. If your book idea is still at an early stage and you would like to discuss it first before writing a formal book proposal, then please contact us; one of our commissioning editors will get in touch with you.

We're not just looking for published authors; if you have strong technical skills but no writing experience, our experienced editors can help you develop a writing career, or simply get some additional reward for your expertise.

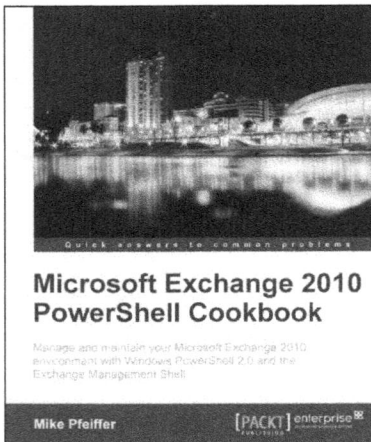

Microsoft Exchange 2010 PowerShell Cookbook

ISBN: 978-1-84968-246-6   Paperback: 480 pages

Manage and maintain your Microsoft Exchange 2010 environment with Windows PowerShell 2.0 and the Exchange Management Shell

1. Step-by-step instructions on how to write scripts for nearly every aspect of Exchange 2010 including the Client Access Server, Mailbox, and Transport server roles.

2. Understand the core concepts of Windows PowerShell 2.0 that will allow you to write sophisticated scripts and one-liners used with the Exchange Management Shell.

3. Learn how to write scripts and functions, schedule scripts to run automatically, and generate complex reports.

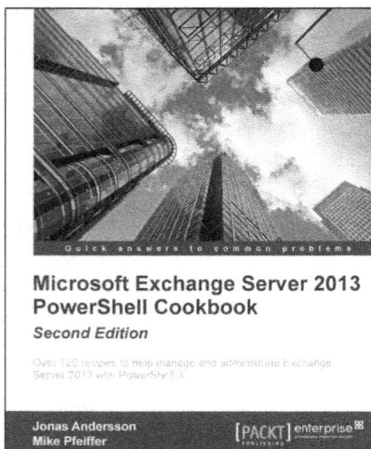

Microsoft Exchange Server 2013 PowerShell Cookbook
Second Edition

ISBN: 978-1-84968-942-7   Paperback: 504 pages

Over 120 recipes to help manage and administrate Exchange Server 2013 with PowerShell 3

1. Newly updated and improved for Exchange Server 2013 and PowerShell 3.

2. Learn how to write scripts and functions, schedule scripts to run automatically, and generate complex reports with PowerShell.

3. Manage and automate every element of Exchange Server 2013 with PowerShell such as mailboxes, distribution groups, and address lists.

Please check **www.PacktPub.com** for information on our titles

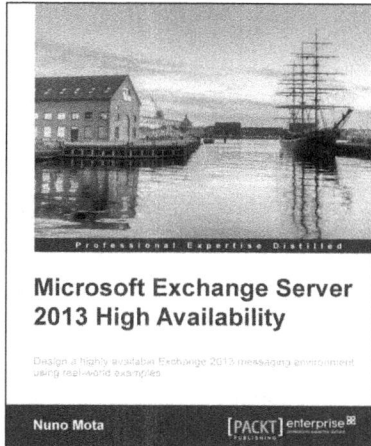

Microsoft Exchange Server 2013 High Availability

ISBN: 978-1-78217-150-8   Paperback: 266 pages

Design a highly available Exchange 2013 messaging environment using real-world examples

1. Use the easy-to-follow guidelines and tips to achieve the highest availability.

2. Covers all the aspects that need to be considered before, during and after implementation of high availability.

3. Packed with clear diagrams and scenarios that simplify the application of high availability concepts such as site resilience.

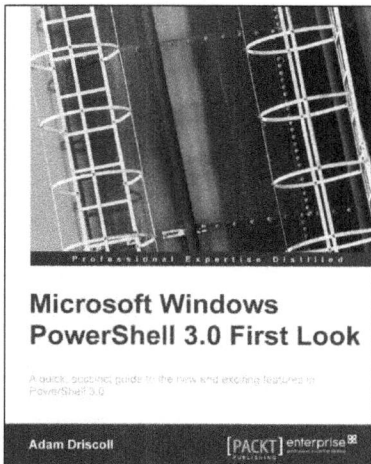

Microsoft Exchange Server 2013 High Availability

Design a highly available Exchange 2013 messaging environment using real-world examples

Nuno Mota   [PACKT] enterprise 🎴

Microsoft Windows PowerShell 3.0 First Look

ISBN: 978-1-84968-644-0   Paperback: 200 pages

A quick, succinct guide to the new and exciting features in PowerShell 3.0

1. Explore and experience the new features found in PowerShell 3.0.

2. Understand the changes to the language and the reasons why they were implemented.

3. Discover new cmdlets and modules available in Windows 8 and Server 8.

Microsoft Windows PowerShell 3.0 First Look

A quick, succinct guide to the new and exciting features in PowerShell 3.0

Adam Driscoll   [PACKT] enterprise 🎴

Please check **www.PacktPub.com** for information on our titles

www.ingramcontent.com/pod-product-compliance
Lightning Source LLC
Chambersburg PA
CBHW080131220326
41598CB00032B/5028